Battle

THE STORY OF THE BULGE

John Toland

INTRODUCTION TO THE BISON BOOKS EDITION BY
Carlo D'Este

UNIVERSITY OF NEBRASKA PRESS
LINCOLN AND LONDON

© 1959 by John Toland
Introduction © 1999 by the University of Nebraska Press
All rights reserved
Manufactured in the United States of America

∞

First Bison Books printing: 1999
Most recent printing indicated by the last digit below:
10   9   8   7   6   5   4   3   2   1

Library of Congress Cataloging-in-Publication Data
Toland, John.
Battle: the story of the Bulge / by John Toland.
p. cm.
Originally published: New York: Random House, 1959.
Includes bibliographical references and index.
ISBN 0-8032-9437-9 (pbk.: alk. paper)
1. Ardennes, Battle of the, 1944–1945.   2. World War, 1939–1945—
Campaigns—France.   3. World War, 1939–1945—Campaigns—Luxem-
bourg.   4. World War, 1939–1945—Campaigns—Belgium.   5. France—
History, Military.   6. Belgium—History, Military.   7. Luxembourg—
History, Military.   I. Title.
D756.5.A7T6   1999
940.54′21—dc21
99-10700   CIP

Reprinted from the original 1959 edition by Random House, New York.

This book is dedicated to all those who were there

Introduction

Carlo D'Este

The Battle of the Bulge took place as a direct result of an unforeseen series of events which began with the D-Day landings by the Allies on June 6, 1944, the first vital step in the liberation of Occupied Europe and the defeat of Nazi Germany. In the aftermath of the sudden, dramatic conclusion to the Normandy campaign in August, there was an inescapable aura of largely unwarranted optimism and self-deception in the ranks of the Allied high command. So crushing was the Allied victory that some began to perceive that the war was virtually over.

The German army was left seemingly in complete disarray, and with the Allies liberating vast areas of France and Belgium at a rapid rate, invasion of the Third Reich seemed only a matter of time. German losses were staggering: nine hundred thousand on the Eastern Front and another four hundred and fifty thousand in the west. What was overlooked was that there still remained some 3.4 million troops in the German army, over a million of whom were to be committed to the defense of the Reich on the Western Front.

The miscalculation consistently made by the Allies during World War II was a failure to anticipate—despite repeated demonstrations to the contrary—the will and tenacity of the *Wehrmacht* to resist, against overwhelming odds and under the most appalling conditions, with any means at their disposal. The resolute German defense of Sicily, Salerno, Cassino, Anzio, northern Italy and Normandy were all examples, as was Operation Market-Garden, the ill-fated Allied airborne and glider landings to secure a bridgehead over the Rhine at Arnhem, Holland, in mid-September 1944.

The original Allied blueprint for fighting the war in Northwest Europe was predicated on the assumption that the Germans would conduct an orderly retreat from Normandy and on a solid defense of the Seine River line. There was no scenario for the rout which resulted from the successful breakout from the Cotentin Peninsula at the end of July by the First and Third U.S. Armies. Hitler's ill-considered attempt to split the Allied armies at Mortain resulted in the entrapment of Army Group B in the Falaise pocket and hastened its withdrawal from Normandy under dire conditions.

Allied strategy after Normandy was an enormously contentious issue. Field Marshal Sir Bernard Montgomery, the commander of the British Twenty-first Army Group, proposed an invasion of Germany via the Ruhr, with his army group and an American army group advancing abreast—in all, some forty divisions, a force so powerful, he argued, that it "need fear nothing." Lt. Gen. Omar N. Bradley, the U.S. Twelfth Army Group commander, proposed an entirely different scenario in which his forces would thrust across central and southern France, through the Frankfurt gap and into the heartland of Germany.

Eisenhower rejected both plans in favor of an Allied advance on a "broad front." If the entire Allied force had been composed of one nationality, Eisenhower might have agreed with Montgomery's plan, but his unwavering maxim was that it was an *Allied* war and would be won by Allied armies, not solely by British or Americans. The result was compromise.

Neither Montgomery, nor Bradley and the Third U.S. Army commander, Lt. Gen. George S. Patton Jr., were appeased by Eisenhower's decision that Montgomery's armies were to thrust northeast through Belgium and Holland toward the Ruhr after capturing Antwerp, the largest and best-equipped port in Europe. Bradley's forces were relegated to protecting the British right flank by simultaneously attacking eastward toward the Saar (Germany's most important industrial region after the Ruhr) and the Frankfurt gap in what were clearly identified as secondary operations.

The other immediate impact of their stunning victory in Normandy was that there was no longer the luxury of a pause at the Seine while the Allied armies regrouped, advanced their logistical bases forward, and made plans to resume offensive operations toward Germany. From the North Sea to the Swiss border, British, Canadian, Polish, and American forces were now as far as four hundred miles from their primary source of resupply, the port of Cherbourg. On D + 100 days (September 14, 1944), the Allies had advanced to where Eisenhower's logisticians thought they would reach only in May 1945.

Once beyond the Seine, logistics, not tactics, became the dominant factor, particularly after the Allies captured the vital port of Antwerp in early September but failed to secure its approaches. German interdiction precluded the use of Antwerp until the end of November. The result was that only a fraction of the chronic shortages of fuel and ammunition required to sustain the Allied advance into

Germany could be alleviated, even though ninety-five percent of virtually all classes of supplies were already positioned in France. Even the heroic but ultimately futile effort by the famed Red Ball Express to keep the wheels from coming off the great Allied war machine itself consumed more fuel than it was able to supply the sixty-five divisions operating in Northwest Europe, each of which consumed an average of seven hundred tons per day. Unable to support both broad front thrusts fully, Eisenhower was obliged to allocate the precious supplies. Priority went to Montgomery's Twenty-first Army Group. One of the immediate effects of Eisenhower's decision was to cripple Patton's promising offensive in Lorraine.

The inability of the Allies to mount a rapid thrust into Germany in the autumn of 1944 provided the Germans with precious time to regroup and resist as Eisenhower's "broad front" advance stalled along the borders of the Third Reich in the mud and cold of the most severe winter weather in fifty years. From the Saar to Aachen, a series of bloody battles accomplished relatively little except to raise the casualty count. The most costly battle of all was an offensive masterminded by Bradley and Lt. Gen. Courtney Hodges, the U.S. First Army commander, to gain a foothold into Germany by seizing the vital Roer Dams. American infantry were flung into the Huertgen Forest in a series of futile attacks, at a cost of thousands of casualties, in what one military historian has described as "a misconceived and basically fruitless battle that . . . should have been avoided."[1]

Despite the growing shortages, which now included winter clothing, Eisenhower elected to continue Allied offensives along the entire front. However, in order to support operations on such a lengthy front, it became necessary to strip Allied reserves down to two veteran but undermanned U.S. airborne divisions. The weakest link in the Allied front was in the rugged Ardennes, with its poor road net and thick forests. There, Bradley took what he later termed "a calculated risk" by lightly defending the so-called "Ghost Front" of the eastern Ardennes. Holding this thinly-held one-hundred-mile sector were only three newly arrived, untested American infantry divisions, part of an armored cavalry group, and three battered veteran divisions in the process of absorbing replacements. In such vile weather it was deemed unlikely the Germans could ever mount a serious offensive threat in the Ardennes in secret.

With Allied operations at a virtual standstill and the Third Reich on the verge of eventual invasion and defeat, Adolf Hitler elected to gamble the fate of Germany on a last-ditch attempt to split the Allied armies with a sudden, lightning *blitzkrieg* thrust through the Ardennes. Hitler's grandiose intent was nothing less than a repetition of the success of the 1940 invasion of western Europe which had worked to near-perfection through the Ardennes. Hitler believed that once across the Meuse River and into the Belgian lowlands beyond the Ardennes, his armies could drive clear to Antwerp and, with the port in German hands, compel the Allies to sue for peace. Hitler named his counteroffensive Operation *Wacht am Rhein* ("Watch on the Rhine").

The German commanders responsible for implementing Hitler's orders had severe misgivings. When they first heard of the plan in late October 1944, both the Commander-in-Chief West, Field Marshal Gerd von Rundstedt, and the commander of German ground forces (Army Group B), Field Marshal Walther Model, strongly opposed Hitler's plan. Both generals believed that the seizure of Antwerp was a hopelessly unrealistic goal and attempted to persuade Hitler to scale down its scope. Their advice fell upon deaf ears. Again, in early December, both Model and his two panzer army commanders, Waffen SS Gen. Josef "Sepp" Dietrich and Gen. Hasso von Manteuffel, spoke forcefully at a conference with Hitler, urging that the plan be reconsidered. Hitler again adamantly refused.

To accomplish such a Herculean task, Hitler assembled in great secrecy a massive force of a quarter of a million men to launch the first and only German counteroffensive of the war in Northwest Europe. Under the cover of the bitter winter weather, more than fourteen hundred tanks, two thousand guns and twenty divisions were quietly moved forward into the rugged Schnee Eifel on the eastern fringes of the Ardennes.

In the early morning hours of December 16, 1944 two panzer armies launched the main attack against the "Ghost Front" of the U.S. First Army, catching the Allies entirely by surprise. The once quiet Ardennes suddenly became bedlam as American units became entangled in a series of desperate battles for survival. The German advance appeared unstoppable. What ensued was called the Battle of the Bulge.

John Toland is one of America's foremost military historians. Originally published in 1959, *Battle: The Story of the Bulge* was Toland's first work of military history. It is the saga of how beleaguered American troops not only resisted Hitler's deadly counter-offensive but, in what became one of the defining moments in the history of the United States Army, turned it into an Allied victory. As Toland writes in his foreword, *Battle* "is the documented story of the greatest pitched battle ever fought by the United States, its only struggle in the dead of winter."[2]

At the time he researched this book the official documents and after-action reports then available hardly even began to tell the incredible story of the Battle of the Bulge. Toland is renowned for finding and interviewing participants, and during his research he traveled nearly one hundred thousand miles and interviewed hundreds of soldiers from both sides, from private to general, as well as civilians. The result was fifty notebooks crammed with first-hand accounts.

Undeterred by a State Department prohibition against travel by American citizens behind the Iron Curtain, Toland and his wife, Toshiko, journeyed with virtual impunity throughout East Germany, Hungary, and Czechoslovakia to interview former participants. Wherever there was someone with information about any aspect of the Battle of the Bulge, Toland managed to locate them—sometimes in such unlikely places as a municipal house of prostitution in Stuttgart, where he spoke with the mistress of a German commander. Whether it was visiting Hitler's mountain retreat, the Eagle's Nest in Bavaria's Obersalzberg, Vienna, Yugoslavia, East or West Germany, Belgium, Luxembourg, Spain or the United States, Toland's diligence paid off. No other military historian then or since has gone to such extraordinary lengths to research an event.

In *Battle*, Toland has combined scholarship with a rousing story to recreate one of the most harrowing battles of World War II. The result is a colorful, human account of the Battle of the Bulge as seen through the eyes of those who fought it. As Toland notes in his epilogue, "the accounts of such men actually make the heart of the story."[3]

Two generals, one American, the other German, held the key to the outcome of the battle. Both were interviewed extensively by Mr. Toland. An obscure, newly promoted Brigadier General, Bruce C. Clarke was the U.S. commander responsible for the hastily assembled defense of the town of St. Vith, which was, next to Bastogne, the most important road and rail center in the eastern sector of the Ardennes. To gain the Meuse, Manteuffel's spearheads had to capture the key crossroads town of Bastogne. However, before the Fifth Panzer Army could capture Bastogne, it first had to overwhelm the besieged Americans defending St. Vith. Although the battle for Bastogne is better known for the heroic stand of the surrounded 101st Airborne Division, and its acting commander's terse rejection of a German surrender demand with the single word, "Nuts!" much of the focus of Toland's account is appropriately on the desperate battle to delay the Fifth Panzer Army at St. Vith.

To gain his unique perspective, Toland also interviewed extensively Baron Hasso von Manteuffel, the able commander of the German Fifth Panzer Army. From this and other interviews, he has drawn sharp portraits of the leaders of Germany's desperate attempt to win the war in the West. Von Manteuffel, an eloquent Prussian and one-time gentleman jockey and modern pentathlon champion, related how the Germans conceived and fought *Wacht am Rhein*, as well as what occurred at St. Vith to thwart that plan. Toland's diligence in persuading men like Manteuffel and Bruce Clarke to talk is one of the reasons *Battle* is such a gripping story.

My interest in the Battle of the Bulge began long before I became a military historian. While stationed in Europe with the U.S. Army in the 1970s, I had the good fortune to meet Dr. Robert C. Larson, a German expert and the Army's civilian liaison officer in Stuttgart who recounted his participation in a little known but unique postwar event.

At approximately the same time as Toland was researching *Battle*, Bruce Clarke, then the four-star Commander-in-Chief, U.S. Army Europe, led a small, select group on a battlefield tour of the Ardennes. Accompanying Clarke was his one-time enemy, Baron von Manteuffel. After the war the two men had forged a friendship based on mutual respect and the shared experiences of combat soldiers. At the scene of their fateful encounter in December 1944, the two generals each recounted the battle for St. Vith from their perspective in what may have been the most memorable battlefield tour ever staged. Toland's lengthy interviews of Clarke and von Manteuffel enabled him to re-create the essence of that event in *Battle*.

When it was first published, *Battle* was both praised and criticized. Toland aroused the ire of the academic and intellectual community for producing a book rich in detail from interviews but not based entirely on official documents. The most absurd criticism of all was that Toland lacked the credentials to be an historian because he had never studied history or earned a doctoral degree. The *New York Times* recently noted that Toland's use of personal interviews "exasperated those who like their history falsifiable."[4]

Among those praising the book was Bill Mauldin, the Pulitzer Prize winning cartoonist and creator of the famous Willie and Joe cartoons for the *Stars and Stripes* newspaper during World War II. Speaking as a former G.I., Mauldin wrote in the *St. Louis Post-Dispatch* that *Battle* was "far more fascinating than any war novel. The pace is rapid, crackling, like battle itself . . . it contains the best description of the American combat soldier I have ever read."[5]

During his distinguished career, John Toland has chronicled many of the major events of the twentieth century as has no other historian. He does not merely recount battles, he lives them! In the process, the reader invariably becomes a willing participant in the events he portrays. Many have tried, but few have ever done it so well. In *No Man's Land*, for example, he has written the story of the tumultuous final year of World War I. But it is the Second World War that has dominated his historical contributions. Toland's other book about the war in Northwest Europe in 1944–45, *The Last 100 Days*, is an enthralling account of the war's final days that has, in my opinion, never been surpassed. I recall vividly reading this book and thinking at the time: this is the way military history should be written. Not surprisingly, *The Last 100 Days* became an immediate best-seller.

The *Chicago Tribune* may have best summed up his work as a military historian with the observation that "Toland weaves the epic tapestry of popular history, meshing together thousands of details into monumental narratives of wartime drama."[6] The ultimate value of any historical account is how well it stands the test of time. Although a number of books about the Battle of the Bulge have subsequently been published, John Toland's account remains a pioneering work which I am pleased to re-introduce to a new generation of readers.[7]

NOTES

1. Charles B. MacDonald *The Battle of the Huertgen Forest* (Philadelphia: Lippincott, 1963), 205.

2. John Toland, *Battle: The Story of the Bulge* (New York: Random House, 1959), ix.

3. Toland, *Battle*, 355.

4. Review of *Battle*, by John Toland. *New York Times Book Review*, 10 November 1997.

5. See John Toland, *Captured by History* (New York: St. Martin's Press, 1997), 152.

6. Toland, *Captured by History*, dust jacket.

7. The U.S. Army official history of the battle was not published until six years after *Battle*. See Hugh M. Cole, "U.S. Army in World War II: European Theater of Operations," *The Ardennes: Battle of the Bulge* (Washington DC: Center of Military History, U.S. Army, 1965).

CONTENTS

Author's Note

This is the documented story of the greatest pitched battle ever fought by the United States, its only major struggle in the dead of winter. It was as great in scale as the Battle of Stalingrad—over a million soldiers and thousands of civilians were actively involved. Unlike any other campaign in World War II, it was conceived in its entirety by Adolf Hitler. It was his last great offensive, his last great gamble.

The dialogue in this book is not fictional. The conversations were reported to me by participants or listeners. For example, the retort of McAuliffe to the German surrender request at Bastogne—suspected by many of being bowdlerized—was told to me by five men who were present.

For over two years I followed the trail of the Battle of the Bulge. It led to interviews with more than a thousand people in ten countries. To make myself familiar with the sprawling battlefield I walked over many miles of the Ardennes. I slept in foxholes and in cellars. I retraced scenes of battle and murder with civilian eye-witnesses. Often and spontaneously these people of Luxembourg and Belgium would suddenly re-enact what had taken place so many years before with harrowing realism.

This book could not have been written without the full cooperation of the Departments of the Army and Air Force. They opened their files and tracked down the whereabouts of Bulge participants without making a single demand or restriction. They had only one request: that I tell the truth.

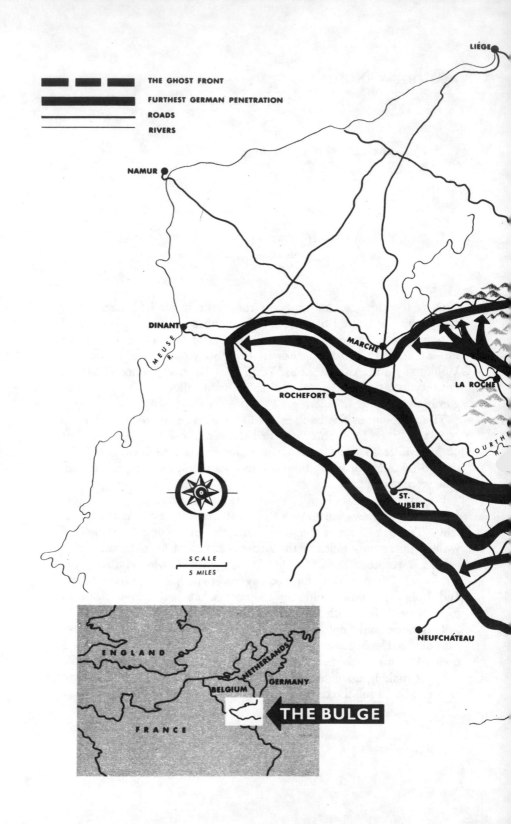

THE GHOST FRONT

FURTHEST GERMAN PENETRATION

ROADS

RIVERS

LIÉGE

NAMUR

DINANT

MEUSE R.

MARCHE

LA ROCHE

ROCHEFORT

OURTHE R.

ST. HUBERT

NEUFCHÂTEAU

SCALE
5 MILES

ENGLAND

NETHERLANDS

BELGIUM

GERMANY

FRANCE

THE BULGE

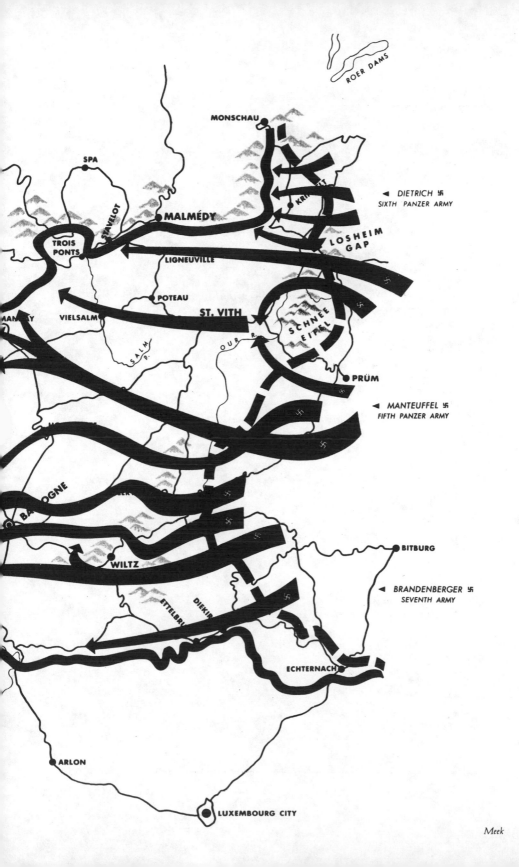

ROER DAMS

MONSCHAU

◄ DIETRICH ⚡
SIXTH PANZER ARMY

SPA

STAVELOT

MALMÉDY

LOSHEIM
GAP

TROIS
PONTS

LIGNEUVILLE

POTEAU

MANHAY

VIELSALM

ST. VITH

SCHNEE
EIFEL

SALM R.

OUR R.

PRÜM

◄ MANTEUFFEL ⚡
FIFTH PANZER ARMY

BASTOGNE

BITBURG

WILTZ

ETTELBRUCK

DIEKIRCH

◄ BRANDENBERGER ⚡
SEVENTH ARMY

ECHTERNACH

ARLON

LUXEMBOURG CITY

Meek

PART ONE
Operation "Christrose"

1. THE GHOST FRONT

15 December 1944

1

The night of December 15, 1944, was cold and quiet along the Ardennes Front.

At 10:00 P.M. the American troops in Echternach, a quaint medieval town in the Grand Duchy of Luxembourg, were abed or going to bed in yellow patrician houses with dormer windows and mansard roofs. They saw no sign of activity from the Germans in the crumbling cliff-top abbey that overlooked them from across the swift narrow Sauer River. They had nothing to stay up for in Echternach itself. Since September, when the Americans had liberated Luxembourg at the end of their wild dash through France, the town's 3,300 citizens had been living in evacuation quarters behind the hills to the west.

Echternach, the southern anchor of the Ardennes Front, was being held by a single company of riflemen. And by 10:30 P.M. all but a few of them were asleep.

Twisting eighty-five miles through terrain reminiscent of the Berkshires and the Green Mountains, the front was held by six American divisions. Of these six, three divisions were brand-new and had been sent here to get "blooded"—lightly tested in combat before being assigned to a major engagement; the other three, exhausted and bled white in battle, were here to be refitted, retrained.

For the Ardennes Front was the "Ghost Front"—a cold quiet place where artillery was fired mainly for registration and patrols probed the enemy lines only to keep in practice. Within rifle range of each other, German observers watched the Americans eat, and the American observers watched the women come at dusk and steal into the pillboxes of the Siegfried Line. For over two months now both sides had rested and watched and avoided irritating each other.

From Echternach, the front swung northward along the winding Sauer River. The hill-straddling American lines were manned by the 4th Division, which the month before had suffered 7,500 casualties in the brief but bitter battle of Hürtgen Forest. On the German side of the river the battlement-like cliff continued, concealing the forward positions of the Siegfried Line.

About five miles north of Echternach the 9th Armored Division took over. Newly arrived in Europe, it had been in position for just a week. Actually only one combat command—roughly equivalent to an infantry regiment—was on the line; the other two were garrisoned in reserve fifty miles to the north. One week up front, and already the officers were worried: how could their men be battle-tested when there was so little action?

At 10:30 P.M. it was drizzling on the 9th Armored front. "I'm living in a dugout," wrote Lieutenant Clifford Penrose to his wife, "and the damn thing is starting to leak tonight. So don't let a few blurred spots bother you, it isn't beer. We had Spam for supper tonight. And then your package came. Thanks a lot, but next time don't send Spam."

After six miles, where the Our River flows into the Sauer from the north, the lines were taken over by the 28th, another veteran infantry division that had suffered heavily in the Hürtgen Forest.

The front continued north along the Our. This fast-flowing river was only fifty feet wide, but the towering bluffs on both sides restricted vehicular crossing to a few places. One of these crossings, eight miles above the Our's confluence with the Sauer, was at Vianden, a picture-book town that crouches beneath the splendid ruins of a huge rambling castle. This fortress, which had held off Vianden's enemies for centuries, was now an observation post for thirty-six American soldiers.

At 11:00 P.M. most of the men in Vianden were asleep. But in the dining room of the Heintz Hotel, on a table that had served royalty, prime ministers, and great authors, several GIs were patching a boat and talking of the one-armed German sergeant who had been picked up earlier that night on the other side of the river. Ever since, the captive had kept crying in terror, "The Germans come tonight! The Germans come tonight!" He begged them to flee to the west—and take him.

About fifteen miles farther north, the front crossed the Our and poked through the Siegfried Line into Germany. From this breach, the 28th Division positions continued almost due east for another seven or eight miles. Then the 106th Division—the Golden Lions— manned the defenses.

This was not only the newest American division in the Ardennes; it was also the newest Allied division on any front. Transported across France and Belgium through cold rain in open trucks, the men had arrived, drenched and miserable, only a few days before. Immediately some encouragement had come their way. As they took over from the 2nd Division, those battle-wise veterans had shouted, "Lucky guys! You're coming into a rest camp!" And a regimental commander of the 2nd had told a regimental commander of the 106th, "It's been very quiet up here, and your men will learn the easy way." By now the young newcomers—these were the first of the eighteen-year-old draftees—were cockier than the veterans and certain they "had it made" for the duration.

"Never expected your little boy to get this far, did you?" nineteen-year-old Pfc. Joe Schectman was writing to his folks in Plymouth, Pennsylvania. "We are billeted as comfortably and safely as we were in England. Of course there's no telling how long I'll be in this paradise. But as long as I am, I'll be safe."

And a few miles to his north 1st Lieutenant Alan Jones, Jr., a regimental staff officer, was staring dreamily from his bunker. He saw nothing but a typical Christmas card scene: icicles two feet long, snow-covered fir trees. At ease in this peaceful world he turned his thoughts to his wife Lynn in Washington, D.C. Soon she would have a baby, their first.

Young Jones's sense of tranquillity was not shared by his father, Major General Alan Jones, commander of the 106th Division. That day he had come up to the front lines and chatted with his son.

Noticing his father's .32 pistol, young Jones had remarked jokingly, "I could use that, Dad."

"I really should give it to you. But I might need it myself." General Jones's tone had been as bantering as his son's, but inwardly he was extremely worried. He had been worried from the first moment he had seen a situation map: his entire division was out on a salient thrust six miles into the Siegfried Line. This area, called the Schnee Eifel (Snow Mountains), was a range of rugged wooded hills, rolling fields, and twisting streams, with tiny villages squatting atop bald ridges or hidden in deep valleys. Through the Schnee Eifel ran miles of Hitler's "dragon's teeth"—concrete tank traps—and hundreds of cleverly camouflaged pillboxes.

As soon as he had taken his positions—"man for man and gun for gun," his orders said—Jones had protested that this whole salient could easily be cut off. Too many of his defense points were located in villages in the valleys, and his men were open to attack from all sides and above.

But Generals Hodges, Bradley, and Eisenhower insisted that this finger sticking into the Siegfried Line would be a valuable bridgehead when Germany was invaded. That it could be bitten off was a risk, true, but only a small one.

Jones was also worried about a long narrow valley which lay just to the north of the Schnee Eifel. This valley was a seven-mile-wide corridor that led from Germany to Belgium. It was called the Losheim Gap.

Even the name conjured up danger. For the Losheim Gap was the classic gateway from east to west. Through it invading German armies had poured in 1870, in 1914, and in 1940. Although no one in his right mind believed the Germans would try a fourth time, Jones fretted. If they did, his men on the Schnee Eifel would be trapped.

All except the northernmost two miles of the seven-mile Losheim Gap was his to guard. Moreover, the five miles that were his responsibility were held by troops he had never seen, the 14th Cavalry Group. Jones had inherited these men from the previous occupants of the Schnee Eifel, the 2nd Division. As yet there had been no time for his officers even to visit their Losheim Gap positions.

In a house on the eastern edge of the tiny village of Krewinkel, a sergeant in this 14th Cavalry Group, John Banister, was holed up with his platoon. Only the day before, while on patrol, he had spied fifty Germans dragging a heavily laden sled to a lonely house. His report of the surprising concentration of men and equipment went up through channels, and he heard no more about it. But toward midnight of December 15, Banister found himself getting out of bed, going to the window, and looking out nervously toward the house to the east.

Beyond the sector of the 14th Cavalry Group, the front bore north again. For two miles there wasn't a single tank or a single foxhole. This area was so lightly patrolled that German soldiers on leave often walked safely through to visit homes behind American lines. And this two-mile hole was the top section of the Losheim Gap.

The storm door between Germany and Belgium, if not wide open, was invitingly ajar. Only nine hundred cavalrymen—ill-suited by training and equipment to a static defense—were guardians of the most important gateway in Europe.

Equally dangerous was the fact that here at this vital spot the lines of Major General Troy Middleton's VIII Corps—comprising the 4th, 9th Armored, 28th, and 106th Divisions—ended and those of his friend, Leonard Gerow, began. As all military men know, the boundary between corps is exceedingly weak. Though two soldiers can shake hands across this boundary, the chain of command separates them by a hundred miles.

Gerow's V Corps began with the 99th Division, which was almost as green as the neighboring 106th.

For the GIs of the 99th, who had been in the Ardennes a month but had seen little action, conditions were far from ideal. They didn't mind the quiet, but foxholes were general accommodation, and why had the hot chow been cut out the last few days? Now they were down to "D" bars, a sickening concoction of concentrated chocolate sometimes called "Hitler's Secret Weapon."

Toward the northern end of the 99th Division sector, a complex maneuver was going on: the 2nd Division, just moved up from the Schnee Eifel salient, was attacking through the 99th lines in a narrow two-mile corridor. The 2nd had been trying the past three days to smash a hole in the Siegfried Line, break through, and knife north to the Roer Dams. These dams, a menace to the entire Allied advance into the Roer Valley, had to be captured before the main attack started. For if their sluices were opened, the advancing army would be flooded and cut off from the rear.

At midnight, the men of the 2nd Division were stalled in front of Wahlerscheid, a heavily fortified crossroads. As they waited, Lieutenant Jesse Morrow passed time talking to Captain Fred Aringdale. It was a desultory conversation, but suddenly Aringdale said, "You know, Morrow, I'm going to be killed tomorrow."

"That's not a good joke."

"I wonder who decided I'd never live to be thirty?"

Aringdale's certainty turned Morrow cold.

North of the 2nd Division attack corridor, the lines of the 99th resumed, ran a few miles farther, and ended at the historic German border town of Monschau, which nestled in a narrow serpentine valley between wooded mountains.

Nowhere along the Ghost Front was the feeling of comfortable confidence stronger than at Monschau, its northern terminus, some eighty-five winding miles above Echternach. Rumor was that Hitler had bicycled through its cobbled streets and stopped to admire its rococo buildings; that he himself had ordered that the whole town be treated as a museum and spared the ravages of war. In any case, no German shell had ever landed in Monschau; and, convinced none ever would, the handful of American cavalrymen in town had gone to bed early in their thick featherbeds. For to them tomorrow would be like yesterday—comfortable, quiet, and a little cold.

All along the Ghost Front, from Echternach to Monschau, the 75,000 American troops made little note of midnight December 15. Those few who did felt only that they were one day closer to a Christmas far from home.

2

Behind the front, division command posts and rest camps were much like stateside garrisons. That night in the dingy village of Honsfeld, Belgium, five miles behind the Losheim Gap, a movie was shown at a 99th Division rest camp. The sound track broke down, and while repairs were being made the men invented dialogue of their own and delivered it in shouts. Later, as they filed out of the recreation hall, a hot rumor went the rounds: Marlene Dietrich would arrive to put on a show next morning. Immediately riflemen scheduled to return to the front at 8:00 A.M. began conspiring to postpone their departure till noon.

Thirty miles behind the Losheim Gap, in friendly Vielsalm, Belgium, the reserve half of the 14th Cavalry Group was watching a USO Camp Show. The men enjoyed the whole show, even the performer who ate crackers and sang at the same time. The GIs' main concerns were food and mail from home; the officers', food, mail from home, and their liquor ration.

Halfway back to the front, General Alan Jones, commander of the 106th Division, sat at his desk in a somber, stone schoolhouse, in the somber town of St. Vith, Belgium. He was still deeply worried. Even St. Vith made him uneasy. Unlike the picturesque towns of Luxembourg, it was an ugly if important road center, a clutter of depressing stone buildings barren of decoration. The shop windows were lettered in German; everything, even the church, was formidably and uncompromisingly Teutonic.

In the past century the entire sector around St. Vith had changed hands four times. Half the people felt they were Belgian, the other half German. Neighbor was suspicious of neighbor. As a result a strange, foreboding atmosphere—half friendly, half sullen—hung over Jones's command post.

So far that night he had received no disquieting reports from the front. All was apparently quiet. But it had not been so the previous two nights. The roar of many motors had been heard from the enemy lines. Jones had quickly reported "heavy armored movements" to his immediate superior, Troy Middleton of VIII Corps. Middleton's staff had only been amused. "Don't be so jumpy," one VIII Corps officer had chided. "The Krauts are just playing phonograph records to scare you newcomers."

This wasn't all. Two fires, both caused by a carelessness infuriating to the well-ordered Jones, had recently destroyed a battalion motor pool and a regimental command post. Two tempting target areas had been lit up. Yet not a single round of enemy artillery had been fired on them. Jones was again suspicious. Again more experienced hands insisted this was only graphic proof that the Germans had no shells to waste.

Jones tried to persuade himself his fears were groundless as he walked to his billet in a nearby house. This was his first time in action. Newcomers to battle were notoriously jittery. Besides, who was he to argue with old campaigners? During World War I he had gone directly from the University of Washington to the army as a second lieutenant. Since then he had worked his way up to command of a division without benefit of West Point training. He was the complete opposite of the Patton type of general. Many of his own troops had never seen him, for he kept in the background, running the 106th Division in a quiet, unspectacular manner.

In bed Jones couldn't sleep. He felt a personal responsibility to every young rifleman sitting out on the Schnee Eifel.

Almost squarely in the middle and six miles to the rear of the Ghost Front, several hundred men of the veteran 28th Division were enjoying themselves that night in the Clervaux Rest Center. This breathtakingly beautiful Luxembourg town, long a tourist's delight with its narrow winding cobblestone streets, its towering monastery and baroque houses, also boasted the romantic ruins of a medieval castle once owned by the ancestors of Franklin D. Roosevelt.

In spite of the peaceful atmosphere, Joseph Geiben, a young townsman who had deserted from the German Army, was troubled. There were too many stories being told of a great Nazi buildup behind the Siegfried Line. Some of them had to be true. If attack did come, his beautiful little Clervaux would be in the path of the Nazi columns. It lay directly behind the main crossing of the Our River on the road to Bastogne, key town of the Ardennes. Why didn't the Americans heed the warnings?

Actually the few Americans who took note of the warnings had a sound explanation for the Germans' moving into the area. Troy Middleton had just conducted a big "rubber duck" operation not far from Clervaux. GIs posing as generals had ridden around the countryside, as if selecting billets for a new division; papier-mâché tanks and guns had been paraded around to simulate the arrival of fresh troops. The purpose had been to decoy German units from the Saar and Roer areas into the Ardennes. Apparently the Germans had swallowed the bait.

That night no Allied commander seriously feared a major German attack. Yet in Bastogne, Belgium, about twenty miles west of Clervaux, Middleton, whose VIII Corps comprised the bulk of the Ghost Front, was uneasy. A woman had been sent up that morning from the 28th Division. She told of seeing, just the night before, a mass of German troops behind the Siegfried Line east of Clervaux. And their tanks were twice as large as anything the Americans had.

Middleton realized that if an attack did fall, his four divisions—two green, two exhausted—would be hard put to defend themselves. So he sent the woman on up the chain of command to *his* chief, Lieutenant General Courtney Hodges, commander of First Army.

But at the famous Belgian resort of Spa, Hodges was too occupied with the slow progress of his own attack toward the Roer Dams to be concerned. It was true that the week before, his intelligence officer, Colonel "Monk" Dickson, had surprised everyone by predicting there would soon be an all-out German offensive and the past few days had made a pest of himself by announcing that the attack might *possibly* come where no one expected it—where it had come in 1870, 1914, and 1940—in the Ardennes. Then at a briefing just the night before, Dickson's hunch had become a conviction as he pounded a map board and said with certainty, "It's the Ardennes!"

Hodges' staff had advised the general not to take Dickson too seriously: Monk was a notorious pessimist; also he was overworked, and three days in Paris would perk him up a bit.

The 12th Army Group, which gave orders to Hodges, had also been displeased with Dickson's prediction. Lieutenant General Omar Bradley's intelligence officer announced in rebuttal: "It is now certain that attrition is steadily sapping the strength of German forces on the Western Front."

Supreme Headquarters of the Allied Expedition Forces (SHAEF) quickly joined Dickson's critics, Eisenhower's G2 issuing a report that the Germans were all but finished.

Even the British ridiculed fear of any enemy attack. That very afternoon Montgomery had stated flatly that the Germans "cannot stage major offensive operations." In fact, things were so dull he asked Eisenhower if there was any objection to his going off to England the next week.

Reassured by this chorus of confidence from above, Hodges had kept busy with his own offensive. He went to sleep around midnight bothered only by a head cold.

Just behind the southern end of the Ghost Front, his immediate superior, Omar Bradley, was getting ready for bed in the Hotel Alfa in Luxembourg City. Early next morning Bradley, leader of more combat troops than any American field commander in history, would be leaving for Versailles to discuss with his superior, Eisenhower, the critical shortage of infantry replacements. He expected no attack but rather wished for one. "If the other fellow would only hit us now!" he had said a few days before. "We could kill more Germans with a good deal less effort if they'd only climb out of their holes and come after us for a change."

In the Versailles Officers' Club far to the rear, talk was of the coming Allied attacks on the Roer and Saar, and the stupidity of sending MacArthur infantry that was needed in Europe. There was also some mention of Major Glenn Miller. That day the famous band leader had left England by plane for Paris. He was now hours overdue.

Not far from the Officers' Club, in the villa occupied a few months before by German Marshal Gerd von Rundstedt, Dwight D. Eisenhower was in a celebrating mood. The Supreme Commander had just been promoted to five-star general. But there was no time to celebrate. Tomorrow he had an important conference with Bradley, and on top of that he had promised to attend the wedding of his orderly Mickey to a WAC. Tomorrow was going to be hectic. The Ardennes was far from his mind.

By midnight of December 15, the facts had been collected. Reports of marshaling east of Clervaux, prisoners' claims of a great offensive, front-line reports of heavy movements of armor, even the capture of German documents revealing the establishment of a school to teach combat troops how to pass as Americans—all these, or part of these, should have revealed something was about to happen in the Ardennes.

They didn't. Everyone responsible for the Allied state of affairs on the Ardennes Front—the master planners Churchill and Roosevelt, as well as the military leaders—slept soundly that night, safe in the feeling that there was nothing to fear from Germany. Hitler was beaten even if he didn't yet know it.

In the Ardennes it was now past midnight. It was December 16, 1944. All was quiet along the 85-mile Ghost Front. Except for a slight mysterious rumbling a few miles to the east.

Over trails and roads matted with straw to muffle the noise, 250,-000 Germans, 1,900 pieces of heavy artillery, and 970 tanks and assault guns were slowly moving west to their final attack positions.

Within six hours "Christrose," the greatest and most deceptive attack ever launched on the Western Front, would begin.

2. "WATCH ON THE RHINE"

31 July–15 December 1944

1

Behind this gargantuan buildup stood one man, Adolf Hitler.

That he must regain the initiative had been obvious to the Führer from July 31, 1944, when word reached him that the Allies had broken out of their Normandy beachheads at Avranches. At first, still shaken by Count Stauffenberg's assassination attempt eleven days earlier, he seemed crushed. But in a few weeks he began to stamp about, to abuse the General Staff, to regain his optimism.

On September 16, after his daily conference at Wolf's Lair, the Führer asked his most trusted generals to come into an inner chamber for a second meeting.

First to enter the new conference room was Field Marshal Wilhelm Keitel, Supreme Commander of all German Armies. He was followed by Chief of Operations Colonel General Alfred Jodl. Then came Heinz Guderian, famed tank leader now in command of the Eastern Front, and General Kreipe, representing Air Marshal Göring. In whispers they wondered what new surprise Hitler had for them.

Finally Hitler walked in, stooped, wan, and dreamy. His blue eyes were watery and distant, his mouth slack.

As usual in these high-level councils, Jodl, by rank Keitel's subordinate but second to none in Hitler's confidence, began the briefing quietly, presenting the ugly facts of the war in an adroit manner.

Politically the Reich was friendless, deserted. Italy was finished; Japan had politely suggested that Germany start armistice negotiations with the Soviet Union; the Rumanians and Bulgarians had switched sides, joining the triumphant Russians; Finland had just broken with Germany.

While the Wehrmacht still listed ten million men under arms, over four million had been killed since the war started and in the last three months it had suffered at least 1,200,000 casualties—almost half of them in the West.

As for the fronts, Jodl went on with a glimmer of optimism, the Russian summer offensive seemed to have run its course. "And on the Western Front we're getting a real rest in the Ardennes."

At the word "Ardennes" Hitler suddenly came to life, raised his hand dramatically and cried, "Stop!"

There was a dead pause of two minutes. Then Hitler spoke: "I have made a momentous decision. I am taking the offensive. Here —out of the Ardennes!" He smashed his fist on the unrolled map before him. "Across the Meuse and on to Antwerp!"

The others stared at him. His shoulders were squared, his eyes luminous, the signs of care and sickness gone. Once again he was the dynamic Hitler of 1940.

2

The next day Hitler pressed preparations for the counteroffensive. He issued orders for the establishment of the Sixth Panzer Army, and initiated into the plan a man who was to play a vital role in it —General Rudolf Gercke, Wehrmacht Chief of Transportation.

On September 25, Hitler told Jodl to draw up a comprehensive plan for the offensive. To Keitel he assigned the task of calculating what ammunition and supplies would be required and when they would be delivered. And he ordered five panzer divisions withdrawn from the front for reorganization and retraining west of Cologne. These five divisions would be the backbone of the offensive.

By early October, Gercke's preliminary work with the transportation system was well advanced. He had given priority to the Rhine River crossings. Bridge pillars and piers were reinforced, tracks laid on highway bridges, ferries modified to carry locomotives and seventy-ton King Tiger tanks. Special heavy spans of military bridging were constructed; these would be concealed along the Rhine for use if permanent bridges were bombed out.

Dumps and depots were prepared east of the Rhine. Here mountains of supplies would be held for transportation to the west bank. But Gercke's most important job was the complete overhaul of the Reichsbahn, the German State Railways. Emergency schedules and controls were set up. Trains were armor-plated to protect the crews and mounted with light antiaircraft guns to keep fighter-bombers high.

On October 11, Jodl presented Hitler with the draft of his plan for the Ardennes Offensive. Symbolically titled "Christrose," it called for the use of three armies—the Sixth Panzer Army, the Fifth Panzer Army, and the Seventh Army—with a combined strength of twelve panzer and eighteen infantry divisions. Operation "Christrose" was based on two premises: complete surprise, and weather that would ground Allied planes. It was designed to break through on a broad front, cross the Meuse on the second day, and reach Antwerp on the seventh day. It would destroy more than thirty American and British divisions.

To insure absolute secrecy only a selected few were told of the plan; a different code name for the offensive was to be used at each command level and changed every two weeks; nothing about the offensive was to be trusted to telephone or teletype; officers, sworn to silence, would be used as couriers.

To lay a firm groundwork for the deception, Keitel released a general order on October 12 to all commanders on the Western Front, declaring that no counteroffensive was possible at this time, that all strategic reserves must be deployed in the imminent defense of the Fatherland.

The morning of October 21, Jodl handed Hitler the revised plan. The Führer was delighted. He bandied a few jokes and affixed to the plan a new sly name of his own choosing—"Watch on the Rhine."

That afternoon, at Hitler's summons, a tall blond man in the uniform of an SS major reported to Wolf's Lair for a private interview. He was Otto Skorzeny, considered by British Intelligence the most dangerous man in Europe. His best-known exploit was snatching Mussolini from the Allies; most recently he had kidnaped Admiral Horthy's son and seized the Citadel, seat of the Hungarian government. Hitler greeted him with a broad smile, an outstretched hand, and an affectionate "Well done, Skorzeny!"

"Thank you, my Führer."

"Sit down and tell me about it—this Operation 'Mickey Mouse.'"

Skorzeny described the kidnaping of young Horthy, and the Führer laughed often. At the end of the story Skorzeny rose to go.

"Stay awhile," said the Führer excitedly. "I am now going to give you the most important job of your life. In December Germany will start a great offensive. It may decide her fate."

Skorzeny, he said, would play a leading role by training picked men to masquerade as Americans. They would work behind American lines—in American uniforms, with American vehicles. They would seize bridges over the Meuse, spread rumors, give false orders, breed confusion and panic.

"I'm giving you unlimited power to set up your brigade. Use it, *Colonel!*" Hitler smiled at Skorzeny's spontaneous grin. "Yes, I have promoted you to Obersturmbannführer."

Hitler rose and offered his hand again. "Good-bye, Skorzeny. I expect to hear great things of Operation 'Greif.'"

3

Early next morning Field Marshal Gerd von Rundstedt, commander-in-chief of all ground forces in the West, and Field Marshal Walther Model, Hitler's personal choice to command the offensive, were sent copies of "Watch on the Rhine."

Rundstedt read the plan with growing dismay and shook his head sadly. Although ingenious, "Watch on the Rhine" was too radical. Besides it was excessively ambitious for the troops now available. The leathery, tired old aristocrat set his aides to work on counterplan "Martin."

Model read the plan eagerly, for unlike Rundstedt, he was young, vigorous, and driven by an incredible ambition. And like Hitler he was a great gambler. But when he finished, he growled, "This damned thing hasn't got a leg to stand on!"

With that, Model went to work on *his* counterplan, "Autumn Fog."

On October 27, the Führer met with Rundstedt and Model.

He heard out all their objections to "Watch on the Rhine."

He listened impatiently as Rundstedt presented "Martin," an attack of seventeen divisions on a twenty-two-mile front.

He paced and grimaced as Model explained "Autumn Fog," an attack of twenty divisions on a forty-mile front.

He had heard enough and motioned for silence. "Don't you even remember Frederick the Great?" he asked sarcastically. "At Ross-bach and Leuten he defeated enemies *twice* his strength. How? By a bold attack." He threw up his hands. It was the same old story. His generals lacked imagination for the Big Solution. "Why don't you people study history?"

Frederick, he explained, had taken his big risk and then, as if in reward for daring, a bolt from the blue had come—an *unpredictable historical accident:* the alliance against Prussia suddenly split apart. And Frederick, doomed to defeat by every European seer, went on to win Germany's greatest victory.

"History will repeat itself," said Hitler. "The Ardennes will be *my* Rossbach and Leuten. And as a result another unpredictable histor-ical accident will take place: the Alliance against the Third Reich will suddenly split apart!"

And so Hitler made the decision—in spite of his generals. On December 7 he approved the final draft. It was almost exactly the same plan he had first proposed. It had even retained its deceptive title, "Watch on the Rhine."

4

"Watch on the Rhine" marched forward.

Commanders and chiefs-of-staff at corps level were brought into the plan. To guarantee security, generals were ordered to draft their own maps, take care of their own secretarial work, and keep all se-cret material on their persons day and night. Radio operators sent coded messages to fictitious headquarters, fictitious messages to gen-uine headquarters, genuine messages to headquarters a hundred miles from their advertised locations. False rumors were spread in lower echelons, in bars, in restaurants for the ears of Allied agents.

Now began the most difficult and dangerous phase of the prepara-tions. Within the next week, tens of thousands of troops and tens of thousands of tons of material had to be transported secretly, by night, from assembly areas to terminals just behind the front.

The great crush was on. By dark of December 7, the first loading had been completed, and every track ran one way—to the Ardennes. By three o'clock the next morning all trains had been unloaded, and were on their way back to the Rhine. Before daylight the round trip was over and another loading began.

The next day would be the same, and the next and the next.

Otto Skorzeny, who wielded more power as lieutenant colonel than most full generals, had now reached midterm of his "School for Americans." His volunteers were doing well. The course: American slang, habits, folkways, and how to spread panic behind enemy lines.

But another special group, under Lieutenant Colonel Friedrich August Baron von der Heydte, was just being organized. A quiet thoughtful man, the Baron would have seemed more at home in the classroom than the battlefield. In fact, in 1935 he had received a Carnegie Fellowship in International Law to teach at Columbia University. He turned it down to become one of Germany's most famous paratroop commanders.

In spite of intellectual doubts, "Watch on the Rhine" excited the soldier in von der Heydte. But when he was told his army commander would be Dietrich, the Baron was appalled. "Sepp"—Joe—Dietrich had been a sergeant in World War I, and a butcher and street brawler after it; at best he was qualified to lead a division. To von der Heydte, he was an uneducated brute. But Hitler was still rewarding him for his rabid support in the Munich Beer Hall Putsch, and now the butcher from Bavaria commanded a great army of nine divisions.

At his headquarters near Münstereifel, Dietrich, a big burly man with a rough voice, greeted von der Heydte disdainfully. "What are you paratroop boys able to do?"

"Anything within reason," replied von der Heydte, leaning away from Dietrich's whiskied breath.

"All right!" Dietrich slapped a map on the desk. "Take these places marked X."

"That's unreasonable," said the Baron.

"General Dietrich," interrupted Kraemer, his chief of staff, "those X's mark all the objectives."

"Why didn't you tell me before?" Dietrich grumbled. "You have your choice, von der Heydte."

The Baron chose the crossroads near Baraque Michel, in the desolate wasteland north of Malmédy, Belgium.

"Now, you will go there and make great confusion," said Dietrich. The Baron frowned.

Kraemer interrupted again. "It's not von der Heydte's group that makes confusion. You have it mixed up with Colonel Skorzeny's Operation 'Greif.'"

When the details had been set, the Baron asked for carrier pigeons in case their radios were broken in the drop.

"Pigeons!" Dietrich guffawed. "Don't be stupid! Pigeons! I'm leading my whole damn army without pigeons. You should be able to lead one kampfgruppe without a damn menagerie!"

In trying to hide his disgust, the Baron gave Dietrich the impression he was afraid.

"Don't worry," said Dietrich good-naturedly, clapping him on the back. "Take my word for it, I'll meet you personally at Baraque Michel. At noon on the first day of the attack."

No insane whim had made Hitler choose Dietrich. The Führer knew his weaknesses, fault by fault. But as with Rundstedt, Dietrich's name was magic with the troops. Hitler also wanted the great victories of the Sixth Panzer Army to be won by a good Nazi.

Besides, Hitler knew there were brains behind Dietrich—Kraemer's.

5

On December 11 the buildup was complete. The Reichsbahn, achieving a miracle in railroading, had delivered the first wave to the Zone of the Offensive.

Early that morning, Hitler moved into his new headquarters near the medieval castle of Ziegenberg in order to keep tight personal control of the offensive. The date for the start of the attack was definitely set as December 16. Now only the wrong weather—good flying weather—could hold back his armies.

Then he called a meeting to initiate the division commanders into the plan.

As these commanders and their staffs arrived, they were stripped of revolvers and briefcases by Gestapo men and forced to swear on their lives that they would reveal nothing of what they were about to hear. Not one knew why he had been summoned; each knew only that every division had been going in circles for weeks.

Hitler, flanked by Keitel and Jodl, walked into the briefing room. The Führer's left arm trembled and he looked worn. But for over an hour he excitedly lectured on Frederick the Great, the history of Germany, and the Nazi party.

Then "Watch on the Rhine" was explained in detail.

Starting at 5:30 A.M. on December 16, three great armies would break through on the Ardennes Front from Monschau to Echternach.

They would cross the Meuse between Liége and Namur, bypass Brussels, and reach Antwerp within a week. The western Allies would never recover from the initial surprise. They would be smashed and sue for a separate peace.

The division commanders listened thunderstruck.

The three attacking armies were: the Sixth Panzer Army, led by Sepp Dietrich; the Fifth Panzer Army, led by Baron Hasso von Manteuffel; and the Seventh Army, largely infantry, led by General Ernst Brandenberger.

Dietrich was assigned the northern flank and the main effort of "Watch on the Rhine." He would also have a preponderance of the best troops—an elite of the Waffen (Weapon) SS scraped together to form an army as formidable as those which had won the great victories on the Russian front. With four powerful panzer and five infantry divisions, the Sixth Panzer Army was to attack from Monschau to the Losheim Gap, rolling over Elsenborn Ridge, across the Meuse River, and on to Antwerp.

On Dietrich's left, to the south, was the Fifth Panzer Army commanded by a descendant of a famous family of Prussian generals, Manteuffel. An ex-gentleman jockey and German pentathlon champion little more than five feet tall, he was tough-minded, had formidable energy, and was one of the few who ever dared disagree openly with Hitler. For the past few months Manteuffel had had the Führer's ear perhaps more than any other field general. And into it he occasionally whispered one of his collection of pungent stories. This, too, no one else dared.

Manteuffel was given two objectives. On his right, two infantry divisions were to encircle the Schnee Eifel salient, trapping the 106th Division, and then capture St. Vith, the most vital rail and road center east of Bastogne. The rest of his army, three panzer and two infantry divisions, would race south of the Schnee Eifel, through Luxembourg.

Brandenberger's Seventh Army, the lightest of the three, was to seize the Vianden-Echternach area and then push west to protect Manteuffel's left flank. Brandenberger—a meticulous, dependable commander—not only looked like a scientist, but ran his army like one. He was eminently suited for his role. Though there was little glamour in the mission, the success of the entire offensive might depend on the wall of defense he could throw up against any counterattacks by Patton from the south.

The briefing was over.

"This battle," concluded Hitler, "is to decide whether we shall live or die. I want all my soldiers to fight hard and without pity. The battle must be fought with brutality and all resistance must be broken in a wave of terror. In this most serious hour of the Fatherland, I expect every one of my soldiers to be courageous and again courageous. The enemy must be beaten—now or never! Thus lives our Germany!"

The division commanders started back to the Ardennes.

6

There, last-minute preparations were under way. Movable ramps were brought up to convey tanks over the dragon's teeth of the Siegfried Line. Corduroy roads to the front were finished and thick beds of straw laid on them to deaden the clank of tanks and half-tracks. To conserve gasoline and hold down the sound of motors, ammunition for the opening barrage was moved up by hand, one round at a time.

Everywhere security was maximum. Radio silence prevailed, civilian phone service behind the lines was monitored. A camouflage officer was assigned to each village. A small army of special police roamed about, halting all unessential movement. Reconnaissance patrols were called off, and all artillery missions canceled. To minimize the risk of deserters, soldiers from Alsace, Belgium, and Luxembourg had already been transferred from their outfits to the interior; and now a strict schedule of roll calls, five or six a day, was begun. The troops were even issued charcoal, lest the smoke of wood-burning fires reveal their presence.

The last phase of "Watch on the Rhine" was about to begin.

7

On December 13, final reports were in from the men who had mounted "Watch on the Rhine."

General Jodl reported that 77,000 replacements had been fed into the three armies. The offensive would start with twenty divisions, but five more would be added shortly.

Marshal Keitel reported that 3.17 million gallons of fuel had been delivered to the front, with 2.11 million on the way and 792,000 in reserve. Each tank had enough fuel to travel ninety to one hundred miles.

As for ammunition, Keitel reported that an eight-day supply—15,-099 tons—was on hand. A second eight-day supply was ready to be brought up.

General Kreipe reported that the Luftwaffe had assembled 350 aircraft, including almost eighty of the new jet planes. More were expected before the foul weather broke.

That night the three German armies began to move in stages, across the ten-mile band of woods and silence separating them from the enemy, to their final attack positions. Infantry divisions moved to a restraining line six miles from the front. Horse-drawn guns and howitzers were brought within five miles of their firing pits.

The next night, while German planes swooped low to drown out the noise, tanks and half-tracks moved forward to within six miles of the front and infantry crept to within three miles. Horse-drawn and motorized artillery rolled secretly to their emplacements.

And now at last it was the night of December 15. Twenty divisions —250,000 men and thousands of machines—completed their last movements to the line of departure.

Near midnight all German soldiers in the offensive were assembled at their assault posts. They stood shivering but listened with avid curiosity as officers read a message from Field Marshal Gerd von Rundstedt:

> Soldiers of the Western Front! Your great hour has come. Large attacking armies have started against the Anglo-Americans. I do not have to tell you more than that. You feel it yourself. *We gamble everything!* You carry with you the holy obligation to give all to achieve superhuman objectives for our Fatherland and our Führer!

The excitement of old victories rose in the men. Once more they were on the attack. Deutschland über alles!

Then it was past midnight. It was December 16, 1944. All was quiet along the 85-mile Ghost Front.

3. ATTACK

16 December 1944

1

Fog hung thick in the Schnee Eifel on the morning of December 16. The men of the Tank Artillery Regiment of the 1st SS Panzer Division, "Hitler's Own," were tense with excitement.

"All batteries ready to fire!" came the report.

On a nearby road, tanks of the division were lined up for attack like a great winding dragon. A commander waved to the man standing in the turret of the next tank.

"Good-bye, Lieutenant, see you in America!"

The lieutenant laughed.

Final checks were made on the range finders. Throats were dry, hands poised at the lanyards, eyes fixed on watches.

Up and down the line the arms of gunnery officers were raised. It was 5:30 A.M.

"Fire!"

An eruption of flame and smoke burst all along the Ghost Front. For eighty-five miles mortars coughed, rockets hissed up their launching platforms, 88s roared. The ground shook. Snow-covered fir trees quivered, shaking veils of white to the ground. Hundreds of tanks rumbled and clanked, and from the rear came the hollow boom of railroad guns hurling their fourteen-inch shells at targets miles behind the American lines.

In his foxhole near the northern end of the Ardennes Front, Private Anthony Thibeau of the 99th Division was awakened by shells shrieking overhead. Then came the sounds of ashcans—"screaming meemies"—and a second later two hollow plunks of mortars a few yards away. After that the explosions blended into each other too fast to be identified.

Half a mile to the rear, officers were stumbling into the Battalion Command Post. The tremendous nonstop barrage awed and confounded them. According to intelligence reports, the Germans had only two horse-drawn artillery pieces opposite their sector.

"Christ!" said the executive officer. "They sure are working those two poor horses to death!"

Even further to the rear, a half dozen men sat drinking coffee in a 99th Division mess tent while the cook, Tyger by name, mixed a batch of pancake batter. Shells began flying overhead.

"Give 'em hell, boys!" one GI said.

A shell landed a hundred yards away.

"That's *incoming* mail!" said Tyger in surprise.

Then came an explosion overhead and Tyger leaped in the air. As the others stared at shrapnel holes in the tent, Tyger slowly, fastidiously withdrew his foot from the can of batter, and started stirring again.

To the south, in the Losheim Gap, Sergeant John Banister of the 14th Cavalry Group was out of bed, staring east through the gloom. No shells were falling in his village, Krewinkel, but the people on the left were catching it. He recalled that house a half-mile away filled with fifty Germans. If they attacked in force, his outfit could do little to stop them.

To Banister's right, out on the tip of the Schnee Eifel salient, there was considerable confusion at the command post of Lieutenant Alan Jones, son of the commanding general of the 106th Division. With telephone wires knocked out and German band music jamming every American wave length, young Jones was completely out of touch. He knew that the barrage was heavy, that so far casualties were light; and that was all he knew.

Just south, in the middle of the 28th Division line, German artillery was pounding the little villages along "Skyline Drive," the macadam highway that ran parallel to and about two miles west of the Our River. But soon this barrage lifted and shells began to land in rear echelon towns. Most important of these was Clervaux.

Here, Joseph Geiben, the young townsman who had escaped the German Army after forced service in Russia, was awakened by the explosions. He dressed and woke up his mother. "Oh, it's just the Americans shooting," she mumbled. "Go back to bed."

Geiben went downstairs. Just as he opened the front door, he heard a high-pitched whistle and dropped to the floor. The explosion rocked the house; clouds of dust rolled over him. Then he got up and looked around. The door was shattered, the front window blown out. By the light of the burning house across the street Geiben saw his mother and two sisters, their eyes large and frightened, coming shakily downstairs. Now there was no doubt about it: the Germans were coming back.

South of the 28th Division, in foxholes strung along the Sauer River, the novices of the 9th Armored Division were braced under their first barrage. It was worse than they had imagined. How could a man live through it?

A few miles further south, the 4th Division's forward positions were being pounded to pieces. In and near Echternach, outposts had been destroyed and all telephone wires were knocked out.

All along the Ardennes Front, this rude reveille had awakened American soldiers, Belgians, and Luxembourgers. Yet in the confusion caused by the breakdown in communications, each isolated group thought it alone was being softened for some local attack.

2

After an hour the barrage stopped. There was a stunned silence, but only for a moment. Then at key points all along the front giant searchlights from the east stabbed through the morning fog. American frontline positions, battered and smoking, were lit up. GIs stared out, faces white in the deathly glow. This was their first terrifying, bewildering taste of the new Nazi fright weapon, "artificial moonlight."

Now ghostly white-sheeted forms came out of the haze toward them, advancing in a slow ominous walk twelve and fourteen abreast.

In the north, infantrymen of Sepp Dietrich's Sixth Panzer Army burst into the 99th Division's forward positions. As they did, planes of a new design came out of the east with a strange crackling roar, streaking by at unbelievable speed. The Germans looked up, suddenly realizing these were the new jets. They cheered, wild with excitement. Hitler's "miraculous weapons" were a fact. Even the hard-bitten veterans who had been pummeled in Russia and chased across France felt new hope. Exultantly they swept forward, leaping and screaming and waving their rifles.

The power, fervor, and surprise of their attack was met by a stubborn if makeshift defense by the green American troops. Cooks and bakers, clerks and musicians, loggers and truck drivers were thrown pell-mell into the line to stem the tide. Some ran; many stood and fought. Though Dietrich had boasted he would overwhelm this untried division in the first assault, the line from Monschau to the Losheim Gap wavered but held.

At the Gap it was a different story. Here there was little to stop the attackers. Already planks had been thrown across selected sections of the concrete "dragon's teeth." These were quickly fastened to underpinning, secretly constructed the previous night. Tanks, armored cars, and assault guns roared over these improvised bridges and through huge holes already punched in the loosely held American lines by infantrymen.

Before dawn the weak link between the 99th Division and General Jones's attached troops, the 14th Cavalry Group, was broken. The little intelligence and reconnaissance patrol of the 99th, which was supposed to make an hourly jeep trip across the two-mile hole that separated their division from the cavalrymen, was cut off by infiltrating Germans. All it could do was report that its part of the Losheim Gap was "crawling with Krauts!" Then there was silence.

Not far south of this patrol, in the heart of the Losheim Gap, Sergeant John Banister of the 14th Cavalry was watching hundreds of Germans streaming toward Krewinkel.

His squad had taken machine guns to the second floor of their house and concentrated fire power on the waves of attackers. The main tide of Germans swept around them and continued to the west.

Banister, a big, solidly built man of twenty-two, could turn a joke

on almost anything. But the situation that morning looked too serious for joking.

Another white-sheeted wave loomed out of the haze and drizzle.
But it was held off, and at 7:30 A.M. drifted back, leaving the yards
littered with dead.

"Take a ten-minute break," a German shouted in English. "We'll
be back."

"Go to hell!" Banister shouted back. "We'll still be here."

Telephones were already jangling in Vielsalm, twenty-five miles
to the rear, where the reserve half of the 14th Cavalry Group was
resting. At 7:30 A.M., as 1st Lieutenant Bob Reppa was finishing a
leisurely breakfast, a message came through from the Losheim Gap.
Five enemy tanks, it was reported, were raising hell with their comrades up front who had pulled back.

Reppa was disgusted. He wrapped his liquor rations in a bed roll
and hopped into his armored car. The reserves, originally part of
Chicago's famous "Black Horse" Troop, would have to put out the
fire.

The report was false, but the nine hundred cavalrymen of Banister's squadron needed help desperately: they were the target not
only of Dietrich's left flank but also of the right flank of Manteuffel's
Fifth Panzer Army.

Already Manteuffel's infantrymen had bypassed the cavalrymen's
strongpoints in the southern section of the Losheim Gap in an attempt to drive a deep wedge to the village of Schönberg which lay
directly behind the Schnee Eifel salient. At the same time other
Manteuffel infantrymen were driving a similar wedge on the other
side of the Schnee. The two forces were aiming for Schönberg like
the jaws of giant ice tongs. And Jones's 106th Division would be
completely encircled.

But this was not Manteuffel's most important operation. At the
moment he was personally supervising a strong five-division tank
and infantry attack aimed at the center of the Ghost Front held by
the veteran but exhausted 28th Division.

Hours before the opening of the early morning barrage, Manteuffel had sent infantrymen across the Our in rubber boats to clear the
way for tank attack. The left flank of the 28th reacted quickly and
although several kitchens were captured, it soon drove back the in-
vaders. Scores of thin-faced Germans now lay dead around the

kitchens, some with their mouths still stuffed with half-eaten frank-furters.

But the center of the 28th Division, bearing the brunt of the at-tack, was already in serious trouble. Village strongpoints all along Skyline Drive were surrounded and under heavy assault. Here the German infantrymen had done their job well. The road to the west —to Clervaux, Bastogne, and the Meuse River—was open.

But the Tiger and Panther tanks, which should have darted into this opening, failed to appear. Something had gone wrong at Das-burg, where the 2nd Panzer Division was supposed to cross the Our River.

Engineers still had not flung a bridge across this river by 7:40 A.M., when Lieutenant Rudolph Siebert and his armored car com-pany came down the winding mountain road to the little border town. Some dummkopf had let the overlay reach the crossing site ahead of the sixty-ton bridge's main section. All was confusion on the narrow road. In desperation Siebert crossed the river in his amphib-ious Volkswagen. On the German side of the Our, miles of tanks and armored cars continued to pile up in a vast traffic jam.

In spite of this mistake, the center of the American line faced mo-mentary disaster. Seventy-five thousand men and more than two hundred tanks were about to burst across the Our River.

Their main obstacle was a single regimental combat team, 5,000 men. Their main roadblock was the lovely castle town of Clervaux. Here, six miles due west of the Dasburg crossing, the townspeople were on the verge of panic. They roamed the streets clamoring for information from the passing soldiers. But the GIs knew less than the civilians. They had come to Clervaux for rest, and they didn't like the idea of being away from their outfits in time of trouble.

In the Claravallis Hotel, just down the street from the battlements of the castle, Colonel Hurley Fuller was trying to make sense out of the confusing reports from the Skyline Drive villages. He knew that the position of his entire 110th Regiment, strung out for seven miles in front of Clervaux, was growing critical, but he could only guess at the details. The opening barrage had knocked out all his com-munications; telephones were dead, radios jammed.

At 7:45 A.M., a messenger from his northern battalion excitedly re-ported that all strongpoints along the Skyline Drive were being hit hard by enemy infantry. So far there were no tanks.

A few minutes later an even more excited messenger came from Fuller's southern battalion. Here tanks *had* crossed the Our and were heading west. Even horse-drawn artillery had been seen racing down the valleys.

There were the beginnings of alarm in the Claravallis Hotel, but the little office of Hurley Fuller remained calm. He issued orders curtly, pungently. It was obvious he was in his element. Word spread from room to room that he was in rare form. The incipient panic died. A reaming from the "old man" was more to be feared than the Krauts.

South of Fuller's regiment, the Seventh Army of General Ernst Brandenberger was attacking all the way to the terminus of the Ghost Front, Echternach. For an hour infantrymen had been boating across the Sauer. Now they were stealing up draws masked by fogs and heavy woods.

American forward positions along the entire southern sector were already either bypassed, as at Echternach, or overwhelmed, as at Vianden. Columns of Germans were moving west up the glens and gorges like armies of ants. In a tiny plane above the battlefield an American artillery observer radioed, "My God, this area is as full of targets as a pinball machine!"

By 9 A.M. "Watch on the Rhine" was developing well. The Losheim Gap was being overrun, and the center of the erstwhile Ghost Front, the gateway to Bastogne, was pierced in a dozen places.

A definite pattern had appeared but no one on the Allied side could see it. With telephone lines knocked out and radios jammed, the battle was on the squad, platoon, and company level; Regiment was hard put to communicate with Battalion up front and Division to the rear; and many would die in ignorance before Division could get intelligence and receive instructions from Corps. The whole process of command had been short-circuited.

By mid-morning conflicting reports had traveled deviously up to the corps level. In Bastogne, Troy Middleton paused many times in his general perplexity to worry about the Schnee Eifel; no matter what its size and objectives, the German attack meant hardship for Jones and his 106th.

Leonard Gerow, commander of the northerly V Corps, had an

even more complex problem. He was not only being attacked, he himself was attacking with one of his divisions toward the Roer Dams. If the German assault turned out to be a big one, his 2nd Division could quickly be cut off, wiped out.

The reports from the northern front grew graver with every hour. At 11 A.M., Gerow put through a call to his superior, Courtney Hodges, at First Army Headquarters in Spa.

"I'd like to halt my attack," he said.

Hodges thought for a moment. Earlier that morning the 2nd Division, after a brilliant infiltration maneuver, had captured a hornet's nest in the Siegfried Line, Wahlerscheid crossroads. The attack on the Roer Dams was finally rolling.

"Keep your attack moving," he told Gerow. From the spotty, conflicting reports it appeared that the German action was only a spoiling attack.

At that same moment Omar Bradley, Hodges' superior, was insulated from even spotty and conflicting reports; he was in his staff car, speeding toward Versailles and the conference with Eisenhower. Two hours before, he had departed Luxembourg City unaware that the Germans were attacking just twenty miles away.

In Versailles, Eisenhower was pausing in his hectic schedule to write a jesting letter to Montgomery. The day before he had been dunned by the Field Marshal for five pounds—the amount he had wagered that the war would be over by Christmas.

"I still have nine days," he answered.

3

By noon every village in the Losheim Gap was either taken, under siege, or about to be attacked. Every road in and to the Gap was in a frenzy.

Colonel Mark Devine, commander of the 14th Cavalry, was now up front seeing for himself what was happening. At a few minutes past twelve he started back to his command post in Manderfeld.

Here he found the narrow streets jammed with service and artillery vehicles heading west for St. Vith and safety. Hysterical civilians ran alongside, begging to be taken along. Others, German at heart, stood by smiling and nodding.

When Devine walked into his command post, he found the place a shambles and his staff packing up. He was enraged. A tough, hard-driving commander of the "spit and polish" school, he soon had everyone unpacking.

In Krewinkel, two miles forward, Sergeant John Banister's Troop C had spent the whole morning fighting off one violent attack after another. Then at 1:00 P.M., with ammunition running out, the survivors were ordered into five jeeps and three armored cars. As the little convoy headed west, Germans in white capes converged from three sides on the wrecked village.

Banister's convoy entered Manderfeld from the east just as the reserve squadron, led by Lieutenant Bob Reppa's Troop A, drove in from the west. Believing a false report that the men up front had fled without firing a shot, the reservists jeered as the two columns passed.

But the men of Troop C, faces gaunt and filthy, ignored the catcalls and followed their officers to a hill facing east where they began digging foxholes.

Through the early afternoon, as supporting infantry followed German assault troops through the Losheim Gap, the American situation worsened rapidly. In panic Colonel Devine's executive officer telephoned Jones's Command Post at St. Vith: "Germans passing southwest of us! They're moving toward the Our!" If the 14th Cavalry did not withdraw at once, he insisted, they would be cut off from the rear.

Permission was given to withdraw, and soon Banister's troop was evacuating Manderfeld covered by the guns of the "Black Horse" Squadron. But the men of this proud unit, who had started the morning so leisurely in reserve, were not far behind. Although they still had seen little action, their colonel had already turned over the outfit to his executive: he was reported to be in a highly nervous state and hurrying to the rear "for ammunition."

In the scramble to get out of town ahead of the Germans, the Americans set fire to several buildings solely in order to burn important papers. The whole town was burning by the time Bob Reppa's Troop A, the last to leave, raced northwest through the gathering dusk.

After several miles Reppa came to the squalid village of Holzcheim, where he was supposed to set up a defense. An Anti-Buzz Bomb battery was just pulling out.

"Krauts!" shouted a lieutenant. "They've cut the main road to Schönberg. They'll be here any minute. You'd better follow us north to Honsfeld!"

"I don't have orders to pull out," said Reppa. He went back to his radio and once more tried to contact the squadron command post. His orders had been vague to begin with, and unless he could check them now, any move he made would be the wrong one.

This time Squadron acknowledged receipt of Reppa's message. But the request for orders remained unanswered.

Reppa set up his little force on the high ground east of town. With nothing to do, the men sat uneasily and stared down into Holzcheim, now growing dim in the dusk. The villagers were cool, almost hostile, clearing their houses of all traces of American occupation.

"In a few minutes," someone said grimly, "they'll be hanging out German flags."

4

By dusk the important conference on infantry replacements was in session at SHAEF headquarters in Versailles. Attending were Eisenhower, his staff, and Bradley.

Midway in the discussion, a colonel came into the conference room and quietly delivered a message to British Major General Ken Strong, Eisenhower's intelligence officer. Strong read it himself, then interrupted to read it aloud: "This morning the enemy counterattacked at five separate points across the First Army sector."

Bradley surmised it was merely a spoiling attack. "The other fellow knows that he must lighten the pressure Patton has built up against him," he said in his calm midwestern accent. "If by coming through the Ardennes he can force us to pull Patton's troops out of the Saar and throw them against his counteroffensive, he'll get what he's after. And that's just a little more time."

"This is no local attack, Brad," Eisenhower said. "It isn't logical for the Germans to launch a local attack at our weakest point."

"If it's not a local attack, what kind of attack is it?"

"That remains to be seen. But I don't think we can afford to sit on our hands till we've found out."

"What do you think we should do, then?"

"Send Middleton some help. About two armored divisions."

"I suppose," Bradley said, "that it *would* be safer that way. Of course, you know one of these divisions will have to come from Patton."

"So?"

"So Georgie won't like losing a division a few days before his big attack on the Saar."

"You tell him," Eisenhower said with some heat, "that Ike is running this damned war!"

A minute later, Bradley was on the phone talking to Lieutenant General George Patton in Nancy, command post of the Third Army. "George," he said, "get the 10th Armored on the road to Luxembourg City."

The line crackled with Patton's objections. If the 10th was stolen from him, he might not be able to break through to the Saar, and what did they want with another armored division anyway?

Bradley patiently explained the situation.

"But God damn it!" Patton said in his high thin voice. "There's no major threat up there. That's just a goddam little spoiling attack. They want to throw us off balance down here. Make me stop my offensive."

"I hate like hell to do it, George, but I'm taking that division. Troy Middleton must have help."

Bradley then called his own headquarters in Luxembourg City and told his chief of staff to order Ninth Army to send the 7th Armored Division down from Holland.

As he was hanging up, Walter Bedell Smith, Eisenhower's chief of staff, put a hand on Bradley's shoulder. "Well, Brad," he said, "you've been wishing for a counterattack. Now it looks like you've got it."

"A counterattack, yes," Bradley said with a tight smile, "but I'll be damned if I wanted one this big."

Within the hour Bradley's orders traveled from Luxembourg City to Ninth Army Headquarters to the 7th Armored Division in Eubach, Germany, twenty-seven miles north of Monschau.

In Eubach, Brigadier General Bruce Clarke of Combat Command B of the 7th Armored was in his quarters packing for a leave in Paris. It hadn't been his idea, though this was his fifth month of continuous combat duty. Brigadier General Robert Hasbrouck, the division's new commander, had insisted he take three days.

Just as Clarke finished dressing, he was called to the phone.

"Bruce," Hasbrouck said, "I'm afraid you can't go to Paris after all. Division just got orders to move down to Bastogne."

"Bastogne! That's practically a rest area. What're we going to do there?"

"I have no idea. General Simpson told me to go down and report to Troy Middleton. You go on ahead and find out what the probable mission is. Maybe they're having a little trouble down there."

Clarke left. A few minutes later the information Hasbrouck had given him was incorrect. The 7th was to head not for Bastogne but for Vielsalm. But even this new order was already outdated. The 7th was needed desperately twelve miles farther east, in St. Vith. Unfortunately the battle could not wait for messages or orders.

In the grim somber stone town of St. Vith the streets were now dark, the houses blacked out. The Americans sensed a hostility on the part of some of the local inhabitants even stronger than that of the day before. Although half the townspeople—those who considered themselves Belgian—were packing their belongings in terror, the German half were quite obviously delighted. Soon St. Vith would be German again.

In his schoolhouse command post, Alan Jones was waiting for some word from corps commander Troy Middleton. Jones was aware the Germans had burst into the Losheim Gap and were close to cutting off his men on the Schnee Eifel, but he didn't know that by now the 14th Cavalry Group was almost completely shattered and that St. Vith itself was being marked on German maps as the next day's main objective.

Though facts were few, the men in this schoolhouse knew a debacle was brewing. Weary and distraught, they filled the halls, talking excitedly.

Into this confusion walked a stern-faced brigadier general, William Hoge, of Combat Command B of the 9th Armored Division. By reputation he was as unshakable as his rocklike appearance. Noncoms were running about and junior officers arguing in loud voices, and he could get nothing but rumors from them. In disgust he went upstairs to Jones's office.

"You've heard about it?" Jones asked him.

"I haven't heard anything," Hoge said in his abrupt manner. "I was reconnoitering up in Monschau. General Gerow told me my outfit was released and I was to report here to you. I came straight on down."

"It's bad," Jones said. "They've hit my whole front around the Eifel. Two regiments are nearly cut off."

"What shall I do?"

"Move your combat command up here right away. I want you to attack toward Schönberg tomorrow morning. Bring my regiments back!"

Without comment Hoge left the office. While trying to find a phone to contact his command post, he ran into Colonel Mark Devine of the 14th Cavalry Group.

"What the devil's happening out there?" Hoge asked.

Devine, who had seen his little force smashed by two divisions, could give no coherent answer.

In the meantime Jones was having his long-awaited conversation with Middleton. Both men were guarding their language carefully: chances were that the enemy was listening in.

"I'm worried about some of my people," Jones said. The connection was bad and he was almost shouting.

"I know." Middleton realized Jones was referring to his regiments out on the Schnee Eifel. "How are they?"

"Not well. And very lonely."

"I'm sending up a big friend, 'Workshop.' It should reach you about 0700 tomorrow."

"Workshop," Jones knew, was the 7th Armored Division's code name. He felt a great relief. "Now about my people," he said. "Don't you think I should call them out?"

Because of the bad connection, Middleton didn't hear this last sentence. "You know how things are up there better than I do," he said. "But don't you think your troops should be withdrawn?"

Jones, in turn, didn't hear this question. "I want to know how it looks from where you are," he insisted. "Shall I wait? Is there time?" He was convinced that Middleton meant him to keep his men on the Schnee Eifel. He felt he should argue, but he hesitated. Perhaps being new to action he was overcautious and overconcerned. He decided to rely on Middleton's experience. He hung up.

With a sigh Jones looked up at Colonel Malin Craig, one of his artillery officers. "Well, that's it!" he said tightly. "Middleton says we should leave them in. Get General Hoge."

As Craig started for the door he told himself the two regiments were lost, and for no good.

Jones, his face brightening, now turned to Lieutenant Colonel Slayden, an VIII Corps officer lent him by Middleton. "But here's some good news. I'm getting the 7th Armored. They'll be here early in the morning."

Slayden started to tell Jones that the 7th was so far north it couldn't possibly arrive before noon, but he said nothing.

The door opened and Hoge walked in.

"The 7th Armored is coming," said Jones. "They'll be here tomorrow around 7:00 A.M." He walked to a wall map. From St. Vith two roads ran east to the Schnee Eifel. He pointed to a village on the northerly road. "I'm going to have the 7th attack Schönberg instead of you. I want you to take Winterspelt." He now pointed to a village between St. Vith and the trapped men on the southerly road.

After hours of tension, Jones finally began to unwind. He had been hit a sledge-hammer blow, and the situation was critical, but in the morning the 7th Armored and Hoge's combat command would drive through to the Schnee Eifel. Until then his men would manage. He had worked hard to make fighters of them, and he was proud of every one of the 8,000. He was particularly proud of 1st Lieutenant Alan Jones, Jr.

In Bastogne a staff officer came into Middleton's office.

"I just talked to Jones," Middleton said. "I told him to pull his regiments off the Schnee Eifel."

5

After 8:00 P.M., fighting gradually slacked off, and all along the front preparations began for tomorrow's action. But the situation was still developing around the two major German breakthrough areas: in the Losheim Gap and east of Clervaux.

It was a night full of motion in the quaint castle town of Clervaux. As small-arms fire broke out in the eastern distance, Colonel Hurley Fuller was telephoning Major General Norman Cota, commander of the 28th Division.

"But I've *got* to have my 2nd Battalion," he said. In his years of service since World War I, Fuller had never bothered to adjust his tone to rank.

"I'm sorry," said the equally explosive Cota, "but the answer is still no. They're my only reserve. I've got two other regiments to think about, you know."

Fuller angrily asked again.

Again Cota refused. "But," he added, "I *will* let you use the officers and men on rest duty in Clervaux."

Fuller hung up and quickly rounded up the three hundred men who had come to Clervaux for a good time. They were armed with rifles, carbines, and grenades and sent hustling to the eastern outskirts. Then cooks, personnel clerks, and Special Service men were assembled at hotels all over town and told to help the MPs defend the castle.

One cook, tears running down his cheeks, was holding a grenade in terror. "I've been in the army three years," he said, "and all I've done is cook. I'll get blown to hell!"

As this pickup brigade reluctantly marched to the castle, once more shells began falling in town.

At 9:30 P.M. Fuller was called to the phone again.

"I'm considering releasing to you the 2nd Battalion," said Cota. "What do you plan to do with it, *if* you get it?"

"I'll counterattack!" was the quick answer. "I'll relieve the surrounded garrison at Marnach." This was the key town that lay between the Our River and Clervaux. "And if that is successful, I'll continue the attack astride the Marnach-Hosingen road and relieve my men at Hosingen."

Cota grunted. "You can have the 2nd Battalion, less Company G which I'm holding in reserve."

Fuller hung up. Now he had something to put out on the ridge east of Clervaux.

But Fuller's plans were more than matched by Manteuffel's plans for him. An entire tank division, the elite 2nd Panzer, and a division of grenadiers were preparing for dawn assault. Manteuffel was determined to have Clervaux by noon the next day.

In the Losheim Gap, twenty-five miles northeast of Clervaux, the situation was more complex and far more urgent.

Dietrich and Manteuffel, shoulder to shoulder, had smashed a broad hole in the Gap and were about to burst out the Belgian side of the corridor. And when they did Manteuffel would surge southwest toward St. Vith and Dietrich would knife due west.

Yet neither Troy Middleton, commander of the corps Manteuffel

was threatening, nor Gerow, commander of the corps through which
Dietrich would make his race to the Meuse, suspected that the
Losheim Gap was wide open.

The 14th Cavalry Group was too shattered, scattered, and confused to send back the correct information to Middleton.

And although the 99th Division knew it had lost contact with the
cavalrymen since early that morning, this intelligence, by an inexplicable oversight, had still not filtered back to Gerow.

At 9:30 P.M. the V Corps commander was actually feeling rather
secure. It had been a rough day all along the 99th Division lines, but
reacting quickly, Gerow had backed up the breaches and weak
points with two reserve battalions of the 2nd Division. Now the entire line seemed in fairly good shape.

His appraisal was based on an oversight. The front door was
locked. But the side door, the southern end of his lines, was wide
open.

The quiet village of Honsfeld stood near this southern terminus.
The road due west to the front lines was orderly. The 99th Division
forward positions were holding and there was nothing to worry
about yet. But the road from Holzcheim, two miles due south, was
fast becoming clogged with terrified VIII Corps refugees from the
Losheim Gap disaster. This mob of assorted anti-aircraft, supply,
and artillery troops now roared into peaceful Honsfeld from the
south, and without stopping headed to the rear. Those watching a
movie in the recreation hall wished the noisy traffic would slack
off.

About to join this panic flight was Lieutenant Bob Reppa's Troop
A of the 14th Cavalry Group. Reppa had fretted in Holzcheim for
two hours without hearing from his headquarters. Now, without orders or regrets, he was leaving the unfriendly town. It was obvious
the Germans would soon arrive. He hoped he and his men would
get to Honsfeld before they were caught from behind.

For the moment they were safe. The Germans were almost as confused about the state of the Losheim Gap as the Americans. By evening Sepp Dietrich was thoroughly disgruntled over the progress of
his Sixth Panzer Army. According to plan the green 99th Division
should have collapsed that morning.

The most exasperating obstacle had come at Losheimergraben, a village at the Belgian opening of the Losheim Gap. Volksgrenadiers had failed to clear out the stubborn Americans, who were managing to hang on to the village. By hanging on, these few men were blocking the main road to the west. The situation was even more aggravated by a blown-up railroad overpass a mile east of the village. Although German engineers had long since arrived, they could do little. One truck containing vital bridge parts was missing.

The 12th SS Panzer Division was to have passed over this bridge long before noon. But at 7:30 P.M. it was fighting traffic, not Americans, in a great jam extending miles to the east. Its tanks, churning clods of mud, were hopelessly trying to clear a path through a solid mass of infantry vehicles.

Behind the stalled panzers sat Obersturmbannführer Otto Skorzeny's brigade, dressed in American uniforms. Knowing that Operation "Greif" needed a breakthrough to succeed, and realizing he would never get it on this road, Skorzeny angrily pulled his three kampfgruppes—battle groups—into a wood to await developments. He sent several jeep-loads of men in American uniforms to look for a hole in the line. But "Greif's" chances waned with each passing minute.

Near the head of this entire clogged line, another obersturmbannführer (SS Lieutenant Colonel) was in a vicious temper. This was Jochen Peiper, commander of the spearhead of the 1st SS Panzer Division. The ardent young Nazi leader of Kampfgruppe Peiper was already a legend, as much for correcting generals as for his daring tank raids in Russia.

Peiper had got this far forward by ruthlessly pushing a horse-drawn artillery outfit off the road. Leading the way in an armored car, he finally reached the bottleneck itself—the unrepaired overpass. Without hesitation he ordered his driver to swerve off the highway. Peiper's car skidded down the steep railroad embankment. The other tanks and cars of the kampfgruppe followed.

At this moment he received a radio-telephone order from Corps: "Swing west to Lanzerath. 3rd Parachute Division has been stopped. Take over and get them moving again."

The road to Lanzerath was rough and deadly. A few of the leading tanks exploded. The preceding parachutists had failed to clear the German mines laid months before. But Peiper was too impatient to wait for mine detectors.

"Clear the road by rolling over the mines," he ordered.

Although six tanks and half-tracks were sacrificed to their own mines, it was almost midnight before Peiper rolled into Lanzerath. It was strangely quiet for a frontline zone. But the colonel in charge of the parachutists told Peiper the woods to the west, which lay between them and Honsfeld, were alive with mines and fiercely defending Americans.

Peiper was bitterly disappointed. This meant another delay of several hours while he regrouped his spearhead. It was a senseless delay. There wasn't a single mine or American in the woods ahead.

Two miles northwest in Honsfeld, trucks at the recreation hall were being loaded with GIs due back at the front after a three-day rest. The word was that there'd been some trouble up front but the situation was now in hand. As his truck started, a 99th Division corporal waved good-bye to a heavy-set Belgian girl. She waved back, so he blew her a kiss and called, "So long, you crummy-looking beast."

Elated, the girl cried, "Danke schön, mein herr!"

As the last of these trucks headed east, Lieutenant Bob Reppa of the 14th Cavalry Group led his little convoy into the dreary village from the south.

Honsfeld was a different world. Reppa saw a GI standing placidly in a little musical comedy candy-striped sentry box; then he met a captain of the 99th Division who smiled and told him to take it easy —the town was a rest area for the 394th Regiment. Here the good word was: relax.

At the captain's suggestion Reppa set up his command post in the Red Cross Headquarters. Then he established one platoon as a roadblock at the south end of town and two others in a perimeter defense. But when he returned he was still uneasy, and the captain was still amused by his nervousness.

"But where the hell is everyone?" Reppa demanded. "How come I'm all alone?"

By way of explanation the captain called his own regimental headquarters and connected Reppa with a staff officer.

"I haven't seen any Krauts yet," Reppa said, "but I know they're coming."

"You have nothing to worry about, young man," said the staff officer. "You're well behind the front lines. And since you'll come under my command at daybreak, I want you to prepare to make contact with the enemy."

"At daybreak," Reppa muttered to himself, "the Krauts'll be here making their own contact."

"What was that, young man?"

"Nothing, sir. Good night."

Then the 99th Division captain smiled and told him to stop this foolishness. In particular he should stop screening vehicles at the roadblock south of town; antiaircraft and tank destroyer units were streaming up from the Losheim Gap, and traffic had to be kept rolling.

Reppa, his fears somewhat allayed, tried to relax. It had been a day of wild alarms and sudden movements and nervous waiting. He wished something would happen.

6

By midnight, fighting had stopped almost completely along the Ardennes Front.

Echternach, the southern anchor, though surrounded, was still in American hands.

In Clervaux, Colonel Hurley Fuller dozed by the phone in his command post.

In Honsfeld, Lieutenant Bob Reppa was waiting for dawn. Orders had finally come from Squadron to move southwest at daylight. The crisis, apparently, was over. Only a few miles to his south, Colonel Jochen Peiper was regrouping his spearhead for the attack toward Honsfeld.

The first German shell had yet to fall in Hitler's beloved Monschau, northern anchor of the line; the little American garrison had turned in early, as if nothing at all had happened that day on the Ghost Front.

Far north of Monschau, men of the 7th Armored Division were loading their trucks, fueling their Shermans and half-tracks, studying road maps of the Ardennes. They were expected in St. Vith in seven hours, but were headed for Vielsalm.

Another relieving American column was already on the road. Although the spate of confused reports at Spa still failed to show a full-scale German attack, Courtney Hodges was being properly cautious. He had ordered those veteran troubleshooters, the 1st Division, to hustle down from the north just in case things were worse than they appeared.

Far to the west, Versailles was being swamped with reports from the front. It seemed a hundred of them used the same language—"All hell just broke loose!" But no one in SHAEF yet realized this was Hitler's greatest gamble, an all-out attack aimed at Antwerp.

And the Allied world teetered on the brink of disaster.

It was well past midnight when the phone rang in German Army Group G Headquarters far south of the Ardennes. The man at the other end claimed to be the Führer, and he demanded to speak personally with the commanding general.

General of the Armored Forces Balck hurried to the phone.

"From this day on, Balck," Hitler said, "not a foot of ground is to be given up. Today we march!"

"Ah," said Balck, and settled himself in a chair to listen.

Hitler told him of the opening successes in the Ardennes. He described how Dietrich—staunch old Dietrich—had punched a hole in the Losheim Gap and, now only a few miles from Honsfeld, was about to break into the open with Kampfgruppe Peiper. He told how Manteuffel was swiftly cutting off the Schnee Eifel with one corps and was driving toward the Meuse with two others; already he stood on the heights just east of Clervaux and promised to pry open the road to Bastogne before the next noon.

And the weather was still "Hitler weather." Fog, drizzle, and haze, it was forecast, would continue to hold down Allied planes.

For five minutes Hitler talked to Balck, and Balck, who had seen the other war too, sat and listened and felt excitement rising in him.

And then at the end, his voice tight with emotion, Hitler cried out, "Balck, Balck, everything has changed in the West! Success—complete success—is now in our grasp!"

4. BREAKTHROUGH

17 December 1944

1

A few minutes past midnight an Allied agent far behind enemy lines tapped out a message: "15 Junkers-88 and 90 Junkers-52 to take off at 0145 Paderborn-Wahn area. Destination ten miles south of Aachen. To return at 0530."

This information, correct but for the exact time and destination, was carefully noted by Allied Intelligence. Its meaning was clear: a major paratroop drop was about to be made, probably in an effort to impede U.S. reinforcements to the Ardennes from the north. Even as the message started up through Allied channels, 1,200 German paratroopers were boarding the big Junker transports at Paderborn and Lippspringe.

Their leader was Baron von der Heydte. He was ready—if far from prepared—to drop in the woods north of Malmédy and try to cut off any reinforcements sent south to the Ardennes.

About 1:00 A.M. on the morning of December 17, the first plane, von der Heydte aboard, took off from Lippspringe. Half an hour later the last plane left Paderborn. Kampfgruppe von der Heydte was airborne.

As the swarm of Junkers roared toward the Ardennes, the Baron watched the raw enlisted men fidgeting. He had seen his troops for the first time only five days before, and they were the sorriest lot he had ever commanded.

The Junkers were now flying in bomber stream, their inexperienced pilots guided by a line of friendly searchlights. In von der Heydte's plane, the enlisted men were whispering, cursing the Amis, then the Luftwaffe. For their benefit the jump-master patiently reviewed the operation once again.

At 3:15 A.M. von der Heydte made a last check of his parachute, a new triangular Russian type that was supposed to be oscillation-free. He'd be the first German to use one on a combat jump. Then, as he tightened the sling on his heavily taped left arm, it occurred to him he'd probably be the first commander to jump into battle with a broken arm.

He hoped that at least the target area had been properly marked. Four naphtha bombs should already have been dropped to form a cross. Three of them were supposed to burn white; the fourth, a red one, would point due west.

Now the air came alive with anti-aircraft fire. They were passing over the front. The flak was so heavy it seemed almost as though the Americans had known they were coming.

With no German searchlights or flares to guide them further, the novice pilots gathered in a crude squadron formation. Red and green flight-lights flashed all over the sky; without these, the pilots would have crashed into each other.

The illuminated Junkers made easy targets, and the flak grew still heavier. Presently the plane behind von der Heydte's heeled over, plunged down, and spaded into the earth with a livid orange burst.

The Baron, hiding his feelings, glanced around. His ten enlisted men—only two had ever jumped before—were deeply shaken. He stood up and gave a few last orders. Then a brilliant burning cross appeared far below to the left—three white lights and one red. They were on target.

At 3:30 A.M. to the minute, von der Heydte tumbled out of the lead plane, his men following in good order. As the next planes passed overhead, the night bloomed with parachutes, pale blobs sailing against the dark. Yet there did not seem to be enough planes or parachutes. Had something else gone wrong?

The night was cold and the wind strong. For a time von der Heydte felt as though he were rising. Then the wind slacked off and he settled into the target area.

A wood loomed up at him, slid away at the last moment. His feet hit hard in the mud of a field. Before the wind could belly out his chute he pressed the two buttons on his chest and unstrapped the belts at his thighs.

Above him, lighted by red, yellow, and green fountains of tracers, his parachutes were still drifting down. But they were scattering in the high wind, and now he knew there were too few of them.

In fact, only ten of the 105 Junkers had followed von der Heydte all the way to the drop area. Most had been dispersed by the fierce anti-aircraft fire. About fifteen plane-loads had been dumped over Bonn, Germany, by overeager pilots.

By 3:50 A.M. the skies were clear of parachutes, and von der Heydte had collected four frightened privates, a sergeant with a twisted ankle, and a young lieutenant full of Nazi zeal who wanted very much to go on the attack.

An hour later another twenty joined von der Heydte in a dense thicket between a peat bog and a long stretch of spongy heather. He knew he would find a few more but not nearly enough. Kampfgruppe von der Heydte would be a small but spendthrift offering to a war that had already been lost. If the bomb plot of his cousin, Count Felix von Stauffenberg, had not gone awry, he would not be waiting on this desolate plateau for an ex-butcher.

Four days previously, Sepp Dietrich had promised to be at Baraque Michel by noon of the first day of the attack. Now it was 5:00 A.M. of the second day, and Dietrich was nowhere in sight.

But ten minutes later the Baron heard the deep rumble of many vehicles. His quickened hope died when he saw a long line of trucks loaded with infantrymen wearing a big red "1." And their trucks wore the American star, not the black cross.

This, he knew, was the elite American 1st Division, a hard enemy. He was supposed to stop them. With what?

2

Well before dawn the little advance party of the 7th Armored Division pulled into Bastogne, still unaware that St. Vith was their actual destination. General Bruce Clarke of Combat Command B was squeezed in the front seat of the old Mercedes-Benz lent him by the division commander, General Hasbrouck. All the way from Eubach he'd had to hold on to the gearshift to keep it in high. It had been a long cold drive, almost ended in Liége by a buzz bomb.

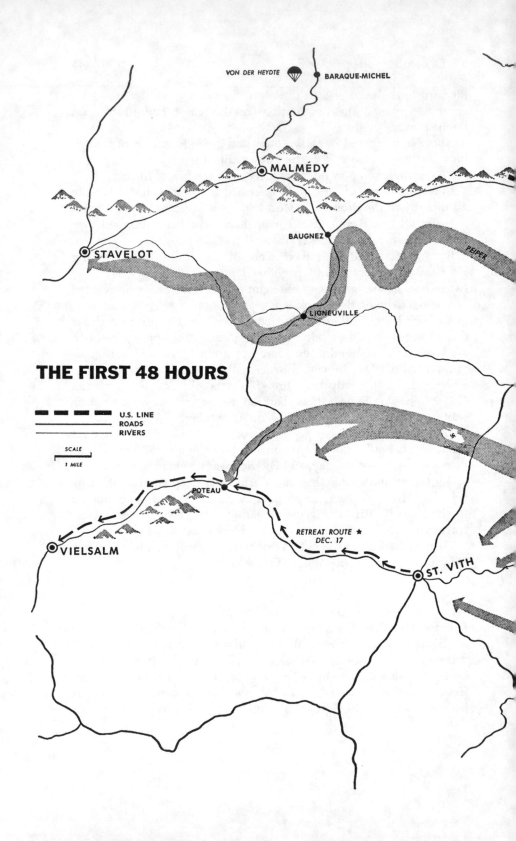

VON DER HEYDTE 🪂 ● BARAQUE-MICHEL

⛰ MALMÉDY

BAUGNEZ

◎ STAVELOT

PEIPER

● LIGNEUVILLE

THE FIRST 48 HOURS

▬ ▬ ▬ **U.S. LINE**
━━━━ ROADS
──── RIVERS

SCALE

1 MILE

POTEAU

RETREAT ROUTE ★
DEC. 17

◎ VIELSALM

● ST. VITH

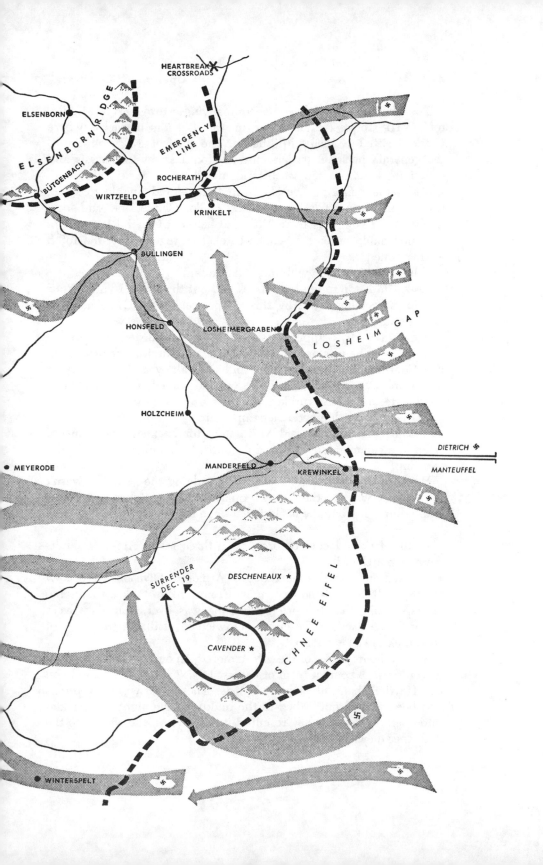

The Mercedes and the jeep accompanying it drove up to Middleton's VIII Corps Headquarters in the Belgian barracks, where Clarke insisted on seeing Middleton. The chief of staff took him to the general's personal trailer, mounted on a six-by-six chassis and containing a built-in bed, washstand, and closet.

Middleton, suffering acutely from bursitis and unable to sleep, was reading when Clarke entered. "Hello, Clarke," he said, cordially. "You're to go up to St. Vith and help out General Jones. He's in some trouble out on the Schnee Eifel. Two regiments of the 106th are marooned there."

"I have just four men with me," Clarke said.

Now Middleton found his glasses and put them on. "I know. Your division is coming south by three separate routes." He smiled at Clarke's surprise.

A native of Mississippi, Troy Middleton had enlisted as a private in 1910. Now he was one of a new breed of American general who, like Courtney Hodges, ran his command calmly and efficiently as if it were a corporation; and the war he waged was logical, dispassionate, and utterly ruthless.

Clarke wearily slumped in a camp chair.

"Go to bed, Clarke," said Middleton, for he knew the value of sleep to a commander. "You can go to St. Vith and see Jones in the morning."

He seemed unconcerned, so Clarke, judging the situation wasn't too serious, went to the officers' quarters and stretched out on an empty bunk. It would be his last real sleep for six days.

In the dark and cold before dawn, three major American units were on march orders.

Blacked-out vehicles of the 7th Armored Division were now rolling south toward the Ardennes. From tank to tank a rumor began spreading that the war in Europe was over, that they were going to the Pacific. The crews scrawled in chalk on the sides of their tanks, PACIFIC BOUND.

Several hours ahead of the 7th Armored, on one of the same roads it would use, a combat team of the 1st Division had just passed von der Heydte's handful of parachutists. These overworked veterans had been yanked out of bed in the middle of the night and packed into open trucks, and they resented it bitterly. All the way in to the Ardennes they shivered and griped.

Far to the south, the 10th Armored, the division "borrowed" from Patton, was in no hurry. It appeared likely the vanguard would not head north for Luxembourg City until that afternoon.

These three reinforcing units would arrive later than the American defenders hoped, but sooner than the German General Staff thought possible.

3

At 4:00 A.M. American vehicles—bumper to bumper—were still coming into Honsfeld from the shattered Losheim Gap sector: stray artillery pieces, long cut off from their batteries; anti-aircraft units which had suddenly found themselves in the front lines; jeeps and half-tracks filled with frightened cooks, engineers, and office personnel; trucks loaded with "201" forms, athletic equipment, clothing, and ammunition.

Not far behind this creeping column were two tanks, wide, low-slung, and much larger than any Sherman. Behind the tanks came armored cars, half-tracks, and more giant tanks. The vehicles were marked with the black cross, and the men in them wore black leather jackets.

In the first armored car rode Jochen Peiper.

After regrouping his spearhead, Peiper had attacked the woods west of Lanzerath. To his surprise and disgust, he met no resistance. Then he had swung onto the road Lieutenant Reppa had taken into Honsfeld and now lurked behind the unsuspecting American column.

A dark jumble of buildings, lit only by an occasional shell-burst loomed just ahead. It was Honsfeld.

In Honsfeld, Lieutenant Bob Reppa of the 14th Cavalry Group was sprawled in a chair, his head nodding. Abruptly he sat up, wide awake. The rumble of traffic outside the Red Cross Headquarters had changed pitch.

"Those don't sound like ours," he said to his first sergeant, William Lovelock, as he leaped to the front door and pulled it open. Vehicles were passing slowly. A shell burst nearby, lighting up the highway.

"Look!" He pointed at a half-track with slanted sides. American half-tracks had perpendicular sides. Then a huge 60-ton Tiger, twice as big as a Sherman, clanked by. "My God!" he gasped and carefully closed the door.

"They *are* German," Lovelock whispered.

Reppa's shock turned to anger. "That regimental commander was really wrong! And God damn it, why didn't Creel warn us?"

As his anger switched to the man he'd put in charge of the roadblock south of the town, Sergeant Creel himself walked in.

"What have you got to say for yourself?"

"I was in my armored car," Creel said calmly. "A guy came walking down the road in front of a big vehicle, swinging a flashlight. Biggest damn tank I've ever seen. With a swastika on it."

"Well, why the hell didn't you shoot?"

"I figured it'd be best to warn everyone. So here I am."

"Get all the men ready," ordered Reppa. "We're moving out of here. It's dark, and we'll just pull into their column. When we come to a crossroads we'll turn right and beat it."

Messengers ran out to prepare the column.

There was a great rumble outside. Reppa peeked out under the window shade and saw that a tank loaded with German paratroopers had stopped. The paratroopers, their guns trained on the house, were rushing for the door.

"Come out!" a German shouted.

Reppa looked at the others. Then he looked at the stairway which led to a second floor filled with wounded. Suddenly he felt like an old man.

"We can't make it," he muttered. "We can't do a damn thing."

He went to the door, opened it, and called, "Kamerad!"

By daylight Honsfeld had fallen; and Kampfgruppe Peiper, its main route to the Meuse lying wide open, was running wild. This was 1940 all over again.

Peiper now faced a weighty decision. Two miles northwest of his own designated course lay Bullingen, site of a big American dump. Again his vehicles were dangerously low on fuel. But he had orders, as had all other spearhead commanders, to adhere strictly to his own road—under penalty of death.

The ordinary German commander, slave to the "book," would have kept to the south and quickly run out of fuel. Peiper turned northwest, and after a sharp skirmish with engineers, fought his way into Bullingen. As he refueled, he kept glancing nervously to the east, half expecting to see the 12th SS Panzer Division. He needn't have worried. If he had not lost radio contact with the rear he would have known that this division, which owned the highway he had briefly borrowed, was still being held up at Losheimergraben by the 99th Division.

But a few minutes after Peiper had swung south, back to his own road, a strong armored reconnaissance party of his own division did roll into Bullingen. It paused briefly and then turned north. Its mission: to probe for enemy; its first objective: Wirtzfeld two miles to the north.

In this village, Colonel Matt Konop, commanding officer, of the 2nd Division's Special Troops was pacing in a farmhouse. At exactly 6:53 A.M. he was called to the phone.

"Listen to me, Konop!" The colonel recognized the voice of Major General Walter Robertson, 2nd Division commander, but he'd never heard him so excited. "I want you to alert all units and organize a last-ditch defense of the command post! Enemy tanks have broken through on our right flank at Bullingen. And we've got reports of a paratroop landing northwest of us. We've got to hold these positions. If they break through here, there's almost no opposition all the way to the coast! I want you to take every available gun and defend to the last man. Understand?"

"Yes, sir. But all I have left are cooks, clerks, and KPs."

"Put them all on the line!"

Shells began falling. As Konop was setting up a defense, Meyer Levin and Morley Cassidy, two reporters who had come to the farmhouse the night before, asked what was going on. Konop told them to forget about a story, to pack their gear and hightail it to the rear. In five minutes it might be too late. The crackle of machine-gun fire underlined Konop's warning.

The reporters stayed.

In a stone house half a mile away, Robertson was now talking by phone to V Corps. He explained that Wirtzfeld was being threatened from the south; in front of him the 99th Division line was crumbling; and to the north, just below Monschau, two thirds of his division was still attacking toward the Roer Dams.

Fifth Corps told him to withdraw his two attacking regiments at once, and set them up as an emergency defense line behind the hard-pressed 99th Division.

Immediately V Corps rang off, Robertson called Colonel Chester Hirschfelder, commander of the forces which had recently taken Wahlerscheid crossroads in the Siegfried Line. He told Hirschfelder to withdraw beginning about 9:00 A.M.

While he was talking, rifle and mortar fire broke out. Six German tanks, followed by half-tracks and infantry, suddenly appeared over the ridge eight hundred yards to the south of Wirtzfeld.

"God!" Robertson shouted into the phone. "The Germans are here!"

He watched out the window as Colonel Konop's three 37-mm. anti-tank guns—operated by his driver, a cook, and another driver—laid a deadly barrage on the advancing column. In fifteen minutes every German vehicle was knocked out. Then the makeshift army of cooks and clerks swept forward, killing the surviving German infantrymen.

Satisfied that Konop could hold Wirtzfeld, General Robertson now headed east in a jeep. His main worry was how to withdraw the men who had just punched a hole in the Siegfried Line.

On the road to the front he met his first retreating units. Officers and men were confused and bitter. They couldn't see why they were pulling out of Wahlerscheid after they'd fought so hard to take it. Already they were calling it "Heartbreak Crossroads."

As each unit withdrew, Robertson placed it in a new defense wall. It was obvious that the green troops of the 99th Division couldn't stand off the three German divisions attacking them much longer.

The alarming reports had not been exaggerated. Strong columns of volksgrenadiers, backed up by tanks of Dietrich's 12th SS Panzer Division, had broken through and were converging on Krinkelt and Rocherath, adjoining villages which lay a short five miles behind the center of the 99th Division lines. Astride the only possible roads to the west for miles, these twin villages were the prime German target of the day. And for the Americans, they were the funnel through which all the retreating men of the 2nd and 99th Divisions must pass to reach the safety of the rear. In a few hours these dingy twin villages would become the most important piece of real estate in the world.

4

To the south, Baron von Manteuffel's pincers biting off the two
regiments of the 106th Division on the Schnee Eifel were now ready
to snap shut at Schönberg, a valley village between the mountainous salient and St. Vith.

Three miles farther to the rear in St. Vith, General Alan Jones
was studying the great map on the operations room wall. Angry
arrows of red now completely surrounded his two regiments on
the Schnee Eifel.

Jones was desperate. Where was the 7th Armored? It should have
reached St. Vith early that morning and gone on to Schönberg. If
he had known the 7th was going to be late, he would have sent
Hoge's combat command to Schönberg instead of south to Winterspelt.

But distraught as he was, Jones kept his feelings well hidden. A
methodical man, preferring to run his division from the background,
he considered displays of emotion unmilitary.

With the Germans only six miles away and few American troops
in between, Jones organized his last men and turned them over to
Lieutenant Colonel Thomas Riggs, commander of the 81st Engineer
Combat Battalion and ex-football star of the University of Illinois.
With this scratch force of about five hundred engineers, a platoon of
riflemen, and three patched-up tank destroyers, Riggs headed east.
His mission: to delay the 18th Volksgrenadier Division until help
arrived.

Still trusting that the 7th Armored would appear at any moment, Jones dictated a message to his two trapped regiments:
"Reinforcements driving through this afternoon. Withdraw from
present positions if they become untenable."

His message, relayed by the division artillery radio network
would not be received until mid-afternoon.

An hour later, at 10:00 A.M., General Bruce Clarke, commander
of Combat Command B of the 7th Armored Division, pulled into St.
Vith. Traffic from Bastogne had been extremely heavy; and a few
miles out of St. Vith, in an attempt to go across a field, the
Mercedes-Benz had broken down. Once in town Clarke went directly to the big church school, St. Joseph's-Kloster, which served as

the command post of the 106th Division. Men were hurrying
about in the corridors, talking excitedly. He threaded his way
through the commotion and reported to Jones.

"Thank God!" Jones said. "I've been expecting you since seven!"

"Since seven?" Clarke frowned. "General Middleton didn't tell me
you were that bad off."

"I want you to attack Schönberg. Two of my regiments are cut off
on the Eifel. You've got to get them out of there! When can you
attack?"

"I can't say."

Jones looked at him in utter disbelief. "What do you mean?"

"I came ahead. I don't know when my men will arrive."

Jones, who had needed so much, so soon, said nothing.

5

By 10:30 A.M., alarming reports were coming into First Army Headquarters at Spa's Hotel Britannica. Swarms of German parachutists
had been seen a few miles to the east; enemy patrols were reported
far behind American lines.

The stream of reports from the front had swollen to a flood. They
were still frantic and fragmentary, confusing and conflicting. Even
so Courtney Hodges now realized he was in serious trouble. Clearly
a number of wide, deep holes had been punched in his front. This
could be a full-scale offensive.

Studying his latest situation report, Hodges concluded that the
heaviest attacks were coming from Sepp Dietrich's Sixth Panzer
Army. Dietrich posed two threats: a drive straight west to
the Meuse or a sudden turn north cutting off not only First Army
but also all the Allied forces in Holland.

The drive due west didn't worry Hodges as much as the possible
thrust north from Bullingen, reportedly in German hands. He had
to throw up a dam, keep the Nazi flood from pouring north. But
where was the best location? If he made the wrong choice, he might
not get a second chance. He studied a map, found himself returning time and again to a series of rolling wooded hills just behind the
twin villages of Krinkelt and Rocherath. These hills, parallel and a
few miles north of the main highway to the Meuse, were not high,
but they could give a formidable advantage to defenders—an advantage that could determine the outcome of the battle. Hodges
decided on these hills.

They were called Elsenborn Ridge.

At 11:00 A.M., Hodges put in a call to SHAEF in Versailles, asking for General Bradley, who had reportedly spent the night in St. Germain at Eisenhower's stone villa.

"Brad," said Hodges, "I want the two airborne divisions."

"But Courtney, the 101st and 82nd Airborne are Ike's only reserve."

"I've got to have them."

"Well, I'll ask."

While Hodges had not yet begun to fear for the safety of his own headquarters in Spa, already the battle was closing in on it. Less than fifteen miles southeast of the Britannica Hotel events of great military import were about to take place at Baugnez, a lonely spot where five roads crossed. It was marked on the routes of two great armored columns: Combat Command Reserve, one third of the 7th Armored Division, on its way to the Ardennes from the north for what reason it knew not; and Kampfgruppe Peiper, racing confidently toward the Meuse. The two columns—one from the north and one from the east—were converging on the crossroads.

But at Baugnez nothing was happening. It rarely did. Most of the inhabitants were at church several miles away in Malmédy. Two weren't. Henri Lejoly was feeding his cattle. A hundred yards away Madame Adel Bodarwé was behind the bar of the Café Bodarwé.

Twenty miles to the north two Americans in a jeep were heading for Baugnez. Major Don Boyer and his driver were an advance party of Combat Command Reserve of the 7th Armored Division. Their outfit, the last of the three combat commands in the division to move, had left Eubach, Germany, just after dawn but was making excellent time on the most direct route, down unobstructed roads.

Boyer looked more like a professor than a tank commander. After graduating from Virginia Military Institute in 1938, he had decided he was better fitted for foreign service and enrolled at the Fletcher School of Law and Diplomacy. But Pearl Harbor had changed his mind again.

He had no idea why the 7th Armored had been so abruptly put on the march. He knew only that he was to report to Vielsalm, an important road junction about twenty miles to the rear of St. Vith.

Since Vielsalm was so far behind the front, he figured the division was probably going into VIII Corps reserve.

An MP, gesturing with a submachine gun, stopped the jeep. "Who's Mickey Mouse's girl friend?" he asked, shoving the muzzle at Boyer's stomach.

Boyer thought the man had gone crazy, but he answered, "Minnie."

"Who are Dem Bums?"

"The Brooklyn Dodgers."

"You're okay," said the MP. "But we got to be careful. Kraut paratroopers landed around here last night. They're wearing American uniforms and using our jeeps, and they speak English as good as me."

Boyer took his driver's M-1 out of the clip holder on the windshield. "Step on the gas. Let's get as far ahead of the column as we can. We've got to find out what's going on."

Twenty minutes later the jeep rolled into the austere town of Malmédy. The people stood about in the streets, staring at Boyer, some with strange smiles, others darkly.

In the main square an MP pointed out the road to Baugnez. "Major, what's going on here?" said the MP. "Something's fishy. Just look at the people. They're so damn surly."

"You've got me, soldier." But as they started forward again it came to Boyer: this unhappy region had changed hands so often between Belgium and Germany that the people were simply resentful at the prospect of another change.

The jeep hurried to Baugnez and its five converging roads. In front of a dreary café bearing the odd name of Bodarwé, Boyer checked his map, then told his driver to take the road leading south.

Half an hour later the two men came to a tiny settlement of a dozen houses and barns. Checking his map again, Boyer discovered that this was Poteau. Here their road should feed into the main highway connecting St. Vith with the west.

The jeep went through Poteau, then suddenly came to a macadam highway running east-west. Trucks, jeeps, guns, tanks, half-tracks, prime-movers—vehicles of every kind— were heading to the rear. The one-way traffic now ground to a stop. Horns blew and drivers shouted; a command car filled with officers pulled out and raced westward down the empty eastbound lane. Its horn blowing, a truck carrying three bareheaded, disheveled men followed the command car, then an armored car, a crane truck, and a prime-mover without a gun. At last the main column swarmed forward again. It stretched out in both directions as far as the eye could see. And nothing was coming east toward the front lines.

Boyer was shocked. This was no convoy; it was wild retreat. He told his driver to break into the surging traffic and follow it to Vielsalm, a few miles to the rear.

The column speeded momentarily, then began to crawl. Again, just as Boyer's jeep was approaching a small village, it stopped dead. The din—horns, angry voices, the roar of motors—was over-powering.

Boyer climbed out of his jeep. Ahead he saw a vast tangle of cars. A great armored column, its drivers shouting angrily, was trying to break through from the other direction but the retreating vehicles now were packed solid in both lanes.

Boyer went up to an ordnance officer wearing a lion's head shoulder patch. "What's your outfit?" he asked.

"Hundred sixth Division."

"Where from?"

"St. Vith."

"What's the score?"

"Two panzer armies—at least six panzer divisions—hit us yester-day!"

"What are you doing about it?"

"Me, I'm leaving."

"What's in front of St. Vith?"

"I don't know. Maybe some cavalry. Maybe nothing. Everyone's pulling out. God, what a mess!"

Boyer pushed forward and soon discovered the armored force trying to break through from the west was Bruce Clarke's Combat Command B. After arriving in Vielsalm by a roundabout route, it had been told to continue east and join Clarke in St. Vith.

Boyer now figured his outfit was also needed in St. Vith, not Vielsalm. But he had to make sure. He ran back to his jeep, moved his driver over, and steered off the road into a muddy field. Maybe he could get his new orders in Vielsalm and return to Poteau in time to head off Combat Command R before it debouched into this traffic jam and turned in the wrong direction.

In St. Vith, General Jones could no longer conceal his fears for the two encircled regiments on the Schnee Eifel. By now, he guessed, they were low on food, ammunition, and medical supplies. It was time for emergency measures.

He called the VIII Corps air officer who agreed that supplies should be parachuted immediately, and relayed the information to the IX Fighter Command. Jones's request ground up through channels, passing through numerous headquarters to the IX Tactical Air Command, back to First Army for approval, on to SHAEF. Finally, hours later, it arrived at CATOR (Combined Air Transport Operations Room). Even then, the IX Troops Carrier Command, whose pilots would fly the mission, would not get its orders until the next morning.

But at 1:30 P.M., Jones radioed his two regiments that air resupply drops would be made that night.

He now turned his full attention to St. Vith itself. First he learned to his consternation that Colonel Devine had pulled back the remnants of the 14th Cavalry Group almost to St. Vith—without orders.

Then at 2:00 P.M., word came that German vehicles had been sighted only two miles to the east. While Jones was discussing this latest development with Bruce Clarke, Devine burst into the office, his face flushed.

"The Germans are right behind us!" he cried. "They've broken through in the north. My group is practically destroyed!"

"Why don't you send the Colonel back to Bastogne?" Clarke suggested. Devine, he thought, was in no state of mind to be useful at the front. "He could report the situation to General Middleton."

Before Jones could answer, a message came in from Riggs. The little task force of engineers had been forced under heavy pressure to retreat from positions just one mile east of St. Vith.

Now heavy firing—this time from big American guns—broke out to the north. A Cub observation plane had spotted a column of German tanks and infantry converging on St. Vith.

A 155-mm. shell exploded on the lead German tank. The column stopped. Fifty more rounds poured in, and the Germans scattered to the rear.

"Getting heavy resistance," radioed the German commander.

The attackers regrouped but were reluctant to advance, little realizing that all that stood between them and St. Vith was a small band of engineers who knew next to nothing about their bazookas and machine guns.

In New York City, few of those eating Sunday breakfast were reading about the great offensive in the Ardennes. The story of the German attack was buried on page 19 of the *Times*. Only a fraction of the few who read it were concerned. For although the headline read, "GERMAN ASSAULTS ON 1ST ARMY FIERCE," the subhead was reassuring: "Enemy Pays Heavy Price in Futile Blow to Stem the Advance of Hodges."

5. DEBACLE

17 December 1944

1

All that morning Kampfgruppe Peiper, on its way to the Meuse, had been heading toward Baugnez. All morning Combat Command Reserve of the 7th Armored Division, on its way to St. Vith to help rescue General Jones's 106th, had been heading toward Baugnez. By noon they were within ten miles of each other and bearing down on the lonely road junction.

At 12:05 P.M. Combat Command Reserve rolled through Malmédy, made a sharp turn east, and labored up a steep hill. In ten minutes it was slowing down at the Baugnez crossroads.

A solitary MP in front of the Café Bodarwé directed it down the southern road toward Poteau. Then, after watching the last vehicle disappear at 12:45 P.M., the MP got into his jeep and started back to Malmédy. He had an hour to kill before the next column from the north, the division artillery, was due.

Fifteen minutes later, a small American convoy of jeeps and trucks crawled up the hill from Malmédy. This was Battery B of the 285th Field Artillery Observation Battalion. Attached to no division as yet, it was a relatively innocent and defenseless outfit. By rare luck it had squeezed into the 7th Armored Division line of march between CCR and the artillery.

As this independent little convoy was passing the Café Bodarwé, one of its jeeps pulled out of line and parked. Three men entered the café.

Henri Lejoly, the farmer from across the road, was alone inside with Madame Bodarwé.

"Vielsalm?" asked the first American, pointing south.

Madame Bodarwé, who considered herself Belgian even though her husband was now doing forced service in the German army, nodded pleasantly.

The American turned to Lejoly. "Avez-vous vu des Allemands?"

Lejoly, who considered himself German in spite of his name, shook his head curtly. He'd have said nothing anyway.

Just then a half-track topped the rise east of the crossroads. Behind it rumbled two more half-tracks and three tanks, the spearhead of Kampfgruppe Peiper.

The young commander was a hundred yards to the rear in a recently captured jeep, questioning an American lieutenant colonel. There was, Peiper learned, an important U.S. headquarters in nearby Ligneuville. It would soon be his for the grabbing.

Peiper was feeling much better than he had the day before. Since leaving Bullingen, he had seen nothing of the Amis but an occasional jeep scuttling for safety. His breakthrough was complete.

The low thudding of 88s and the sharp chatter of machine guns suddenly broke out ahead. The spearhead had caught sight of the American column slowly heading south past the Café Bodarwé. Peiper raced forward and ordered the spearhead to cease firing. Any more noise, he told them, might alert the unsuspecting Amis in Ligneuville.

Henry Lejoly stood boldly in the doorway of the café and waved as Peiper's spearhead turned south. A few moments later he saw about 125 American soldiers come back along the same road, hands in the air. The entire little observation convoy had been captured.

German guards herded the Americans into the open field next to the café. Hands still in the air, they chatted with an unconcern that baffled Lejoly.

Now more vehicles, the main body of Kampfgruppe Peiper, began rolling out of the east and turning south at the café. A half-track stopped. A man in the rear stood up, aimed a pistol, and fired into the group of prisoners. One fell.

"Stand fast!" cried an American officer. The prisoners, suddenly terrified, huddled together.

An armored car skidded to a stop. There was a second pistol shot, then the dry hacking of a machine gun.

The Americans moaned and screamed.

Lejoly saw them falling. He watched in horror as they were all cut down.

The machine gun stopped firing.

Several Americans tried to crawl away. They were shot by pistol. Others were writhing in pain. They were shot by pistol. In two minutes the 125 men were a tangled, blood-spattered mass of still bodies.

Next Lejoly saw Germans setting fire to the café of his friend, Madame Bodarwé. He stole across the road to his farm.

Three miles south of Baugnez, the last units of Combat Command Reserve of the 7th Armored were now rolling past Ligneuville. This pleasant village was best known for the Hotel du Moulin, an inn famous with tourists for its trout, Ardennes ham, and its amiable host, Peter Rupp. An elderly but ardent Belgian and a violent anti-Nazi, Rupp had helped smuggle out twenty-two Allied aviators during the German occupation.

The men in the trucks were sleeping; a few standing up in the tank turrets waved and whistled at the girls dressed up for Sunday.

The last vehicle passed; the clouds of dust settled; the heavy gas fumes dissipated. Then it was quiet again—too quiet. The townspeople began to wonder. Ever since early morning American soldiers had been fleeing south. Then just a few minutes ago the not so distant rumble of guns had been heard. Were the Boche coming again?

They buttonholed the few soldiers bivouacked in town and asked what was happening. These soldiers, who had arrived late the night before, driving the supply trucks of General Bill Hoge's Combat Command B of the 9th Armored Division, shrugged their shoulders. They had no idea what was going on.

Their commander, Captain Seymour Green, only knew he had been ordered to proceed to Ligneuville and meet two other supply trains. He didn't have the slightest hint that a zealous obersturmbannführer, was only half a mile away.

Suddenly a bulldozer roared down the hill from Baugnez at twice its safe speed. "German tanks!" shouted the driver to Captain Green who stood near the Hotel du Moulin.

"Captain, I was shot at by German tanks!" the engineer shouted.

"Get the outfit ready to move," Green called to his first sergeant. Then he jumped into a jeep and headed north up the winding hill toward Baugnez. To make plans he had to see just how close the Germans were.

At a sharp bend in the road Green stopped the driver. "I'm going ahead to do some snooping. If anything happens, go back." Carrying a carbine, he crept around the bend.

Twenty-five yards away, a German scout car was crawling toward him, followed bumper to bumper by a long armored column. Green stopped. So did the column.

First Green was stunned. Then he felt silly, crouching there, one man with a carbine.

A German officer motioned him to the other side of the road. As the column passed, several SS men raised their machine pistols and laughed.

Soon the lead vehicles of Kampfgruppe Peiper were edging cautiously around the bend and down the road. Far below them, the first of Green's service trucks were scrambling out of Ligneuville to the south. Peiper's armored cars and trucks spurted down the hill to wipe them out. It would be a shooting gallery.

Suddenly one of the lead German cars burst into flames and slewed around blocking the road. Peiper's column stopped.

A lone Sherman, one of its tracks removed for repairs, stood near the Hotel du Moulin pumping round after round into the column, trying to hold off the Germans long enough for the American vehicles to escape.

Finally an 88 scored a direct hit on the Sherman. Kampfgruppe Peiper raced through town, destroying the last laggard trucks in Green's column. The advance guard continued down the main highway for a mile, crossed the Amblève River, and turned west into the dirt road leading over a rugged hill to Stavelot, the next objective.

In Ligneuville, a command post was already being set up in the Hotel du Moulin. As prisoners were herded into the lobby, hotelowner Peter Rupp, his arms flailing wildly, accosted a German sergeant. A few minutes before, Rupp had seen him executing Americans behind the hotel.

"Murderer! You killed eight of them! I saw you put the pistol in their mouths!"

The sergeant punched the old man in the jaw, knocking out two teeth.

An officer approached. "Shoot them all," he said. "The Belgian swine too."

The sergeant started herding the Americans and Rupp outside.

"Leave them alone, Sergeant!" A second officer, wearing SS insignia, pushed forward. He put his hand on Rupp's back. "You're right, mein herr. It's a shame how some people treat prisoners." He looked with distaste at the other officer. Then turning he said in a hard voice, "Sergeant, put these men in that room and treat them as you'd want the Amis to treat you."

Three miles to the north, half-tracks of Peiper's column were still passing the smoldering ruin of Café Bodarwé. Some of the troops, seeing the Americans' bodies, fired their rifles into the mass, just for practice.

But not all were dead. Ken Ahrens, wounded twice in the back, was still alive. The long motionless wait seemed to have frozen every part of him but his pain.

Then he heard whispers. Others were alive!

In undertones they made plans for escape. About twenty said they thought they could walk. It would be hard leaving the other wounded: obviously the Germans would make a closer examination and kill them off. But that was the reason they had to make a break for it.

"Let's go!" someone cried.

The twenty scrambled to their feet. There were surprised shouts from the passing Germans. Rifles cracked. The Americans scattered. Ahrens ran toward woods two hundred yards off. It seemed like a mile. Behind him survivors were dropping, bullets in the back.

Finally Ahrens and two others reached safety among the trees. They caught their breath and then, leaving a dribbled trail of blood, staggered through the underbrush toward the west—toward the town whose name would soon be a synonym for massacre: Malmédy.

In Ligneuville, the fourteen captured Americans were huddled in a room on the main floor of the Hotel du Moulin. Captain Seymour Green found the temper of the Germans hard to gauge. Some treated him diffidently, some casually, and others seemed ready to shoot at the first opportunity.

The German sergeant who had murdered Staff Sergeant Abraham Lincoln and seven others from the 14th Tank Battalion entered, nodded curtly to Green and escorted him to another room, where the SS officer, who had recently saved them all, offered a cigarette and asked pleasantly in English, "How do you like our tanks, Captain?"

Green shrugged his shoulders.

"Are you Jewish?"

"No. I'm early American stock."

The German put his hand to his mouth and whooped like an Indian. Then he asked where the division command post was located. After a moment's silence he said, "We never find out anything from you officers, but some private always tells us what we want to know." He picked up a book. "Now I'm going to enjoy myself with some reading. It's got a perfect title, don't you think?" Grinning, the German held the book for Green to see.

It was *An American Tragedy*.

Hotel-owner Peter Rupp still feared for the fourteen prisoners: the Germans were in a dangerous mood; if one thing went awry, the murdering might start again. Then an idea occurred to him. He had hundreds of bottles of the finest cognac and champagne in a secret wine cellar. He'd use them to keep the Boche happy.

He crept down into his cellar, filled his arms with bottles, and returned to the kitchen.

"Mary," he told his daughter, "give the guard a good cognac so I can talk to the prisoners."

Without question she left the room. A moment later Rupp went to the prisoners' room and was admitted. He held out two bottles.

"Just a minute," Green said suspiciously. "Are you Belgian or German?"

"Belgian, of course!"

A GI hid the bottles.

"Thanks for the cognac," Green said, "but we're hungry."

Rupp left the room and returned with eight plates on a huge tray. On his way back with six more meals he was stopped in the corridor by an angry SS officer.

"What's the idea?"

"Well, you're not feeding them, so I have to."

Rupp's wife, Balbina, had entered the hotel in time to hear the last exchange, and like her native Switzerland, she was small, strong-minded, and independent.

"See here," she said, looking up at the officer. "I'm from the Swiss Red Cross. I have orders to look after all prisoners. And they get that food!"

Rupp, his round face beaming, hurried in to the prisoners, while his wife continued haranguing the SS officer.

The meals delivered, he then stood guard in the lobby, surreptitiously handing out bottle after bottle of cognac to Germans, regardless of rank. The atmosphere of the Hotel du Moulin grew cordial, then jovial. Rupp knew the crisis had passed. His fourteen Americans would live.

2

The surrounded troops of the 106th Division on the Schnee Eifel were more confused than concerned that afternoon. So far, except for the men on the flanks, they'd seen little action.

Colonel George Descheneaux, Jr., commander of the 422nd Regiment and one of the youngest regimental commanders in the army, knew little more than his men. Ever since the first hours of the offensive, communications with Division had been sparse.

At 2:00 P.M., Descheneaux phoned Colonel Charles Cavender, commander of the regiment on his right. By now their only communication was this single telephone line.

"What are you going to do?" asked young Descheneaux.

Cavender, a veteran of the First World War, replied that he was not sure. He had just received the orders from Jones sent hours before to "Withdraw from present positions if they become untenable."

"Well," said Descheneaux, who still hadn't received an order, "until Division tells me definitely to move, I'm staying right where I am."

There was a slight pause at the other end. Then Cavender said, "So am I."

In St. Vith there was an air of impending disaster at the 106th Division's command post. The clamor in the corridors of the stone schoolhouse had stopped, but the crack of rifles sounded sharp and dry in the near distance. Jones and Clarke went to the top floor of the building. They saw tiny gray figures advancing in a crooked line from the edge of nearby woods.

Jones, his jaw set, his face expressionless, looked past the attacking Germans toward the Schnee Eifel. Out there were his two trapped regiments, and his son. He should have pulled them back last night in spite of Middleton. He should have followed his intuition. Now it was too late.

"Clarke," he said heavily, "I've thrown in my last chips. You take over the defense of St. Vith."

Clarke knew what Jones was going through; in less than two days his division had been smashed, and probably his career with it. On top of this he was suffering the anguish of a father. Clarke had three sons, and he vowed never to put them in his own outfit.

"All right," said Clarke curtly. "I'll take over." But with what?

Both the stand of St. Vith and the march of the 7th Armored were faring worse than Clarke imagined. The left flank of the town's defenses was just now beginning to disappear. Colonel Mark Devine, again without consulting Jones, had ordered his 14th Cavalry Group to retreat once more. Without having fired a shot all day the cavalrymen were getting as far west as possible.

The town, now defended only by Riggs's few engineers, depended solely on the arrival of Clarke's own Combat Command B.

Still short of Poteau, Combat Command B was battling frantic westbound vehicles on the St. Vith-Vielsalm highway in a spectacular traffic jam extending for almost twenty miles.

In Vielsalm, Major Don Boyer was in a cold rage. He had arrived at 2:05 P.M., and ever since he had been trying to unsnarl traffic and get information at the same time. At 2:40 P.M. he gave up. Swinging his jeep around the stalled armor of Combat Command B and plowing through muddy fields, he worked his way four miles toward the front. Here he learned that General Clarke had ordered the 31st Tank Battalion to launch an attack east of St. Vith early that afternoon. It was now 3:15 P.M. and the commander of the 31st was still struggling wildly to extricate his vehicles from the muck and muddle.

Boyer volunteered to clear a way. He commandeered a thirty-ton tank and moved onto the road, waving and shouting. Slowly a hole opened up. When a westbound weapons carrier refused to move, Boyer ordered the tank to charge. The weapons carrier turned into the ditch to avoid being crushed.

Boyer's tank rumbled forward a hundred feet, then halted. A retreating command car full of colonels was trying to dart into the space Boyer had just cleared.

He jumped in front of the **car.** "Get back! I don't give a damn who you are! Nothing's coming through unless it's going to the front!"

"Go get 'em, Major!" a GI shouted. "Give 'em hell!"

The tanks and armored cars of Combat Command B crept toward St. Vith, the men clinging to them clearing the way with shouts. They had been told, "Take no orders from any officer, regardless of rank, unless he wears the 7th Armored patch. If anyone gets in the way, run over the son of a bitch."

Then they broke into a stretch of clear road. It gave Boyer a shiver of pride to hear the 7th Armored men gun their motors, to see them head for St. Vith in a shower of mud. They were going into a fight that others were running away from.

A first sergeant jumped out of an artillery jeep headed to the rear. "I'm going with these damned tanks!" he shouted to his companions. "I'm in this here army to fight, not run!" The sergeant climbed up behind the turret of an eastbound tank.

"Hi, Mac," said a tanker. "You just joined the 7th Armored."

In St. Vith, Bruce Clarke was still waiting. Two hours had passed since he had taken over the defense of the town from Jones, and he knew that if his Combat Command B didn't arrive in a few minutes, and the rest of the 7th Armored after it, there would be nothing left to defend.

A messenger ran into his office on the first floor of the schoolhouse and reported that the crossroads a few hundred yards to the west was hopelessly snarled. Clarke's traffic control officer had been pushed aside by senior officers fleeing to the rear.

Within minutes Clarke himself stood at the crossroads, and he soon had the panic under control. The eastbound lane was cleared.

As dusk thickened, the sound of rifle fire from the east grew louder. It was difficult to tell how much longer Riggs's engineers could hold. Where was the 7th Armored?

"Here they come!" his driver shouted.

Around the bend to the west came a muddy jeep leading a column of filthy, overheated Sherman tanks.

"Take the Schönberg road!" Clarke called out to the tank commander. "Go east until you contact the engineers."

A few minutes later three Sherman tanks clanked down the hill east of town. Out of the growing darkness suddenly loomed a Panther. Its first shot went wild. The lead Sherman pivoted and fired. The German tank burst into flames. Others behind it spun and fled.

The 7th Armored had started its defense of St. Vith.

West of town, Clarke was still on traffic duty, positioning his troops as they dribbled in. Troop B of the 87th Reconnaissance Squadron had already been sent north of the engineers' roadblock. Company B of the 23rd Armored Infantry Battalion was rushed to the south of town. Slowly, improvising as he went along, Clarke set up a thin mobile arc of defense between Manteuffel and St. Vith.

In town, officers and men of Combat Command B began to take over the schoolhouse. A 7th Armored corporal and a 106th Division sergeant, bedrolls on their shoulders, passed on the stairs. "What the hell's wrong with you guys?" the infantry sergeant said. "Don't you know the Jerries are right on the edge of town?"

"Sure. But, man, we didn't march sixty-five miles just to turn around and go back."

It was dark when Major Don Boyer neared the western outskirts of St. Vith. He had spent all afternoon sending tanks to the front and making himself unpopular with high-ranking officers hurrying to the rear. Now he was guiding a lost company into town, swimming upstream in a tide of vehicles that was being swollen by both squadrons of the 14th Cavalry Group.

At the edge of St. Vith, Boyer slid off the hood of his jeep and went down the line repeating his orders: "If anybody gets in the way—" Usually he got no further than that before the tankers shouted back, "Run over the son of a bitch!" As he waved the column forward, a light tank raced by, its track plates ripping his pants clear across the seat.

The little column crawled the last dark, agonizing mile into St. Vith. Near the great dour church, Boyer jumped down to the road. A sharp crack sounded, a bullet whistled past his ear. He dropped face down into the muck. From that position he glimpsed a white face in a second-floor window across the street. It was a civilian sniper.

Boyer hailed a passing assault gun. A .50-caliber machine gun swung around and opened fire. What looked like the top half of a man's body tumbled out the window into the street.

Then a motorcycle roared down the road from the north and skidded to a stop near Boyer. An MP, his face cut and bleeding and his uniform ripped, staggered toward him. Boyer recognized him as one of Colonel Church Matthews' motorcycle escorts.

"Ambushed," the MP mumbled in shock. "Couple miles up the road. Ran into a Kraut column. What the hell were they doing *behind* us? I crawled in a ditch. The colonel, he ran up a hill. They machine-gunned him."

Boyer could hardly believe what he had heard. Not only had they lost their chief of staff, but St. Vith was cut off from the north.

As bad as that news was he was unaware that St. Vith was also being cut off from the south by Manteuffel's 2nd Panzer Division. A second pocket, much larger than the Schnee Eifel salient, was now in the making.

3

Baron Hasso von Manteuffel decided to spend that night with his right-hand corps for he was far from pleased with the slow progress toward St. Vith. It was true the town was outflanked to the north and south, but this was not enough. For St. Vith was excepted from Hitler's explicit orders to bypass all heavily defended towns. St. Vith had to be taken: five important highways extended from the town like spokes in a wheel; more important, it was the only rail center west of the Rhine capable of supporting the Fifth Panzer Army drive.

Manteuffel chose to spend the night in Schönberg at the headquarters of the 18th Volksgrenadiers; his presence might put some iron in their attack the next morning.

About mid-evening Manteuffel put on his overcoat and left his billet. Outside he paused for a moment. The traffic crawling past him was so heavy it would be faster to walk. He struck out across a muddy field for the 18th VG Headquarters.

Deep in thought, Manteuffel emerged at a crossing east of Schönberg and bumped into another pedestrian almost as small as he was. It was Field Marshal Model.

"Good evening, Marshal."

"Heil Hitler," Model said. "And how is your situation, Baron?"

"Mostly good."

"So? I got the impression you were lagging, especially in the St. Vith sector."

"Yes, but we'll take it tomorrow."

"I expect you to. And so that you'll take it quicker, tomorrow I'm letting you use the Führer Escort Brigade."

Manteuffel hesitated. He had planned to use the Führer Escort, an elite armored brigade, much further west. But Model had a point: first things first; the stronger force is half the battle.

"You disagree?" Model said casually.

"Not really. We've got to take St. Vith tomorrow. And," he added a bit reluctantly, "the brigade may swing the balance."

They walked a short way together. Theirs was a strange relationship, but a good one. Manteuffel respected Model for his drive and generalship, and Model returned the respect for much the same reasons. Yet it went little further: Model remained cool, aloof, impersonal. There was not much between them but the profession of war. This suited the Baron. After all, Model's father was a schoolteacher.

"I turn off here, Marshal," Manteuffel said. "Good night."

"Heil Hitler," Model said. "And good luck tomorrow."

Several miles north, in Manderfeld, Sepp Dietrich was pounding a table and laying down the law to commanders of five divisions. He was very unhappy about the progress of his army. The 12th SS Panzer Division should be racing for the Meuse, but it was still stalled in front of the twin villages of Rocherath and Krinkelt. And while Kampfgruppe Peiper had driven past Ligneuville, the rest of the 1st SS Panzer Division was lagging far behind.

Heatedly he ordered the 12th SS Panzer to break through the next day at all costs, but he did not tell the division commander precisely how this was to be done. Immediately a quarrel broke out.

Colonel Otto Skorzeny listened to the arguments, recriminations, excuses, threats. Finally he raised his voice and began talking: since his Operation "Greif" stood no chance without a full-scale breakthrough, and since they didn't have one, let the original plan be dropped and his three battle groups be used for some standard operation.

His suggestion was glumly approved.

Skorzeny, of course, couldn't know that seven jeeploads of his American-dressed commandos were actually working havoc. The leader of one team was directing an American regiment down the wrong road while his men were changing signposts and tearing up telephone wires. Another team, stopped by an American column for information, feigned fear so convincingly that the column turned tail. Another team tore up the main telephone cables connecting the headquarters of Hodges and Bradley.

But the greatest damage was done by a team that had been captured. When the four men confessed their mission to an American intelligence officer, the news was quickly broadcast that thousands of Germans in American uniforms were operating behind the lines. At once this new information was associated with the many reports of parachutists: von der Heydte's men had been scattered so widely that it was easy to believe at least a division had dropped; and all of them, it was assumed, were part of the plot.

Out of two fiascos was developing a formidable success. Hitler's dream of spreading chaos and terror could still be realized.

4

By mid-evening, the dam Hodges was throwing up on Elsenborn Ridge to hold back a possible surge to the north was beginning to take shape. The 1st Division had raced to Bütgenbach, and, arriving only moments before a German column, had dug in.

By a few minutes Hodges had won an important victory.

Northeast of Bütgenbach, as engineers frantically extended the Elsenborn Ridge defenses, exhausted shocked survivors of the 99th Division were already straggling back.

These men, after upsetting Dietrich's plans in front of Krinkelt and Rocherath, had drifted back to the twin villages late that afternoon. Here they had been directed by 2nd Division MPs to the rear.

Just before dusk the streets of the two villages had still been clogged with 99th Division men trying to get to the west and with 2nd Division men trying to set up a temporary defense line to hold back the Germans until Elsenborn Ridge was ready.

As shadows of evening began to fall, a battalion of the 2nd Division, commanded by Lieutenant Colonel Frank Mildren, was approaching the twin villages to fill a hole which existed between two other battalions of the 2nd in Krinkelt.

Mildren's men were disgruntled and disgusted. Yesterday they had helped take Wahlerscheid—Heartbreak Crossroads. Today they had been told to turn around and give up the stronghold that had cost so much blood.

As they slogged south, Christmas packages hanging from their belts and dangling at the ends of their rifles, they wondered what new foul-up the brass had invented for them.

A German scout of the 277th Volksgrenadier Division watched them pass from his hiding place in the woods. To him they looked more like postmen than soldiers.

But now as the dim outlines of Krinkelt and Rocherath loomed up in the fast-fading light the "postmen" suddenly turned into alert soldiers. For a rumor swept down the line that hard fighting had just broken out to the south and they might have to force their way into the twin villages.

Already the cloudy skies were darkening. Across the rolling fields, the outlines of the villages—Rocherath in the north, Krinkelt to the south—could be seen above shreds of fog clinging to the snow. Krinkelt's church tower rose black and menacing.

Mildren's men were supposed to dig in near this ominous-looking church, and he had already sent his executive ahead to reconnoiter. It would be like blindman's buff getting into position in the dark.

Without warning a monstrous barrage suddenly enveloped them. Trucks burst into flames and careened into the lines of men. Jeeps and weapons carriers ran wildly off into the fields. The riflemen lay helpless as mortar shells burst among them with terrible accuracy. Then came screaming meemies—multiple rockets—to add to the slaughter.

"Aringdale!" Mildren shouted to his adjutant. "Bring up the rear, pick up stragglers. I'm going to the head of the column."

Captain Aringdale started toward Mildren, staggered. He was pulled to the ditch. A GI tried clumsily to bind up the gaping wound in his chest.

On the night of December 15, Aringdale had told his friend Jesse Morrow that tomorrow he was going to die. He had been wrong by one day.

Mildren pushed his way forward through the snarl of screaming men and blazing machines. He had to get into Krinkelt and find out what the situation was.

A shell landed near by, knocking Mildren flat. He picked himself up, stumbled on into the outskirts of the first village, Rocherath, and weaved through its squalid streets to adjoining Krinkelt. He looked in vain for his executive officer. Confusion ran the streets. Stragglers—some armed, some empty-handed and helmetless—were scrambling from the fields into Krinkelt. Brilliant flashes lit the east, each one followed by a deep hollow boom. The petulant snapping of machine guns came from the woods beyond town.

Fifteen minutes later Mildren finally found the regimental command post on the southern outskirts of Krinkelt.

"For God's sake," he asked, "what's going on?"

The adjutant of the 38th Regiment pointed out the positions Mildren was to take up in front of Krinkelt.

"But who's on my left? Who's on my right?"

No one knew. And no one knew where the enemy was coming from.

They were coming from the woods to the east.

So were front-line survivors of the 99th Division. In small groups and large, they struggled through slippery snow, looking desperately for refuge, keeping together in the darkness by hanging on to each other's cartridge belts. By now mortar squads had thrown away tubes, base plates, and ammunition; riflemen had dropped their Christmas packages, bedrolls, shelter halves, overcoats—even their food and rifles.

Some groups discovered they had been traveling in circles for hours. Others found themselves heading east instead of west. Every noise was terrifying. For they knew Germans were on all sides.

When they were too exhausted to go on, they bedded down in the snow or in shallow foxholes, but they were too cold and miserable to sleep. They wished it were tomorrow, but they dreaded the light of day.

Many felt guilty about retreating. There was no basis for guilt. These green troops had already held up the powerful 12th SS Panzer Division for a day and a half. They didn't know it but their job was finished. From now on the burden would rest on the veterans of the 2nd Division.

The dark had brought fog but no respite for the 2nd Division defenders of the twin villages. Just east of Rocherath, Lieutenant
Colonel William D. McKinley—grand-nephew of the president—
was inspecting his lines. General Robertson had placed McKinley's
battalion on a knoll overlooking the main road from the east, with
the warning that if it didn't hold until the Elsenborn Ridge line was
firmly set up, the entire corps might be wiped out.

Around 8:30 P.M. three big tanks lunged out of the fog and drove
through McKinley's roadblock, a platoon of infantry on their decks,
before anyone realized they were German. Soon they roared into
Rocherath and began roaming the streets.

Half an hour later more German tanks rumbled up the road, but
this time McKinley's men were waiting. The first two tanks struck
mines. The next two swerved off the road and were easy prey for
bazookas. As German infantrymen milled around in disorder, American artillery hit the road. Confounded by such heavy resistance—
their Intelligence had told them the entire 2nd Division was in
reserve far to the rear—the surviving tanks scurried for safety.

But the Germans reorganized, striking again in a combined tank
and infantry attack. McKinley's foxhole line was pierced as tanks
rolled into the next line of defense. Frantically McKinley phoned
for help.

In three minutes seven artillery battalions, newly placed on Elsenborn Ridge, saturated the road area. Many of the Germans fled back
to the east.

But a dozen Panthers and Tigers and hundreds of infantrymen
surged ahead, then swung south through the thick fog.

The first three German tanks soon reached Krinkelt, stopping in
front of the dour old church while the troops riding the decks built
an enormous bonfire. As the flames—a signal for their artillery—
rose high, the tanks clanked off about town, through streets ablaze
with confused battle, through other streets that were calm and
empty.

Colonel Frank Mildren, formerly of Heartbreak Crossroads, was
still looking for his advance party. It was about 9:30 P.M. when
finally, at a junction east of the Krinkelt church, he spied a big familiar figure—his executive officer.

"I'm damned glad to see *you!*" said the executive.

"What's happened?"

"Christ, what hasn't? When Able Company started for their positions out in front of town all hell broke loose. The Krauts were there!"

"Where did you put Able?" Mildren asked.

"I set them up in farmhouses on the outskirts. We're tied in with 3rd Battalion. Now if Baker and Charlie would only get here."

"Where's the battalion C.P.?"

"I've set it up near the church—a combination farmhouse and slaughterhouse. It smells *great*."

As the two men hurried toward the church, a young lieutenant from Baker Company came running down the street without gun or helmet. The executive reached out and grabbed him.

"Tanks!" the lieutenant babbled, his eyes wide with fright. "Tanks came through before we could dig in! Tanks with infantry on them came through our hedgerow! All my men crushed!"

"Stop it, boy!" The executive shook him roughly.

"Dead! Everyone killed in my platoon!"

Mildren looked to the east. It was fairly quiet there, and he decided the lieutenant, like so many new men, had been panicked by a few shots. "Go back and find your platoon."

"But they're all dead! I'm the only survivor!"

"Go back and find your platoon," repeated Mildren without raising his voice.

At once the young lieutenant calmed down. "Yes, sir," he said sheepishly, and he turned and trotted east toward the front.

Mildren hurried into his new command post.

"Things are in a mess," reported the operations officer. "I couldn't control Baker or Charlie Companies. Able is the only one in position. They're out east a couple of blocks."

A messenger told Mildren that 2nd Battalion had embodied the remnants of C Company. Then another messenger came with word that a dozen German tanks had caught B Company while they were chipping out foxholes in the frozen ground. The tanks had steamrolled over the terrified men, riddling them with machine guns, reducing them to a platoon. Mildren grimaced. The young lieutenant had had reason to panic after all.

Now at last the whole battalion picture was pieced together. Mildren summed it up: "B Company's been shot to hell. The 2nd Battalion has what's left of C Company. So our total strength is one company, one machine-gun platoon, and a few mortars. There's a big gap in our lines, and here we sit in our command post exactly two blocks behind it."

"Anyway," a very young, very new lieutenant said brightly, "we're still tied in with the 3rd Battalion on our right."

"Yes," said Mildren wryly. "And on our left we're tied in with the Krauts."

Silence overtook them. It was going to be a rough night.

Meanwhile First Lieutenant Jesse Morrow, Mildren's communications officer, was trying to lay telephone lines out to the companies. Morrow, Sergeant Hunziger, and Sergeant Cutter had just left A Company and were taking a short cut through a field when a machine gun opened up. Hunziger dropped in the snow.

"I've been hit bad," Hunziger grunted.

The machine gun kept raking the area, kicking up bits of snow. Hunziger was too heavy to lift, so Morrow dragged him to a small barn.

"Get a medic," Morrow told Cutter. "Bring a stretcher."

A minute later he heard German voices. He pulled Hunziger behind the barn, stretching him out against the back wall. The voices grew louder. A burp gun coughed inside the barn; bullets ripped through the wall. One of them creased Morrow's forearm, but he ignored it. Then footsteps left the barn, crunched through the snow, and went away.

In the dark Jesse Morrow ran his hand under Hunziger's coat, over his chest. His fingers touched the wound. It was big, wet, and round. He listened to the heart beat; it wavered and faded.

Cutter came back with a medic.

"I wish you'd verify," Morrow said, "but I think he's dead."

The medic felt Hunziger's pulse; then, without a word, took his dog-tags.

Morrow climbed to his feet. He felt a deep, hot anger.

6. END AT CLERVAUX

17 December 1944

1

Five towns tell the story of what was happening in the Ardennes on the night of December 17.

The twin villages of Krinkelt and Rocherath were on the brink of a tremendous attack; the industrial town of Stavelot, just over the hill from Ligneuville, was to be the first objective next morning of Kampfgruppe Peiper; and grim, moody St. Vith was being threatened from three sides.

Important as these four Belgian towns were, the most crucial action of the day had taken place in the middle of the Ardennes Front, at and near the scenic Luxembourg town of Clervaux.

Clervaux was important because it was the main obstacle in Manteuffel's great tank drive on Bastogne. It was an obstacle because of its peculiarly strategic location on the Germany-Bastogne highway.

This road, after crossing the Our River at Dasburg, runs eight miles west through spectacular mountain country. Then, with dramatic suddenness, an even more spectacular sight appears. Straight ahead, down in a little winding valley, lies Clervaux, which is dominated by the moss-covered ruins of a medieval castle.

To reach castle and town, the highway must be followed for a precipitous drop of a mile around three startling hairpin curves.

At the bottom of the hill the highway passes over the tiny Clervaux River. Highway and river both now double back to the east, detouring around a rugged hogback ridge. Sitting on the eastern end of this ridge, overhanging the shops, homes, and hotels of Clervaux, stands the castle, huge, many-turreted, and eight hundred years old.

Once the tip of the ridge is turned, the road again heads west. Then, after less than a mile, it abruptly climbs a steep hill where another breathtaking sight appears: gently rolling country extending all the way to Bastogne—a tanker's dream.

At dawn of December 17, hundreds of keyed-up German tankers in leather jackets sat expectantly in Panthers and Tigers just a few miles east of Clervaux. On their timetable, Clervaux—key to the ridge—would fall before noon.

Dawn broke cold, gray, and threatening in Clervaux. And in the Claravallis Hotel, command post of the 110th Regiment, Colonel Hurley Fuller's mood matched the weather. Fuller had just received a blow. His 2nd Battalion, lined up east of the hogback a mile away, was being hit hard by an infantry regiment. The attack he'd planned for 8:00 A.M. to relieve the village strongpoints to the east was already doomed. And already he had phoned General Norman "Dutch" Cota at the 28th Division Command Post in Wiltz; Cota had promised to send him some tanks.

Slowly at first, but then faster and faster, the bad news came in. Germans had seized a hotel across the little Clervaux River and were machine-gunning the castle, which was garrisoned by only 200 cooks, bakers, clerks, Special Service men, and MPs. If the castle surrendered, the men on the eastern outskirts of town would be cut off from the rear.

But Fuller wasn't worried about this ragtag garrison. He'd ordered them to hold at all costs; he expected only the best and usually got it. His men, though some feared or disliked him, expected nothing but the best from him.

Fuller wanted it that way. The veteran of World War I had never tried to be popular with his men, and he'd been frank with too many high-ranking officers to get his general's star. Disdainful of army politics but impeccably professional, he just went on soldiering.

And now he knew that on his shoulders rested the heaviest burden
of stopping a major drive to the east.

To regain initiative, Fuller ordered a reserve tank platoon in the
nearby village of Munshausen to load up with infantry and go to
the relief of Marnach, which sat on the high ground a few miles
east of Clervaux.

But where was the help from Dutch Cota? Without reinforcements he could do little but sit and wait. He waited.

An hour later Fuller was called to the radio. The young tank commander from Munshausen had reached Marnach but could not
break through to the besieged garrison; also, the infantrymen
aboard his tanks had been mauled. He wanted permission to return
to Munshausen.

"No," said Fuller brusquely. "Proceed here to Clervaux. Attack
the enemy along the Marnach-Clervaux road."

Then a message came in from the castle: somehow the Germans
had managed to drag a light cannon over the hill, and they'd just
knocked out a nest of sharpshooters in the witch tower.

Messages also came pouring in from strongpoints in the villages
to the east of Clervaux. Most were surrounded; Heinerscheid was
ready to fall.

Fuller waited, and still no sign of those reinforcements. And
where was his tank platoon from Munshausen via Marnach?

It was clanking off the last of the three hairpin curves and
coming into the eastern outskirts of Clervaux with guns blazing.
The sudden charge from the rear panicked the German infantrymen attacking the 2nd Battalion east of the hogback.

"Good," Fuller said when he got this news. "Now attack!"

But at 9:30 A.M., just as the depleted 2nd Battalion went on the
attack, thirty German tanks were breaking through the rubble-
littered streets of Marnach and beginning to roll slowly, cautiously,
down the twisting road to Clervaux.

Five minutes later the commanding officer of the 1st, the battalion
holding the left-flank strongpoints, phoned Fuller that his whole
front was shaky, that he'd had to pull back his command post. If
help didn't come soon Heinerscheid would fall.

But there was no help.

At 10:20 A.M. the reinforcements sent by Cota—sixteen medium
tanks—finally rolled into Clervaux from the west. Immediately

Fuller sent five Shermans to relieve Heinerscheid and the rest to defend the eastern side of the hogback.

Meanwhile the side door to Clervaux was standing open. This was Urspelt, a tiny hill village two miles north of Clervaux, and connected by a secondary road. Several German tanks had bypassed the few Americans in Urspelt and, with hundreds of infantrymen, were closing in on Clervaux. Their objective was the bridge at the railroad station. If they could seize it, Fuller's command post, the castle, and the 2nd Battalion just east would be cut off and trapped.

By 11:30 A.M. Fuller's strongpoints on the right flank—Hosingen, Holzthum, Consthum, Weiler, Merscheid—were falling fast. On the left flank the situation was even worse: two strongpoints had been taken and a battery of artillery captured. Of the five tanks sent to relieve Heinerscheid, two were destroyed in a savage little battle and three driven to cover before reaching the surrounded village. And just east of the hogback, the thirty German tanks had arrived from Marnach, smashed the 2nd Battalion's attack, and knocked out the eleven relieving Shermans. Fuller's reinforcements had made not a dent before being swallowed up in battle.

At noon he put through a second call to General Cota in Wiltz. "I need more artillery support, more tanks," he said.

"I'll send you a battery of self-propelled guns," Cota said. "And that's *all* I can spare."

"It's not enough."

"I've got two other regiments screaming for help."

"And we've got twelve Tigers sitting on the high ground east of town, looking down our throats."

"Sorry, Fuller, one battery is all I can give you," repeated Cota. "Remember your orders. Hold at all costs. No retreat. Nobody comes back."

There was a silence.

"Do you understand, Fuller?"

"Yes, sir. Nobody comes back."

Eight miles due east of Clervaux, Manteuffel's tanks continued to roll steadily over the bridge at Dasburg toward Clervaux. For a while Manteuffel himself stood at the bridge, regulating the traffic across the Our River. Every so often he would flag down a unit straining to drive forward. It was a source of satisfaction that he did not have to push his troops; instead they were pushing him.

With luck these tanks would roll through Clervaux in an hour or two.

The advance was going equally well seven miles south of the Dasburg bridge. His Panzer Lehr (Tank Demonstration) Division was finally crossing the Our at Gemünd. Yesterday these tankers had boiled with impatience as their long lines sat stalled on the east bank of the river. Thousands of horse-drawn vehicles, most of them driven by Russian "volunteers" who understood not a word of German, had clogged the roads; and when someone tried to unsnarl the traffic jams, the Russians went about their work as if they had all the time in the world.

But at last Panzer Lehr was rolling. It should take Bastogne the next day. Major General Fritz Bayerlein, its commander, had told his officers this offensive was the decisive battle of the war. He had put himself at the head of the advance guard, saying, "It's not important whether I'm killed." There was a sense of abandon in Panzer Lehr—abandon and a ruthless will to win.

2

By 3:00 P.M. the iron ring around Clervaux was almost closed. German infantry and tanks had bypassed the last crumbling strongpoints along the Skyline Drive, and were converging from three directions on the town. Already a Panther from Urspelt, the "side door" to Clervaux, had crossed the little bridge near the railroad station and destroyed a Sherman at the post office; and a German panzerfaust (bazooka) team had crossed the river undetected and set fire to another Sherman parked in front of the Claravallis Hotel.

On the eastern edge of Clervaux, German infantrymen had broken through the lines of the 2nd Battalion and were loping toward the large sanatorium that dominated the last steep curve in the highway leading into town. The hospital matron and a nurse, watching the battle from the front door, ran down a long corridor, around a corner, into a cellar jammed with 150 refugees.

A German bore down the corridor after them, his machine pistol chattering hollowly. They heard his footsteps pass overhead. Then came more footsteps and a series of loud shouts. A moment that seemed like an hour crawled by. Then the running footsteps faded, and the sound of gunfire drifted down the hill toward town.

By 3:30 P.M. the defense of the Claravallis Hotel had been reduced to half a platoon of riflemen and one antitank gun. The men figured they'd all die there if Fuller didn't pull out right away.

In his office, a call had just come in from the commander of the 3rd Battalion on the battered right flank.

"Well, what now?" Fuller snapped.

"Give me authority to withdraw the men I've got left. I'll take them back to Wiltz."

"Division knows what you're up against and Division knows what we're up against here in Clervaux. But the order still stands—hold!"

A few minutes later the commander of the 1st Battalion on the left checked in: "We're completely surrounded here at Urspelt. Send some relief!"

"There's no relief to send you. Take the tanks you've got and fight your way south to the 2nd Battalion."

As Fuller hung up, the self-propelled guns, promised by General Cota at noon, rolled into town. The battery commander was ordered to get up the ridge and knock out the twelve German tanks on the high ground overlooking Clervaux.

By 4:00 P.M. the few remaining strongpoints in front of Clervaux were falling one by one. The garrison at Munshausen, a mile and a half southeast, reported it was being attacked heavily from east and north. Held jointly by two companies, the town was rubble. Platoon organization had long since ceased; command now began and ended at the squad level. Captain Irving Warden, commander of Cannon Company, told Fuller they were dead ducks if help didn't come soon.

And Fuller's supply officer phoned, "Jerry patrols have reached Weicherdange! I'm having a tough time saving my trucks!" Now, on top of everything, Fuller would be unable even to supply those few strongpoints not surrounded.

In desperation he turned to his most pressing problem—Munshausen. When this village fell, the life of Clervaux could be counted in minutes.

He scraped together five tanks and told the platoon leader—a jittery young lieutenant—to highball it to Munshausen over the back way, picking up as much 105-mm. howitzer ammo as he could carry. Then he radioed Cannon Company.

"Warden! You still there?"

"Barely."

"Well, hang on! Tanks on the way with ammo—five of them."

"Where in hell did you find five tanks?"

As Fuller talked there was a rumble in front of the hotel. Looking out the window, he saw his new battery of self-propelled guns scuttling to the rear.

Fuller swore long and eloquently.

3

In outflanking St. Vith from the south, the 2nd Panzer Division had also cut off Clervaux from the north. And below Clervaux, completing the isolation of Colonel Hurley Fuller's 110th Regiment, more of Manteuffel's troops were driving straight west toward Wiltz. By dusk, General "Dutch" Cota's 28th was no longer a division. It was three disconnected regiments, each cracked along its whole front and struggling to survive in the German rip tide.

The middle regiment, Fuller's, was no longer a regiment—only scattered groups of men falling back onto the final defense point, Clervaux. Fuller was well aware that all his strongpoints to the east were either swamped or about to fall. Soon the only resistance would be at Clervaux. Here there were many casualties, little ammunition, and no hope for victory.

Fuller knew this. He was buying time for those in the rear. The only question was: when would Clervaux fall?

Opposite Fuller a small man with a lean inquisitive face, Hasso von Manteuffel, was asking the same question. According to plan the strongpoints in front of Clervaux should have fallen long before noon, and some of them were still holding out. Marnach and Munshausen were particular tartars.

Three miles east of Clervaux, Lieutenant Rudolph Siebert of the 2nd Panzer Division stood by his armored car, waiting for word to attack Marnach again. That morning thirty heavy tanks had made a dash through the village, but sharpshooters had kept his own armored car company pinned down.

At the time of the tank breakthrough, Captain Heinz Nowak had decided to follow on foot. Swinging a souvenir American bayonet like a baton, Heinz had strolled gaily toward the village. He didn't return. Everyone, even the battalion commander, was anxious to liberate good old Heinz.

At 5:00 P.M. the word came to storm Marnach. The men shouted, cranked their vehicles, piled in and started rolling. The lead tank crashed through the barricade, tanks and armored cars rolling into the village after it. As they started cleaning out snipers, someone shouted to Siebert, "They found Heinz near the church!"

Siebert ran to the church. Heinz, once so full of life, was sprawled in a doorway, his skull bashed in, his teeth knocked out, and the souvenir American bayonet sticking through his throat.

Siebert cried.

Near 6:00 P.M. at the Claravallis Hotel in Clervaux, Colonel Hurley Fuller was talking on the phone to the commander of the 1st Battalion. Lieutenant Colonel Paul said that he and a few men from his headquarters had fought their way to the 2nd Battalion east of the hogback ridge.

"What about Company B in Marnach?" asked Fuller.

· "Maybe they're still fighting," said Paul tiredly, "but I think all my strongpoints are wiped out."

"Don't *think!*" Fuller said. "Find out. Use everything you can lay your hands on to defend that road junction on the 1st Battalion's left flank. Now let me speak to someone from 2nd Battalion."

Lieutenant Colonel Hughes, second-in-command of the defenses in front of the town, picked up the phone.

"How does it look?" asked Fuller.

"I think we can hold till morning."

"Good! Stick with it."

But a few minutes later Fuller heard heavy firing just to the east. He hoped the 2nd Battalion could hold out, but from the increased volume of fire he guessed the entire position on the outskirts of town would soon be encircled or overrun.

He went to the window, looked out, and then pulled back quickly. A Tiger was slowly passing on the street below. Minutes before, it had rolled down the hill from Urspelt in the north, crossed the bridge near the railroad station, and turned sharply east. Now it cruised cautiously past the Claravallis Hotel, heading back toward the castle. A rifle bullet pinged harmlessly on the turret.

"No resistance in the lower town," radioed the Tiger commander. "Only small-arms fire from the castle."

Spurred on by the good news, other tanks of Manteuffel's 2nd
Panzer Division hurried downhill from Urspelt for the kill.

4

In Nancy, far south of Clervaux, General George Patton was still
angry because Bradley had ordered his 10th Armored Division to
the Ardennes; and he intended to stay angry for quite a while.
Then an idea came to him. He rang up General Eddy, one of his
corps commanders.

"Matt," he said, delighted at his own idea, "engage the 4th Armored fast. I don't want to lose them too."

As he rang off, his 10th Armored Division was rolling through
the antique streets of Luxembourg City some seventy miles straight
north. Its commander, Major General William Morris, Jr., walked
into the headquarters of "Tubby" Barton, commanding general of
the 4th Division.

Barton, ill and worried, threw his arms around Morris. "Thank
God you're here!"

A few blocks away Omar Bradley's staff car, lights out, was just
returning from Versailles. He was driven through the black streets
to the advance tactical headquarters in the brownstone State Railway Building.

As Bradley walked into the war room, General Sibert, his intelligence officer, was posting on the great war map those enemy divisions identified on the Ardennes Front. There were already fourteen, half of them panzer. Bradley looked at the map, turned to his
chief of staff and said in dismay, "Lev, just where has this son of a
bitch gotten all his strength?"

"I don't know," Major General Leven Allen said, "but we've certainly got our hands full of Germans."

They were discussing the latest situation reports when Bradley
was called to the phone. It was Courtney Hodges, who since morning had been phoning regularly from Spa, pleading for the two
airborne divisions that Eisenhower was holding in reserve.

"I was about to call you, Courtney," said Bradley. "I've finally
got good news for you. Ike just released the 101st and 82nd Airborne. Where do you want them?"

"I want one at Bastogne and one thirty miles north of there at

Werbomont." Hodges' sigh of relief was audible. "And the sooner the better!"

That evening, the men of these two airborne divisions were enjoying the wine and women of Reims, France.

Pfc. Edward Peniche, a native of Yucatán, Mexico, was sitting at a bar with a group of 101st men. "Throw a beer at that table, Peniche," a buddy suggested, nodding at a group wearing the "AA" patch of the 82nd. "AA—All-American crumbs!"

Peniche obliged.

The can hit a big 82nd man. He picked it up and walked over to Peniche. "Well, who threw it?"

A French girl pointed at Peniche.

"It just fell out of his hand," Peniche's buddy explained.

The 82nd man hit Peniche, and the riot began.

Soon the whistles were blowing, but not primarily to stop this latest skirmish between the two rival divisions.

"Okay, 101, back to Mourmelon!" shouted an MP. "Trucks are outside!"

The men of the 82nd were also ordered to their camp at Suippes.

All over Reims men were being dragged from boîtes, bistros, and bordellos. Some dead drunk, some still fighting, others not quite dressed, they were thrown into trucks and hustled home to camp. What was up? Where were they going? Everyone had a different idea: a new jump; rest camp in the south of France; back to England. But they were going somewhere, and the brass was in a terrific heat to get them there.

A few miles away, in Suippes, some of the 82nd Airborne men were still watching a ballet (their youthful division commander, Major General James Gavin, was a balletomane). At 9:30 P.M. the performance was halted and the men told to report to their units on the double.

Lights were popping on in every barracks. Those asleep woke up angry or sullen, threw shoes at the CQs or got dressed in alarm. Officers arrived, and the word was passed: "Get ready to roll. Get ammo and supplies. We're pulling out in a few hours!"

At nearby Mourmelon, the staff of the 101st knew only that the Germans had broken through near St. Vith. The division might go to a town named Werbomont.

Lieutenant Colonel Paul Danahy, the Division intelligence officer, returned at 11:00 P.M. to his quarters from the staff meeting. His weekend guest, Fred MacKenzie, correspondent of the Buffalo *Evening News,* was waiting for him.

"Something's happened, Fred," Danahy said. "We're leaving in the morning."

"How about going with you?"

"Fine. We owe you a story."

Lieutenant Colonel H. W. O. Kinnard, who looked far too young to be the Division operations officer, joined them.

"This one's going to be rough," said Danahy. "I bet we'll be shooting Krauts right in headquarters this time."

Kinnard pointed to a shoulder patch just sewn on his battle jacket. "How do you like the white thread?" he asked.

"Pretty sharp," said Danahy. The two colonels laughed.

5

As the night wore on, the attack on Clervaux was reaching its climax.

Colonel Hurley Fuller had long since lost contact with his 3rd Battalion on the right. He knew the 1st Battalion, on the left, was shattered. And the 2nd Battalion's lines just in front of Clervaux's hogback ridge were sagging badly under the constant pressure.

Munshausen, less than two miles southeast of Clervaux, was falling. The men of Company C were scattered and fleeing to the west.

Cannon Company, the other unit in Munshausen, was barely hanging on to one edge of town. Its commander, Captain Irving Warden, was cut off from his men; he lay sprawled behind a hedgerow with no ammunition and a company of Germans all around him.

Then he heard a faint clanking. Slowly one Sherman, then four more, hove to and came crawling up the dark road toward him. They were reinforcements from Fuller.

Warden saw one of his noncoms run down the hill, waving the tanks into position. A German stood up and fired his panzerfaust at the leading tank. Although this bazooka shot missed, the Sherman spun around and trundled full speed down the hill, followed closely by its four mates.

The men of Munshausen stood up and shook their fists and screamed obscenities after them.

From his tank fleeing southwest, the frightened leader of the reinforcements radioed Colonel Fuller: "Town of Munshausen burning. It's in the hands of the Jerries. I'm pulling back!"

"Get back to Munshausen!" Fuller ordered.

The tank commander did not answer.

"Did you hear me?" stormed Fuller. "Get back to Munshausen!"

Still no answer. The five Shermans clanked to the rear.

Fuller sat down. He felt drained, feverish, half dead.

Now a sudden and foreboding quiet settled over Clervaux. The few riflemen left in the Claravallis Hotel were ready. They knew the next attack would be their last.

Time inched by.

Then it began again, and for the last time, with the phone ringing in the operations room. Fuller answered. It was Hughes of the 2nd Battalion, on the other side of the hogback less than a mile away.

"I'm being hit by a lot of German armor." His voice was drawn. Only yesterday he'd been released from the hospital. "Six of them just passed my C.P. heading for your C.P."

Fuller hung up and called Division. There was a maddening delay. By now the six German tanks were probably rolling past the castle. At last Colonel Gibney, Cota's chief of staff, came to the phone.

"It's hopeless here," Fuller said. "I want permission to pull back everything I can and defend along the high ground west of town."

"Impossible," snapped Gibney. "Your orders are to defend in place. Don't give up any ground, do you hear?"

"Let me talk to General Cota," Fuller said, struggling to control his anger.

"The General's at dinner and can't be reached by phone."

An officer burst in, crying, "Colonel! Six Kraut tanks coming down the street from the castle!"

"All right, Gibney," said Fuller. "You're transmitting the General's orders, and I've got to obey them. But I'm telling you"—here he had to raise his voice over the roar of tanks—"it's going to be the Alamo all over again!"

A loud explosion below shook the hotel. Quickly two more explosions followed. From fifteen yards out a German tank was firing into the room below Fuller.

"What's going on there?" asked Gibney.

"A Kraut tank just laid one in my S-1 office!" Fuller shouted. "I'm getting out of here before they lay one in my lap!"

"Now wait a minute—"

"I've got no time for conversation!" Fuller banged down the receiver, picked it up again. "Get me the 2nd Battalion C.P."

A machine gun cut loose from below; bullets ripped the plaster over Fuller's head. A dozen hollow booms drowned out the machine gun. The walls shimmied, the lights went out, but the room was still lit by flares shooting from tanks in the street.

Fuller jiggled the phone. It was dead.

He hurried out of the room, bumping into his operations officer. "Colonel, we're trapped!"

"Looks like it."

"What the hell are we going to do?"

"I'm going to try and get out," said Fuller. "We need live soldiers. I'll scrape up as much of the regiment as I can behind town."

Now they heard the Germans bellowing on the first floor.

In the cellar, forty wounded GIs were huddled next to the ladies' room. In one corner two officers were frantically burning papers. In a small cellar behind them sat Jean-Pierre Gillen-Kohner, proprietor of the hotel, with his wife and daughter. The roar of shells, the rattle of machine guns, the smell of smoke, and the raucous cheering of the Boche struck terror in them. This was the end of the world. They went to their knees and prayed.

Fuller ran up to the third floor, picked up his carbine and trench coat. Then he saw figures—maybe a dozen—lurking in the dark room.

"Who's in here?" he shouted.

A panzerfaust shell came through the window and exploded, knocking a few men to the floor. Fuller helped a wounded officer into a bed, covered him with a blanket.

"I'm blind," said a voice from the floor. "I'm blind in both eyes."

Fuller groped around, bandaged the man's eyes with his first-aid kit.

"Colonel Fuller," someone said from the hall, "I've found a way out of the building. Do you want to take the chance?"

"Hell yes," Fuller said. "Does anyone else want to go?"

"Me," they all said.

The blind man grasped Fuller's hand tightly.

"Yes, you too," Fuller said. "Hold on to my belt and come along."

The man in the hall took them to a window at the back of the hotel. One by one they crossed over a narrow iron ladder to the cliff. Fuller guided the blind man across, then up the steps cut into the cliff. It was a strenuous climb, and when Fuller reached the top he flopped to the ground—exhausted.

As he caught his breath, twelve more refugees from the hotel joined them. Then, with a compass in one hand and the blind man's hand in the other, Fuller said, "All right, men, we're going to Eselborn. Follow me."

Single file they clambered to the top of the hogback ridge, past the huge Benedictine monastery, and into a dark thick woods. At the last moment Fuller turned and glanced down into the town. Clervaux was dying in a holocaust. It wouldn't live to see midnight.

Now German infantrymen were swarming over Clervaux. Well armed and warmly dressed in long leather jackets, they loped through the streets in packs, broke open locked doors with bullets and rifle butts. The civilians were terrified.

When the pounding began at Joseph Geiben's front door, he thought a long time before he opened it. Then in bounded a friend, another young Luxembourger who had deserted from the German Army; and after him staggered a wounded American soldier, an acquaintance from the rest center. Geiben slammed and bolted the door.

"Geiben," his friend cried, "it's terrible!"

"Damn Krauts," the GI gasped. "They want to go over the Meuse." He stood there gray-faced, swaying. His rifle slipped from his grasp and he fell to the floor.

"Look at your hand," Geiben told him.

The three looked at the GI's right hand. It was a bloody pulp. Geiben bandaged it.

The rumble of tanks was now a din.

"We've got to go, Geiben," his friend shouted.

Geiben finished the bandage, picked up the rifle.

"No," the GI cried. "You can't use a rifle—you're civilians. Give it to me and get out of here before it's too late."

"Aren't you coming with us?" asked Geiben.

"I'd never make it," the GI said.

They shook his good left hand.

"Bonne chance," said Geiben.

"Same to you—you'll need it. Good God, we'll all need it!"

The two young Luxembourgers ran out. Shells were exploding everywhere. Flames were licking up from the castle, and the Villa Collette was on fire as they ran past it.

A German tank came careening down the street, shooting wildly. They turned away from it, up the narrow road leading to the monastery. They climbed over felled trees and shook off the branches cut free by shell bursts. They ran for their lives—up the hill, past the monastery, and beyond.

Suddenly they were in the clear, out of the target area. They dropped to the ground. With trembling hands Geiben lit a Camel. Then he gazed around him. The eastern sky glowed blood red with fire. Urspelt, Marnach, Munshausen and Hosingen were burning. Clervaux was burning below. Over the whole valley hung a veil of smoke, greasy smoke darker than the night, with German search-lights probing ghostly white fingers through it. The wind from Clervaux carried up the stench of cordite and corruption.

As it died down, the fire in the castle of Clervaux added a layer of ashes and charred beams to the rubble knocked down by the German guns. But the heavy walls of the castle still stood firm. And its American defenders—the same cooks and clerks who had taken up guns for the first time the night before—still stood firm.

Several young Luxembourgers were helping the Americans. One of them, Jean Servé, had carried ammunition and messages all day.

He thought it ironic that the last defense of the castle was being made by Americans, for one seigneur had been the Count Claude de Lannoy—an ancestor of Franklin Delano Roosevelt.

Now it was 11:30 P.M. The barrage had risen to a crescendo, tanks were roaring in the streets below, and in the dungeon the women and children were praying frantically, wailing. The old townsmen came to the commander of the castle forces and begged him to surrender. He shook his head: Fuller had told him to fight to the end.

From the depths of the castle came the sound of piano music. Half believing it was a hallucination, Servé followed the sound down into the large "knights' room." There he saw an American soldier sitting at a piano, playing calmly, thoughtfully. A shell exploded on top of the witch tower, and rubble rained down at Servé's feet, but the soldier missed not a note. Was it Chopin? No, Debussy—"Reflections in the Water."

Down below tanks jammed the streets. They rolled in over the side road from Urspelt, and they came down the winding road from Marnach. First came the Panthers of the 2nd Panzer Division. Then, with an earth-shaking rumble, came huge Tiger tanks and finally monstrous Tiger Kings. On through the night tanks came, nose to tail, twisting and turning, banging balustrades, porches, and gables on both sides of the narrow street.

The troops, infantry and panzer, were in a frenzy of excitement. They pressed forward feverishly, almost desperately, not wanting to waste a minute. At last they had broken through. The enemy had been rocked back on his heels, and he could not be given a moment's rest.

PART TWO
"Hold the Reins Loose"

1. SPEARHEADS THROUGH BELGIUM

18 December 1944

1

By the morning of December 18, more than fifty German columns were probing into the Ardennes from Echternach to Monschau. Some had gone only a mile; half had pierced as far as ten and twelve; and one had raced almost thirty.

At the southern end of the battlefront, Brandenberger's infantry columns had made only short gains near Echternach. But further north, near the confluence of the Our and Sauer Rivers, they had pushed forward almost three miles in the drive on Diekirch. And near Vianden, the 5th Parachute Division had knifed ten miles, almost to the outskirts of Wiltz.

A little north, where Manteuffel's army began, the Baron's three tank divisions had made even greater advances. Between Wiltz and Clervaux, Panzer Lehr had traveled east ten miles against no opposition; the 2nd Panzer had rolled through Clervaux and now topped the ridge beyond town; and a battalion of the 116th Panzer—after wasting a day in a vain effort to drive a wedge just below the Schnee Eifel—had detoured south and followed the trail of the 2nd Panzer through Dasburg, Marnach, and Urspelt, making an advance of fifteen miles in twenty-four hours.

Manteuffel's gains in the Schnee Eifel were almost as deep and just as sensational. Here he had surrounded most of the 106th Division and was approaching St. Vith from three sides.

Above the Schnee Eifel, Dietrich's army boasted the greatest penetration: the thirty-mile gallop of Kampfgruppe Peiper to the outskirts of Stavelot. But his other columns had ground forward only a mile or two and were causing great concern in the Führer's headquarters.

In spite of his generally slow progress, Dietrich insisted he was about to score a great victory near the center of his line. The 12th SS Panzer and the 276th Volksgrenadier Divisions had smashed through the stubborn 99th Division to the outskirts of Krinkelt and Rocherath and had now assembled for a combined assault on the twin villages. Once these key towns were taken, Dietrich assured Hitler, the log jam would be broken and the 12th SS Panzers could make their run to the Meuse.

Defending the villages was a regiment and a half of the 2nd Division. If these men didn't hold, the rest of their division and the survivors of the 99th Division would not have time to dig in behind them on Elsenborn Ridge. The Germans would make a clean breakthrough to the northwest.

Lieutenant Jesse Morrow, communications officer of Colonel Mildren's 1st Battalion, could understand now that no one knew what was going on in Krinkelt; but he resented bitterly that so few seemed to give a damn.

Shortly after dawn, as he peered from behind an upturned jeep just outside of Mildren's command post, a Tiger with a dozen grenadiers aboard approached. He waited till it had closed to fifty yards, then raked the decks with his sub-machine gun. Half of the grenadiers were knocked off; the rest jumped and fled to the rear. Morrow grabbed an M-1, attached a rifle grenade and fired at the oncoming Tiger. It passed him, and swerved around, looking for the gnat attacking it. Morrow ran up closer, and fired another grenade from five yards out.

The Tiger swerved into a ditch. As it tried to back up, Morrow took careful aim and fired again. This time the grenade hit the ammunition rack and the tank burst into flame. Tankers wearing black tams jumped out of escape hatches, their clothing ablaze. Across the street in Mildren's command post, staff officers, expecting momentary capture, were burning papers. Mildren himself was disturbed by a message he had just intercepted which had been sent by his regimental commander to Division: "1st Battalion badly disorganized, of little help. Action quieting." What did Colonel Boos know about Krinkelt, sitting up there in Rocherath? For eight hours Mildren's people had been knocking out tank after tank with bazookas and rifle grenades. And every time he called Boos to tell him the streets of Krinkelt were crawling with Jerry tanks, the colonel mollified him, as if he were seeing bogymen. Firing outside increased abruptly. There was a deafening roar of tanks.

"Call Colonel Boos and ask for tank destroyers," Mildren shouted above the din.

A junior staff officer made radio contact with Colonel Boos. "Sir, we've *got* to have TDs. We're being overrun by Jerry tanks!"

"How many tanks?" Boos asked calmly. "And just how close are they to you?"

There was a roar. The house shook, plaster fell in hunks.

"Well, Colonel," said the officer at the radio, "if I went up to the second floor, I could piss out the window and hit at least six!"

Half a mile to the northeast in Rocherath, not far from Boos's command post, morning fog hung over Lieutenant Colonel William McKinley's battalion. His position, just east of town, was being heavily attacked by tanks and infantry. The GIs let the panzers roll over their holes, hoping to knock them out from the rear with bazookas. But grenadiers followed too closely, and hand-to-hand struggles with bayonets, knives, and even fists were raging all along the little front.

Suddenly the fog lifted like a theater curtain. Three Tiger tanks whirled and headed along the foxhole line, blasting McKinley's men hole by hole.

"I'm overrun," radioed the commander of Company A. "Lay a barrage right on top of us!"

For half an hour the company area was plowed up by an American battalion of artillery.

On the north flank B and C companies wavered. Several men broke in terror and ran to the rear. But McKinley met them and drove them back with his pistol. The lines held.

German tanks, camouflaged white, followed by packs of white-sheeted infantrymen were now roaming the streets of Rocherath.

Tank duels were fought from street to street; infantry fought from
house to house.

Behind McKinley, Colonel Boos, an eyewitness of the Rocherath
fight, was frantically trying to bring the 2nd Battalion into a defensive position. "It'll take me an hour," he radioed McKinley.
"You'd better pull back."

"Two of my companies are already surrounded," McKinley replied. "The rest are pinned down. It would take a miracle to pull
me out now!"

Instantly there was a rumble behind him and the miracle showed
up—the high silhouettes of five Sherman tanks jutting over the rise
from the north.

They charged recklessly toward the surrounded companies. In
minutes two of the three Tigers ravaging the foxholes were blazing
wrecks. Twenty-three GIs, the remnants of the two trapped companies, scrambled from their foxholes and ran back to Rocherath to
join their comrades. Of the entire battalion only 240 were left.

The battle for Mildren's command post in neighboring Krinkelt
was still raging. The defenders, low on bazooka ammunition, were
filling wine bottles with gasoline and stuffing in cloth wicks. As
Nazi tanks roared toward them, the GIs lit their "Molotov Cock-
tails" and threw them at the turrets.

Lieutenant Jesse Morrow, at the heart of the confusion, ran from
house to house. He rooted terrified men out of cellars, and put them
in doorways, threatening to shoot them if they left their posts.

A Tiger roared past him. At the same moment a jeep came out
of a side street, turned and suddenly faced the tank. Two GIs
jumped from the jeep, and with a great screech of rending metals
the Tiger steamrolled over it, leaving behind a flattened tangle of
junk.

Now to jar its jammed turret free, the Tiger pulled to the right of
the road and sideswiped a telephone pole with its long 88. The
pole snapped. Like a prehistoric monster in torment, the Tiger
moved to the next pole and banged it with the 88. The second pole
snapped. The Tiger, its turret finally free, spun around and headed
straight for Mildren's command post.

Morrow picked up a bazooka, aimed at the rear of the tank and
fired. The tank veered, crashed into a house at the end of the street,
rolled into a ditch, and lay there immobilized.

A head popped out of the turret. The Tiger's 88—hand-cranked—slowly turned toward the command post. Morrow pulled out his .45, ran toward the Tiger and shot twice at the man in the turret.

The German gaped at him and then called down orders to his mates in the tank. Morrow stopped fifteen feet away; his pistol was empty. Finally he flung it at the German in disgust and darted into an alley.

Down the alley came a 99th Division jeep, armed with a bazooka.

"Just hold it a minute," ordered Morrow. He seized the bazooka, raised it to a ready position and jumped around the edge of the house. To his consternation he was looking down the barrel of the Tiger's long 88. He thought he saw a round coming out of the muzzle, and there was a shattering explosion behind him. A black blanket fell over him, suffocating him.

When he regained consciousness, he saw the enemy tank standing a few yards away, its gun still yawning at him, tendrils of smoke drifting from its mouth. Sure he was going to die, he slumped back and relaxed. He was going to enjoy his last few minutes. Then as the Tiger's gun slowly turned away and Morrow realized he'd been reprieved, he crawled back around the corner. Minutes later he stumbled into the battalion command post.

Mildren looked down at him and shook his head. He had seen Morrow rush the Tiger, waving a pistol and screaming. Minutes later he'd seen the Tiger's 88 shoot him point-blank. Morrow couldn't possibly be alive.

"Am I hit bad?" asked Morrow as blood poured from his neck.

"Not bad at all," Mildren lied.

"Don't kid me."

At the regimental aid station the medics bound Morrow's wound. "My God," one told a newcomer, "the Lieutenant here was grazed with an 88 round and he's still alive!"

He was loaded into an ambulance with three badly burned German tankers.

"These guys," explained an aid-man to the groggy Morrow, "were in the tank that shot you. A GI threw a thermite bomb down the turret."

One of the bandaged Germans smiled at Morrow. "Do you have a cigarette?"

"Cigarette?" Morrow swore as he tried to fling himself out of his stretcher. Then, his fingers still clawing at the German, he dropped back, unconscious.

2

Alarmed by Kampfgruppe Peiper's dangerous thrust to Stavelot, Hodges was rushing reinforcements to contain the German drive. The 82nd Airborne Division was racing from France to stop its forward progress; the 9th and 30th Divisions were coming from the north in parallel columns to keep the enemy from turning up toward Holland.

The Germans were well aware of these American movements. On her early morning program to GIs, Axis Sally told of the great Nazi victories in the Ardennes. "And now," she said, "just to let you boys in khaki know we're always keeping track of you, here are the latest troop movements. Roosevelt's fanatic 30th Division is on its way south to rescue the First Army."

But by dawn none of the reinforcing American units was as yet a threat to Kampfgruppe Peiper as it stood poised at the southern outskirts of Stavelot, only 25 air miles from its goal, the Meuse River.

Peiper's men had bivouacked on the heights just south of the Amblève River. First they would cross to the north bank over an ancient stone bridge, into the center of Stavelot, an industrial town of 3,000. After a hundred yards they would reach the market place and the main highway to the west. They would turn sharp left onto this road and continue to the next town on their route, Trois Ponts.

Peiper's primary concern was the stone bridge. The night before an attempt to cross had brought a volley of rifle fire. But no matter how strongly defended, the bridge had to be seized before the Amis blew it up. The swollen Amblève River was deep enough and swift enough to stop his tanks.

Before dawn Peiper was ready to make his dash to the Meuse. He remembered his final instruction from General Kraemer, Dietrich's chief of staff: "Drive fast and hold the reins loose, Peiper."

He got into his armored car and waved a platoon of tanks to precede him. In a few minutes the spearhead curved around the top of the steep hill overlooking Stavelot, passed the ruins of an old castle, and rumbled down toward the stone bridge.

He saw two American tank destroyers aim tentatively at his first tank. There was an orange blast from the Tiger. One tank destroyer burst into flames. Then there was a second blast, a second blaze.

Now Peiper saw several American infantrymen scrambling back across the bridge. He ordered his giant Panthers and Tigers to give chase. The tankers maneuvered carefully to fit their broad vehicles onto the bridge. One by one they eased across.

To Peiper's amazement and relief, there was no explosion. (It had not occurred to the American engineers to prepare the bridge for demolition.) Now he had a clear path to his next objective. But as his tanks approached the center of Stavelot heavy bazooka fire broke out. The first tank spun out of control into a house. Then the roar of antitank guns came from the market place. Two more German tanks burst into flames. Peiper angrily ordered a task force to detach itself from the main column, blast through the nest of resistance in the market place and secure the right flank.

Then he ordered the main group to head west toward Trois Ponts and the Meuse. Over an hour had been senselessly lost already.

The market place was defended by a company of infantrymen and a platoon of tank destroyers, commanded by Major Paul J. Sollis. They had entered Stavelot at 4 A.M. Their mission: to hold the town until the 30th Division arrived from the north.

Sollis held off the detached task force for another hour, knocking out two more tanks. As the Germans deployed for a frontal attack, he ordered a retreat. His two remaining tank destroyers headed east along the main highway to Malmédy, eight miles away. Sollis and the infantrymen hurried north up a steep winding mountain road. After several miles his jeep was flagged down by a Belgian officer.

"There is a great petrol dump all along this road!" The Belgian excitedly explained that he and handful of civilians were the sole protectors of thirteen million liters of fuel.

While they were talking, Sollis heard the low rumble of German tanks at the foot of the hill. He looked around helplessly. He had no more antitank guns—just a tired platoon of infantrymen. As the German tanks struggled up the the steep grade with a deafening roar, an idea occurred to Sollis. In several minutes his men and the Belgians had stacked gasoline cans in a sharp curve in the mountain road.

Just as the first tank, a Panther, appeared, the gas was ignited. The Panther, trying to go around the blaze, teetered at the edge of a steep precipice. It quickly backed away from the flaming road-block and spun around. The other fourteen tanks also turned around and, since the roadblock was of no apparent danger to Kampf-gruppe Peiper, rumbled back to Stavelot.

Unaware that his detached task force had just narrowly missed capturing enough fuel to take the entire division far beyond the Meuse, Jochen Peiper was approaching Trois Ponts. It was 11:30 A.M.

This town, he knew, could be his greatest obstacle: here the Amblève met the Salm River. But once the highway bridges over these two rivers were crossed, he would have an almost unobstructed path to the Meuse.

Just in front of an underpass which led into the outskirts of the town, tiny figures were laying mines on the road. He gave the order to attack.

German pioneers—engineers—recklessly ran ahead and cleared away the mines. Then Peiper's tanks roared forward. As the first one reached the underpass, its turret exploded. The tank swerved, stopped. Behind it piled up nineteen Panthers and Tigers.

The fire had come from a 57-mm. antitank gun which was there only because of an accident. That morning its half-track had broken down en route to Stavelot. The defenders of Trois Pont, C Company of the 51st Engineer Battalion, had commandeered the gun, placing it near the underpass. As Peiper's tanks were heard rumbling in the near distance, the four-man gun crew was ordered to delay the onrushing Germans until the bridge over the Amblève could be prepared for demolition.

For fifteen minutes the puny 57-mm. piece held off the German column which tried in vain to locate its exact position. Then there was a great explosion behind the defenders. The ground shook. Rocks and rubble rained down. Finally the smoke cleared. Where the highway bridge spanning the Amblève had been was now a gaping hole. A few Americans had just won an important victory.

When Peiper heard the blast he guessed that one of the two bridges had been blown up. Angrily he ordered his tanks to press the attack. Soon an 88 shell hit the base of the American gun. The entire crew was killed: McCollum, Hollenbeck, Buchanan and Higgins.

Peiper raced through the underpass, then looked to his left. Several hundred yards away, the ruins of the Amblève River bridge were still smoldering. The main road to the west was closed. The few minutes' delay by a single gun and a few GI engineers could prove to be disastrous. But Peiper controlled his anger. He looked at a map and found he could detour to the north over a narrow mountainous road. It was a bad stroke of luck but perhaps would mean only a delay of a few hours.

After Peiper and the spearhead headed north, a small group turned south toward the destroyed bridge. Here, as had happened before in Baugnez and Ligneuville, without knowledge of their commander, they found a savage outlet for frustration. They dragged civilians from houses on the bank of the river and, as anguished friends and relatives on the other side of the Amblève watched helplessly, twenty-two men, women, and children were murdered.

Only ten air miles north of Peiper, the American First Army Headquarters at the famous watering town of Spa was his for the grabbing. The approaching gunfire from his reconnaissance patrols caused panic among the townspeople and even undisguised fear in the lobby of the Hotel Britannica. But upstairs the office of Courtney Hodges was calm. For Hodges was deliberate and incapable of panic. He had been through too much.

Major General J. Lawton Collins, commander of VII Corps, entered the room.

Hodges, a courtly man, rose and shook his hand. "Nice to see you, Joe. Big Simp is letting me borrow you until we straighten out this mess down here. The Germans have broken through all along the front," he explained in a quiet drawl. "Things are pretty vague and confused."

A mustached colonel walked quickly into the room, leaned over Hodges' shoulder and said, "General, if you don't want to get captured you'd better get out of town! The Germans are only a mile away."

"Later, later."

The faint sound of small-arms fire could now be heard.

"But General," said the Colonel, "Monk" Dickson, Hodges' intelligence officer, "there's no time to lose!"

Hodges politely waved Dickson out of the room. "Joe," he continued calmly, "you're going to be my strategic reserve."

3

In Germany noon broadcasts were filling the air. "Our troops are again on the march," said an announcer. "We shall present the Führer with Antwerp by Christmas!"

At Wolf's Lair, Hitler was elated with the victories of Kampfgruppe Peiper and the breakthrough at Clervaux. Major penetrations had been achieved just as he had predicted.

In Paris, there was near panic in many French government offices. The blitzkrieg of 1940 was still a fresh memory. At SHAEF headquarters in Versailles an excited delegation of high-ranking French officers headed by General Juin had just arrived to find out what was happening in the Ardennes. General Bedell Smith, Eisenhower's chief of staff, was conducting the group to the war room to look over the battle map.

As they passed down the hall, Smith noticed the Frenchmen looking with puzzlement at the calm orderly offices.

"I don't understand," exclaimed an agitated French general. "You're not packing!"

In one of these quiet offices Eisenhower was making a decision. Though many disagreed with him, he was now convinced this was an all-out German offensive.

He made up his mind. He would call off Patton's attack on the Saar scheduled for the next day. Instead he would turn Patton north, and hit the German flank with six divisions. He sent word for Bradley and Patton to meet him in Verdun the next morning. There they could work out the details of the American counterattack.

It was a decision that Hitler had been sure would take Churchill and Roosevelt at least a week to make.

4

By noon of December 18, the battle of St. Vith was in full swing. Early that morning as Bruce Clarke was about to launch his drive on Schönberg to rescue Jones's troops on the Schnee Eifel, German tanks and infantry attacked a village only a mile north of St. Vith.

Clarke canceled the attack on Schönberg and rushed reinforcements up to Hünningen, where, after a sharp engagement, the

Germans were thrown back. But he knew this had only been the overture to trouble. Heavy traffic could be heard traveling further north. St. Vith was obviously being bypassed by the Germans and would soon jut into their lines like a peninsula.

The morale of his men also worried Clarke. He was still strange to them, and they were strange to him. They had been moved so many times the proper recommendations for medals had been lost; promotions had been neglected.

Clarke had a third concern: General Jones. Although he still commanded the 106th Division and Hoge's combat command, he had turned over the immediate defense of St. Vith to Clarke. And Clarke didn't like to have a man who outranked him constantly asking him to attack Schönberg and bring back his surrounded troops. Clarke understood Jones's preoccupation, but it was impossible to think of attack now. His sole job was to hold St. Vith.

Jones's staff was even trying to persuade the General to pull the 106th Division Command Post back to Vielsalm. With the division cut off, they were only in the way up front. But Jones insisted that it was his duty to stay as near to his surrounded men as possible. At 2:42 P.M. he was still in St. Vith. He called in his operations officer and ordered him to continue dropping ammunition, food, and medical supplies to the men on the Schnee Eifel.

Jones didn't know, of course, that not a parachute had yet dropped. The IX Troop Carrier Command hadn't received orders from SHAEF until that morning.

Twenty-three C-47s, loaded in England, were just now approaching Florennes, Belgium. There they were to be briefed and pick up fighter cover. It was already cloudy and threatening but with luck they could make their drop on the Schnee Eifel before the weather closed.

They circled, awaiting landing orders. But there were none. Florennes knew nothing about the drop. "Too busy to take care of you here," radioed the tower. "Why don't you go to Liége?"

In the Schnee Eifel, Colonel Cavender had already passed on to young Colonel Descheneaux a joint order from General Jones to the two encircled regiments to turn around and attack a strong panzer force moving along the Schönberg-St. Vith road, and then fight their way back to St. Vith.

Accordingly, a little before noon Descheneaux's regiment had
started moving northwest. Kitchen trucks were destroyed, weapons
too heavy to carry abandoned. On the ground lay strewn the personal and military possessions of a regiment. The distance to travel
to the new assembly area was only three miles, but it was over
rough hilly country. The men, dragged down by weapons and
ammunition, slogged through mud, up slippery hills, and through
dense forests. It was hot work and soon the trail was littered with
overcoats.

Descheneaux personally led the regiment. He was the point.

"You're crazy, Colonel," protested his operations officer. "You're
going to get yourself killed."

"I've got to be sure we're going in the right direction," he said.
He had a strange, excited feeling. His whole career had been leading to the coming action and he was anxious for it to begin.

Behind Descheneaux his men plodded through dense beautiful
forest, the trees laden with tons of snow. "Why all this running and
no fighting?" they griped. They hadn't been driven from a single
position by the enemy. Why pull out?

Then a rumor passed down the line that the 331st Medical Battalion had been captured in Schönberg. The slow pace of the men
quickened. They wanted to free their comrades. The riflemen in the
van set a rugged pace. Without stopping heavy loads were passed
from man to man. But the service troops continued to drop, exhausted, by the wayside.

At 3:00 P.M. firing could be heard to the southwest. Descheneaux
plunged out of the woods onto a road. The noise of battle grew
louder. Deciding it was too dangerous to move further in daylight,
he told his men to hide in the woods until dark.

This noise to the southwest was Cavender's regiment. Starting at
noon, the leading battalion, the 2nd, had run into a strong German
roadblock. Cavender ordered the 3rd Battalion to detour around the
resulting fierce fire-fight. A moment later, an exciting rumor passed
down the line, from man to man, from company to company: some
armored outfit had broken through from the south. Their worries
would soon be over.

The fact was: no reinforcements, no air supplies were coming to
the men on the Schnee Eifel. They were on their own.

At dusk Cavender received another long delayed radio message from General Jones: "Attack Schönberg. Do maximum damage to enemy there, then attack toward St. Vith. This mission is of gravest importance to the nation. Good luck."

Cavender read the order to his staff. Several bristled; the appeal to patriotism was insulting and unnecessary. Soon the artillery started toward Schönberg, prime-movers dragging the howitzers. Then infantrymen followed. Their last march had begun.

A mile and a half to the northeast, Colonel Descheneaux was giving his battalion commanders final instructions for the morning attack. "I don't know the strength or location of the enemy in the Schönberg area," he said. "But I do know that the 423rd will attack on our left. We will attack three battalions in echelon to the right rear. Now move individually cross-country by compass to your final assembly areas. Be prepared to attack at 0700. Good luck, gentlemen."

The three battalions moved out through the dark forest, guided only by compass. There were frequent stops as patrols searched the area front for Germans. It turned cold and those who had dumped overcoats shivered. Riflemen, cooks, clerks, and mortarmen slogged through the dark woods, sleepy, exhausted, hungry, and cold. The wounded in the improvised aid stations heard their comrades move out into the darkness. For they, and volunteer aid-men, were being left behind—to certain capture.

Descheneaux led his regiment across an open field. Suddenly he heard German vehicles. Everyone dropped to the snow. It was so quiet Descheneaux could hear those behind him breathing. The noise of vehicles stopped. Now it was too dark to continue. He ordered his men to hide in the nearest woods until the daylight attack.

Descheneaux lay on the ground. He was too exhausted to dig in. Even with his heavy parka he had never been so cold in his life. Behind him the battalions bunched up in patches of woods. The men were also too tired to dig foxholes. They flopped on the snow and tried to rest.

About six miles northwest of Descheneaux, on the other side of Schönberg, one of his artillery officers, Lieutenant Eric Wood, Jr., was wandering in dense woods. The day before, although three of his guns escaped, he and his last howitzer had been ambushed in

Schönberg. His men had stayed in a ditch to be captured. Wood
had run.

He and a wandering GI were now less than a mile from the isolated village of Meyerode, nestled among hills five miles northeast
of St. Vith. The day before Germans had seized this undefended
town, and marked its fifty-two houses as billets for Sepp Dietrich's
personal command post.

Although the townspeople spoke only German, they were ardent
Belgians.

Near dusk Peter Maraite, whose house was on the edge of
Meyerode near a thick forest, went into the woods to get a Christmas tree. In spite of the war, he wanted to celebrate the holiday
season. He walked up the road which wound through the thickly
planted fir trees. As he was approaching a six-way dirt crossroads,
two dim figures came out of the woods. They beckoned. When he
saw they were Americans, he felt relieved.

"Can I help you?" he asked in German. He offered the hospitality
of his house for it was as yet unoccupied by the Boche.

They couldn't understand. With gestures he told them he was their
friend. The two soldiers looked at each other. Then the taller one,
Eric Wood, nodded. Wet, cold, and tired they followed Maraite
through the woods toward the village. The three sneaked from the
woods into the back of Maraite's house.

"Well," said Maraite to his 25-year-old daughter Eva, "I've
brought you two Americans."

"I hope they really are," she said, for there were rumors of Boche
in American uniforms. Eva motioned the men to sit down, and
served them bread, butter, and coffee. Then Maraite remembered
there was a villager, Jean Schroeder, who spoke English. While he
was gone, the two Americans dried cartridges and made jokes. Eva
couldn't understand the words, but Wood's gestures and expressions
made her laugh.

Finally Maraite returned with Schroeder.

"I was the only one of sixteen to get out of Schönberg," Wood told
Schroeder. "I have to go to St. Vith. I'll get help there and go back
to Schönberg."

"That's impossible," said Schroeder, who had learned his English
as a bellboy in an English hotel. "There's a great battle all around
St. Vith. From our windows you can see it burning."

Wood turned to his companion. "Guess we'll have to get back to the woods and start a little war of our own."

In a house only two hundred yards away sat Sepp Dietrich, drinking some of the local schnapps. There were rumors of great victories to his south—Manteuffel's victories. But he was still bogged down east of Elsenborn Ridge.

The only bright spot on his front was Kampfgruppe Peiper, on the loose somewhere near Hodges' command post in Spa.

By now the streets of Spa were clogged with retreating First Army Headquarters jeeps, trucks, and staff cars. Many lights were blazing in buildings, oblivious of the blackout regulations.

Except for a few officers excitedly roaming the halls, the Hotel Britannica was now almost empty of Americans. But the office of General Hodges was still as peaceful as a well-run library. Hodges was examining reports. He then packed his important papers and walked sedately through the big salon on the second floor, the room where Kaiser Wilhelm had signed his abdication after World War I. Now it was his turn to abdicate. But even amidst chaos, he made his exit as a man of dignity.

The direct cause of this chaos, Jochen Peiper, had no interest at all in Spa. Though only ten miles to the southwest near the mountain village of Stoumont, he was again headed west for a much bigger prize, the Meuse.

The day's frustrations hadn't ended at Trois Ponts. By a fluke chance, an American liaison plane from Spa saw the head of the column through a momentary break in the clouds. Before Peiper could hide in the woods fighter-bombers of the IX Tactical Air Command had knocked out ten tanks and half-tracks.

But in spite of the day's run of bad luck Peiper had advanced another fifteen miles. He decided that the next morning he would push through the little village of Stoumont which sat on the dark hill less than a mile ahead. With Sunday's luck, he would reach the Meuse by nightfall.

He went from group to group pumping new life and hope into his men. Young, strong, and zealous, they needed only these few words. Soon they were talking excitedly of Antwerp, Paris, and London. They ate and drank, and sang songs of the Homeland.

2. SPEARHEADS THROUGH LUXEMBOURG

18 December 1944

1

The northern tip of the little Grand Duchy of Luxembourg sticks between Germany and Belgium like a wall.

By daylight of December 18, Manteuffel's tank columns were driving deep wedges into this Luxembourg wall, all aimed at a Belgian town on the other side: Bastogne, the most important rail and road center in the Ardennes.

By now Manteuffel's 2nd Panzer Division had climbed the ridge beyond Clervaux. Between them and Bastogne lay twenty miles of rolling, open country and two small roadblocks, manned by Task Forces Rose and Harper of the far-flung 9th Armored Division.

About seven miles to the south, Manteuffel infantry columns were racing for Wiltz. Once this town, command post for the 28th Division, was taken, the southern route to Bastogne would also be wide open.

The 707th Tank Battalion, protecting its northeastern approaches, was already falling back on Wiltz with its last eight tanks. Engineers of the 44th Combat Battalion, deployed in a curving line from north to east, now formed the main bastion of defense.

Wiltz itself was in a fever of hesitation. The children were sent off to school as usual, but the people stood about fearfully, ready to flee. As the sounds of battle grew louder, Mayor Joseph Simon went through the streets, telling everyone to go to their cellars. The Germans would be stopped.

But Eugène Weber, the druggist and leader of the local Boy Scouts, didn't believe him. Weber had been told by a French officer attached to the 28th Division that a staff meeting was being held that morning to decide whether the town could be defended. Now Weber was hurrying to the Villa Adler to wait till the meeting let out.

Sergeant Henry Nathan had heard firing as he dressed and shaved in his bedroom above Goebel's tobacco shop, but it wasn't until he stepped out onto Grand' Rue, the main street of Wiltz, that he realized something had gone seriously wrong. Townspeople rushed by him in both directions, and down the street he saw the mayor, stopping the passers-by, gesturing fiercely as a companion excitedly rang a bell. Nathan's first thought was that in the emergency they'd be looking for him: against standing orders, he'd left the barracks last night and spent the evening with the Goebel sisters, the two middle-aged spinsters who ran the tobacco shop; he had stayed to sleep in the soft civilian bed they saved for him.

Nathan followed the curving main street past the shops and homes of Wiltz's leading citizens, past the old castle, which commanded a rocky ridge overlooking Lower Wiltz. One wing of the castle was now occupied by an army field hospital, the other by a Catholic school for girls. Then he went down the steep road and entered the division command post.

The little office of the Order of Battle Team had been turned upside down. Sergeant Lester Koritz was burning captured German documents. The captain, commanding officer of the three-man team, whose main function was to keep track of enemy strength, was packing.

"What's going on here?" Nathan said.

"Henry, we're moving out," the captain said. "The Germans have broken through! They'll be here any minute!"

"But Captain," Koritz said wearily, "nobody else in Headquarters is going."

"Get the jeep and no arguments!"

"Then we'd better take the trailer too," Koritz said. It contained most of their equipment and documents.

"No time for that. Park the jeep outside and keep the motor running!"

A few minutes later the three men were driving up the steep road, past the castle and onto Grand' Rue. Nathan and Koritz said they wanted to stop at the tobacco shop and warn the Goebel sisters, but the captain wouldn't hear of it. They weren't going to stop till they reached Bastogne.

In the back seat Koritz looked to the rear, watching the homes and shops flash by. The 28th had come here battered and bloody from the Hürtgen Forest; the townspeople had welcomed them like sons, given them comfort, hospitality, and friendship; and now, a month later, leaving them was like leaving home all over again. He would never forget the kindness of the Goebel sisters, the pleasant evenings spent talking and singing with the Luxembourgers in the little cafés.

At 11:00 A.M. they left the town behind them and were speeding on toward Bastogne. But they had not seen the last of Wiltz.

Before the 28th Division Command Post, the druggist, Eugène Weber, was still waiting for his friend. At last the meeting ended and officers poured out of the Villa Adler. The Frenchman shook his head: the Americans could not hold Wiltz.

Weber ran to the Red Cross building, warned his Boy Scouts to leave, then hurried home and told his parents to pack a few clothes. He stroked his cat for a moment, put him in a pail, dropped in a piece of chloroform-soaked cotton, and clapped on the lid. Now he was ready to leave Wiltz.

2

By now, 3:30 P.M., Manteuffel's 2nd Panzer Division, which had come through Clervaux, was only ten miles from Bastogne. The few hundred men of Task Force Rose of the 9th Armored Division, after a fierce one-sided fight, had finally been overwhelmed and the panzer column was now approaching the second, and last, roadblock in front of Bastogne, Task Force Harper.

Two other German divisions were also converging on Bastogne. Coming over muddy secondary roads a few miles to the south, Panzer Lehr was churning forward as fast as possible, its march hampered only by men of the 26th Volksgrenadier Division who were using the same roads.

But in spite of their relatively slow progress, the corps commander of these three divisions, General Heinrich von Lüttwitz, was satisfied. A large paunchy man of fifty-six, seldom without his monocle, he appeared to be the typical arrogant Prussian. Actually he was considerate of his troops and, in spite of his rather gross exterior, a daring commander. This was why Manteuffel had put him in charge of the main attack.

Lüttwitz had just intercepted a typically careless American radio message. Two American airborne divisions, the 82nd and the 101st, were moving to the Ardennes from France. It pleased him that elite airborne troops were being used as infantry. This meant American reserves were dangerously low.

He guessed that the 82nd and 101st were bound for Bastogne—his own destination. This didn't bother him in the least. He was sure Panzer Lehr would get there first. The most important rail and road center in the Ardennes would soon be his without a fight.

It had to be taken at all costs. "Otherwise," he had told his commanders, "it will remain an abscess on our line of communication."

Lüttwittz was only half right about these reinforcements. The 101st Airborne alone was bound for Bastogne. That morning Courtney Hodges had ordered the 82nd, the first on the road, to bypass Bastogne. It was to go instead to Werbomont and stop Peiper's drive to the Meuse.

There was, however, a second American column heading for Bastogne. This was Combat Command B of the 10th Armored Division. The night before as they were about to enter battle near Luxembourg City at the southern end of the great front, their commander, Colonel William Roberts, had been called to the phone.

"Crank up, Bill," he was told. "You're to go north to a little town in Belgium called Bastogne."

Soon after 3:00 P.M., Roberts, preceding his troops by jeep, reported to Troy Middleton in Bastogne. A big dignified man who had seen much war, he told the VIII Corps commander that his first troops should be arriving from the south any minute.

Middleton was relieved. "There is already a battle going on for Bastogne," he explained. And he added that the only two roadblocks

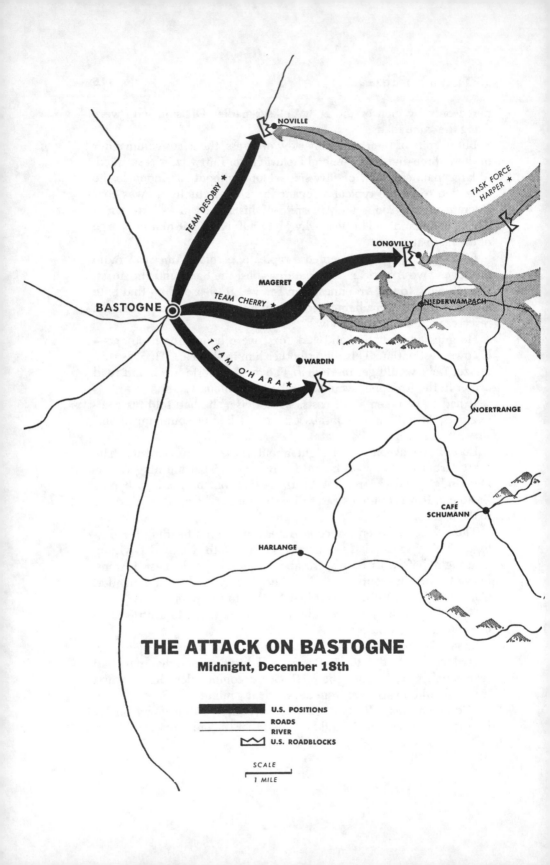

NOVILLE

TEAM DESOBRY *

TASK FORCE HARPER *

LONGVILLY

MAGERET

BASTOGNE

TEAM CHERRY *

NIEDERWAMPACH

TEAM O'HARA *

WARDIN

NOERTRANGE

CAFÉ SCHUMANN

HARLANGE

THE ATTACK ON BASTOGNE
Midnight, December 18th

▬▬▬▬▬ U.S. POSITIONS
───── ROADS
───── RIVER
〰〰〰 U.S. ROADBLOCKS

SCALE
1 MILE

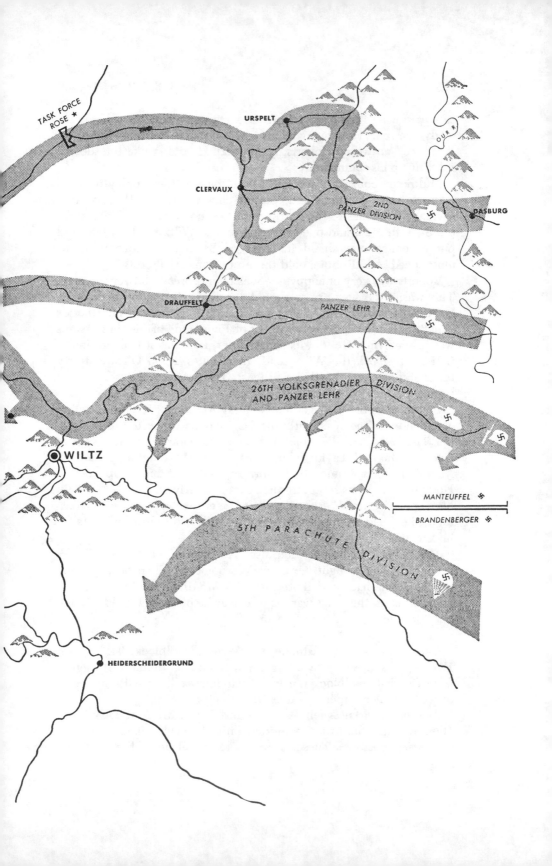

TASK FORCE
ROSE ✱

URSPELT

CLERVAUX

2ND
PANZER DIVISION

DASBURG

OUR R

DRAUFFELT

PANZER LEHR

26TH VOLKSGRENADIER DIVISION
AND PANZER LEHR

WILTZ

MANTEUFFEL

BRANDENBERGER

5TH PARACHUTE DIVISION

HEIDERSCHEIDERGRUND

east of town—Task Forces Rose and Harper—were very likely already overrun. "How many teams can you make, Robbie?" he asked.

"Three," answered Roberts, concerned. He didn't like the idea of splitting up his command.

Middleton pointed at a map. "You'll move without delay in three teams to these positions and counter enemy threats." He indicated a village five miles to the north; one the same distance due east on the St. Vith road; and one southeast on the Wiltz road. This would put a semicircular shield in front of Bastogne. "Move with utmost speed. And Robbie, hold these positions at all costs."

Roberts was very unhappy. He was being spread all over the map. This wasn't the way armor should be used. He made no protests, however; evidently Middleton was facing a desperate, unorthodox situation. He hurried to the center of town. One of his three teams was just arriving. He told its commander, Lieutenant Colonel James O'Hara, to block the Wiltz road. In minutes Team O'Hara, thirty tanks and 500 men, headed southeast. The defense of Bastogne had begun.

In the meantime, Brigadier General Anthony McAuliffe, acting commander of the 101st Airborne Division, had reported to Middleton. The division artillery officer, he was temporarily replacing Major General Maxwell Taylor who was then in Washington, D.C. McAuliffe had left France that morning ahead of his troops before Hodges' new orders rerouting the 101st had arrived, and still thought his destination was Werbomont. But at a crossroads just west of Bastogne, he'd had an impulse to come to Middleton's headquarters for information.

Middleton told him his impulse had been a lucky one. "You're probably going to fight here, not Werbomont." Then he explained that as yet he had no definite plans for McAuliffe for he still didn't know whether the 101st was his to use as he pleased. Until he found out, McAuliffe would have to wait.

Ten miles east of Bastogne, the second roadblock, Task Force Harper, was uneasily awaiting its first attack. Infantry stragglers from the first roadblock ran into their lines, telling wild stories of overwhelming numbers of tanks and infantry.

As soon as darkness fell, Panthers and Tigers struck at Task Force Harper. The attack was so sudden only three Shermans could get into firing position. These were knocked out in a few minutes.

American half-tracks and armored cars were quickly set ablaze with tracer bullets. In the pink glare the defending infantrymen were silhouetted and easily shot down.

The roadblock quickly collapsed. Survivors piled into the few remaining vehicles and raced back in panic to Longvilly, only five miles in front of Bastogne. Here Colonel Gilbreth, commander of Combat Command Reserve of the 9th Armored, gathered up his few remaining resources—Headquarters Company, stragglers from his two overwhelmed roadblocks, and even a few survivors from Colonel Hurley Fuller's regiment—and formed a skirmish line in front of his remaining artillery battalions. Tension rose in the town as the patched-up force waited for the attack from the east.

But the 2nd Panzer Division, which had crushed both the roadblocks, had no intention of coming through Longvilly. A mile short of town they swung north onto the road leading to Noville, a village five miles above Bastogne.

Longvilly's real danger came from the southeast. Lüttwitz's other divisions—the 26th Volksgrenadier and the elite Panzer Lehr—were rapidly approaching, expecting to grab Bastogne before the Americans could dig in.

At 8:00 P.M. the commander of Roberts' second unit, Team Cherry, walked into Gilbreth's hectic headquarters. Lieutenant Colonel Henry Cherry had left the advance guard of his team parked 1,000 yards west of Longvilly next to a roadside shrine. In a few minutes Cherry learned that no one in town knew anything definite and fear was mounting fast. He told his advance guard to stay in place and hurried back to report the dangerous situation to Colonel Roberts.

By the time he returned, the streets of Bastogne were jammed with trucks and jeeps streaming from Middleton's headquarters and heading southwest. Word swept all over town. Eighth Corps Headquarters, on orders from Hodges, was pulling out. The desperation that had already gripped so many towns farther east came over Bastogne.

The tension was increased by the steady line of trucks, guns, and men retreating from the front. Dazed terrified stragglers, faces black with powder burns, eyes red from loss of sleep, all spoke of disaster. What was out east? Tanks, tanks, tanks.

When Colonel Roberts, a veteran of the rout at Chateau-Thierry, saw these haggard men drifting through town, he asked General Middleton for authority to use them.

As Middleton was writing a note of authorization, McAuliffe came in. The airborne commander told Middleton he felt all the troops in Bastogne should be commanded by one man.

"Sir," he said, "I think Colonel Roberts' Combat Command B should be attached to me."

Roberts bridled. "What do you know about armor?"

The short stocky McAuliffe looked up at Roberts and said, "Maybe you want my entire division attached to your combat command?"

Middleton quickly stopped the argument. They would both operate independently, he said. Their mutual cooperation was Bastogne's only hope.

With this uneasy truce the meeting broke up. Roberts went back to his temporary command post, a farmhouse a mile below Bastogne. He had other things to worry about. His second unit, Team Cherry, had arrived and was already in Longvilly. But the last team was still to come. It was scheduled for Noville, the village five miles to the north; and there were rumors that a panzer division, probably the 2nd, was fast approaching this key road junction.

A young major entered the farmhouse and reported to Roberts. This was William Desobry, commander of the third team. They had been friends for years, and Desobry looked on the older man as a second father.

The Colonel pointed to the map. "You're to hold Noville, Bill. You're young, and by tomorrow morning you'll probably be nervous. Then you'll probably want to pull out. When you begin thinking like that," he said, putting an arm around the young man's shoulder, "remember I told you *not* to pull out."

They shook hands and Team Desobry headed north. Now Roberts' first job was finished. His three teams were in place. The next step was up to Cherry, O'Hara, and Desobry. "Remember," he had often told them, "I'm one of the oldest colonels on the front. My brain and not my body will have to pay off. I need proper rest. You see that I get it."

He went to bed, confident his three commanders would give him that rest.

Several miles west of Bastogne an old scarred staff car was crawling through thick fog. An impatient major general was sitting next to the nervous driver. Half a dozen times in the past hour the driver had barely missed crashing into the tail gate of the truck ahead.

Matthew Ridgway, commander of the XVIII Airborne Corps, had been in England that morning. He had flown to Reims where he learned that two of his airborne divisions had already left for the Ardennes. No one knew what the situation was, except that the Americans, taken by surprise, had been knocked sprawling. This situation appealed to Ridgway, a natural fighter. He was already working out a plan of attack. His theory of battle was simple. If you're knocked down you get up quickly and flatten the enemy. Otherwise you're licked.

The car again jerked to a stop. Ridgway's forehead almost hit the windshield. "What's the matter, sonny?" he asked sharply. "Can't you see?"

"Not too good I can't, sir."

Ridgway, unable to stand anything done badly, edged over impatiently and said, "Let me take the wheel."

Many miles behind Ridgway's sedan, 380 big open "cattle" trucks, loaded with 11,000 men of the 101st Airborne Division, were also hurrying to Bastogne. Here there was no fog. Stars were shining. Even so all lights were blazing.

The illuminated convoy was an inviting target for the Luftwaffe. But the risk had to be taken. If the 101st didn't get to Bastogne by morning it might be too late.

Another column, this one with lights blacked out, was moving toward the same destination, but from the opposite direction. At 10:00 P.M. it slowly pulled into the Luxembourg border village of Niederwampach, eight miles east of Bastogne. At the head, in an armored half-track, was Major General Fritz Bayerlein, commander of the Panzer Lehr Division.

He stopped the car. Behind him the advance guard of the division ground to a halt. Bayerlein studied his map. All day he had been struggling over muddy secondary roads, and his corps commander, General von Lüttwitz, expected him to take Bastogne by a coup de main that night.

Bayerlein had three choices. He could go a mile to the north and reach Longvilly on the paved St. Vith road; he could go south to the equally good Wiltz road; or he could drive straight ahead on a secondary road to Mageret.

He looked at the map again. The road straight ahead, according to the map, was fairly good. It saved mileage and it probably wasn't protected. "Straight ahead," he told his driver.

Bayerlein, followed by fifteen tanks and four companies of infantry in half-tracks, headed for Mageret. After a mile the paved road became dirt. He thought it was just a bad stretch, but in another half mile the dirt road had deteriorated into a simple cow path.

Now it was too late to turn back; he had to keep going. One by one vehicles stalled and were left behind. But Bayerlein forced his driver to push forward, on toward Mageret.

Over the rugged hills a mile to the north, Colonel Gilbreth was having a hard job holding the makeshift American defenses of Longvilly together. By now infantrymen of the 26th Volksgrenadier Division were making stabs at his slender line from the west. He had long since been outflanked on the north, by the 2nd Panzer Division, which was now nearing Noville. And, though he didn't know it, Bayerlein was swinging up from the south and was about to cut him off from the rear.

Firing was heard not far away. Then rumors swept town that the Germans were either in Mageret or rapidly approaching it. Gilbreth ordered his exhausted remnants to retreat to Bastogne. He would leave the job of stopping the avalanche to Team Cherry, coiled up for the night just west of town.

The panic was on.

3

As midnight approached, the Ardennes battlefield was a writhing mess, a scene of indescribable confusion to those involved in the hundred of struggles.

No one—German or American, private or general—knew what was actually happening.

In the north, even though Kampfgruppe Peiper was only a day's good march from the Meuse, Dietrich's main drive was stalled in front of Elsenborn Ridge. Hitler, disgusted at the slow pace of the Sixth Panzer Army, now ordered Dietrich to shunt his two reserve divisions—the 2nd and 9th SS Panzer Divisions—to the south and go through the great holes Manteuffel had made in and below the Schnee Eifel.

Manteuffel himself had a heavy program for the next day. He

ordered his troops to wipe out the 106th Division men trapped in the Schnee Eifel and storm three key towns: St. Vith, Bastogne, and Wiltz.

Wiltz was also a target of one of Brandenberger's divisions. Men of the 5th Parachute Division were heading for Café Schumann, a little crossroads settlement just three miles southwest of Wiltz. This cluster of buildings and its four roads would soon become one of the most important half acres in the world. Once it was seized, the main escape route from Wiltz to Bastogne would be cut.

The Americans in Wiltz had no idea their great threat came from this direction. Only a handful of GIs, feeling safe and secure, guarded Café Schumann, their eight guns aimed to the north.

In fact, the German High Command had no idea Wiltz was being threatened by their Seventh Army troops. Neither did the new commander of the 5th Parachute Division, Colonel Heilmann. He had specifically ordered his men to pass below Wiltz and head straight west.

But Heilmann had little control. The young, hungry zealots of the 5th Parachute Division had minds of their own. They knew Wiltz was a great storehouse of food and clothing. They decided to break into this storehouse from the rear, through little Café Schumann.

They loped through the woods that night, shivering in their thin coats. They were on the prowl for food, clothes, and warm beds.

4

It was midnight in Germany. Excited citizens were reading and re-reading the thrilling news of the great offensive. Their radios were full of triumphant reports:

> The speedy collapse of every organized Allied defense has considerably eased our tasks!

> We have all been asking ourselves why is the Führer so silent. Perhaps he is ill? Now we can tell you. The Führer is enjoying excellent health, but he has been preparing this new offensive down to the minutest details. His silence had been worth it. The enemy has received a shock!

> We must force the enemy to throw in the sponge. He must realize that the battle no longer pays!

Many in and behind the Allied lines had the same thought. There was a wave of panic in hundreds of towns and cities not only in Luxembourg and Belgium but in France and Holland. These people remembered the blitzkrieg in 1940.

They were asking themselves: was another even greater blitzkrieg in the making?

3. SURRENDER

19 December 1944

1

In the Schnee Eifel, dawn of December 19 was breaking as young Colonel Descheneaux's 422nd Regiment of the 106th Division began its last-ditch assault on Schönberg, three miles to the northwest.

Major William Moon led the attack, moving his 1st Battalion from a dense woods up a rolling snow-covered hill to a paved highway running along a ridge. As Moon sent his first company across the highway, four German tanks rolled down the road from the east and spotted the rest of the battalion bunched closely together in the woods. Their 88s swung into action, and shrapnel from tree-bursts showered the frightened men.

Moon ran back to the woods. "Move out to the left," he shouted. The men raced toward the protection of a small ravine. Their only hope was to advance up it, cross the ridge road, and join the first company.

As the first men ran across the road, other German tanks and infantry moved up from the other side, catching Moon's men in the open. Now the four tanks on the ridge road moved forward, their guns blasting. Moon's men, caught in the open between two fires, could only hug the ground and pray.

D Company set up a heavy machine gun and sprayed the German infantrymen coming from the left. But in less than a minute, gun and crew were blasted by an 88 shell.

Then a bazooka team ran forward and aimed at the leading tank. As they were launching their first rocket, machine-gun bullets tore them apart. The pinned-down riflemen kept firing, even though the situation was hopeless. Then a GI stood up, waving a white handkerchief, and slowly walked toward the German tanks. Fire ceased as other Americans stood up, raising their hands.

Moon got to his feet. Then he suddenly raced across the ridge road, followed by his staff and a handful of men. They disappeared in the woods.

A mile further west, Colonel Cavender's regiment was already across the highway. Long before dawn Cavender had visited his three battalions, checking on the condition of his men. Now as he prepared to start a meeting of his battalion commanders, he looked up at the skies. They were clearing. Today they would surely get the long-promised air drop. And then he could blast his way through Schönberg and on to St. Vith.

"We will attack at 1000 hours in a column of battalions," he told his commanders. Then he turned to Lieutenant Colonel Klinck of the 3rd Battalion. "You're in the best shape. You'll carry the burden of the attack." He looked at his watch. "Gentlemen, it is exactly nine o'clock."

As the commanders turned to leave for their units, the woods seemed to burst apart. Branches showered down. The ground shook; a hail of steel fragments ripped through the area. Lieutenant Colonel William Craig, commander of the 1st Battalion, fell, badly wounded.

The deadly barrage stopped as suddenly as it had started. Cavender dropped to one knee. "Take it easy," he told Craig.

"If I could only catch my breath," Craig gasped, "I'd get back to my battalion."

"That's all right," said Cavender.

Craig struggled to rise, dropped back. Soon he was dead.

A few minutes later Company L of the 3rd Battalion led off Cavender's attack, advancing along the Schönberg road. Soon the point saw a Sherman tank heading in their direction. The 7th Armored Division, they thought, had finally punched its way through.

But the Sherman was manned by Germans. It suddenly opened fire. At the same moment rifle fire broke out in the rear. Attacked on two sides, Company L fought its way up a hill and dug in. The re-

maining companies pushed on toward Schönberg, reaching the outskirts of town. Here they waited for artillery support, not knowing
that a mile behind them the 590th Field Artillery was smoking
wreckage, completely destroyed by the recent tank barrage.

Now the 1st Battalion started its attack. But the commander, William Craig, who had gone to Cavender's meeting alone, had just
died. The executive, knowing no details of the attack plans, led the
men toward Schönberg. He was also unaware that German tanks
and infantry were closing in from two sides.

Then the 2nd Battalion, riddled by yesterday's fight at Radscheid,
moved down a ravine. Heavy small-arms fire broke out from the
right. Badly shaken at first by the unexpected attack, they re-formed
and answered the fire. The enemy was their sister regiment, Descheneaux's 422nd.

Confusion ruled the Schnee Eifel.

2

Back in St. Vith, Bruce Clarke was beginning to feel more confident
of his men. On his visits to the front lines he found a spirit of dogged
resistance. The men weren't cocky, but they felt they could hold St.
Vith as long as the ammunition lasted. Clarke began to hear fantastic
stories of the 275th Armored Field Artillery commanded by Lieutenant Colonel Roy Clay. This was the VIII corps outfit which had
refused to pull out of St. Vith in the great retreat and for two days
had been Clarke's only artillery support, firing in three directions.

Major Don Boyer was just out front of St. Vith, commanding a
task force of two companies. At 10:30 A.M., taking advantage of a
lull, he was leading an officers' patrol into the woods ahead. He
wanted to see the scene of three vicious attacks of the day before.

As he crept forward he passed piles of German bodies. Many had
died trying to scoop shallow holes with their helmets, bayonets, and
even hands. The slaughter was appalling at one firebreak: nineteen
paratroopers stretched out in almost parade-ground intervals, five
yards apart, their throats and chests ripped by machine-gun slugs.

To Boyer's surprise, under the camouflage jackets of the dead paratroopers were shoulder straps with the Gothic "GD"—the insigne of
the famous Gross-Deutschland Division, an outfit supposedly on the
Russian front.

Boyer counted 249 dead bodies in front of the battalion. Then he

led his patrol back. This was only the beginning. Out east ominous
rumblings were already starting again.

Behind St. Vith, in Vielsalm, Brigadier General Robert Hasbrouck
was trying to make sense out of confusion. The defense of the entire
sector was roughly in the shape of a great arc curving in front of St.
Vith with its open end to Vielsalm.

Hasbrouck's 7th Armored Division held the northern half of the
arc. It was a well-knit line that gave him no immediate concern. The
southern half, beginning just below St. Vith, was a different matter.

General Alan Jones commanded this sector but he had little to
work with. His left flank, tying in with Bruce Clarke at St. Vith, was
held by Hoge's Combat Command B of the 9th Armored. To Hoge's
right, but separated by a hole of several miles, was Jones's only other
force—the 424th Regiment of the 106th Division. Although it had
originally been positioned just below the two Schnee Eifel regiments, Manteuffel's pincers had narrowly missed trapping it with
the others. Luckily its commander, Colonel Alexander Reid, had
pulled back from the closing jaws without waiting for instructions.

Now, nearly out of food and ammunition, Reid held the right flank
of the great arc. Below him were no known American forces—only
a vague no man's land. In short the entire St. Vith-Vielsalm sector
was completely open to attack from the south.

Yesterday Middleton's last words of instruction to Hasbrouck had
been, "You and Jones carry on up there." In other words, he and
Jones were to act as equals, with neither in full charge. Jones, whose
headquarters were also now in Vielsalm, was a major general. Hasbrouck was only a brigadier and yet commanded the bulk of the
troops. It was a command problem for some future army manual.

But Hasbrouck's chief problem that morning was a possible German attack from the south, for a reconnaissance patrol had reported
that a strong force was attacking Gouvy, a village only ten miles
below Vielsalm.

Although Jones commanded this area of the defensive arc, Hasbrouck's own safety was involved. He ordered a tank company to
rush south, and prayed the attack was only a light one.

At 11:00 A.M., while he was trying to figure out what to do in case
of a breakthrough at Gouvy, an exhausted colonel was brought into
his office. The newcomer said he was Gustin Nelson, of the 112th
Regiment of the 28th Division.

Hasbrouck was astounded. "What are *you* doing way up here?" he asked. The 112th was the 28th Division regiment just north of Hurley Fuller's. "And where the hell's the rest of your division?"

Nelson, face lined with exhaustion, shrugged. "Don't ask me. I just found out where *I* was this morning when I ran into one of your patrols."

His regiment, he explained, had been severed from Hurley Fuller's on December 16. Almost all contact with the 28th Division was soon lost and he had been drifting back to the west and north on his own. Although he hadn't had too many casualties, his men were exhausted from constant marching, cold, and hunger.

Nelson pointed out on a map his approximate position—the northern tip of Luxembourg. Hasbrouck felt a surge of hope. Nelson was only five miles south of Reid. If these two groups could tie in and pull northwest until they joined Hoge, the unstable arc would become a solid horseshoe. He telephoned Jones about the unexpected reinforcements from the 28th Division. "Why don't you attach Nelson to the 106th?" he suggested.

Jones quickly accepted. It was the only good news he'd had since December 16. Now he had three units—Hoge, Reid, and Nelson. And there was still a chance his two regiments on the Schnee could fight their way back.

Just before noon, at Wallerode Mill, only five miles east of St. Vith, three men were planning the seizure of the town.

"It has to be taken fast," said Model angrily. "It's a stumbling block to my whole offensive."

"I know," Manteuffel said. He turned to Lucht, the corps commander directly responsible for taking St. Vith. "Encircle the town. Put your heaviest weight on north and south. And do it fast."

Lucht nodded. What had looked like an easy job was turning into a nightmare.

"We've got to have St. Vith within twenty-four hours," went on Model. "Dietrich is making complaints all the way back to Wolf's Lair. He says even his 1st SS Panzer Division is being tied up because of the road jam."

"Dietrich!" Lucht couldn't hide his anger. "His people have been using my roads since yesterday. How can I mount an attack with him fouling up my rear? Yesterday I had to go out personally and arrest some of his officers." He turned to Manteuffel, whose face had hardened. "This morning my horse-drawn artillery couldn't get through because Dietrich's people were stealing my roads. And they still are!"

"Kick them off so they stay off," cut in Manteuffel abruptly. "Without artillery you'll never take St. Vith."

Model got to his feet. He had as little respect for Dietrich as the others. "I'll take care of it," he said.

The little field marshal strode out of the conference room and was soon at the heart of the great traffic jam. Thousands of vehicles were hopelessly tangled. Everyone had a vital job that had to be done instantly.

Model, monocle in eye, stood in the highway. He called out orders and waved his arms. Finally the tangle became a slow orderly line. Two days before it had taken General Bruce Clarke to control traffic west of St. Vith. Today, east of town, it had taken a feldmarschall.

3

At 3:30 P.M. the end was approaching on the Schnee Eifel. By now almost 10,000 Americans were hemmed into a few square miles of woods near Schönberg. As German artillery and mortar fire concentrated on this small area, the mass of trapped men milled around in confusion, ignorance, and terror. Scouts were sent out to find an escape route. But Germans were found on all sides. There could be no escape.

An epic disaster was imminent.

Descheneaux's regiment was still a mile short of its goal, Schönberg. The young colonel and his staff were conferring in a slit trench on the fringe of woods. As they crouched in the 25-foot-long trench, trying to make sense out of conflicting reports, the rumble of tanks came from the north. The rumor again spread that the 7th Armored had finally arrived. There was a moment of desperate hope.

Then tanks poked their noses over the ridge road. Even from a distance they looked too large to be American. They were panzers of the Führer-Escort Brigade. Soon shells from the tanks' 88s exploded in the trees, and the woods became a charnel house for the thousands of Americans as shrapnel rained down.

Descheneaux called together his officers. The dressing station next to the command post in the trench was filling up. The wounded moaned and cried out in pain.

"We're sitting like fish in a pond," said Descheneaux. He was debating with himself. There was no food, no water, no bandages, and little ammunition; but surrender was unthinkable. A litter passed the trench. In it Descheneaux saw his M Company commander, Perkins. One of his legs had been shot off. Blood gushed onto the snow.

He felt sick. "My God," he said, "we're being slaughtered!" His throat was dry. "We can't do anything effective." He looked at the men crouched in the trench with him. "I don't believe in fighting for glory if it doesn't accomplish anything. It looks like we'll have to pack in."

Reluctantly, sadly, they agreed.

There was an embarrassed pause. Then Lieutenant Colonel Frederick Nagle said, "Do you want me to take the white flag?"

Descheneaux nodded.

Nagle, weak from a wound in the back, took the flag. It was the hardest thing he'd ever had to do. He selected a soldier who could speak German. Then under the white banner the two moved cautiously down the hill.

Colonel T. Paine Kelly, commanding officer of Eric Wood's artillery battalion, was digging a foxhole when he heard the report that Descheneaux was surrendering. He hurried to the trench command post.

"Jesus, Desch," he said. "You can't do this! It'll be dark in an hour. Then we can break out to the west."

Descheneaux shook his head slowly.

Kelly looked at him accusingly. "Desch, you can't surrender!"

"No?" Descheneaux was bitter. "What the hell else can I do? You name it."

"But—"

"As far as I'm concerned," said Descheneaux, "I'm going to save the lives of as many as I can. And I don't give a damn if I'm court-martialed." He came out of the trench. "Break up everything you've got," he called. "Break up your guns and pistols."

Several young officers looked at him cold-eyed. It made him feel sick. He didn't know whether it was pity or hate but either way he didn't like it. In a West Point classroom no one surrendered. Out here it was different. You finally reached the point where you couldn't shed another drop of another man's blood.

A private looked at Descheneaux with unbelief. The Colonel's personal courage had become legend to the doughs the past three days. He was wherever things were hottest.

"You heard me. Break up your guns and pistols."

The private held up his M-1. "I've carried this goddam thing for months. I've never even fired it once in anger!" Then he viciously swung it at a tree.

Descheneaux started to cry. Hiding his face, he crawled back into the trench.

Soon a young German lieutenant and several grenadiers returned with Nagle. He explained in French what he wanted. Descheneaux, a French-Canadian, replied in French. He saw the grenadiers relieving some of his men of cigarettes and watches. "Let my men keep one pack apiece," he insisted.

The German lieutenant nodded. "Everything will be correct, Colonel."

Soon hundreds of Americans filed down the slope, passing streams of grenadiers, well armed and full of spirit; there were dozens of mortars and light field pieces. Descheneaux turned and looked at the array of arms and men surrounding his hill.

Kelly, behind him, nodded dejectedly. "You were right, Desch," he said. "There was nothing else you could do."

Less than a mile to the west in another part of the crowded woods, Cavender's men—like Descheneaux's— were without food, water, or ammunition.

At 3:45 P.M. Cavender called a conference.

"There's no ammunition left," he said, "except for a few rounds for the M-1s. I was a GI in the First World War," Cavender continued when several began to grumble, "and I want to try to see things from their standpoint. No man in this outfit has eaten all day and we haven't had water since early morning." He looked around at the small group. "Now what's your attitude on surrendering?"

Half of the officers wanted to break out to the west.

"I'm expecting enemy artillery at 1630," said Cavender.

"I know it's no use fighting," said one officer miserably. "But I still don't want to surrender."

Cavender was silent. He knew the lives of the remnants of his regiment depended on his decision. So did his reputation. He said, "Gentlemen, we're surrendering at 1600."

The news drifted from group to group. Lieutenant "Rip" Collins, executive of Company I, was sitting on a hill digging a trench when his commanding officer returned.

"We're cut off," said the captain. "In ten minutes the regiment is going to be surrendered. Have the men destroy their weapons."

Collins was shocked. This was crazy. "Did someone panic?" he asked. The more he thought, the angrier he got. He called the men of Company I together. "Destroy your weapons," he ordered bitterly.

Some of the men were glad to surrender. Others were indignant. Sergeant Dowling came up to Collins. "All my men want to break out," he said. "Will you lead us, Lieutenant?"

Collins silently argued with himself. Then he said, "I'm sorry, Sergeant, the orders are to surrender."

A short distance away, Lieutenant Alan Jones, Jr., son of the division commander, refused to believe the rumors of surrender. The fifty stragglers he'd rounded up milled around him, dumfounded.

A Negro sergeant, tommy gun hanging around his neck, came up to Jones. "We haven't even started fighting, Lieutenant," he said. "Let's go out and kill some Germans!"

Just then a runner reported to Jones. "All weapons will be rendered inoperable, sir," he reported. "And all units are to stand fast."

In a few moments Germans marched up the hill and began rounding up the stunned men. Jones felt absolute disbelief. It couldn't be happening. He didn't want to look his men in the face.

The Germans were military, well organized and brisk. Commands were brief and answers monosyllabic. There was nothing to talk about.

The tragedy of the Schnee Eifel was concluded.

Eight thousand Americans—perhaps nine thousand, for the battle was too confused for accuracy—had been bagged.

Next to Bataan, it was the greatest mass surrender of Americans in history.

Now the Germans had full control of the road net east of St. Vith. Traffic moved ahead fearlessly, bumper to bumper. The advancing Germans talked with loud enthusiasm. As they passed long lines of despondent prisoners, they grabbed watches, rings, and coats. Young Nazi officers rushed about, shaking hands, congratulating each other. Their eyes glistened as they watched the seemingly endless lines of prisoners walk to the east.

Descheneaux was one of those slogging to the rear. "Did I do the right thing?" he kept asking himself. The answer was, "If I had to do it again, I'd still surrender." But he was eaten by bitterness. He felt a cold loneliness amidst the great captured mob.

One of the men, recognizing him, called, "Hey, Colonel Descheneaux!" Descheneaux turned and saw an unshaven infantryman looking at him with red weary eyes. "I've got a message for you, Colonel."

The GI stuck out his tongue and made a "Bronx cheer."

In Vielsalm, hope was given up for the two regiments on the Schnee by all but a few stubborn optimists.

At 4:00 P.M., General Alan Jones was handed a radio message from Middleton. He read it, then let it flutter to his desk. No food, no medical supplies, not a bullet had been dropped to his men on the Schnee.

Jones now knew his two regiments were lost. His son was lost.

4

North of Vielsalm, Kampfgruppe Peiper was again close to a complete breakthrough by late afternoon. It had burst through Stoumont, overwhelming a 30th Division battalion and ten supporting tanks.

American infantrymen were now running in terror down the hill to the west, shouting that masses of Jerry tanks were on their heels.

A few miles ahead of Peiper's advancing column, Captain Berry of the 740th Tank Battalion had just learned of the breakthrough and was hurrying toward Stoumont from the ordnance depot near Remouchamps with fourteen patched-up tanks. He hoped the recently installed guns would traverse but there had been no time to test. He did know the radios wouldn't work. They were British and his tankers didn't know how to operate them.

As Berry's fourteen tanks pushed through fog and drizzle toward the Stoumont railroad station, other American tanks rolled past them to the rear.

"We're low on ammo and fuel!" shouted one of the retreating tankers.

"And guts," mumbled Berry.

It was now up to the 740th. Having no radio, he gave Lieutenant Powers a hand signal to take the lead with his five tanks. Powers pushed through the fog, almost immediately spotting a Panther 150 yards ahead at a curve in the road. His first shot hit the German's gun mantlet and ricocheted down, killing the driver and bow gunner. The Panther burst into flames.

Powers slowly pushed on, having no idea what lay ahead. A second big tank loomed up. Before the German could fire, Powers sent a round into the Tiger's front slope plate. The shell bounced off harmlessly.

Powers' gun jammed. Since the radios were useless he hand-signaled the tank destroyer behind to move in. The Tiger, jarred by Powers' first shot, fired two wild rounds. Then the American tank destroyer's big 90-mm. roared. The Tiger flamed.

Powers' gun was now cleared. He dodged around the burning tank and saw an unsuspecting Panther. Once more Powers got off the first shot. It blew the muzzle off the Panther's gun. The Panther, trying to back up, was set afire.

The Germans had had enough. Under cover of the blanket of fog, the remaining panzers spun around, climbed the steep hill leading up to Stoumont, and hid behind a stone sanatorium.

The 30th Division infantrymen, encouraged by this American victory, surged back up the hill. In thirty minutes a few determined tankers had stemmed the tide. Peiper was stalled again. He didn't know it, but he was also completely cut off. Fifteen miles to the rear the men he'd left in Stavelot to hold that town had just been driven back across the Amblève River by another regiment of the 30th Division.

5

Twenty-five miles east of Stavelot, the defenders of the twin villages of Krinkelt and Rocherath were exhausted, out of food, and almost out of ammunition.

Behind them, other men of the 2nd and 99th Divisions were digging gun emplacements and foxholes in the frozen ground of Elsenborn Ridge. Nearby fields and farmhouses were rummaged for fence posts, pole gates, planks—anything that could be used as frameworks for sandbags. The men worked feverishly, hoping their comrades out front could hold just a little longer.

It was dark by the time the diggers and builders were finished. The final defense dam was ready for any German attack.

Word was passed to the front: withdraw.

The defenders of Krinkelt and Rocherath had done their job.

Their new job was to save their necks—if they could. Long lines of men and machines began slowly pulling out of the twin villages. Behind they left gutted buildings, streets clogged with the tangled charred wrecks of German tanks, alleys filled with the rotting dead —German and American. Now it was every man for himself.

The move to Elsenborn Ridge soon became a race with death. The leading troops quickened their pace to escape blasts of artillery and screaming meemies. Overshoes and overcoats became heavier with each mile. Even though it was freezing the roadside was soon lined with coats and boots and guns. By now it was an old story in the Ardennes. The cold was nothing compared to the Nazi death at their heels.

4. A CALL TO MONTGOMERY

19 December 1944

1

On the southern half of the Ardennes battlefield, the most significant event of December 19 was developing near Bastogne long before dawn.

The advance guard of Panzer Lehr did not roll into Mageret, a village five miles west of Bastogne, until 2:00 A.M. The back road that had looked good on the map to Lehr's commander, General Bayerlein, had proved to be little more than a path.

In Mageret, Bayerlein's men soon stumbled onto American trucks and ambulances; firing broke out, and the Germans discovered they had captured a hospital unit.

A frightened Belgian was brought to Bayerlein. "Have you seen other Americans?" asked the General.

"A very great force went through a few hours ago," said the civilian, pointing east down the main highway to Longvilly. "At least fifty tanks and forty armored cars. They were led by a major general!" (This was Team Cherry, thirty tanks led by a captain.)

Suddenly Bayerlein lost his usual dash. He heard faint rumbles from several directions. He was afraid American armor had cut him off and was converging on him. Actually he was hearing two different columns: his own tanks closing in behind, and retreating American vehicles which had passed through the village moments before Bayerlein's men cut the Longvilly-Bastogne highway.

Bayerlein did not start down this highway toward Bastogne until 5:30 A.M. Then, after creeping a cautious mile, his lead tank struck a mine and blew up. The tankers cleared the mines and the column again inched forward. When the van finally reached the Neffe railroad station, gray light was beginning to show in the east.

Not a single shot had yet been fired. But Bayerlein again hesitated. He was worried about the impenetrable fog all around him and the "very great force" of enemy tanks in his rear. He decided to stop and wait for more light.

Four miles west, in Bastogne, Colonel Julian Ewell was just leading the 1st Battalion of his 501st Parachute Regiment out the road toward Neffe. After driving most of the night in open trucks from France, Ewell's men had pulled up cold, tired, and hungry in Bastogne. Since they were the first outfit of the 101st Airborne to arrive, to them fell the first and most hazardous mission.

"Ewell," General McAuliffe had said, pointing to the same highway Team Cherry had taken the night before to Longvilly, "move out along this road, make contact with the enemy, attack, and clear up the situation."

Ewell, a droll poker-faced man who reminded his troops of Ned Sparks, said only, "Yes, sir." A few minutes later his chaplain, Father Sampson, reported for duty and asked what the situation was. "Well, Father," drawled Ewell, "if I knew more, I'd be confused."

At dawn Ewell's men were on their way. Many were without helmets; some without rifles were pulled out of ranks; few had overcoats; but their step was quick and jaunty as they pressed their strange march to an unknown destination to fight an unknown foe.

Retreating armored cars, artillery, and half-tracks which had passed safely through Mageret before Bayerlein had cut the road from Longvilly, began slowly passing the double file of paratroopers. Then, eyes red, faces gaunt and filthy, some infantrymen from the 28th Division slumped by.

"What the hell are you guys doing?" one asked.

A paratrooper, his only weapon a stick, waved it menacingly toward the east. "We're going to fight Germans," he said.

"We've had it," the infantryman said, "and you'll get it."

Colonel Ewell plodded along in the middle of his column. By chance in November he had spent two days' leave in Bastogne, wan-

dering over the naked hills among the occasional pine plantations
outside town. Now this knowledge of the country paid off, for in the
dense fog the head of the column turned down the wrong road.
Ewell hurried up front, steering his men back on the right road.

Suddenly the quick chatter of a German machine gun broke
out. Ewell and Bayerlein had collided in the fog.

Ewell called together his commanders and ordered one company
to deploy to the right. To the left, he remembered, was Bizory, located near a rolling hill that could be easily defended; he sent word
for the 2nd Battalion, which was following, to seize this village.

"Clear up the situation," he concluded drily, in imitation of Mc-
Auliffe. "But gentlemen, I don't want you to beat the enemy to
death." Ewell's decision to stand and fight was to determine the defense of Bastogne. It was based on the assumption that he had run
into a minor German roadblock.

When Bayerlein heard the answering fire of Ewell's paratroopers,
he guessed he had run into an entire division. When he heard the
roar of the special glider artillery howitzer, the M-3, he was sure he
was opposed by a heavy armored force. To try to bull his way
through would be too costly and dangerous.

A man ordinarily of great personal courage, Bayerlein now saw
disaster behind every bush. He ordered his men to dig in.

Six miles north of Bastogne, in the dreary treeless village of
Noville, Team Desobry, the last of the three armored task forces
Colonel Roberts had sent out to slow down the German drive, had
spent a sleepless night and a morning of sporadic tank attacks.

The densest fog in the Ardennes had settled over this low-lying
village since dawn. A few minutes after 10:00 A.M. it suddenly
lifted. Major Desobry was astounded. The entire countryside was
alive with German tanks.

To the north fourteen hurried along a ridge, looking desperately
for cover. Like targets in a shooting gallery, they were knocked off
one by one by Desobry's gunners. More tanks appeared on the hills
to the west.

Ammunition was running low. Desobry radioed Colonel Roberts
and asked permission to pull back several miles.

"You can use your own judgment about withdrawing," said Roberts, recalling his last words to the young man the night before. "But I'm sending a battalion of paratroopers to reinforce you."

Desobry replied, "I'll get ready to counterattack."

It was the answer Roberts hoped he'd get. The 101st Airborne men needed every minute the armored teams could give them.

Southeast of Bastogne in the area Colonel Roberts had assigned to Team O'Hara, there was tension but, as yet, no action. O'Hara ordered three men to take a jeep and explore to the north.

It was near noon when the jeep, driven by Lieutenant John Drew Devereaux, descendant of America's most famous family of actors, crept into the fog-bound village of Wardin. People slowly came from doorways, and, when they saw the jeep was American, crowded around it.

"There are Germans all around!" cried an old man.

Devereaux, who had been playing to Broadway audiences not too long before in *Life with Father,* jumped on the jeep's hood. "Don't be afraid," he said in French. "We Americans are here to stay. Keep to your cellars but don't be afraid."

The people were calmed by the young man's confidence. They cheered. Devereaux got back to the driver's seat, guiding the jeep through Wardin and out to the east. When the fog lifted momentarily Devereaux spotted what appeared to be an American half-track and an armored car coming toward him. He stopped the jeep; something about the approaching vehicles bothered him.

"My God, those are *Krauts!*" cried the man next to Devereaux. There was a flash of light from the "American" half-track. The jeep, hit in the bumper, rocked and almost tipped over. Devereaux made a sharp turn and raced back toward Wardin. Civilians still stood in the square talking about the reassuring young American.

"The Germans are coming," shouted Devereaux, slowing down. "Get back to your cellars!"

Devereaux gunned the jeep and disappeared. The people of Wardin hurried back to their cellars.

The half-track that had put a hole in Devereaux's bumper came from a reconnaissance patrol of Panzer Lehr. But most of that division was now headed back east. Bayerlein, convinced he was in a jam, had turned his back on Bastogne momentarily. First he would wipe out the Americans to his rear in Longvilly. Then he would take Bastogne.

At 2:00 P.M. he launched his attack on Longvilly from the southwest. At the same moment, acting independently, the 26th Volksgrenadier Division hit the town from the southeast. Hearing the noise, a battery of 88s from the 2nd Panzer Division, bypassing Longvilly to the north, also opened fire.

The immediate target of this unplanned concentration was the conglomerate column of stalled American vehicles stretching from Longvilly to Mageret. The slaughter was great.

The advance guard of Team Cherry, still positioned a mile west of Longvilly at the grotto of St. Michael, fought so aggressively that the 26th Volksgrenadiers reported a counterattack. But the rest of the long column—the stragglers from the two 9th Armored Division roadblocks and other refugees from the front—were panicked by the heavy bombardment and the roar of approaching tanks. Without even a show of resistance they scattered toward Bastogne on foot.

In spite of the lonely, tenacious stand of Team Cherry, almost every American vehicle in the long column was destroyed or abandoned by 3:30 P.M. The highway was a mass of wreckage. The greatest damage was at the roadside grotto. Here a great junk heap of American tanks, armored cars, self-propelled guns, trunks, and jeeps burned brightly. Scores of dead GIs sprawled among the stone crucifixes and sacred images.

In all, more than two hundred vehicles had been destroyed or captured intact. But the Germans had paid a high price. Bastogne was given a day of grace.

2

Late that morning, Eisenhower's staff car was approaching the limits of Verdun. All during the trip the General had been mulling over the Ardennes problem. It was a weird battle, with many surprising facets. One of the most amazing was the strange hysteria that had suddenly sprung up behind the American lines.

It had spread all the way to Paris. That morning as he was about to leave, an excited security colonel had insisted he use a bulletproof car. "I have positive knowledge," he was told, "that Otto Skorzeny has sent special teams of American-dressed commandos to assassinate you." Five German parachutists had already been sighted in Eparnay. They were now said to be speeding toward Paris in a civilian car.

Eisenhower's car rolled into the streets of the famous battle town, and up to the formidable Verdun caserne. At 11:00 A.M. he walked into the chilly squad room which had been chosen for the conference. He looked around at a semicircle of solemn faces. "The present situation," he said, "is to be regarded as one of opportunity for us, and not of disaster." He scanned the council members again. "There will only be cheerful faces at this conference table."

Patton's face exploded into a big grin, exposing short dingy teeth. "Hell," he said, "let's have the guts to let the sons of bitches go all the way to Paris. Then we'll really cut 'em off and chew 'em up!"

The solemnity was broken. Everyone smiled.

Eisenhower shook his head. "No, the enemy will never be allowed to cross the Meuse." The gravity of Hodges' situation had to be faced. Unless a big diversionary attack were launched fast, the First Army line might collapse completely. "George," he said, turning to Patton, "I want you to go to Luxembourg and take charge. When can you start up there?"

"Now," snapped Patton.

"You mean today?"

"I mean as soon as you've finished with us here."

"How soon will you be able to attack, George?" asked Omar Bradley.

"In forty-eight hours."

Eisenhower frowned. Patton would have to turn his army ninety degrees. "Don't be fatuous," he said.

"Never mind dates." Patton waved his arms expansively. "I'll get there on time."

There was a murmur of excitement. Some thought Patton was merely boasting; others, like Bradley, were delighted with his brash air.

In his element, Patton lit a cigar and pointed to the great bulge on the map of the Ardennes. "Brad," he explained, "this time the Kraut has stuck his head in a meat grinder." He held up his fist. "And this time I've got hold of the handle."

Even Eisenhower grinned. "All right, George," he said. "Start your attack, no earlier than the twenty-second—and no *later* than the twenty-third." Then he raised a cautioning finger. "And remember, the advance has to be methodical, sure."

Patton blithely waved aside difficulties. "I'll be in Bastogne before Christmas," he said. Eisenhower warned him of the great strength of the German assault and then turned to Devers, who commanded the army group south of Bradley. "Jake," he said, "you'll have to thin out your lines so you can take over the big gap left by George. And if you're attacked, give ground even if you have to move completely back to the Vosges Mountains."

As soon as the meeting ended, Patton told a staff officer to telephone his chief of staff, General "Hap" Gay. Before leaving Nancy that morning, he had sketched out three possible plans for the Ardennes crisis and given Gay a code name for each. In minutes, on the basis of one telephoned word, Patton's army began to wheel and turn north toward the Ardennes.

Eisenhower approached and pointed to his new fifth star. "You know, George," he said with a smile, "every time I get promoted I get attacked."

"Yeah," said Patton. "And every time you get attacked I have to bail you out."

Seventy-five miles to the northeast, the 28th Division still held Wiltz even though the German wave had already surged far past to the edge of Bastogne. General "Dutch" Cota, after turning over the town's defense to Colonel Dan Strickler and promising to send back ammunition and replacements, had reluctantly retreated in a jeep to the division's new command post only two miles south of Bastogne.

Strickler's motley force of about 1,500 men knew they were in for a hard fight. But they had no suspicion an envelopment of the town was already in progress. A Manteuffel column from the north had already cut the main highway seven miles behind Wiltz. Coming up to meet it was a Brandenberger column from the south. When the two columns met—and they were only a few hours apart —Wiltz would be surrounded.

A few miles northeast of Wiltz, Colonel Hurley Fuller and four of his men—among the last survivors of Clervaux—were stumbling through a dense forest infested with briars and underbrush. Fuller, like so many others in his shattered regiment, had been putting up an isolated rear guard fight since the fall of Clervaux. But he now knew the Germans were closing in.

Suddenly he heard a sharp command in German. They had stumbled into an enemy assembly area. Fuller leaned against a tree; the others squatted tensely in the snow. The crunch of snow grew louder.

Without warning one of Fuller's men jumped up in terror, shouting, "Kamerad!"

The other four sprinted to the west. Then Fuller felt something hit him in the back of the head. When he regained consciousness he was lying in a ditch, his four men looking anxiously down at him. He felt a sharp pain in his groin and realized he'd been bayoneted. A bored German stood guard over them.

"Are you hurt, Colonel?" asked one of the men.

"I'm bleeding." He lowered his voice, signaling the others to come closer. "Remember," he whispered, "don't tell the sons of bitches anything."

A German officer standing behind Fuller angrily slammed a pistol butt on his skull. Fuller was then brought to a German command post and escorted by a sergeant to a little room where an officer of the 2nd Panzer Division sat.

"How do you feel?" asked the German sergeant solicitously in a British accent.

"As well as could be expected with a bump on the head and a cut in the groin."

"We'll take care of it later." He pointed to the map. "Do you recognize where you are?" Fuller nodded. "Take this pointer, Colonel, and mark on the map the headquarters of the 28th Division."

Fuller sat and looked and said nothing.

"Don't you understand?"

"Sure, but I'm not pointing out a damn thing."

The sergeant conferred with the officer, then turned to Fuller. "Colonel, I've got some bad news. We're going to shoot you."

"Why shoot me?" answered Fuller, feigning indifference.

"You ordered German prisoners killed at Hosingen. We found their bodies. And when our aid-men went to carry out the wounded under a white flag, your men killed them. That's why we're going to kill you."

The Germans sat, smoking Camels, staring at Fuller. He stared back.

Five miles south of Wiltz, the three-man Order of Battle Team, which had left town the day before in panic, was now returning to the town to pick up its abandoned trailer. A few hours earlier the two sergeants, Koritz and Nathan, had finally convinced their captain they should redeem themselves by returning to Wiltz for their secret papers and equipment.

As they crossed the bridge over the Sauer at Heiderscheidergrund, they had no idea that Germans of the 5th Parachute Division were hiding only a few hundred yards away, preparing to launch an attack.

Twenty minutes later they were speeding down the steep hill to Wiltz. Perhaps things weren't as bad as everyone imagined. They hadn't seen a single German or heard a sound of war. Wiltz, except for GIs, was now a ghost town. There was no panic. Squads of men were digging foxholes at strategic positions and tanks were maneuvering as the three men hurriedly loaded their trailer.

Soon they were heading south, along the same road they had recently come and going down the hill to the bridge at Heiderscheidergrund.

The jeep and trailer turned a sharp curve. Suddenly Koritz, the driver, saw a long line of Germans in blue uniforms lounging along the roadside.

These were men of the 5th Parachute Division. After taking the bridge the paratroopers had just split into two groups. One headed due west toward Harlange where it would soon link up with the Manteuffel column coming down from the north and surround Wiltz.

This, the second group, was heading directly for Wiltz. Their commander, Colonel Heilmann, had given definite orders to bypass the town and drive west. But these headstrong young paratroopers had made up their minds the night before to make a personal raid on Wiltz for booty.

The sudden appearance of the Ami jeep stunned them and they shouted in amazement as it raced by. Koritz stepped on the accelerator. His one chance was to run the gantlet. Parachutists further down the road picked up rifles and machine pistols and fired. Bullets flew from both sides of the road. Koritz ducked. The jeep swerved dangerously. Nathan, in the back seat, fired his carbine with one hand and leaned forward with the other to help Koritz keep the bouncing jeep from crashing into the river.

Koritz saw Germans ahead. He knew they couldn't get through. "Hold tight," he shouted. "I'm going to crash into the snowbank!"

The jeep raced across the bridge. Then, instead of following the curve, Koritz aimed the car at a snowbank. His last thought before the crash was, "I hope they can't use the jeep."

When he opened his eyes, he saw a crowd of Germans staring down at him. He crawled out of the wrecked jeep, amazed to find himself unharmed. He looked around. His captain was sitting holding his forearm. Nathan was motionless, blood running from his leg.

A young round-faced German pulled Koritz's .45 from its holster, yanked off his wrist watch, and then asked for chocolate.

By dusk Wiltz was surrounded. With darkness came all-out assaults from three directions. Communication with Division at Sibret, its new command post near Bastogne, had been long since lost. Ammunition was almost gone, and the few surviving tankers were numb with exhaustion.

At 10:00 P.M. a scout from Division, after sneaking through several enemy roadblocks, limped into Strickler's command post. His message was brutally simple: no reinforcements were coming; Wiltz was considered lost; all supplies, all reinforcements had to be sent instead to Bastogne.

A few minutes later, Germans were reported moving from the south. Strickler sent for all his commanders. He told them the withdrawal to Bastogne would have to start at once. "We've done all we can here. Now I want you to break up into small groups of ten men. Infiltrate back through the Germans independently to Sibret. Be sure to take only necessary equipment and ammunition. Destroy the rest. Any questions?"

"Yes," grinned Major Milton, commander of the last few infantrymen of Hurley Fuller's regiment. "When do we eat?"

Strickler went on: "The withdrawal will start in twenty minutes." He turned to Colonel Linus T. Hoban, an elderly judge from Scranton, who commanded the provisional battalion—700 assorted troops including cooks, clerks, anti-aircraftmen, and musicians. "Hoban, you've reconnoitered these roads. You take the lead and the column will follow."

The meeting ended. The commanders, grim faced, started back to their units, where they passed on the orders for withdrawal.

Artificial moonlight now flooded the eastern and northern approaches to the town as Judge Hoban led the command group up Grand' Rue. Near the west end of town the road branched, both routes leading eventually to the Café Schumann crossroads. Hoban's command car took the left branch. At the first road junction he waited for the main column. But after fifteen minutes he realized the others must have taken the other branch.

"Turn around, Byers," he told his driver. The command car speeded back toward Wiltz.

By now the main column of the Command Group was several miles up the right branch, stalled in front of a roadblock.

"We're going through," called a man at the wheel of an anti-aircraft half-track. The half-track, its .50-caliber guns blazing, raced headlong at the roadblock. As it struck a mine field there was a great explosion.

The wreckage of the half-track was pushed off the road and the column proceeded cautiously, soon approaching the most important crossroads in the area, Café Schumann. Here, where several buildings clustered around an inn, the main road to Bastogne continued to the west. Two other roads led south and southwest.

As the command group neared Café Schumann, it was also approaching a platoon of freebooters from the 5th Parachute Division dug in at both sides of the road—a machine gun on the north side, a self-propelled gun on the south.

As soon as the lead American vehicle, an armored car, reached the crossroads, there was a sharp blast. The armored car, hit in the side, turned over, bursting into flames.

A captain leaped from one of the half-tracks. "Let's clear them out!" he called. A platoon of Negroes piled out of the trucks and advanced on both sides of the road. Those south of the road moved methodically, without hesitation, cleaning out foxhole after foxhole and finally knocking out the self-propelled gun with grenades. Those on the north side crawled under the fire of the German machine gun, then made a sudden charge, bayoneting the crew.

The crossroads cleared, the column took the road toward Bastogne; but after several hundred yards it came to a third road-block.

Fire suddenly poured from both sides of the road. Men leaped from vehicles in panic flight. Many were killed, some captured. Only a few escaped.

A mile behind, their commander, Judge Hoban, was now just approaching Café Schumann, unaware of the disaster. But when he heard firing ahead he told his driver to stop.

He got out of the car and walked forward to the crossroads.

It seemed deserted. He went back. A half-track armed with a .50-caliber gun had pulled up behind. Three infantrymen from the 110th Regiment jumped out.

"Colonel," said one, "we're your fire power. We're going with you." They jumped into the Judge's command car.

"We'll follow," said the driver of the half-track, "and cover you."

The two vehicles went past Café Schumann full speed and continued west toward Bastogne. Suddenly there was an explosion behind Hoban. He felt a sharp pain in his shoulders and the back of his neck. He was sure he was going to die. There was a screech of tires, a loud crash. The next thing Hoban knew he was surrounded by Germans. By some miracle he was still alive. He looked to his left. His driver, a great hole in his back, was moaning in pain. In the rear seat two of the infantrymen were dead, one wounded. Hoban, his left leg throbbing, painfully got out of the car.

The Judge's battle was over.

It was almost midnight. Shells were exploding in the streets of Wiltz as the rear-guard defenders fell back toward the town. Engineers waded across the Wiltz River and ran into the stone houses at the eastern edge to make a last stand. The survivors of the band had joined forces with men from the Quartermasters. Now a group of sixty, they were retreating from Lower Wiltz to the upper town. They stumbled up the steep hill past the division command post. "Our only hope of escape," said their leader, "is down the road to the Café Schumann crossroads."

Colonel Dan Strickler was still in the command post destroying important papers. He tore off a piece of map from the wall and stuffed it in his pocket. Then he burned the rest of the map and went outside. Men were drifting past, firing to the rear. His jeep, the "Dangerous Dan," was waiting in the street. His driver, Bob Martin, greeted him cheerfully.

"Bob," said Strickler, "I want to take a last look." The jeep turned down an alley to avoid Grand' Rue which was jammed with vehicles and foot soldiers and climbed to the western heights of Wiltz. As they passed through a wooded ravine, firing burst out. Riddled by machine-gun bullets, the jeep swerved into a ditch.

Strickler saw a German tank slowly advancing, leveling its 88. The Americans ran into the woods. There was one thing to do: circle through the woods around the roadblock. Strickler checked his compass and led the way.

Behind them Wiltz was now almost deserted. A few engineers were the last defenders. The Germans, crowding from all sides, hesitated. They would make the final assault at dawn.

3

Ten trucks, lights out, were now slowly approaching Bastogne from Wiltz. They had escaped that afternoon in a hectic trip over the back roads, narrowly missing the German columns surrounding the town.

In the lead was a half-ton truck filled with mail. Next to the driver sat Lieutenant Walter Grogan. Like so many others in the 28th Division, Grogan was a stubborn man with a one-track mind. He had been told to get the mail back safely because of its great morale value.

Grogan directed the driver to the police station in Bastogne. There an MP advised him to keep moving west and out the other side of town. The 28th Division Command Post, the MP thought, was several miles out that way.

The ten trucks headed west. At a road junction, Grogan halted the convoy. "I don't like the looks of things," he said. It was foolish for this was the road to the rear. But he had a premonition. Taking two men he walked to the crossroads. Figures jumped from the ditch and overpowered the three Americans.

"Now just a minute," said Grogan in a serious dignified manner. "This is the U.S. mail. And I'm sure you know what the Geneva Convention says about mail."

The leader of the Germans, a sergeant, was perplexed and led Grogan down the highway to an armored car. Inside was an officer.

"I'm only carrying U.S. mail," explained Grogan. "It's of no use to you." He again mentioned the Geneva Convention. "Now if you'll just let us go, everything will be okay."

The officer was bewildered by Grogan's indignation and argument. Suddenly firing burst out on the main road. Grogan recognized the deep low rattle of an American machine gun. Someone in the convoy had apparently become suspicious at their long absence.

The German column burst into life, and in minutes the American trucks were flaming. Grogan's mission to bring the mail through had failed. But he hoped the burning convoy would warn the defenders of Bastogne of the danger at their back.

In nearby Bastogne the blaze of Grogan's trucks in the west went unnoticed. Over much of the town was a pall of fear and depression. Survivors of the disastrous ambush near Longvilly were still drifting through the streets, their faces spreading the message of German invincibility.

Colonel Roberts' straggler lines caught most of these men, but soon lost them. After being fed, the majority sneaked to the rear. They had no real idea what had happened. All they knew was that they had been hit again and again by mobs of panzers. To try to stand up against such an irresistible force was insanity. But some of them remained and willingly joined forces with the men of McAuliffe and Roberts.

In spite of the day's setbacks the men of the 10th Armored and the 101st Airborne were little affected by the mounting terror. And the Longvilly ambush hadn't been the only hard punch. Team Desobry at Noville, just north of Bastogne, had been mauled in the day's attacks. The climax had come not long after a battalion of paratroopers, commanded by Colonel La Prade, marched into town to help out the tankers. A few minutes after it was decided La Prade would command the combined units, an 88 shell fell in the command post. La Prade was killed, Desobry badly wounded.

Colonel Ewell's regiment had also been hit hard. In Wardin, the town where the former actor, Lieutenant Devereaux, had made his speech, Company I had been attacked first by Royal Tigers, then by a battalion of infantrymen. Of the entire company only eighty-three had survived.

That night those in Ewell's Bastogne command post, the huge

five-storied stone seminary, were silent and gloomy. Father Sampson, Ewell's chaplain, noticed a group of fifty teen-age boys milling nervously in one of the great halls.

A Belgian priest recognized Sampson's insignia. "I am the Abbé Musty," he said. "What will I do with my boys? Everyone says there will be a great battle in Bastogne. Should I take them out of town?"

Sampson hesitated. "I'll have to ask Colonel Ewell," he said.

He went into Ewell's office. The regimental commander was sitting behind a desk. Outwardly unmoved, he was recovering from the shock of learning Company I had been practically wiped out. He pulled a teabag from his pocket, dipped it into a cup of hot water and handed it to his friend.

Sampson, a big rawboned man, somewhat resembling Irvin S. Cobb, knew the hidden torments Ewell was suffering over his lost men. It had taken some time to understand Ewell but now the two men—one taciturn and wry, the other hearty and jolly—were close friends. Sampson asked what should be done with the boys of the seminary.

"That's up to Division," said Ewell. "All I can tell you is to keep them under cover."

Just outside the monastery a jeep from the front stopped. Three cavalrymen jumped out. One was Sergeant John Banister of the 14th Cavalry Group. That morning the three cavalrymen had been drafted by the 7th Armored Division for the battle of St. Vith. But in the day's confusion they got separated from their new unit and decided to head west.

An MP stopped the three cavalrymen. "Get up the street to that building," he ordered. The three men went into the building, finding it filled with stragglers from the 106th and 28th Divisions and a dozen assorted artillery and engineer units.

"What the hell's going on?" Banister asked a filthy, bleary-eyed infantryman from the 28th Division.

"They call us Team Snafu and we sure are," said the man dejectedly. "But you can be sure of one thing. Us doughs will get the dirty end of the stick no matter what happens."

Banister nudged his friends. This was a good town to leave. The three walked out of the building. On the main street they saw a 2½-ton truck slowly passing.

"Where you going?" asked Banister.

"Out of this place," said the driver.

The three men hopped into their jeep and followed the truck to the north.

An hour later their guide made a turn to the right. The jeep tagged along, its occupants not realizing they were now headed back toward the battlefield. The truck was bringing supplies to the 7th Armored Division.

Its destination: St. Vith.

4

In Paris a stormy session was taking place at the regular SHAEF nightly briefing of war correspondents. The correspondents were angrily demanding that public relations officers release details of the Ardennes offensive.

Major James Hughes, SHAEF briefing officer, tried to explain that security necessitated the news blackout.

"Why don't you step down and let us hit at General Allen," shouted a correspondent. "It's his place to answer these questions."

Brigadier General Frank Allen, public relations chief of SHAEF, quickly mounted the rostrum. "We're withholding news," he said, "to prevent the enemy from knowing the whereabouts of his forward elements."

George Lyons, SHAEF representative of the Office of War Information, stood up. "May I say that SHAEF's policy on this matter is stupid? And that's no reflection on you, sir. Everyone across hell and forty acres knows what's going on. The American people are entitled to know what's going on."

The meeting broke up, the correspondents angry, indignant, and still uninformed.

A few miles away Eisenhower was puzzling over the Ardennes crisis. Since his return from Verdun alarming reports of further German advances had come in: St. Vith and Wiltz were falling; Bastogne would probably be taken in hours.

How should the attack be countered? Already Bradley at Luxembourg City was cut off from normal communications with Hodges in Belgium. Coordination between the northern and southern sections of the American front was impossible.

He looked at the big situation map. Then just above Bastogne he drew an imaginary line through the middle of the Ardennes battle-ground.

This was the solution. Two commanders: Bradley for the southern half and someone of comparable stature for the northern half. The logical man for the north was Montgomery. But Eisenhower was well aware that such a choice would be unpopular with many of his generals. For months the Field Marshal had been sharply critical of American leadership, insisting the only way to final victory was a single attack on Germany.

Many Americans would consider Montgomery's appointment an insult to Bradley; many British would use it as an excuse to demand Montgomery be made Deputy Commander of SHAEF.

But Eisenhower knew it had to be done. In addition to the military, there was another consideration. It was possible, he and a few others knew, that German scientists had almost completed an atom bomb. Perhaps the entire offensive was only an attempt to give these scientists a little more time. No matter what the cost, the battlefield had to be split and the final victory speeded.

A few minutes later, in Luxembourg City, Bradley was called to the phone.

"Ike thinks it may be a good idea," said Bedell Smith, Eisenhower's chief of staff, "to turn over to Monty your two armies in the north."

Bradley was amazed. He hesitated, then said, "I'd question whether such a change-over's necessary."

"It seems the logical thing to do," said Smith. "Monty can take care of everything north of the Bulge and you'll have everything south."

"Beetle, it's hard for me to object," replied Bradley slowly. It might discredit the American command but the change was logical. "If we play it the way you suggest," he admitted, "we *will* get more help from the British in the way of reserves."

Stilling further objections, he hung up.

In Zondhoven, Holland, two canaries and a slender man were sleeping in a trailer. The man was Bernard Montgomery—Britain's highest ranking officer and a constant source of irritation to many of America's highest ranking officers.

For some time Montgomery had been opposing Eisenhower's two-pronged attack against Germany with his usual vocal frankness. It was not sensible, he'd insisted, to hit the enemy hard in two places when men and equipment were both scanty. He wanted the big effort to come in the north, spearheaded by his own 21st Army Group.

The telephone in the trailer rang. It was Eisenhower. The Ardennes situation was very serious. The Field Marshal was to take command of the northern half of the battlefield.

Montgomery hung up the phone. He wished the Americans had listened to him before. Then they wouldn't be in such a mess. But it was no time for recriminations. He called for his six liaison officers. These were young bright officers, all devoted to the "Master." Their job was to get on-the-spot information from the front lines. Montgomery had copied the idea from Napoleon.

He told the young men to contact the various American units involved in the fight, gather information, and meet him the next day at 1:00 P.M. at Hodges' new command post in Chaudfontaine. He sent another batch of officers to the Meuse area, then went back to bed, for he was an old soldier who knew the value of rest. Soon he was asleep again.

In Versailles Eisenhower's phone rang. It was Churchill. He wanted to find out how the battle was going.

Eisenhower told him of the new command setup.

Churchill was delighted. "I assure you," he said, "that British troops will always deem it an honor to enter the same battle as their American friends."

Eisenhower was relieved. What could easily have been an unpleasant situation had come off smoothly. Perhaps in this moment of real crisis, the constant friction between Montgomery and certain American generals would end. Pleased with the night's work, Eisenhower finally went to bed.

5. FOG OF WAR

20 December 1944

1

A few miles north of St. Vith, Bruce Clarke, while inspecting a front-line unit, was captured on the morning of December 20.

"I'm General Bruce Clarke of CCB," he kept saying.

"Like hell," said one of his captors, an American MP. "You're one of Skorzeny's men. We were told to watch out for a Kraut posing as a one-star general."

Clarke argued vehemently. The decisions of the next few hours could determine the battle of St. Vith. The MPs ignored his protests and locked him in a building. Only a Kraut would have insisted the Chicago Cubs were in the American League.

All over the Ardennes half a million Americans were quizzing each other on lonely roads, in dense pine forests, and in deserted villages. Passwords and dog-tags no longer had a meaning. You were an American only if you knew the capital of Pennsylvania, the identity of "Pruneface," or how many homers Babe Ruth had hit.

Bruce Clarke wasn't the only general being questioned. At every crossroad the big staff car of Omar Bradley was held up by MPs who seemed to like stopping generals. At the first stop he was asked the capital of Illinois; at the second, the position of guard in a football line; at the third, the name of Betty Grable's newest husband.

Bradley had no idea how to answer the third question.

"It's Harry James," said the MP triumphantly, and then waved on the general's car.

Reporters were also being quizzed. Not far from Chaudfontaine, Hodges' new command post west of the Meuse River, two newspapermen, Lewis Gannett of the New York *Herald Tribune* and Lou Azrael of the Baltimore *News-Post,* were stopped by a jittery MP.

"What state do you come from?" the jeep driver was asked.

"Maryland."

"What's the capital?"

"Baltimore."

"Okay," said the MP. "Go on."

"Hey," protested Azrael, "that's not right. It's—" But the jeep was already far past the MP.

In Paris terror of Otto Skorzeny and his men had reached panic peak. Thousands of pictures of Hitler's favorite commando were distributed. Described as the "most dangerous Nazi," he was given the gangster title of "Scarface" Otto Skorzeny. (The great scar inspiring this name came from a duel over a ballet dancer during his Vienna student days.)

According to French police, an unknown number of Skorzeny parachutists had already landed at Port Marly near SHAEF headquarters. Another report told of two hundred near Bohain. A third hysterical alarm came from Valenciennes: Skorzeny men dressed as nuns and priests had just floated to earth.

The destination of all these men, according to the confession of a captured "Greifer," was the Café de la Paix. There they would join forces and kidnap Eisenhower.

American security officers firmly believed this fabricated story. SHAEF headquarters was surrounded with barbed wire and the guard quadrupled. Tanks stood at the gates, passes were examined and re-examined. If a door slammed, Eisenhower's office was pestered with calls asking if he was still alive.

The only one unperturbed was the intended target. Although Eisenhower discounted the assassination story and tried to cancel the elaborate protective measures, security officers and his own staff begged him to move out of the "von Rundstedt" house. It was isolated from the Trianon, they argued, and Germans were familiar with the grounds.

Eisenhower, in disgust, finally bowed to the pressure, moving into the barricaded compound to become a virtual prisoner. "But only," he said, "so you'll all forget this damned business and go back to the war."

Skorzeny's twenty-eight men had done their work well.

2

A British staff car was speeding from Holland down toward the Belgian resort town of Chaudfontaine. In the back seat were Bernard Montgomery, wearing a red beret and a camouflaged parachute jacket, and his acting chief of staff, Brigadier David Belchem.

For weeks Montgomery had been depressed. But since Eisenhower's phone call the night before, assigning him the northern half of the Ardennes battlefield, he had recovered his old intensity and certainty. Master was again infectiously jaunty.

Belchem had seen him react like this in other tight situations. Like the time he took over the defeated British forces in Africa.

"It's a sad thing," Montgomery had then remarked to Lord Ismay, Churchill's chief of staff, "that a professional soldier can reach the peak of generalship and then suffer a reverse which ruins his career."

"Don't be depressed," said Ismay. "It may be you will win through."

"My dear fellow," replied Montgomery, "I'm not talking about myself. I am talking about Rommel."

In Chaudfontaine, General Courtney Hodges was waiting for Montgomery. A man of natural dignity, Hodges was considered colorless copy by most of the war correspondents. Compared to the ebullient George Patton, the grenade-carrying Ridgway, or "Gravel-Voice" Harmon he was difficult to write about. Hodges himself was deliberately responsible for this. He shied away from publicity.

As a result, the achievements of the First Army received far less publicity than the successes of Patton's Third Army. Like Bradley, Hodges was a soldier's soldier. Few civilians realized he was one of America's finest generals, comparable in temperament, courtesy, and strategic skill to Robert E. Lee.

His military career, like that of his friend George Patton, had started bleakly. Both had flunked as plebes at West Point in 1905. Patton, held over a year, finally did graduate. But Hodges, found "deficient" in mathematics, started at the bottom again, enlisting as a private.

Like everyone else, Hodges had been completely fooled by the Ardennes offensive. Until the morning of December 17 he was positive the attack was merely a spoiling one. Then he changed his mind, and without wasting time making excuses, switched over instantly from attack to defense. Within hours thousands of men and machines were turned toward the danger zone. This movement on wheels was so decisive that by now a strong northern shoulder of defense had been thrown up from Monschau to Stavelot.

But that morning Hodges was once again thinking of attack. Like other American generals—all graduates of the Command and General Staff School at Leavenworth and of the Army War College—he had been raised on the vigorous American military doctrine of constant, relentless attack. He decided to have Ridgway's corps strike southeast toward Vielsalm and smash headlong into the German salient.

A moment later Montgomery stepped spryly into Hodges' headquarters. He was confident, airy, and supremely cheerful. To one amused British officer he seemed to stride into the building "like Christ come to cleanse the temple."

"Well, gentlemen," he said crisply as he entered Hodges' conference room and surveyed the serious faces, "I gather that a difficult situation has arisen." With birdlike quickness he sat down. "Now do tell me the form."

While he was being briefed he sent out for his wicker luncheon kit, and as the battle situation was unfolded sat thoughtfully munching sandwiches. He suddenly rose like a jack-in-the-box. "Gentlemen," he said, "will you excuse me a few minutes."

Montgomery and Belchem went into another room where his young liaison officers had been told to congregate. All six were there. Knowing no passwords or American comic-book characters, several had been arrested as Skorzeny spies or von der Heydte paratroopers. But all had managed to talk themselves out of jail. One by one they reported first-hand news of the battle. The only area not covered was St. Vith.

Montgomery returned to the conference and laid out a general plan. The German, having passed through Stavelot, he predicted, would wheel north across the Meuse near Liége. Therefore an immediate Allied counterattack was out of the question. "I propose,

Hodges," he said, "that you assemble a corps northwest of Marche for a counterattack. But first we must sort out the battlefield, tidy up the lines." The primary job, he concluded, was to pull everyone out of the great St. Vith pocket.

Hodges couldn't believe the Field Marshal was serious. The St. Vith "bulge," he argued, would be a valuable bridgehead for the counterattack.

But Montgomery persisted. The salient was messy and dangerous. It would be simply a waste to send Ridgway's corps to St. Vith.

At this moment an exhausted officer, wearing the patch of the 7th Armored Division, was brought into the room. It was Lieutenant Colonel Fred Schroeder, Hasbrouck's chemical warfare officer. He handed Brigadier General William Kean a letter.

Hodges' chief of staff glanced at it. "Gentlemen," he said with rising excitement, "I think you'll find this news from St. Vith interesting." He read aloud:

> Dear Bill: I am out of touch with VIII Corps, and understand XVIII Airborne Corps is coming in. My division is defending the line St. Vith-Poteau inclusive. CCB, 9th Armored Division (Hoge), the 424th Infantry Regiment of the 106th Division (Reid), and the 112th Infantry Regiment of the 28th Division (Nelson) are on my right, and hold from St. Vith (exclusive) to Holdingen. Both infantry regiments are in bad shape. My right flank is wide open except for some reconnaissance elements, TDs, and stragglers we have collected into defense teams at road centers as far back as Cheram, inclusive. Two German divisions, 116 Panzer and 560 Volksgrenadier, are just starting to attack northwest with their right on Gouvy. I can delay them the rest of today *maybe* but will be cut off by tomorrow. VIII Corps has ordered me to hold, and I will do so, but need help. An attack from Bastogne to the northeast will relieve the situation and, in turn, cut the bastards off in the rear. I also need plenty of air support. Am out of contact with VIII Corps so am sending this to you. Understand 82nd Airborne Division is coming up on my north and the north flank is not critical.
>
>   Bob Hasbrouck.

Hodges cleared his throat. "In the light of this new information," he said politely but firmly, "Ridgway's XVIII Corps will have to keep driving forward toward St. Vith to Hasbrouck's relief."

Montgomery made a quick decision. "I agree that the chaps in St. Vith must be helped," he conceded. But it had to be done his way. Ridgway would keep driving southeast until he reached Vielsalm, opening up an escape corridor. Then as soon as the St. Vith people had retreated to the northwest, the defense line had to be drastically shortened. "After all, gentlemen," he concluded, "you can't win the big victory without a tidy show."

3

By dusk the battle for St. Vith was approaching its crisis. The 18th Volksgrenadiers and the Führer Escort Brigade were closing in on the east; the 62nd Volksgrenadiers were on the south; and two fresh, eager panzer divisions, the 2nd and 9th SS, were closing in. Originally slated to exploit Dietrich's expected breakthrough, Hitler had ordered them shunted down to Manteuffel's sector.

Pressure was increasing all along Bruce Clarke's thin line. A mile east of town Major Don Boyer was visiting the foxholes of his battered task force of 450 men. Two engineering units had been added to his command. Their assigned commander had never shown up and Boyer, a man who liked responsibility, had snapped them up.

"We're in a tough spot," he told a rifleman in a lonely forward position deep in the woods. "And I feel you should know it. We're like a thumb sticking in Fritz's throat." Boyer crawled to the next hole. There was little food, little ammunition, and everyone felt the sharp pains of frostbite. But all were standing fast.

As Boyer was returning to his own dugout, seventy men sneaked into his lines from the east. They were the remnants of Colonel Cavender's 423rd Regiment. These exhausted survivors of the Schnee Eifel debacle were questioned, taken to the schoolhouse in St. Vith, fed, and given beds.

A few miles away another American was being liberated. The MPs who had "captured" Bruce Clarke were finally convinced, after five hours, that he was American.

"May I have your autograph, General?" asked one MP.

Clarke impatiently signed a scrap of paper and then told his jeep driver to hurry to his new command post at Neundorf, several miles southwest of St. Vith.

It was dark when Clarke walked into the gasthaus that was his headquarters. After being quickly briefed by his staff, he addressed the waiting unit commanders. "Information is vague," he said. "We've got to save rations and ammunition. We're running very low. Issue only two thirds of a ration daily. Use artillery only if the situation looks critical."

After the meeting, Clarke walked outside. A sergeant, his face almost black from powder stains, went past, his feet dragging painfully.

"How're things going?" asked Clarke. "Pretty rough?"

"Yeah," said the sergeant grimly.

"Well, things are looking up," said Clarke with a confidence he didn't feel. "General Patton is driving up from the south."

The sergeant's face broke into a grin. "Well, now," he said, "that makes it a different story. If old Georgie is coming, we've got it made!" The sergeant saluted and went off down the road.

Back in Vielsalm, Hasbrouck was wondering what had happened to Schroeder, his courier to Hodges. At a few minutes after 8:00 P.M. there was a flurry of noise outside his door as voices were raised in surprised pleasure. The door opened and Schroeder, returned from the busiest and most important day of his army career, walked in.

Hasbrouck wrung his hand and called out for coffee and food. Schroeder handed him a message from Hodges.

> Ridgway with armor and infantry is moving from west to gain contact with you. When communication is established you come under command of Ridgway. You retain under your command following units: 106 Division (R.C.T. 112) and CCB 9th Armored Division.

It was very, very good news. But the command setup was becoming even more complicated. Hasbrouck, a brigadier general, was now in command of Hoge, who outranked him, and Jones, who had two stars.

A few blocks away Major General Alan Jones was being handed a message from Troy Middleton:

> There is a large attack on Bastogne from the direction of Houffalize. It has reached a point six kilometers east of Bastogne. Can you send something small to attack the enemy in the rear? The 112th Infantry has a battalion near Gouvy. If it is not engaged, ask the command-

ing general to have it advance in direction of Bastogne and hit the enemy from the rear.

Jones passed the order on to Colonel Nelson. Although the Gouvy area was itself being hit by two divisions, Nelson detached G Company and ordered it to march southwest on Bastogne. Like David marching forth against Goliath, George Company rushed to the attack.

At 8:55 P.M. another message came to Jones from Middleton. Dated the day before, it relayed an order from First Army stabilizing a defense line from St. Vith to Echternach: "Enemy in rear of line will be isolated and destroyed where found. There will be no withdrawal."

4

Bastogne was the storm center of the southern half of the battlefield that day. By 3:30 P.M. Noville, the village defending its northern approaches, had been completely abandoned and the American survivors of the bitter two-day battle were retreating in bad shape to Bastogne.

Chaplain Francis Sampson was just then leaving Bastogne in his jeep. He had learned that the division hospital, located at a crossroad several miles to the rear, had been captured by the Germans and that there were still about fifteen wounded men lying near the ambush.

After an hour Sampson saw wreckage in the road ahead.

"I think we're past our last outpost," said his driver nervously.

"Keep going."

They came to the scene of the ambush. Medical supplies were scattered over the road. Three dead Americans sprawled in a ditch. Two German armored cars, filled with dead, were charred wrecks. Sampson and his assistant began gathering supplies. With the hospital gone, the men of Bastogne would need every bandage.

A Belgian hurried over the hill. "There are wounded over there," he said, pointing to a village in a hollow. A moment later the chaplain's jeep was entering the village.

As they neared a parked vehicle, the driver said, "I don't think that's ours."

"Move into the town," said Sampson, intently looking for

wounded. Germans suddenly poured from the side streets. "Turn around and step on it," he cried. "No, stop!" Germans, guns at the ready, surrounded them. "I'm sorry," he said sheepishly. "We're captured."

"That's all right, Father," said the driver in a sick voice.

Sampson could now see that the side streets were jammed, bumper to bumper, with German tanks and cars. Shouting soldiers were throwing musical instruments out of the schoolhouse. Others were pitching bags of grain from windows.

Someone grabbed Sampson's wrist watch. "I'm a chaplain," he said indignantly, taking it back, "a Catholic priest."

A German officer, inspecting the jeep, opened Sampson's kit and strewed its contents on the road. He took a chalice and a box of cookies.

"Give me back the chalice," said Sampson. He was pushed into a half-track. An old Belgian priest watched, horrified. "I'm an American priest," called Sampson in Latin. "If you get a chance, tell the priest in Bastogne, the Abbé Musty, I've been captured."

"Take the other priest along too," said the German officer.

The Belgian priest, waving his arms, cried out in terror. The officer laughed. "Oh, let the old man go." He looked at Sampson. "But take that one to the rear."

Less than a mile away, Sampson's friend, the Abbé Musty, was leading the boys of the Bastogne Seminary in the opposite direction —to the west. He had spent all morning in Bastogne, going from office to office, finally getting permission to leave town. The boys were excited. This was real adventure. And now that Bastogne was behind them, there was no real danger. Musty, scolding good-naturedly, hurried them forward. He wanted to cross the bridge at Ortheuville before dark.

The fate of Bastogne was being discussed at that moment, 4:00 P.M., twenty miles to the southwest at the VIII Corps's new command post in Neufchâteau.

"There are three German divisions in your area," Troy Middleton was telling Anthony McAuliffe. "And the 116th Panzer is on its way. You're going to have a rough time staying there."

"Hell," replied McAuliffe, "if we pull out now we'd be chewed to pieces."

"Well, I certainly want to hold Bastogne," said Middleton. "But in view of recent developments I'm not sure it can be done."

"I know we can hold out for at least forty-eight hours," insisted McAuliffe. The short stocky artilleryman got up and walked to the door. On paper he and Roberts still shared the command at Bastogne. So far Roberts' armored men had shouldered the main burden. But now that Team Cherry had been chewed up, and Team Desobry was scrambling out of Noville, it was up to the 101st Airborne to take over. Defending a town would be quite an experience for an artilleryman.

"Good luck, Tony." Middleton smiled. "Now don't get yourself surrounded."

Soon McAuliffe's jeep was rolling up the Neufchâteau-Bastogne highway—the only road into Bastogne not controlled by the Germans. Within an hour he entered his command post in the Belgian barracks.

He had narrowly missed capture but didn't know it. A few minutes after he'd used the Neufchâteau highway, it was cut by the Germans. Bastogne was now completely surrounded.

By 10:00 P.M. the temperature had dropped sharply. From his command post at the Le Brun Hotel, Colonel Roberts of the 10th Armored Division watched a flurry of snow falling on Bastogne. The hardening ground foretold a new danger: soon German tanks, until now roadbound, would be able to move freely across fields.

Roberts' telephone rang. It was Middleton. He had just learned Bastogne was surrounded. He said, "I'm putting Tony in full command."

There was an embarrassed pause.

"Your work has been satisfactory, Robbie, but I have so many divisions I can't take the time to study two sets of reports from the same area."

"I understand," said Roberts. "It's the right move." He paused. "But I hope McAuliffe uses CCB sensibly. Most paratroopers think tanks are forts. They want to use us only for roadblocks."

Then he hung up. He packed his gear and started for the Belgian barracks. He wanted to be at McAuliffe's elbow at all times.

5

Twelve miles behind Bastogne, the Abbé Musty and his students had just crossed the most important bridge in the Ardennes—the big Bailey bridge spanning the Ourthe River at Ortheuville. It was important because once it was crossed by the Germans only a few companies of American engineers, anti-aircraft and antitank troops would stand between them and the Meuse.

Germans were not far behind Musty. The spearhead of the entire invasion, Manteuffel's 2nd Panzer Division, was hiding in woods on the east bank of the river. These troops had smashed through Clervaux, pushed aside the two armored roadblocks in front of Bastogne, and taken Noville.

Now they were preparing to assault the Bailey bridge and make a dash to the Meuse. This was their second attempt. Early that morning they had momentarily captured the bridge when American charges underneath had failed to explode. But when the first panzer to cross had been knocked out by one of the eight American tank destroyers hiding on the west bank, the Germans, fearing a trap, had retreated and hidden in the woods.

At 11:30 P.M., panzers again approached the bridge as German infantrymen plunged into the icy water. Across the Ourthe an American engineer pushed the explosive plunger.

For the second time that day nothing happened.

Tigers and Panthers rolled across the bridge. The defenders—a few GI engineers and the 9th Canadian Forestry Company—held off the first attack. But it was soon obvious that they were far outnumbered. They were ordered to retreat.

As soon as the bridgehead was secure, a young German lieutenant, Ernst Gottstein, was instructed to take two armored cars and patrol the main highway ahead as far as the key crossroad, Barrière de Champlon, where five important roads met at the edge of a great woods.

Instead of driving directly up the main road, the impetuous Gottstein dashed across fields, quickly reaching his objective. Seeing a café, he entered alone, his pistol drawn. The taproom was filled with rear-echelon GIs, eating and drinking.

When the Americans saw Gottstein, most escaped through the windows. Two surrendered. Not a shot was fired. Gottstein, elated at the victory, radioed his commander at the bridge: "Road junction clear of enemy."

6

In the north, Dietrich's only advancing column was fighting for its life. Kampfgruppe Peiper now knew it was completely surrounded in the scenic mountainous area near Stoumont. Fifteen miles to its rear the rest of the 1st SS Panzer Division was still unable to drive across the Amblève River into Stavelot and bring up desperately needed fuel, food, and ammunition.

Since morning Peiper had been assaulted from three directions. Task Force Jordan, a column from the 3rd Armored Division, had fought to within 500 yards of Stoumont from the north. Two miles to the south, across the Amblève River, the 82nd Airborne Division had pushed SS troopers back into the village of Cheneux after a bitter, bloody, all-day fight. But the main threat was coming from the west. By dusk a battalion of the 30th Division and Captain Berry's tank company had slugged their way up the steep mountain road to St. Edouard's Sanatorium, a large stone building which stood like a fort at the outskirts of town.

In the cellar of the sanatorium two priests and nuns wearing huge winged caps were trying to calm two hundred terrified children, tubercular patients. Shells crashed, machine guns jabbered; soldiers shouted and screamed.

Father Hanlet led the children in prayer. Then there was an abrupt silence. The children stopped praying. A single shot rang out, followed by a groan. Then more silence. The tension in the cellar was almost unbearable.

The cellar door swung open and a burst of shots rattled in the stairway.

"Civilians! Civilians!" cried the children and nuns.

A bulky man clumped down the steps. The children rushed to him, shouting with relief, "Sammy! Sammy!"

Other Americans came into the cellar and were greeted with the same wild abandon. To calm the frenzied children, the mother superior recited a dozen rosaries in thanks. Then she asked for eternal rest for all those fallen in battle, both American and German.

While the Americans took over the ground floor, the two priests and the nuns brought them hot water, coffee, and chocolate.

"It's been a rough day," said one tired infantryman.

"Yeah," said another, his face black with powder burns, "but they took a real licking. And tomorrow," he added, "we leave for Stavelot, Malmédy, and—Germany."

But soon heavy enemy tank fire burst out. While the GIs were hiding from this barrage, Germans broke into the cellar, shouting, "Heil Hitler!" They lined up the Americans, searched them, and smashed their weapons.

"Ach so," said their leader mockingly as he waved the identification card of one of the prisoners. "Here is even a lieutenant."

Thirty-two Americans, hands on head, were marched into the adjoining bakery. One, badly wounded in the right arm, remained on the floor. A nun was trying unsuccessfully to stop the flow of blood with a tourniquet. Father Hanlet knelt down to administer the last rites.

The wounded man looked tiredly up at the priest. "Thanks," he said. "I'm not a Catholic but my wife is. She'll be happy—in case I die."

The German leader put a cigarette between the wounded man's lips and lit it. The American, smiling wanly, took a few puffs. The cigarette seemed to revive him. He fumbled in his pockets with his left hand and handed a small piece of chocolate to the priest. "For the German comrade," he said.

The big German took it with a brief formal bow and smiled. "But I can't eat it," he whispered apologetically to the priest. "It's covered with blood."

6. THE BATTLE SHAPES

21 December 1944

1

By the morning of December 21 the battle had assumed a recognizable shape. It was a giant bulge.

On the southern shoulder—Bradley's—there was more suspense and threat than battle. But the activity was endless. Patton's Third Army was rolling north to attack on a twenty-mile front. Trucks and tanks continually rumbled through the streets of Luxembourg City. Its citizens, momentarily expecting Germans to break into their city, greeted the vehicles with relief.

"Patton! Patton!" they called.

The busiest man in the entire sector, the man marshaling the Third Army into its attack position, was George Patton. He was visiting every division and corps headquarters, warning commanders to rush into attack or be relieved. He was mingling with the enlisted men—one pearl-handled revolver strapped outside his coat, another stuck in his waist—laughing, wisecracking. He drove his army northward, dashing by jeep from place to place like a man possessed.

While waiting in traffic, his driver, Sergeant Mims, turned and said, "General, the government is wasting a lot of money hiring a whole general staff. You and me are running the whole Third Army and doing a better job than they do."

2

In his command post in the Belgian barracks, former artillery officer Anthony McAuliffe was reviewing the Bastogne situation. By a series of circumstances he found himself not only commanding general of the 101st Airborne Division but of all forces in Bastogne.

Bastogne was intact that morning primarily because the 501st Parachute Infantry Regiment, just a mile and a half to the east, had held against violent attacks of the previous night. Mounds of Panzer Lehr infantrymen were now piled up on a hillside in front of the paratroopers. Trapped between barbed-wire fences—feeder pens for cattle—they had been slaughtered in evenly spaced lines.

The fact the garrison was surrounded didn't depress McAuliffe. In one respect it made his job easier. All he had to do was hold in place.

The artillery situation was good and bad. Besides his own artillery and the big guns of the 10th Armored, he had picked up several wandering artillery units, including a battery of Long Toms manned by Negro gunners. By early morning all the guns had been placed so that they could fire around the clock at any attacking target. That was all to the good. On the bad side, ammunition was fast running out.

Two new forces had found their way into town the day before: the 705th Tank Destroyer Battalion, which had already plugged holes at Noville and Mont, and fourteen Sherman tanks from the 9th Armored Division. These tanks, refugees from the Longvilly ambush, had escaped to Neufchâteau. There they had resupplied and been led back to the fight by a determined lieutenant, John DeRoche.

McAuliffe's biggest ally, of course, was Colonel Roberts. Now that the touchy problem of command had been resolved and their personal feelings set aside, the two men were working closely.

In addition to advising McAuliffe on the use of armor—and he was never slow to speak his mind—Roberts was in charge of the garrison reserve. He combined the remnants of Team Cherry and Team Desobry, eight tanks, into one team and organized a second force of fifteen light tanks and four tank destroyers which could be sent at a moment's notice to any threatened sector.

Roberts had a third force, sixteen half-tracks each mounted with four .50-caliber machine guns, also ready for quick counterattack. But he deliberately neglected to tell McAuliffe of this unit. As an old campaigner he wanted an ace in the hole.

Against the defenders of Bastogne, Baron Hasso von Manteuffel was maneuvering an almost equal force—the 26th Volksgrenadiers and one regiment of Panzer Lehr. Although he knew Bastogne in enemy hands could influence all his movements, he couldn't afford to hold up his main attack to the Meuse.

The remaining two regiments of Panzer Lehr were already finding little opposition in their sweep below Bastogne. That morning they had captured a convoy bound for the encircled Americans— fifty-three trucks and fifteen jeeps, all undamaged. But after this easy victory Bayerlein's lead tanks slowed down, and finally stopped at a log barrier hastily set up by American engineers.

Manteuffel, hearing this, hurried to the front. He was furious. All that was needed was a little determination and dash. He jumped into the first of five stalled tanks. "Go around the roadblock," he ordered the driver. "Head for St. Hubert. I tell you we have a clear road."

The driver circled the log barrier and rolled forward. The other four tanks followed. For an hour Manteuffel led the patrol into what was supposed to be "heavily defended enemy territory." Not a shot was fired, not an American seen. At last they stood on heights overlooking St. Hubert, an important town twenty-five miles beyond Bastogne. Here was a prize that needed only grabbing.

The 2nd Panzer Division, which had finally taken the bridge at Ortheuville, twelve miles northwest of Bastogne, was not as bold as it had been at Marnach and Clervaux. It too was stalled by its own timidity.

The night before, young Lieutenant Ernst Gottstein had routed Americans at the Barrière de Champlon crossroad single-handed and then radioed that the road to the Meuse was clear. At dawn the division had moved forward expecting an unopposed march. After a mile the leading elements ran into a weak, hastily flung-up roadblock. The surprised and disappointed Germans pulled up and radioed back, "We have been stopped by strong enemy forces."

Young Gottstein had, quite understandably, missed the roadblock. He had come over the fields. Now instead of the Ritterkreuz for his daring feat, a court-martial awaited him. There would also be one for the overcautious commander of this stalled spearhead. Only one hundred stubborn Americans were manning the road-block.

3

On Montgomery's northern front there was explosive action that morning. Starting before dawn Dietrich launched a series of fierce attacks from Bütgenbach to Malmédy. He was probing for a soft spot in the northern shoulder.

It wasn't at Malmédy. By dawn Otto Skorzeny's attack on this town had ended in complete failure. Using his "Greifers" as conventional tankers and infantrymen he had tried to smash into Malmédy from two directions. But the fog covering the attacks suddenly lifted and the 30th Division completely smashed the 150th Brigade.

Skorzeny had to order a general retreat. Then he walked back toward his headquarters at the Hotel du Moulin in Ligneuville.

Innkeeper Peter Rupp saw him approaching, head slightly bowed. Suddenly there was an explosion. When smoke cleared, Rupp saw Skorzeny staggering, hand over eye. Blood seeped through his fingers. The big man waved away a soldier who ran up to help him, and walked unsteadily into the hotel.

While the attack on Malmédy was ending in failure, to the east the American 1st Division was battling desperately to hold its positions in front of Bütgenbach. Wave after wave of Tigers and Panthers had been banging at this key point in front of Elsenborn Ridge since 1:30 A.M.

Soon after dawn five tanks of the 12th SS Panzer Division broke through the American lines and began to ravage company and battalion command posts. For an hour it looked as if Dietrich had found a weak spot. But even as more tanks and grenadiers were rushed to the breakthrough area, the hole was sealed and the attacking tanks knocked off one by one.

It had been close and a fresh panzer regiment could already be heard marshaling behind the woods.

That morning the full effect of Bernard Montgomery's personality was being felt all over the northern half of the great battlefield. Many American officers were delighted to hear that the veteran professional had been called in to bring order out of chaos. Others, particularly generals, were dubious. For their taste Monty was too cautious. But the GIs, almost to a man, were encouraged as he rode past their foxholes in an open car, disdaining escort. The very picture of assurance in his red beret and paratrooper's jacket, he spread confidence wherever he went.

His influence was felt on higher levels too. He had already devised a defense plan. He ordered the VII Corps, commanded by "Lightning Joe" Collins, to circle behind the German salient and assemble in the Marche area, avoiding all contact with the enemy. Then as soon as the offensive had slowed down, Collins was to hit the attackers at the "point" of the bulge.

But a sudden change in the plans of one of Manteuffel's panzer corps was about to upset Montgomery's strategy. The commander of the 58th Panzer Corps, General Krüger, was a sound reliable man. But since he lacked the drive of Lüttwitz, Manteuffel had given him only the 116th Panzer Division and the understrength 560th Volksgrenadier Division.

Krüger had launched his original attack on December 16 at an area just below the Schnee Eifel defended by Colonel Nelson's 112th Regiment. Like the other 28th Division regiments, the 112th put up a stubborn defense, delaying Krüger's entire corps for two days. But on December 18, Nelson had been forced to drift to the northwest, where he eventually joined up with the defenders of St. Vith.

With Nelson out of the way Krüger had a clear path. Passing below the St. Vith salient, he raced west, rolling into Houffalize, a town twelve miles above Bastogne, by dawn of December 19. He continued west and by noon reached the Ourthe River, the last natural obstacle of importance this side of the Meuse.

But American engineers had blown up the bridge. A reconnaissance patrol was sent to the next crossing, eight miles to the southwest. Here a Bailey bridge, capable of supporting the heaviest equipment, was found intact. But this news did not excite the cautious Krüger. He reasoned that by the time his main column reached it, the bridge would be blown up by the Americans. It would just be a waste of time and fuel.

He made a decision that was to affect the whole course of the battle. He turned his two divisions to the north, ordering his advance guard to head for a village named Hotton.

It was the decision of a cautious reasoning man. But success in battle often eludes the cautious. The Bailey bridge in question was the one at Ortheuville. A day later it was crossed by the 2nd Panzer Division. In fact, it was never destroyed by the Americans.

At eight o'clock on the morning of December 21, a jeep raced up to the command post of Colonel Robert Howze at Soy, a village twenty-five air miles due west of St. Vith. An excited officer jumped from the jeep and ran into Howze's office. He reported breathlessly that he'd heard heavy firing near Hotton. Howze was astounded. Hotton was three miles to the west. Who would be attacking his rear from the south?

The day before his outfit, Combat Command Reserve of the 3rd Armored Division, had been given its most important mission. Since the other two combat commands of the division were busy fighting at Stoumont and Malmédy, it alone was to delay any Germans coming from the east, while Collins hastily assembled the VII Corps.

Howze realized that if this unexpected German thrust broke through at Hotton behind his back and continued north, Collins would never be able to get into position. He called Division, telling them he would assume personal command of the Hotton garrison which consisted only of a few engineers, signalmen, clerks, and ordnance men. He asked permission to muster an emergency force and send relief to Hotton. Permission was granted.

But Howze had few men of his own to send. The day before he had formed all his fighting troops into three task forces, each composed of about 400 men and eight tanks. He had sent these three task forces down separate roads. They were to throw themselves in the path of the onrushing enemy.

One of these expendable groups, Task Force Hogan, had soon run into Germans near La Roche, a spectacularly beautiful resort town about midway between Bastogne and Marche. When Hogan radioed back this information, Howze told him to coil up for the night at La Roche and then personally report next morning to Soy for further instructions.

And so, at 8:00 A.M.—at the same moment Howze was learning of the attack on Hotton—two jeeps were leaving La Roche and heading north up a hill. The second jeep, Hogan's, flew the flag of Texas from its antenna.

Lieutenant Colonel Sam Hogan was already well known in the division. A slow-talking Texan, reminiscent of a young Will Rogers, he had carried the Lone Star flag on his jeep and tank through France and Belgium.

A private jumped from a ditch, flagging down the two jeeps. "You're crazy to go through here," he said.

"We're going," drawled Hogan.

"Well, you'd better go fast then. The Krauts on the bluff up there are rolling hand grenades down onto the road."

Hogan signaled his lead car to keep moving north. Nothing happened for several miles though he noticed absently that tracked vehicles had torn up the road.

Then his jeep stopped suddenly. Hogan looked up and saw his first jeep facing another American jeep and a half-track. Then he saw twenty soldiers standing in the road eating K-rations from cans. Eighteen were Germans but two others seemed to be Americans. He supposed the Germans were prisoners.

Lieutenant Clark Worrell in the first jeep turned around and whispered, "They're *all* Germans, Colonel!"

The twenty soldiers on the road were staring at them with surprise as Hogan got out of the jeep to hear what Worrell was saying.

Major Travis Brown, Hogan's executive, leaped from the first jeep and fled to the right, followed by Worrell.

The men on the road, shouting in German, ran to their vehicles for weapons. Hogan didn't know it but he had collided with the tail end of Krüger's northbound panzer corps—the head of which was assaulting Hotton.

"Turn around," he called to his driver.

Private Gast started to turn around but the jeep stalled. He and Hogan's orderly, Phil De Orio, leaped from the jeep. Hogan, wearing fleece-lined RAF boots, followed them across a wide field as shots flew overhead. At the end of the field he jumped down a sharp 20-foot drop, almost landing on Worrell, De Orio, and Gast. A few seconds later Travis Brown tumbled over.

"Not very good shots, were they?" said Hogan slowly. "The best marksmen must have been looting our jeeps." He had been carrying a fruitcake, soaked in brandy, from his aunt in Texas.

The men crept to a clump of woods while Germans searched the adjoining fields. Hogan lit a cigarette and lay back. He made it a practice to rest as hard as he fought.

4

That noon a distracted SS man in the mountain village of Stoumont was talking by radio to another distracted SS officer fifteen miles to the southeast on the heights overlooking Stavelot.

"We're in a very bad condition," said the man from Stoumont, Jochen Peiper. His kampfgruppe was cut off and the Amis were pressing in from several sides. "Very urgently need Otto. Without Otto we can't do anything."

"Will do what we can," replied the man near Stavelot. It was his responsibility to get supplies up to Peiper. But it seemed hopeless. A relief force had tried a dozen times to break into Stavelot and re-open the road to Stoumont. The men had even waded across the icy swollen Amblève River but none had reached the other side alive.

Now Peiper was almost out of "Otto"—fuel. Cans had been dropped into the Amblève in the desperate hope that some would drift down river to Stoumont. None had. Several air drops had been made but only a few canisters fell within Peiper's lines. The rest, because of the division commander's stubbornness, had dropped in American lines. Peiper had sent back the correct coordinates but General Mohnke had insisted that Peiper didn't know where he was.

The troops closing in on Peiper at Stoumont were now led by Brigadier General William Harrison. The undisciplined retreat the day before had angered Hobbs, the 30th Division commander. He had replaced the regimental commander with his own assistant, the most respected man in the division.

By noon Harrison had devised a plan of attack. Two battalions, supported by tanks, would make a holding assault from the west. The third battalion, led by Major Hal McCown, would circle north cross-country and cut the road east of Stoumont.

By early afternoon, Major McCown had cut the highway and set up a roadblock. Then he started his men on the surprise attack back toward Stoumont. Soon he heard firing from that direction. The other two battalions had already started their attack, and it suddenly occurred to him that the two American forces might fire at each other. Since this was his first command in battle, he felt he had to do everything personally. He selected two men as escorts and started to circle back to the west to give the other battalions his exact position.

As the three men pushed up a rugged, heavily wooded slope, a German soldier jumped from behind a bush. McCown swung up his machine pistol and killed him. A minute later, firing came from two directions. McCown and his two men dropped to the ground.

"Kommen sie hier," called out a voice to the rear.

McCown swiveled his head. Less than fifty yards away a long line of Germans was covering the three Americans with rifles.

A few minutes later McCown was led into a stone house on the eastern outskirts of Stoumont. There he was questioned by Colonel Peiper and then taken to a cellar. He was seated where an electric light shone in his face. A big sergeant silently loaded and unloaded a Lüger.

Meanwhile the battle for Stoumont was reaching its height. In the sanatorium cellar three little girls kneeled in a narrow vault where vases were kept as Father Hanlet gave them sacrament. To the roar of exploding shells he asked God to have pity on these children.

Then an American tank destroyer, only 150 yards away, began pouring shells into the sanatorium. The aim was deadly—a GI hiding in the sanatorium annex was adjusting fire. Two hundred forty shells from the destroyer pulverized the walls.

Finally a shell pierced the granite of the ground floor, collapsing parts of the ceiling onto those in the cellar. One large group of screaming children huddled around the nuns, whose great white hats bobbed in reassurance. Others, eyes big with terror, hugged the floor.

The elderly chaplain was constantly praying, begging the children and the few adult refugees from Stoumont to be calm. "I will give all general absolution," he cried.

Everyone recited with a single voice the act of contrition. Then rising above the din, the grave voice of the priest asked pardon in the name of God for all sins.

There was a horrifying noise. A shell crashed through the ceiling of the vault itself. The entire cellar was filled with the acrid fumes

of powder and smoke. Children and grownups screamed in panic,
"Help! Help! We are civilians!"

Father Hanlet dashed up the stairway to the kitchen. He would
ask both sides for a truce so that the people in the cellar could escape. Above, a German soldier, seeing a dim form run toward him,
aimed a machine pistol and fired. Hanlet staggered back to the
cellar. To his amazement he found he hadn't been hit.

"Be calm," he called out. "I promise you no evil will come." The
others, thinking he had received reassuring word from the Germans, calmed.

The firing subsided and then died out. The children relaxed.
Candles were lit. Father Hanlet looked up and saw the shell that
had pierced the vault. It stuck halfway through—a dud.

5

Although the battle had now shaped into a great bulge, a long
American finger was sticking into the German salient from the
northwest. This was the St. Vith peninsula.

The current slackening action over much of the Ardennes battlefield was caused by this bulge within the Bulge. The German High
Command knew this finger had to be severed before further advances were made.

And so almost the full fury of the Nazi offensive was falling on St.
Vith.

7. DEATH OF A TOWN

21 December 1944

1

It was almost 2:00 A.M., December 21, in Vielsalm. General Robert Hasbrouck fought sleep. Since leaving Eubach he hadn't been able to afford the luxury of a bed. In addition to his heavy battle worries he had a personal one. Fearing his message of the day before to Bill Kean, Hodges' chief of staff, might have given the wrong impression of General Jones's status, he now wrote a personal note to Kean:

> General Jones is a major general and I am a brigadier. His being attached to me makes it look as though he had failed in some respect and I want to put myself on record as saying he is in the saddle in control of his outfit and that we are cooperating in the best possible way. If my note gave any other impression, I want to correct it at once before an injustice is done.

Hasbrouck then wrote a footnote to Jones on a carbon copy: "This is being dispatched at once with a copy to General Ridgway. I hope it will correct any misimpression my note to General Kean may have caused."

A general's hardest problems were not always concerned with the enemy.

By dusk, after hours of bitter fighting, the lines east of St. Vith were buckling badly in two places. Manned only by 1,000 Americans and a handful of tanks, this sector was now facing 200 panzers and almost 10,000 Germans.

At 5:15 P.M. German mortar fire was plowing up the woods just in front of the town near Major Don Boyer. Ahead Boyer saw shadows drifting through the darkness. Soon he heard the angry voices of German sergeants talking it up among their squads as they headed for Lieutenant M. A. Jamiel's platoon.

At 5:35 P.M. Boyer's phone jangled. It was Lieutenant John Higgins, of B Company. "My God," he yelled, "my men are being slaughtered! Where the hell are the TDs?"

Boyer tried to ring Lieutenant Colonel W. H. G. Fuller who commanded this shattered sector. But the radio and phone hookup with the battalion forward command post were both cut. He got through to one of his own commanders, Lieutenant W. R. Holland, and shouted above the battle noises, "Tell Colonel Fuller if we don't get some TD support damn fast those Jerry tanks will get through."

A few minutes later Boyer's phone rang. "Don, I need help fast!" It was Jamiel. "That tank section from Company A that's supposed to be covering the Schönberg road, they're either knocked out or pulled out. Two Panthers are going up and down my foxholes!"

Boyer had nothing to send Jamiel. The phone rang again at 6:44 P.M.

"We knocked out one Panther," cried Jamiel excitedly. "And the other's pulled back."

"Nice work." Boyer felt a load fall from his shoulders. He called Colonel Fuller, this time making direct contact. "Our lines are still holding," he told the battalion commander. "A few Krauts got through but we'll take care of them. I believe we can hold through the night. But we've got to have relief in the morning."

A few minutes later, at 7:05 P.M., a blackened face appeared at the top of his foxhole. It grinned. It was Higgins.

"Things are looking up," said Boyer. "Now all we have to do is sweat out the night." He wiped his glasses and tightened his helmet. "I'm checking the lines." As Boyer started to climb out of the foxhole, a shell exploded, knocking him against Higgins. Screaming meemies, artillery, and mortar converged on the area in the worst barrage Boyer had ever experienced.

"Well, John," he said grimly as they crouched, "we can forget sweating out the night. Get back to the battalion forward CP. Tell them how desperate things are up here. I don't think we can hold off another big assault. We need tank and tank destroyer support reinforcements. And we need them in one helluva hurry."

As soon as Higgins left, Boyer's phone rang. "God damn it, they've got two more tanks here on the crest!" It was Jamiel. His voice was so choked with emotion Boyer could hardly understand him. "They're blasting my men out of their holes one by one. The same thing is happening on the other side of the road. Damn it, Don, can't you do something to stop 'em? Please!"

Over the radiophone Boyer could hear the barking of 88s.

"One of the tanks is on the other side of my house," shouted Jamiel above three quick explosions. "We're getting the hell out of here!"

Several hundred yards north, Jamiel, Sergeant Knight, and three men dashed from their house into the nearby woods. All about them infantrymen were scrambling from their foxholes and racing for the rear.

More German tanks pulled up, over the crest of the hill. From the opposite direction five American tanks unexpectedly loomed out of the darkness. They spread out, looking for the marauding Germans. Suddenly white flares shot toward the Americans. Blinded by the brilliant lights, the American tanks groped helplessly, easy targets in the glare. Within minutes they were all aflame.

Jamiel and Knight, unable to round up the 1st Platoon, ran toward St. Vith. There, they hoped, they could pick up reinforcements and return.

As they withdrew, Boyer was sprinting down the southern flank of his line. He had spotted a platoon, led by a lieutenant, sneaking to the rear.

"Where the hell do you think you're going?" he cried angrily.

"To the rear," said the shaken lieutenant.

"Why?" Boyer glared through his glasses like an angry professor. He raised the muzzle of his M-1 until it stuck in the lieutenant's stomach. "Now turn your platoon around or you'll eat lead."

"But Major," protested the lieutenant.

"I'm going to count ten and then shoot. One . . . two . . ."

"C'mon, Lieutenant," said a short bowlegged sergeant, "let's do what the Major wants."

The platoon went back to its foxholes.

Just to the north, Jamiel and Knight, after hurriedly picking up a company of engineers at Fuller's forward command post, were returning to the front. At a bend in the road near their original positions, a huge German tank, rattling as though every screw was loose, came toward them. The GIs ran into the woods. Other panzers followed, raking the road with machine-gun fire. The engineers were now scattered in all directions, some running to the rear, some in wild confusion to the front. Jamiel and Knight, exhausted, turned and trudged back toward St. Vith.

2

Lieutenant Colonel Robert Erlenbusch, commander of Bruce Clarke's northern flank, was in a jeep heading toward St. Vith. He had just made a tour of his lines, and knowing his men couldn't hold much longer, had just drawn up a plan of withdrawal. His whole front, pivoting on C Company, would swing back like a door to prepared positions on the high ground west of town.

Erlenbusch walked into his St. Vith command post. Lieutenant Colonel Robert Rhea, of the 23rd Battalion, telephone to ear, beckoned him. "We just got a frantic message from Troop B of the 87th," said Rhea. "They're getting a heavy attack from infantry supported by tanks and assault guns."

While they were talking, another message came in. Colonel W. H. G. Fuller urgently requested Erlenbusch to lend him some help. German tanks and infantry were streaming down the road from Schönberg. Captain Dudley Britton's Company B, just to the right of Boyer, was being shot to hell.

"Okay," said Erlenbusch. "I'll crank up my reserve." Five Shermans, commanded by Sergeant John Blair, were rushed to Britton's area.

Britton's command post was about to be overwhelmed. A panzerfaust blasted the stone house. The walls shook but held.

"Cumzieout," shouted a German.

"C-cumzieout hell," replied Britton in his slight stammer. "What've you g-got out there I want? C-cumzie in, Mac!"

The panzerfaust blasted again at the house, setting its furnishings

on fire. Several men crept out the back and climbed the hill behind the house where they laid down a withering fire. Britton and
the others in the house, under this cover, ran out the back, escaping
into the woods.

By 8:00 P.M. Clarke's defenses were pierced in three places.
Panzers and grenadiers converged on St. Vith as a thick curtain of
snow began to fall.

Lieutenant Jamiel and Sergeant Knight ran across the railroad
tracks and reached the edge of town. Shells were exploding. Vehicles, loaded with dead-eyed men, were careening through the
streets from the north and east, and heading to the west and south.

Colonel Rhea, out on the street organizing stragglers, stopped
Jamiel and told him to take a tank destroyer loaded with men up
the railroad tracks to the northeast and try to plug up one of the
holes. Jamiel and Knight jumped on the vehicle and it disappeared
into the white haze of snow.

At that moment Captain Britton staggered into St. Vith from the
southeast. He was looking for Rhea to find out what the situation
was. There was a great flash to his left and an American tank destroyer on the corner burst into flame. White parachute flares
floated down like aerial jellyfish.

Britton, caught in the middle of the fire-fight, jumped into a drugstore. Haggard Americans, faces weird in the glare of flames,
rushed past. Then he saw Rhea dart out and shout angrily at the
retreating men. German infantrymen, just as confused as the Americans, now ran down the streets, looking for targets and cover.

Britton went up to Rhea. "W-what do you want me to do?" he
asked.

"Take your people west. We're setting up a new line about a
mile the other side of town. Good luck!"

At 8:05 P.M. Boyer was still in position east of St. Vith. He heard
heavy tanks clanking and creaking down the Schönberg road.
Quickly he shifted machine-gun and mortar fire to the road. Dark
enemy forms running behind the tanks dropped or ran to the rear.
Boyer figured if he could stop the infantry, someone else could take
care of any tanks that punched through. He telephoned the forward
observer of the 275th Armored Field Artillery, Lieutenant Shanahan.

Hitler congratulating Otto Skorzeny on his daring rescue of Mussolini in 1943. A year later, the Führer's favorite commando led a brigade of Germans, disguised as Americans, in the Battle of the Bulge. His mission, the Allies believed, was to assassinate Eisenhower.

Obersturmbannführer (SS Lieutenant Colonel) Jochen Peiper, whose kampfgruppe made the first deep breakthrough.

Baron Hasso von Manteuffel, commander of the Fifth Panzer Army.

A few of the frozen victims of the "Malmédy Massacre." The outcome of the resulting trial is still bitterly argued in Europe.

These Luxembourg women hid an American soldier, Sergeant Lester Koritz of the 28th Division, for several weeks in the German-occupied town of Wiltz. (Left to right standing) The spinster sisters: Mariechen and Elise Goebel. (Left to right sitting) Their married sister, Susanne Disberger, her two daughters, Thesy and Maria, and Betty Hoentges, a neighbor.

Peter Rupp and his wife, Balbina, in front of the monument to GIs murdered near their hotel in Ligneuville, Belgium. They helped save fourteen other captured Americans from the same fate.

Troy Middleton, commanding general of VIII Corps.

Field Marshal Bernard Montgomery (left) ordering Major General Matthew Ridgway, XVIII Airborne Corps, to "tidy up" his lines by withdrawing from the Fortified Goose Egg. Many U.S. generals vehemently objected.

(Left) *Lieutenant General Courtney Hodges, commander of the First Army.*

(Right) *Colonel Hurley Fuller, commander of the 110th Regiment, 28th Division.*

O P P O S I T E :

(Top) *A chance meeting, two days before the Battle of the Bulge started, in the Schnee Eifel between Brigadier General Eric Fisher Wood, of Eisenhower's staff, and his son, Lieutenant Eric Wood, Jr., of the 106th Division.*

(Middle) *Major Donald Boyer, Jr., 7th Armored Division.*

(Bottom) *Robert Hasbrouck, commanding general of the 7th Armored Division.*

Two weary infantrymen of Colonel Hurley Fuller's 110th Regiment (28th Division) who escaped to Bastogne. (Left to right) Private Adam Davis (Philadelphia, Pa.) and T/5 Milford Sillars (Morrisville, Ind.).

OPPOSITE:

(Top) *A 35th Division infantryman, Sergeant Joseph Holmes (Cumberland, Md.), battle-worn from the savage struggle near Bastogne in the first days of 1945.*

(Bottom) *GIs of the 26th "Yankee" Division marching toward Wiltz.*

Near Houffalize, Belgium, where the First and Third U.S. Armies met on January 16, Pfc. Frank Vukasin (Great Falls, Mont.) loads his M1 with another clip. Like thousands of other GIs, he learned winter warfare in the school of battle. The two dead Germans are wearing camouflage snow suits.

The only reporter in surrounded Bastogne, Fred MacKenzie of the Buffalo Evening News.

Pfc. John Fague, 11th Armored Division.

Christmas dinner in surrounded Bastogne. (Left to right) Colonel William Roberts; Lieutenant Colonel Ned Moore; Brigadier General Gerald Higgins; Brigadier General Anthony McAuliffe (commander of the garrison, whose one-word reply to the German surrender request infuriated Hitler); Colonel Thomas Sherburne, Jr.; Lieutenant Colonel H. W. O. Kinnard; Lieutenant Colonel Paul Danahy; Colonel Curtis D. Renfro.

Maurice Rose, commanding general of the 3rd Armored Division. Killed in Germany a few weeks later while far up front.

Maxwell Taylor (left), commanding general of the 101st Airborne Division, congratulates the man who temporarily took his place at Bastogne, Anthony McAuliffe.

Three U.S. generals inspect battle-torn Bastogne. (Left to right) Omar Bradley, Dwight Eisenhower, and George Patton.

Lieutenant Colonel Sam Hogan of "Hogan's 400 (3rd Armored Division).

Major Hal McCown, 30th Division, temporary prisoner of Jochen Peiper.

In German-occupied Wiltz, Luxembourg, Meisy Steiner hid Private Ralph Ellis, 28th Division, for almost a month in her combined grocery store and home. Her son was then doing forced service in the German army.

The Abbé Jean-Baptiste Musty (right) identifies his four young students of the Bastogne seminary, among the thirty-two massacred by Himmler's secret police in Bande, Belgium, on Christmas Eve. Leon Praile (left) struck a guard and escaped.

"Mike," he cried, "give me all the fire you can on the Schönberg road from the main line of resistance east."

In two minutes shells ripped overhead and exploded on the road. But German tanks kept coming through. Each gun and bazooka along the road had already been manned by several crews, no team lasting more than ten or fifteen minutes. As soon as one team of GIs was killed, another crawled into position. Boyer felt like an executioner and telephoned B Company. "Hold up replacing teams along the road. I won't let your people pay the price any longer."

A call came from Higgins. "I tried to send a patrol across the road. They couldn't make it. I don't know what the hell's the situation over there. I'm getting a lot of infantry and tanks! Jamiel's platoon is wiped out—the whole damned platoon!"

Another enemy tank plunged full speed past Boyer as if its driver could see in the dark. Boyer guessed it was equipped with some new kind of infrared lights.

At 9:30 P.M. five American tanks slowly ground through the darkness from the west past Boyer's position. This was Sergeant Blair's platoon loaned by Erlenbusch to plug up the Schönberg road. Blair lined up his tanks so that all guns would be trained on any panzer coming over the hill. In a moment Panthers and Tigers rumbled over the crest. Before Blair's men had a chance to fire, high-velocity flares shot out from the German tanks. The shells burst, throwing out a tremendous light. Blair's men were blinded, their vehicles silhouetted.

The fight was ferocious but one-sided, for Blair's men had to strike out blindly. Blair, catching brief sight of a Tiger, headed his tank for it, firing. The Tiger, hit, swung angrily toward Blair and roared full speed at the light American tank. There was a terrific crash. Blair's tank tipped over and crashed. There was an explosion. The bottom of the American tank blew off and Blair stumbled out through a gaping hole. Eleven other American tankers were scrambling from their burning wrecks. Blair collected them. They headed west.

3

In Vielsalm, Hasbrouck was trying to piece together what was happening out front. He knew that St. Vith was being abandoned.

Clarke, whose command post was now halfway back to Vielsalm in Commanster, was setting up a new defense arc just behind St. Vith. Hoge, south of Clarke, and battered back slowly since morning, was doing his best to tie in with Clarke once more.

Luckily the rest of the southern half of the horseshoe was holding up. Reid's 424th Regiment and Nelson's 112th were in good shape. They had had a relatively easy day. And Task Force Jones, the 7th Armored outfit defending the extreme right wing near Gouvy and Cherain, was still holding. Hasbrouck knew that if it folded, everyone in the horseshoe would be outflanked—and trapped. "Delay enemy, drop back on Gouvy," he ordered the small task force, "and hold like grim death towns of Beho and Bovigny. We must have the road."

Not far east of St. Vith, Baron von Manteuffel, impatient at the long siege, was exhorting his corps and division commanders to smash through the town and drive west. He had a grudging admiration for the unexpected fight the defenders of St. Vith were putting up. An artillery outfit (it was the 275th) was doing a particularly damaging job. But the most troublesome unit, it seemed to him, was a group of British defending the eastern approaches.

These troublesome "British" were Colonel W. H. G. Fuller's motley collection of GIs. By now Fuller's defenses were crumbling. Of his original 1,142 men, only 269 were left. Some of these survivors were drifting to the rear. But almost half of them—those commanded by Anstey and Boyer—were still in their front-line positions.

At 10:50 P.M. Captain Anstey, holding out with a few men on the left of Boyer, got a radio call. It was from 1st Sergeant Norris Burns in the company command post back in St. Vith.

"Our building's on fire," said Burns. "How's chances moving the command post out of town?"

"Get it out of there."

"Your left flank's like open house, Captain," said Burns. "Your right flank isn't much better."

"Thanks so much," replied Anstey sarcastically. "By now we're practically the rear echelon of the German troops."

At 10:50 P.M. Boyer was getting arguments from his men. It was apparent to everyone but him that the situation was hopeless.

"We're not pulling out of here," he said, "until General Clarke gives us the word."

A few moments later he scribbled out a message for Clarke and transmitted it through the artillery network. "Road cut," it read. "At least eight heavy tanks and infantry in town. What are our orders?"

Clarke's answer came almost immediately.

Boyer read it and called in his commanders: Higgins, Holland, and Rogers, the new commander of B Troop of the 87th Cavalry Reconnaissance Squadron. When they were assembled he looked at the three men, knowing almost exactly what they would say. Then he read the message: "Re-form. Save what vehicles you can; attack to the west through St. Vith; we are forming a new line west of town."

"But my men aren't in shape for an attack," protested Higgins.

"Mine have had it," said Holland.

"Mine too," said Rogers.

Boyer sighed. "I know, I know." He was too tired to argue; besides, he agreed with them. They would be lucky to escape with their lives. But orders were orders. They would retreat *and* attack. "We'll peel off to the right. Send a messenger to the mortar platoon. Tell them to destroy vehicles but salvage their mortars and tripods."

"That damned tank section supporting me took off already," reported Holland.

"John." Boyer turned to Higgins. "Try to get word across the road to A/23. Tell them what we're doing. Have them peel off to the left through Anstey."

"I have five badly wounded men who can't be moved," said Rogers. "An aid-man has volunteered to stay with them. In the morning he'll try to surrender to a German medic."

Boyer didn't like that, but nothing else could be done. "Tell the medic to stay in the woods until afternoon. If he surrenders to front-line Germans that have been badly hurt it might go rough on the boys." He looked at his watch. It was 11:10 P.M. "Move out in one hour."

"That's too damned late!" objected someone. Someone else said it was too damned early.

"Stow it, we're moving in an hour," said Boyer sharply.

"How about *our* four prisoners?" asked someone. "Let's kill the bastards."

Boyer shook his head. "You can do anything you damn please to the Krauts—until you take them prisoner. Put gloves on their hands so they won't freeze, then tie them up. The Germans will find them tomorrow morning."

"I say kill them!"

Boyer paid no attention. He turned to Higgins. "You and I'll work our way to the right and pass the word. Let's go, John."

Boyer crawled out of the foxhole and headed south. It was 11:15 P.M.

A series of dull roars came from the rear. Boyer, turning, saw a fantastic orange glow through the thick wall of snow. St. Vith was burning.

4

Halfway back to Vielsalm, in Commanster, General Bruce Clarke, eyes heavy from lack of sleep, was pulling together the battered pieces of his command at 11:55 P.M. He had set up half a dozen straggler lines, and retreating men and tanks were being placed on the high ground southwest of St. Vith. Even cooks, bakers, communication men, and clerks were thrown into the new line.

Clarke, seated at a table in a gasthaus, heard a loud insistent voice outside the door: "I won't see anybody but General Clarke."

"The General is busy. You can't see him." Clarke recognized the voice of his aide.

He went to the door. Big flakes of snow were slowly falling. A sergeant—unshaven, eyes bloodshot—was glaring at the aide. It was Sergeant Leonard Ladd of the 87th. When he saw Clarke, he pushed forward. "I want to get it from you personally, General, that Troop B was ordered out of the position we are holding." He wobbled, weak from fatigue. "Me and my men didn't like the idea of leaving the front. So now I just want to get it straight that we were ordered out by you."

"Yes, Sergeant, I ordered you out. There were Germans in your rear. I need you here."

"Okay, then. That's all I wanted to know."

The two men walked down the road. Through the falling snow
Clarke saw remnants of Ladd's troop, forty men. Their faces were
covered with mud, powder burns, and blood. Their tired eyes were
like holes.

"If you'll move down the road," Clarke forced himself to say, "an
officer will lead you to your new position." He watched them plod
down the road—now white with fresh snow.

About a mile north of St. Vith five tanks of C Company of
Erlenbusch's tank battalion were sitting in a field. Tankers huddled
next to them, grumbling but motionless. Snow had already made
white mounds of the tanks and whitened the men's helmets.

Flares shot up in the south. The tankers turned and watched dark
figures, guns at the ready, advancing toward St. Vith. The figures
drew closer and passed the tanks not ten yards away. Other flares
shot up. Their neighbors were Germans.

Sergeant Wallace Hancock crept to another tank commander, Al
Ettinger. "Al," he whispered, "let's get the hell out of here."

"But they haven't called us yet. They told us to stay put until we
got orders to pull out."

Hancock decided to break the long radio silence. Cautiously he
climbed into his tank and switched on the radio. "Charley Seven to
Charley One," he said softly. "Have you moved out yet and if you
have, what's your location?"

There was a pause—then static. "Charley One to Charley Seven,"
came the scratchy answer. "We are clearing St. Vith on the south
side. Withdraw and meet us south of town."

Hancock swore. They'd been forgotten. "What'd I tell you?" he
said angrily. "Snafu."

The five tanks slowly, cautiously, headed for St. Vith. Hancock,
standing in the turret of the first vehicle, saw a pinkish glare in the
distance. As the tanks rolled on, he saw it was St. Vith: houses
burning, tanks and half-tracks blazing in the streets. Heavy snow-
fall covered the dying town in a surrealistic cloak.

"All right," Hancock called to his driver. "Give me all the speed
you've got!"

Single file the tanks dashed down the main street, spraying
machine-gun bursts. Rifle shots cracked as men in civilian clothes
leaned out of windows and shot at the retreating Americans.

In the center of town a burning half-track blocked the road. Hancock's driver stopped. "Want me to go left or right of the vehicle?" he asked.

"Grab a handful of right lever," called Hancock.

Suddenly GIs swarmed from the buildings and covered the five tanks like flies. Hancock was already carrying two Germans—captured several hours before. The Germans, as eager to escape from the burning town as the Americans, crowded together to make room and gave a hand to the newcomers. Hancock's tank swung to the right, cleared part of the half-track and rolled over part. The column was once more on the move.

German grenadiers ran out from between buildings and shot at them. Hancock couldn't use his bow gun—ten GIs were clinging to it. The only free piece was his .50-caliber machine gun. It raked the passing houses. The grenadiers fled.

The tanks rolled through the town at twelve miles an hour, then swung southwest toward Krombach. Behind them the town of St. Vith, once the home of St. Vitus, glowed eerily, like hell in a nightmare. The rifle shots had ceased, the chatter of machine guns was distant.

Blanketed by the heavy snow the tanks, safe for the moment, plowed west. One of the GIs started singing:

> Silent night, holy night,
> All is calm, all is bright.

Other voices picked up the song. Soon all the men on the tank were singing. The two Germans were singing in their tongue.

> Nur das traute, hochheilige Paar,

Hancock thought of home. Five of his seven brothers were in service—four in the Army and one in the Marines. All were in combat. He hoped they were as safe as he was.

> Schlaf in himmlischer Ruh,
> Sleep in heavenly peace.

The song was ended. The tanks, with clanking treads muffled by the rising drifts of snow, disappeared into the dark.

It was midnight—the end of St. Vith.

PART THREE
Black Christmas

1. THE FORTIFIED GOOSE EGG

22 December 1944

1

On December 22, "Watch on the Rhine" picked up its pace. The rate of speed would have been even faster but for two obstacles. Standing athwart the German flood tide were an island and a peninsula.

The island was Bastogne, seriously hindering the attack by forcing Manteuffel to detour above and below it. The peninsula was the new horseshoe defense being hastily thrown up just behind fallen St. Vith. It was almost an island, for its escape corridor to the northwest was being dangerously narrowed every hour by a second wave of attacking German troops.

Just east of St. Vith, Major Don Boyer and his last 100 men were surrounded by Germans.

"Break up into groups of five," he told Lieutenant Higgins and his remaining sergeants. He was exhausted and depressed. "Infiltrate through the Krauts. Travel only at night." He gave them the compass bearings to the rear. Groups quickly formed and disappeared. Boyer wearily handed his binoculars to Higgins. "You can make better use of these, John."

"Who are you going with?" asked Higgins, helping Boyer to his feet.

"You, I guess."

Boyer's five-man group trudged to the south through snow almost up to the knees. A dull gray light appeared on their left. Now the quiet was broken by rifle shots as the Germans began to pick off survivors of the Battle of St. Vith in the opaque first light of day.

Skirting a stone fence, Boyer climbed a rise. Below lay the main road from Prüm to St. Vith. He ordered his four men to hide behind the fence. They'd have to sweat it out until dark and then sneak across the highway.

One man, impatient, crawled forward.

"Stop," whispered Boyer. But it was too late. A rock was loosened and fell onto the road. Instantly there were loud shouts from below.

"Surrender," called someone in English. "I've got you surrounded." There was a pause. "If you don't, I'll start shelling you with mortar."

Boyer and the others conferred quickly. "Maybe we could make a fight for it," he said.

"It's suicide!" protested one man; two others agreed. Boyer sighed. He stood up dejectedly, yet defiantly. A German sergeant on the road ordered him to climb down the bank.

The Americans were marched east. German staff cars, jeeps, and trucks sped by. An infantry regiment looking fresh and confident passed them, heading toward St. Vith.

Boyer's captor smiled sympathetically. "Just the fortunes of war," he said. "Maybe I'll be a prisoner tomorrow."

They were taken into a gasthaus. Four guards with burp guns stood near the doors. There was an excited humming, then one guard whispered, "Feldmarschall von Rundstedt is coming!"

A moment later a car stopped in front of the gasthaus. A young colonel wearing a gray coat lined with fur stepped out. Another officer, an old man with an incredibly wrinkled face, joined him. Heels clicked, someone called for attention.

The old officer strode into the gasthaus, glancing at Boyer and the other prisoners without changing expression. Boyer recognized Rundstedt.

Boyer measured the distance to a machine pistol in the corner. He wondered if he'd have enough time to grab it and pour a few

rounds into Rundstedt. But it was a crazy idea; if he killed the
marshal, probably every American prisoner in the area would be
murdered in retaliation.

Rundstedt turned sharply on the young colonel. "Where did you
get those slovenly guards?"

"They've been fighting all night, sir."

"This place is a disgrace. Look at it!" Rundstedt wheeled about
and strode out of the room. The colonel reprimanded a major, then
left. The major shouted at a lieutenant. A few minutes later a
corporal was swearing at the filthy guards.

Boyer smiled for the first time in five days. They passed the buck
in every army.

2

To the northeast, surrounded Kampfgruppe Peiper was fighting
for survival in a shrinking area. The Germans now held only two
mountain villages—Stoumont and La Gleize. The key to the first
was the Sanatorium of St. Edouard which stood like a fort at the
western outskirts of town. Once it was taken, Peiper would have to
abandon Stoumont and fall back a few miles to his last stronghold,
La Gleize.

The sanatorium was now a shell. Pounded by tanks, antitank
guns, and a big 155-mm. cannon located several miles to the west,
its roof had already tumbled in and its perforated walls were
tottering. But Peiper's stubborn men refused to withdraw.

In the cellar, 250 children, nuns, priests, and adult refugees tried
to sleep. The firing became sporadic. After the terrible bombardment of the afternoon, the relative calm seemed peaceful.

Exhausted SS men climbed down to the cellar from the
kitchen. "The reinforcements didn't come," said their big leader dis-
consolately to Father Hanlet and then dragged himself up the
stairs followed by his nineteen men. In a few minutes enemy tank
fire came from a new direction, from the north. The SS men were
surprised and confounded for there was nothing back there but
rugged woods.

GIs of the 704th Tank Battalion and 30th Division had secretly
built a corduroy road from the main highway, up over a steep embankment and behind the sanatorium.

The big building shook as American tanks fired from above. The cellar ceiling swayed, threatening to collapse with each explosion. Those in the cellar heard the gun the Germans had dragged into the hallway on the main floor fire regularly every ten minutes for over an hour. Then there was a strange quiet.

The upper rooms were now deserted. The twenty surviving SS men had just sneaked out of the building to the east, toward La Gleize. In a cellar in that picturesque little mountain village, an American was deep in conversation with Jochen Peiper. It was now almost dawn and they had been talking since midnight.

Hal McCown, the recently captured major of the 30th Division, wanted to learn the extent and aim of the German offensive in case of escape. He encouraged Peiper to tell the details of the recent Nazi successes.

"We can't lose," Colonel Peiper was saying earnestly, in good English. "Himmler's new reserve army has so many new divisions your G-2s will wonder where they came from."

Major McCown said nothing. He had been fascinated by the long talk with a man who admitted he was an ardent Nazi and was proud of it. To his amazement he found Peiper amiable and good-natured. He even had a sense of humor. How could such an obviously intelligent, cultured man be a Nazi?

"Oh, I admit many wrongs have been committed. But think of the great good Hitler is accomplishing. We're eliminating the Communist menace, fighting *your* fight. And the Führer's concept of a unified, more productive Europe! Can't you see what good that will bring? We will keep what is best in Europe and eliminate the bad." He said Americans didn't realize how warmly the Germans had been welcomed when they first went into Russia; how eagerly millions of French, Belgians, Dutch, Norwegians, and Finns had accepted the Führer's idea of "One Europe."

McCown now turned the subject to prisoners of war for he was worried about the fate of the 131 Americans Peiper now held in La Gleize. He asked about the notoriously ruthless treatment of Russian prisoners.

Peiper smiled. "I'd like to take you to the Eastern Front. Then you'd see why we've had to violate all rules of warfare. The Russians have no idea what the Geneva Convention means. Some day, perhaps, you Americans will find out for yourselves. And you'll have to admit our behavior on the Western Front has been very correct."

But in spite of these reassurances, McCown recalled the stories of massacres in Stavelot and Baugnez. "Colonel Peiper," he said, "will you give your personal assurance that you'll abide by the rules of Land Warfare?"

"I give you my word," said Peiper solemnly.

The 250 in the cellar of the Stoumont sanatorium were stirring, awakened from brief uneasy sleep by a new outbreak of firing. The two priests and the mother superior agreed the situation was intolerable. At any moment the shaky ceiling would fall and crush them all to death.

The nuns—looking like capital Ts under the two great white wings of their hats—woke up the children and told those that were fasting they could receive the sacrament. The chaplain led them all in the morning prayer, then he and Father Hanlet went from mattress to mattress giving Holy Communion to the kneeling children who wished it.

Bundles of personal possessions were tied up in the flickering candlelight. Outside there was an abrupt calm. The mother superior, another sister, and the sanatorium gardener volunteered to go upstairs with a white flag. The three left.

After a few minutes another violent barrage began. The building shook. There were great thuds from above as huge beams fell. Dust sifted into the cellar through holes. The tortured ceiling groaned.

A white flag was quickly made from a curtain rod and a tablecloth. An American soldier, slightly wounded in the knee, took the flag and hobbled up to the main floor. A few minutes later an excited villager ran down the stairs.

"The soldiers want two sisters or two civilians to be parlementaires!" he cried.

"Are they German or American?" asked a man.

"I don't know," said the confused man.

A tiny nun, her hat flapping grotesquely, hurried up the stairs followed by two citizens of Stoumont. There was an anxious wait of several minutes.

Then the cellar door opened. An American officer stood on the landing, looking down at the terrified children.

"You can all leave in a few minutes." His battle-weary face broke into a smile of reassurance.

Two aid-men came down the stairs and lifted the GI who had been given the last rites two nights before. He was frantic with happiness. "Everyone thought I was a goner," he kept saying. "A goner."

Now the children—some chattering, some crying, some dumb with joy—slowly came up the stairs, led by Father Hanlet.

The priest was shocked by the scene. Beams lay at crazy angles. The walls were full of holes. He passed the altar. It was untouched. But the chapel was a mass of wrecked statues.

He dazedly stepped over a dozen bodies—some American, some German, some crouching, some kneeling, some stretched out with mouths open as if sleeping; all bathed in a sea of blood. Hanlet stopped and recited a prayer for the dead. "God, who has saved us, welcome in your mercy the fallen fighters of this place."

American soldiers climbed over the mountain of rubble, picked up the children and carried them across the sagging floor. One soldier carrying a barefoot girl took a pair of socks from his pocket and slipped them on the child's icy feet as she looked at him with solemn trust.

Father Hanlet surveyed the wrecked sanatorium—graveyard of so many. It didn't seem possible a soul could have survived the three-day battle. But of the 250 children and refugees not one had been injured. It was a miracle.

The Battle of Stoumont was over.

3

Twenty-five miles to the east an even more decisive battle was reaching its climax all along snow-covered Elsenborn Ridge. For the third straight day Sepp Dietrich was trying to drive a hole to the north.

At 9:00 A.M. the 99th Division section of the line was a hell of exploding 88s, 105s, and screaming meemies. The GIs huddled in their foxholes, hoping they would be alive when this preliminary to attack ended.

Sergeant Jim Revell was going from foxhole to foxhole. Two days before, during another heavy barrage, he had found himself in a state of exultation. "Lord," he had said, "you know what to do with me. If you want me to live, I'll live. If you want to take me, take me."

He had lived. And now he was dedicated to the service of God. When the war was over he would become a preacher. But Elsenborn Ridge on this morning was his first pulpit.

Word had spread in the company that Revell's life was charmed. No matter how much he exposed himself, apparently no bullet, fragment, or shell could hit him. Every foxhole wanted him as a guest.

Revell, once the butt of the company, crawled from hole to hole on his self-appointed mission. The men—even the officers—listened to him and tried to keep him in their holes as long as possible.

He was talking to Lieutenant Faraday. "You remember the words of Jesus to Nicodemus: 'Ye must be born again.'"

"Look, Jim," said Faraday earnestly. "I feel a good life is enough to get into heaven."

"But you need the experience of salvation."

"Well, I may be wrong, I don't know." Faraday dismissed the subject with a wave of the hand. "I just want to go back and be the best insurance man in my home town."

Revell now started back for his own hole. A shell exploded beyond, then in front.

"Hey!" A soldier raised his head from a hole and beckoned.

Revell was amazed. It was one of his greatest ridiculers. Once while drunk he had broken Revell's nose. Although Revell asked the court to be lenient, the man had been reduced to private and fined.

"Come on in here, boy, and read your Bible to me."

Revell crawled into the cramped hole and read from his Bible for a long time. Finally the other man shook his head slowly. He closed his eyes and said, half to himself, "Is it possible I've been as bad as I have?"

Suddenly the shelling stopped all along Elsenborn Ridge and along the 1st Division defenses in front of Bütgenbach. Tigers, Panthers, and waves of infantrymen charged forward.

The 99th and 2nd Division lines held, but to their right the 1st Division lines were pierced. A dozen Panthers and Tigers began shooting down rear-echelon troops in Bütgenbach. More tanks and infantry poured through an 800-yard gap in the lines.

For several hours it looked as though Dietrich finally had his breakthrough to the north. But other 1st Division GIs rushed into the gap, destroying tanks with bazookas and picking off the white-clad grenadiers. The 800-yard hole was sewed up and every one of the German breakthrough tanks became a funeral pyre for its occupants.

In three days Dietrich had lost over a hundred tanks and thousands of men in his efforts to drive through the men of the 99th, 1st, and 2nd Divisions. He would not try again. The Battle of Elsenborn Ridge was over.

Just north of Elsenborn Ridge and only two miles west of Hitler's favorite town of Monschau, three ragged shivering German paratroopers were stumbling up a hill. They were Baron von der Heydte, his executive, and his orderly. The day before, the Baron had decided his situation was impossible. He had wounded, prisoners, and no food. There was only one thing to do—break through to the German lines. Before ordering the starved remnants of the kampfgruppe to split into groups of three, he had written a note in English to the man he mistakenly believed commanded the opposing force, Major General Maxwell Taylor:

> We fought each other in Normandy near Carentan and from this time I know you as a chivalrous, gallant general. I am sending you back the prisoners I took. They fought gallantly too, and I cannot care for them. I am also sending you my wounded. I should greatly appreciate it if you would give them the medical treatment they need.

The three men staggered to the top of the rise. Now in the gray light of dawn they could see houses—the outskirts of Monschau. Von der Heydte's feet were numb. He was afraid they were frozen. A festering wound on his wrist was bothering him even more and his mind was hazy from exhaustion and hunger. He hadn't eaten since leaving Germany.

"I'm going straight to Monschau," he said hoarsely. The two others, who were in better physical condition, wanted to keep going. "Go on without me," ordered the Baron. "I'm too weak." He headed painfully for the first house and knocked. No one answered. He staggered to the next house, then a third.

A man, a schoolteacher, led von der Heydte into the house.

"Paper and pen, if you please," said the Baron.

The teacher's son—a fourteen-year-old—examined the Baron's paratroop gear admiringly. "I am a Hitler Youth," he said proudly.

Von der Heydte handed the paper to the boy. "Take it to the Americans," he said. "I'm surrendering."

With mixed regret and relief the Baron watched the boy go. It was the end of Kampfgruppe von der Heydte. A ridiculous end to a ridiculous mission. Yet he was glad everything was over. He, like so many other Germans, had known the end was inevitable for many months. Now at last he could speak his mind. He had been one of the earliest members of the great conspiracy against the Führer—the conspiracy known as "Walküre." Only luck had saved him from the fate of his cousin, Count von Stauffenberg, and the other leaders.

Now it was over for him. He prayed it would soon be over for everyone. Dr. Friedrich August Freiherr von der Heydte, professor of international law, husband and father, ex-soldier, fell asleep in a chair.

4

Although the battle of Elsenborn Ridge was over, a new and dangerous German drive was being mounted in the northern half of the Ardennes battlefield. Pressure was increasing all along Ridgway's long, winding XVIII Airborne Corps front. The line started at Malmédy with the 30th Division, going along the Amblève River to Stavelot, Trois Ponts, and Stoumont. South of the river at this point, the 82nd Airborne Division assumed responsibility and the line turned sharply back, thus surrounding Peiper. At Trois Ponts the line again turned, this time to the south, following the Salm River to Vielsalm. Here Ridgway's line bulged far to the east, encompassing the conglomerate forces of Hasbrouck and Jones, and then turned again, extending back to the crossroad of Baraque de Fraiture ten miles west of Vielsalm.

At this road junction began the lines of Ridgway's last division, the 3rd Armored, extending for another twenty miles to the west, all the way to Hotton. Actually this entire area was almost completely dominated by Krüger's panzer corps. Even Hotton, supposedly the 3rd Armored's rear, was under heavy attack, and the

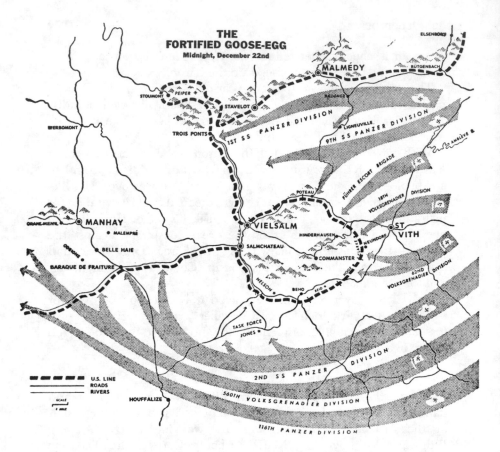

THE
FORTIFIED GOOSE-EGG
Midnight, December 22nd

MALMÉDY

STOUMONT · PEIPER
STAVELOT
TROIS PONTS
1ST SS PANZER DIVISION

WERBOMONT

LIGNEUVILLE
9TH SS PANZER DIVISION

ELSENBORN
BUTGENBACH
BAUGNEZ

AMBLÈVE

FÜHRER ESCORT BRIGADE

POTEAU
18TH
VOLKSGRENADIER DIVISION

ST
VITH

MANHAY
MALEMPRÉ
BELLE HAIE
BARAQUE DE FRAITURE

VIELSALM
SALMCHATEAU
HINDERHAUSEN
NEUNDORF
COMMANSTER

GRAND-MENIL

NELSON
BEHO
REID

62ND
VOLKSGRENADIER DIVISION

TASK FORCE
JONES

2ND SS PANZER DIVISION

HOUFFALIZE

560TH VOLKSGRENADIER DIVISION

116TH PANZER DIVISION

U.S. LINE
ROADS
RIVERS

SCALE

three weak armored task forces sent out to screen the assembly and deployment of "Lightning Joe" Collins' VIII Corps were fighting for their lives. One, Task Force Hogan, had already disappeared and was given up for lost. That morning Colonel Sam Hogan and two of his men, separated from the rest of the task force by an ambush the day before, walked into the mountain village of Marcouray, three miles north of La Roche. There to his surprise he found his own unit, surrounded and almost out of ammunition.

This weird corps line, extending like a snake for about a hundred miles, would have confounded the average commander. Ridgway was a man who liked problems, thrived on trouble, and welcomed the unusual. By late morning he had all three in plenty. In addition to the two Krüger divisions attacking the 3rd Armored Division, two powerful panzer divisions from another corps were now threatening the center of his corps line.

These two divisions, originally slated to follow Dietrich's expected breakthrough in the far north, had already been shunted to Manteuffel's area by an impatient Hitler. The day before they had helped seize St. Vith. Now the 9th Panzer Division, circling above the American salient, was aiming at Vielsalm. The 2nd SS Panzer Division had already circled south of the salient, bypassing Vielsalm in a rapid, unopposed march. Now it was swinging north and was only a mile below the highway that connected Vielsalm with the west.

When the panzers reached this highway, Ridgway's corps line would be cut in the middle.

It was not quite noon when Ridgway's jeep pulled up in front of the schoolhouse in Vielsalm. He hopped out, the grenades strung around his belt bouncing.

A few minutes later he was in conference with Jones and Hasbrouck. Standing in front of a map, the corps commander drew a large goose egg between Vielsalm and St. Vith. "What do you think of making a stand inside this area?" he suggested. Hasbrouck and Jones bent over the map and studied the goose egg. "You'd hold out until a counteroffensive caught up with you. You'll soon be surrounded, of course, but we'll supply you by air."

"I don't like it," said Hasbrouck promptly. "The area is heavily wooded with only a few poor roads. Besides the troops have had over five days of continuous fighting in very trying weather. My people are only fifty per cent effective. And I'm sure that goes for the infantry too."

Ridgway was troubled. A man who drove everyone, himself above all, relentlessly, he believed the only way to win a war or battle was to be aggressive and then more aggressive.

Jones turned to Ridgway. "I think it can be done," he said.

Hasbrouck was exasperated. It was the old story. To an infantryman a tank was a place of refuge. But to a tanker, a dug-in tank was only a metal death trap containing a ton of high explosives and many gallons of gasoline. It was nonsense, he thought, making a useless stand on that terrain. The fight should be on ground of their own choosing under the most favorable conditions for armor.

"Tanks can't maneuver in there," he protested, pointing at the goose egg. It could mean the end of his entire division. "We could only use them as pillboxes."

Ridgway was displeased at the widely divergent opinions of the two commanders. He was never slow to relieve a man—the day before he had relieved a good friend. But he never took such drastic action until he had a thorough knowledge of all the facts. There was only one place to get these facts—up front.

He picked up his helmet. "Come on, Bob," he said to Hasbrouck impatiently. "The two of us will go up front and see just what the hell the situation is."

A moment later, the two men, both irritated, were driven toward the front.

Near the front, General Bruce Clarke sat in a jeep on a hill east of Commanster, presently his command post. He thoughtfully surveyed the rolling hills and patches of forest. This was his new line. It was a thin improvised arc, threatened at every point.

The north flank had already been pierced by tanks and infantry of the Führer Escort Brigade, cutting Clarke off from Combat Command A. This fight had been so desperate that wounded men in an American aid station were given arms and thrown into the struggle.

By now the American artillery was down to its last rounds, dozens of tanks and trucks were stranded for lack of fuel, and many of the defenders hadn't eaten for over a day.

It was a bleak picture—for three reasons: Ridgway forbade retreat; there was almost no gas left; and the ground wasn't hard enough to support armor.

At 3:00 P.M. Clarke got out of the jeep and strode across the snowy field to test the ground. It felt solid but he knew it would sink under a Sherman or even a half-track. He saw a car, abandoned and lonely, in the middle of the field. It was the Mercedes-Benz Hasbrouck had lent him. Turning he called to his driver, "There's a brand-new star on that car. Get it, please." It was his first star and he didn't want some Kraut souvenir hunter to have it.

A few minutes later he walked into the Commanster command post. His aide was smiling broadly.

"What're you so happy about?" asked Clarke.

"A convoy of 90 supply trucks just pulled in. They had to fight their way but they made it."

Clarke smiled. It was the first good news all day. He felt a wave of gratitude for the supply people.

"There's a message from Division, sir," continued the aide. "General Hasbrouck is on his way up with General Ridgway. They want to hold a commanders' conference here."

An hour later Ridgway was pacing the floor. He turned, looked piercingly at Colonel Reid. "What's the combat efficiency of your unit?"

The commander of the 424th Regiment thought a moment. He'd lost all his kitchens and almost all his heavy equipment. "About fifty per cent, sir."

Ridgway looked at him coolly, then turned to Clarke.

Clarke didn't hesitate. "Forty per cent, sir."

Ridgway was silent. He knew little of these men or Hasbrouck. They might have panicked. What he needed was a reliable estimate from a man he trusted. Bill Hoge was such a man. They'd been good friends at the Point.

When he learned Hoge was still on the road, heading toward Commanster, Ridgway concluded the conference. A few minutes later he reached his friend by radio. Using doubletalk allusions to the days when he was football manager and Hoge a member of the West Point team, Ridgway gave the grid coordinates of a farmhouse, where the two met.

"Bill," said Ridgway, "this position is too exposed to try to hold any longer. We're not going to leave you in here to be chopped to pieces little by little." He eyed Hoge closely, watching for a reaction that would give him a clue to the real situation. "I plan to start a withdrawal of all forces tonight. We're going to get you out of here."

Hoge looked at his friend in silence. He'd been battered by almost constant combat for five days. His men had done well in this, their first battle, but the strain was telling. In one battalion alone, the 27th, there had already been three commanders. Colonel Seeley had suffered a heart attack; his replacement was soon overcome with battle fatigue; and the third man, already cracking fast from responsibility, was imagining orders that had never been issued.

All he said was, "How?"

This one word gave Ridgway the complete story. The situation was hopeless. "Bill," he said, his mind now made up, "we *can* and we *will*."

They shook hands. Ridgway left.

An hour later he stormed into the 106th Division Command Post in Vielsalm. "I want to speak to General Jones," he said. "Alone."

When the office was cleared, Ridgway bluntly told Jones he didn't like the way things were going in Vielsalm. Ridgway and Jones then traveled the few blocks to Hasbrouck's command post in the schoolhouse. Here Ridgway sent everyone from the room except the two generals who shared the command of the goose egg area and his deputy chief of staff, Colonel Quill. Once more Ridgway asserted his extreme unhappiness with the complicated command setup in Vielsalm.

Then as Quill scribbled in pencil on a scrap of paper, the corps commander dictated an order clarifying the situation: Jones was made his assistant and all units in the Fortified Goose Egg were put under the sole command of Hasbrouck.

Ridgway turned to the one-star general who now commanded the equivalent of more than two full divisions. "Bob," he said, "start pulling your people back as soon as possible. I want them all withdrawn under cover of darkness tonight."

2. "NUTS"

22 December 1944

1

On December 22, the Battle of the Bulge was one week old. In Washington at his press conference, President Roosevelt refused to make any comments about the great German offensive. He did state that the "end was not in sight," and those on the home front should exert every effort at this critical time to back up the fighters.

In Paris, civilians were more than ever alarmed over Skorzeny's "trained assassins." Parachutists had been seen in Mayenne. The convergence of Skorzeny men on the Café le la Paix was expected momentarily.

In Versailles, Eisenhower was still a prisoner of his own guards. But the new reports of German parachutists only irritated him. "Hell's fire," he told his secretary, Lieutenant Kay Summersby, "I'm going for a walk. If anyone wants to shoot me, he can go right ahead. I've got to get out."

He strode into the courtyard, and under the anxious eyes of guards, enjoyed his forbidden walk. When he returned he was feeling better. He sat down and wrote one of his rare "orders of the day." It was defiant and confident:

> By rushing out from his fixed defenses the enemy may give us the chance to turn his great gamble into the worst defeat. So I call upon

every man, of all the Allies, to rise now to new heights of resolution and of effort. Let everyone hold before him a single thought—to destroy the enemy on the ground, in the air, everywhere—destroy him! United in this determination and with unshakable faith in the cause for which we fight, we will, with God's help, go forward to our greatest victory.

In Luxembourg City the daily target conference was in session at the Ninth Air Force Advanced Headquarters War Room. Major Stuart Fuller was reading his weather forecast. A front had settled east of the Ardennes in the Rhine Valley and showed no signs of leaving.

"For the next few days," he concluded, "there will be unrelieved gloom. No break can be expected until about 26 December."

The gloom in the war room was as heavy as the forecast. Lieutenant General Hoyt Vandenberg, commandant of the Ninth Air Force, and Fuller mulled over the most remote possibility of a break. There were stagnant high areas to the east and west but it was extremely unlikely that they would move.

"That means no ops," said Vandenberg grimly. From the cobblestone streets the rumble of a passing Patton armored column deepened his frustration. What help could he give these men in their coming fight?

A few blocks away George Patton was reading a sheaf of reports. At six o'clock that morning tanks and infantry of his III Corps had jumped off in the first American counteroffensive of the Bulge.

Through thick swirls of fog, and gusts of snow, three divisions had flung themselves up against the great Ardennes salient. On the west flank was the 4th Armored, its goal Bastogne; in the center the 26th was aimed at Wiltz; and on the east, or right flank, the veteran 80th Division, led by the hard-driving "Hairless Horace" McBride, expected to recapture Ettelbruck in a day and drive up to St. Vith.

Patton was delighted. His critics had been confounded. The three divisions had moved one hundred miles over strange roads, under icy conditions, in less than forty-eight hours. As predicted, his attack was on schedule.

Now he gave an even more startling prediction. "We'll be in St. Vith," he said, "by December 26."

The week before, Patton had ordered his chaplain to publish a prayer for good weather for his Saar attack. "See if we can't get God to work on our side."

"Sir," replied Chaplain O'Neill, "it's going to take a pretty thick rug for that kind of praying."

"I don't care if it takes a flying carpet."

"Yes, sir," replied O'Neill reluctantly. "But it usually isn't customary among men of my profession to pray for clear weather to kill fellow men."

"Chaplain, are you teaching me theology or are you the chaplain of the Third Army? I want a prayer."

The prayer was written:

> Almighty and merciful Father, we humbly beseech Thee of Thy great goodness, to restrain these immoderate rains with which we have had to contend. Grant us fair weather for battle.

Patton, delighted with O'Neill's prayer, ordered thousands of copies printed. But before they could be distributed, the Saar attack was canceled and the entire Third Army pivoted ninety degrees toward the Ardennes.

Now, as Patton's III Corps headed north to bite into the great German offensive, the prayer was being passed out, even though Patton's chief of staff, General Gay, had reminded him that it had been printed for an earlier attack.

"Oh, the Lord won't mind," was Patton's answer. "He knows we're too busy right now killing Germans to print another prayer."

That morning it was being read by men of three divisions in a driving snowstorm.

2

In German-occupied Wiltz only a few civilians dared to walk the streets that morning. One was an elderly woman, climbing up the steep hill, over rubble and wreckage, to the hospital. Mme. Balthasar-Wagener was trembling, but not from age or cold. She and her husband, Jean-Pierre, had a wounded GI hidden in their attic. Why had they had the misfortune to find him? Ironically many of their neighbors considered them collaborators, for their daughter, Mariette, had married a German officer, Fritz Schultheiss. Already a dozen German soldiers were billeted in their home on the Rue Plank. And what if Fritz should suddenly come home on leave?

She walked into the big modern hospital which looked over the valley, wandering a few minutes in the sterile hallways, not knowing what to do.

"I'm a volunteer nurse," said a young fragile-looking woman. "They call me Mlle. Anna. Can I help you?"

Her sympathetic face encouraged Mme. Balthasar-Wagener. "I have an American soldier named Georges," she blurted out. "He's wounded!"

Mlle. Anna took the old woman's arm and led her to an empty room. "First we'll get some medicine for your American," she said. "Then we'll go to your house."

Half a mile away, several trucks marked with big red crosses were pulling into the courtyard of the ancient castle. A few days ago the castle had housed an American field hospital. Now it was German. Aid-men of both sides were carrying wounded American prisoners into the castle.

Directing the operations from one of the German trucks was an unwounded GI, Sergeant Lester Koritz, formerly of the 28th Division Order of Battle team.

Koritz, self-styled "interpreter" for wounded Americans, looked around. It seemed incredible, but he was back where he had started four days before. He looked through the ancient archway to Grand' Rue. A hundred yards up the street was the tobacco shop of his good friends the Goebel sisters. He wondered if they were still alive.

Three days previously the sisters had fled south to Boulaide. But when the Germans took this town, all refugees were ordered to return to their homes. Now the Goebels and hundreds of other citizens of Wiltz were walking, through a driving snowstorm, past Café Schumann. Their arduous round-trip flight was almost over.

3

That morning, a thick white mantle covered the somber buildings of Bastogne, giving the town an air of peace and security. In the northwestern outskirts, at McAuliffe's command post, there was an atmosphere of confidence.

Two encouraging messages had just arrived. One read, "Hugh is coming." This meant that General Hugh Gaffey's 4th Armored Division was driving up toward the beleaguered town on the left flank of Patton's III Corps attack. The other message was from VIII Corps: "Resupply by air will start coming at 2000."

The men in the foxholes and in lonely company command posts on the edges of the defense circle felt a growing confidence too, but for a different reason. When word spread that they were surrounded, rivalry among the various units was suddenly forgotten. The paratroopers now grudgingly admitted that the 10th Armored Division teams had put up one hell of a fight and had saved the bacon during the first two days.

The sharp rivalry among the regiments of the 101st also ceased. Of course no self-respecting 501st man would want to be in the Five-O-Deuce, the 504th, or the 327th Glider. But those were pretty good outfits to have at your side.

Negro artillerymen of the Long Tom outfit which had wandered into town were stuffing the bottoms of their trousers into their boots. "What the devil kind of uniform is that?" a 101st officer asked curiously. "Man," was the answer, "we're airborne!" So was their spirit.

Even the stragglers, Team Snafu, had finally caught the spirit. They had stumbled into town exhausted, shocked in mind and body, but several days of sleep and food had revived them.

Three miles south of Bastogne, Sergeant Oswald Butler, of the 327th Glider Infantry Regiment, was standing in the basement of a lonely farmhouse overlooking the highway to Arlon.

At exactly 11:30 A.M. he saw four figures coming up the road from the south carrying what looked like a bedspread on a pole. They were Germans. He picked up a phone and called his commanding officer, Captain Adams. "There're four Krauts coming up the road. They're carrying a white flag. It looks like they want to surrender."

Butler, followed by two of his men, went out to meet the Germans. A short stocky captain, with medical insignia, stepped up to him. "We are parlementaires," he said in careful English, "and we want to talk to your officers."

An artillery major, wearing Panzer Lehr markings, said something in German to the captain. "We want to talk to your commanding general," said the captain.

Butler tore off several strips from the white flag and blindfolded the two officers. He told Private Gommell to stay there with the two

German enlisted men, and then led the officers up the hill toward the rear.

Half an hour later Colonel Joseph Harper, commander of the 327th, was talking on the phone to Lieutenant Colonel Ned Moore, McAuliffe's acting chief of staff.

"I have some Germans," said Harper. "They have a request for surrender. I'll bring them up to the command post."

"Good," said Moore. Then he opened the door to a small room where McAuliffe was sleeping. He shook the General awake and told him Harper was on the way with a surrender request.

A few minutes later Colonel Harper walked down the steep steps to the division command post and handed Moore two typewritten sheets of paper—one in German, one in English.

Moore read the English translation:

> To the U.S.A. Commander of the encircled town of Bastogne.
>
> The fortune of war is changing. This time the U.S.A. forces in and near Bastogne have been encircled by strong German armored units . . .
>
> There is only one possibility to save the encircled U.S.A. troops from total annihilation: that is the honorable surrender of the encircled town . . .
>
> If this proposal should be rejected one German Artillery Corps and six heavy A.A. Battalions are ready to annihilate the U.S.A. troops in and near Bastogne . . .
>
> All the serious civilian losses caused by this artillery fire would not correspond with the well-known American humanity.
>
> The German Commander

McAuliffe, yawning, came out of his room. "What's on the paper, Ned?" he asked.

"They want us to surrender."

McAuliffe, after glancing carelessly at the papers, laughed and said, "Aw, nuts." He let the two papers fall to the floor and drove out to the front to personally congratulate some men who had just wiped out a German roadblock.

When McAuliffe returned to his command post, Colonel Harper was there. "Say, Tony," he said, "those two Kraut envoys are still at my command post. They say they brought a formal military communication and they're entitled to an answer."

"What the hell should I tell them?" McAuliffe sat down, thought-fully fingering a pencil.

"That first remark of yours would be hard to beat, General," suggested Colonel Kinnard, the youthful operations officer.

"What'd I say?"

"You said, 'Nuts.' "

Everyone in the room, officers and enlisted men, liked this answer.

McAuliffe wrote and then handed the paper to Harper. "Here's the answer."

Harper read:

> To the German Commander:
>   Nuts!
>   —The American Commander

"Will you see that it's delivered?" said McAuliffe.

Harper grinned. "I'll deliver it myself. It will be a lot of fun."

At 1:30 P.M. Sergeant Butler, who had just finished checking his lines, walked into the farmhouse overlooking the Arlon highway. He was amazed to see the two German privates of the surrender team sitting on the basement floor, machine pistols propped against the wall. Private Gommell, their guard, was proudly fingering a P-38 pistol.

"What the hell's going on?" asked Butler.

"They just surrendered to me," said Gommell innocently.

"Give them back their guns."

Reluctantly Gommell handed the P-38 to one of the privates, a frightened youngster who looked less than sixteen. The boy was just as reluctant to take it.

Butler heard a jeep approaching. Followed by the others, he hurried outside. In the jeep were Colonel Harper and the two German officers.

"But what does it mean?" the medical officer was asking in bewilderment.

"If you don't understand what 'Nuts' means," said Harper, losing his temper, "in plain English it's the same as 'Go to Hell.' And I'll tell you something else. If you continue to attack we'll kill every goddam German that tries to break into this city!"

The Germans saluted sharply.

"We will kill many Americans," said the medical captain regretfully.

"On your way, Bud," said Harper. Then, without thinking, he added, "And good luck to you."

About ten miles southwest of Bastogne, comrades of the German surrender team had made almost no western progress that day. At an advance command post of the Panzer Lehr Division, Baron von Manteuffel, who had personally taken a tank all the way to the approaches of St. Hubert the day before, was berating General Bayerlein.

"There's nothing out west," he stormed. "Get your damned people moving!" Manteuffel was also angry with his corps commander, Lüttwitz. For the Baron had learned of the surrender note to Bastogne too late to stop the envoys. Besides being in poor military taste, it contained hollow threats. The artillery battalions which were to lay waste the town existed only in Lüttwitz's mind.

Now the hollow threats had to be made good. Manteuffel picked up a phone.

It was midnight in Bastogne. In McAuliffe's command post the mood had suddenly changed. The air drop promised for 10:00 P.M. had been called off because of bad weather.

McAuliffe and his staff again reviewed their situation. So far three things had kept the Germans from overwhelming Bastogne: lack of artillery, uncoordinated attacks, and the stubbornness of the defenders. As yet the Germans had hit only one sector at a time, giving the defenders time to rush reserves to the threatened spot.

McAuliffe studied the latest "sitrep"—situation report. There was bitter fighting at Marvie; reports of rumbling traffic at other points presaged other attacks. When these came he would have little to stop them. Infantry commanders all around the perimeter were calling for artillery and getting almost none. Ammunition was rationed to ten rounds a day per gun.

To one commander who continued to plead for artillery, McAuliffe drily replied, "If you see 400 Germans in a hundred-yard area, and they have their heads up, you can fire artillery at them. But not more than two rounds."

Colonel Robert's big 105s, the heavy punch of the town's defense, were so low on ammunition that three of his tanks and two half-tracks were now making a break for the south. This desperate force, led by Captain McCloskey, hoped to fight its way back to Bastogne with an ammunition train. But before McCloskey had gone a mile all five vehicles were knocked out.

As news of this reached Bastogne, the unfamiliar hum of German bombers could be heard. Their roar grew louder, then deafening. There were shrill whistles, followed by explosions. Manteuffel was carrying out von Lüttwitz's threat to devastate the town.

The men in the foxholes around Bastogne were bitter. If Germans could fly over, why not the Allies? The confidence of that morning was waning. This bombing was an indication that the end was near.

3. THE RUSSIAN HIGH

23 December 1944

1

A few minutes after midnight of December 22, an ambulance was leaving Vielsalm, heading northwest for Liége. In it was Major General Alan Jones.

Soon after his last meeting with Ridgway, during which he had been relieved of command of the 106th Division and made Ridgway's assistant, Jones fell to the floor, unconscious. His heart—strained by worry, overwork, and tension—had given way.

At the schoolhouse Hasbrouck was still working. His detailed plan to withdraw the 20,000 men and hundreds of tanks and trucks of the Fortified Goose Egg back across the Salm River, and to the northwest in the wake of Jones, was now being radioed to the front.

Starting at 3:00 A.M. Hoge and Reid were to pull back through Beho, follow the main highway up to Salmchâteau, and then pass through the escape corridor held open by the 82nd Airborne Division. Three hours later, at 6:00 A.M., Clarke was to funnel his men through Commanster and over a rough dirt road—little more than a logging trail—to Vielsalm. Task Force Boylan was to cover Clarke, and Task Force Jones was to protect Hoge and Reid. Nelson's 112th Regiment was to form a defense line just east of the Salm River and stay in place until all retreating forces in the southern sector had pulled through. On the north, the other two combat commands of the 7th Armored Division, CCA and CCR, were to hold their lines until Clarke had escaped and then make a run for it.

It was a concise, efficient plan—on paper.

General Clarke had just walked into his Commanster command post when he was handed a copy of the plan. Although he, like everyone else in the Fortified Goose Egg, had been praying for a withdrawal order, he realized the roads were in no condition for a general retreat. He had just returned from a tour of the front. On the main road from Hinderhausen, his jeep had sunk into mud over the hub caps. It had taken a dozen men to push it out. What would happen when trucks, tanks, and half-tracks tried to come through this sea of mud?

General Bill Hoge entered the gasthaus. He was even more perturbed. "I'm supposed to start moving at 0300," he told Clarke. "But I'm getting hit hard in at least two places. I can't possibly disengage."

And so both men radioed Hasbrouck that a withdrawal at the scheduled time was impossible. Neither knew, of course, that the eastern area of high pressure, the Russian High, had just started moving toward the Ardennes. If it arrived soon enough its cold winds would blow fog and clouds off the battlefield; fields and mud roads would freeze; and trucks, half-tracks, and tanks could escape to the west.

Several miles away Lieutenant Colonel Robert Erlenbusch was trying desperately to shore up the northeastern arc of the Fortified Goose Egg. Driving through Braunlauf he saw a candle flickering in a house. He went into the house. A dozen men, their barracks bags piled in one corner, were sitting on the floor staring vacantly at the burning candle.

"What the hell are you doing here?" he asked.

Nobody knew. They were from the 424th Regiment but had no idea what they were doing in Braunlauf.

"Come with me," he said. The men, grateful that someone was taking charge of them, followed him to the street. In a few minutes Erlenbusch had routed several hundred more confused infantrymen from the houses.

A dozen empty 2½-ton trucks plowed through the mud from the south. Erlenbusch flagged them down.

"The Jerries have broken through!" shouted a sergeant in the first truck. He told Erlenbusch he was from Hoge's combat command and trying to get back to Beho.

"I can use these trucks," said Erlenbusch. The sergeant was only too glad to be relieved of responsibility and in a few minutes the trucks were filled with the infantrymen from the 106th Division. "Now move back to Commanster," ordered Erlenbusch.

He hurried to his own command post, radioed General Clarke, and excitedly told him of the breakthrough.

"Yes, yes, I know. The Jerries have broken through at several places." His tone calmed Erlenbusch. "Just hold *your* lines."

A few minutes later Erlenbusch was called back to the radio. "This is General Hoge," said another unperturbed voice. "I can't get through to General Clarke. Part of my front has been broken through. If any of my units come through your area, take charge of them."

"Sir, I just took over fifteen of your trucks trying to get back to Beho. I'll keep an eye out for anything else."

Now bad news came from Erlenbusch's own two commanders. Lieutenant Colonel Wimpel, who held the right flank, reported heavy action and Major Lohse, commanding the left flank, was being shelled by artillery and tanks.

Alarmed, Erlenbusch called Clarke. "Sir, my whole area is being surrounded. The Jerries are softening up Lohse and will hit him at any minute. Wimpel is already under heavy attack. Don't you think they should pull out now, sir?"

"I can't authorize a withdrawal yet. General Hoge is getting heavy action in the south. If you pull out first, he'll be outflanked."

"But, sir, if my people are going to get out at all, it'll *have* to be at the very first light."

"You've got to hold on," said Clarke firmly. "The area in the south has to be cleared first. Besides the roads to the rear are awfully muddy."

Erlenbusch was near physical collapse from the week-long exhaustion and tension. "But, sir," he protested, "my men will be sitting ducks."

"Don't worry. I'll do everything to get them out—just as fast as possible."

It was now Erlenbusch's turn to soothe. He called Lohse. "We're not moving out right away. Get ready for a Jerry attack."

Lohse was astonished. His men couldn't hold much longer. "Do you know what it's *really* like out here?" Loud explosions could be heard in the background.

Erlenbusch borrowed Clarke's calm tone. "Don't worry. We'll get you out."

At 5:00 A.M. Clarke was handed a radio message. It was from Hasbrouck.

> The situation is such on the west of the river south of the 82nd Airborne Division that if we don't join them soon, the opportunity will be gone. It will be necessary to disengage, whether circumstances are favorable or not, if we are to carry out any kind of withdrawal with equipment. Inform me of your situation at once.

Clarke was still concerned about the muddy roads, but he knew Hasbrouck was right. He was called to the radio.

"There's a fire-fight just south of me," reported Erlenbusch excitedly. "We've got to get out now!"

Clarke hesitated. He hated to start his people over muddy roads. They'd be such easy targets. "You'll probably be able to take off at daylight," he promised. "If you'll hang on another ten minutes I can give you the good word."

Clarke hung up and went to the door of his command post. The sky in the east was just graying. He went outside. Bitter gusts blew from the east. He stepped onto the road. A thrill shot through him. The ruts were frozen solid.

The Russian High had arrived.

Inside, Erlenbusch was again on the radio. "Sir—"

"All right, Bob," interrupted Clarke, "crank up."

In the dull morning light, cold tank and truck motors coughed, sputtered, and then roared to life. Soon vehicles of all kinds were moving west over roads and fields frozen rock-hard. Two tanks bogged down and were set on fire. The rest rolled across the hard terrain.

In Braunlauf, Erlenbusch couldn't find a jeep. In the excitement his driver had taken off. Sheet-covered German infantrymen filtered out of the woods and ran toward town. Shells began digging up the fields and streets. It was obviously an artillery concentration before an attack. Seeing a jeep parked in a farmyard, Erlenbusch darted across the road, ran hunched-up behind a wall, and jumped in the driver's seat. In the back were two figures in sleeping bags.

The jeep started with a jerk for its wheels were frozen in ruts. As it spun around and headed west, Erlenbusch heard a distant "burp-burp-burp." The left sleeve of his jacket was pocked with holes. His two passengers—a chaplain and his assistant—were still sleeping, oblivious of the hail of fire.

In Vielsalm, General Robert Hasbrouck was watching the first retreating vehicles stream past his command post toward the bridge across the Salm River. There they would pass through the thin lines of the 82nd Airborne Division and continue to the northwest and safety.

It was a sunny, crystal-clear day. It occurred to Hasbrouck that he'd been given a similar problem at Fort Leavenworth. His solution, as now, had been to withdraw at once, even though it was daylight. He had been given a very poor mark. The school solution had been to wait for darkness.

Six miles to the east, in Commanster, General Bruce Clarke was standing in a field directing traffic over a corduroy road. He watched his men pass—red-eyed, unshaven, filthy. A week before, he'd had his doubts about them. He wouldn't trade them now for any outfit.

The last vehicle passed; only Boylan's rear guard was left. Clarke slowly climbed into his jeep. Every muscle ached. His mind was exhausted. For seven days he hadn't had a real peaceful moment of sleep. He loafed back in his seat. A pleasant drowsiness came over him. His men were safe. His job was finished. As the jeep bounced over the rough road his eyes closed. He was finally asleep.

2

It was a cold bright dawn all over the Ardennes. For the first time since the great offensive had begun, flying weather was perfect. Ceiling and visibility were unlimited.

On the southern front swarms of B-26s and P-47s were over Luxembourg City. The people, wakened by the unaccustomed noise, rushed to the streets. They craned their necks and watched the

Americans speed to the attack, leaving behind skies filled with snakelike vapor trails.

When Patton looked out his window on the Boulevard Paul Eyschen and saw the sun, he was jubilant. "Hot dog!" he said. "I guess I'll have another 100,000 of those prayers printed. The Lord is on our side and we've got to keep him informed of what we need."

He called for his deputy chief of staff, Colonel Harkins. "God damn, Paul, look at that weather! O'Neill sure did some potent praying. Get him up here. I want to pin a medal on him."

But soon Patton's morning jubilation was clouded by rumors of a great general withdrawal in the north. Montgomery, according to vague reports, was pulling back everyone in the St. Vith salient.

Then news of trouble along his own attacking III Corps front began to come in. Although the 26th Division, in the center, was making good progress, the 4th Armored Division, on the left flank, was stuck at a railroad far from Bastogne. And the 80th Division, on the right, had been given a severe beating miles below its objective, Wiltz.

One thing was finally obvious to Patton: the German was still tough and dangerous. The roads to Bastogne and Wiltz would not be easy ones.

3

In Wiltz, where Brandenberger had just set up his new headquarters, shells from Patton's long-range cannons were falling in the streets. Josephine Thein, wife of a schoolmaster who had fled the day before to avoid arrest by the German secret police, was alone in their cellar with her two children—Nicole, eight, and Edy, four. Wrapped in blankets, they had slept on a coal pile.

With each explosion the children whimpered and clung closer to their mother, who tried to hide her own fear. The shelling grew worse. Terrified by the loneliness, Josephine led the children up the stairs. She would take them to the stone house of her mother's cousin, several blocks up the hill leading to the castle.

Quickly she dumped a few belongings into a baby carriage. With the children hanging on to her skirts, she pushed the carriage out of the house and up the cobblestone street. A shell exploded a hundred yards to her right. Debris fell in front of them. Then American planes suddenly appeared in the bright blue sky.

Josephine was now at her cousin's house, banging on the door.

After a minute a window opened. A woman peered out fearfully and asked, "What do you want, Josephine?"

Across the street Germans in blue-green uniforms scurried toward the big post office building. A plane swooped down. There was a chatter. Machine-gun bullets ricocheted off the cobblestones, flying over Josephine's head. Edy sobbed, hiding his face in his mother's skirts.

"We want to stay in your cellar," cried Josephine hysterically. "Our part of town is deserted. We're all alone!"

"I don't know, I'll have to ask my husband first." The cousin closed the window.

Another shell fell behind the post office building. Bombs began landing near the same place. A tank passed. A German standing in the turret laughed at the terrified Josephine. "What are you doing out here, beautiful woman?" he said mockingly.

Josephine burst into tears.

Finally the window opened again. "Albert says we have no room for you. Besides he couldn't take the responsibility." The heavy shutters slammed.

Another tank rattled up the hill. Josephine pulled the children from the tank's path just in time. The three stood, backs flat against the post office door.

"What are you doing on the streets?" called a voice through the peephole in the door. "Don't you have a home?"

"We're all alone!"

"Well, come on in here. Do you want to get killed?" The door opened. The three refugees hurried inside. Then she saw her host was M. Kremer, the porter of the building.

"My God, it's you, Josephine," he said. "I didn't recognize you. You looked so upset." He led her into the basement apartment.

Mme. Kremer comforted Josephine and the trembling children. "First you must eat," she said. "Then you and the children go to sleep in our bed."

4

In the foxholes circling Bastogne the bright sun was bringing welcome warmth to the town's cramped frozen defenders. They had never before been so glad to see dawn. It had been a night of misery. Their foxholes had been refrigerators. Awake all night, they had danced up and down to keep from freezing. A half dozen times they had taken off tight paratrooper's boots to massage their numb feet. Now they were trying to thaw out not only themselves but their pieces. One man's M-1 rifle wouldn't work. Checking, he found the ejector frozen. He resorted to the old soldier's solution: he urinated on the cold metal.

Distant hums in the west became shrieks. Sleek American fighter planes knifed overhead, bound northeast for missions in the Fortified Goose Egg. The men of Bastogne stood up and cheered.

At 9:35 A.M. there was a deeper roar as several lumbering transports appeared and circled the town. Parachutists drifted to a snow-covered field. They explained they were pathfinders who were to guide in resupply planes which should start arriving in an hour and a half.

While the pathfinders were assembling their radar sets, Captain James Parker, an air force officer who had made his way into Bastogne the day before the encirclement, was getting more good news by radio. Supporting planes were on the way. A few minutes after 10:00 A.M. Parker, whose radio jeep was located just outside McAuliffe's basement command post, was talking to the approaching planes, telling them where to strike. Without warning they dove at German columns converging on Bastogne, knocking out scores of tanks and armored cars.

At 11:50 A.M. sixteen big C-47s approached the encircled town. German anti-aircraft threw up a wall of flak. Several planes plunged to the earth in flames, but the oncoming flight never wavered. Over Bastogne hundreds of gaily colored parachutes blossomed and drifted onto the open fields.

Civilians, in spite of regulations, poured out of their cellars and stared up in awe at the carnival sight. These Americans were like people from another world.

GIs seized each other. They shouted and danced in the streets.

5

That day the London newspapers featured alarming reports from the Ardennes. The *Daily Express* headline asked, MONTHS ADDED TO WAR? and printed a German claim that Liége had been reached and that there was "fighting in the city's suburbs."

According to the Paris correspondent of the *Daily Telegram,* English-speaking German women, equipped with knives, had just been dropped inside the American lines. Reportedly seven had already been arrested, confessing that their mission had been to seduce GIs and then put knives in their backs.

But the conclusive proof of the seriousness of the battle was revealed by the *Daily Mail:* "There is not enough beer in some parts of the country to last over the holidays. Many public houses may have to shut down on Christmas Day and part of Boxing Day."

Even so, London was calm compared to Paris, which was in the grip of its greatest spy scare. Lynchings were reported in several places. A fifth column was reported ready to rise from the sewers.

Versailles was still an armed camp. No one was allowed to enter the gates to see Eisenhower, who was becoming more and more irritated with his restricted existence. Without his knowledge, an elaborate trap was being set for his assassins. A colonel, Baldwin B. Smith, who bore a striking resemblance to Eisenhower, had put on one of the Supreme Commander's uniforms and was being driven back and forth between the "von Rundstedt House" and Versailles. The hook for Skorzeny was baited.

Actually there wasn't a Skorzeny man within several hundred miles. There were, however, thousands of "saboteurs." These were the Americans AWOL in the European Theater of Operations. Most had congregated in Paris and lived by hijacking American supplies, including an average of 1,000 gallons of gas a day.

In one Paris detention barracks alone, there were 1,308 Americans under arrest, more than half charged with "misappropriation." In another cage 181 officers and three enlisted men were charged with stealing an entire trainload of soap, cigarettes, and other supplies. Each of the prisoners had at least $5,000 when picked up.

"This place is getting to be like Chicago in the days of Al Capone," said Colonel E. G. Buhrmaster, provost marshal of the Seine base section. "They hijack trucks right off the road. One major sent home $36,000 in a few weeks."

Almost 19,000 men, more than a division, were plundering supplies needed by their comrades in the Ardennes. They were stealing everything from food to trucks. They would have stolen bullets and tanks—if there had been buyers on the black market.

6

By late morning the great retreat from the Fortified Goose Egg was well under way. The survivors of the far-flung Battle of St. Vith were now passing in a steady orderly stream through Vielsalm, across the Salm River, and on to the northwest.

Threatening these men from the south was the 2nd SS Panzer Division. Originally scheduled to follow Dietrich, it had been routed below the salient to exploit Manteuffel's breakthrough. The day before, after following the trail of Krüger's panzer corps, it had suddenly swung back north and was now behind Vielsalm.

Though this powerful panzer unit could have burst through the 82nd Airborne Division lines protecting the American withdrawal, the German High Command had a much greater objective than the destruction of the 20,000 men fleeing from the Fortified Goose Egg. Their plan was to head for Baraque de Fraiture, a tiny isolated settlement ten miles west of Vielsalm. Here the highway from Vielsalm crossed the most important road in Belgium, the trunk-line running north from Bastogne to Liége. The 2nd SS Panzers were to seize this crossroad and then continue straight north up a wide paved highway perfect for tanks.

The first step, of course, was to take Baraque de Fraiture. Although this was apparently a simple chore, the settlement had already held out for over two days under sporadic attacks by preceding Krüger units. This was puzzling, for according to patrols, it was protected by only a few guns and a few mixed troops. Intelligence officers decided the patrols had done a poor job of spying.

They hadn't. Four days previously, Major Arthur Parker III had rolled up to Baraque de Fraiture in the general retreat from St. Vith. He had been ordered by the artillery officer of the 106th Division to establish a roadblock with his three remaining 105-mm. howitzers. These guns had narrowly escaped from the Schnee Eifel, mainly through the dogged efforts of their battery commander, Lieutenant Eric Wood, Jr., who was still roaming the forests east of St. Vith, fighting a lonely guerilla war.

When Parker arrived he found a deserted crossroad, marked only by a few crude stone houses, sitting on high marshlands, surrounded by pine forests. His original mission had been to protect the vital supply route back to the St. Vith area. But Parker concluded, after studying a map, that this road junction was of much greater importance: it was the strategic key to the northwest. Consequently he persuaded several other passing units to join him: an anti-aircraft battalion with three multiple .50-caliber machine guns and a self-propelled 37-mm. gun; a reconnaissance company from the 7th Armored Division; and several dozen assorted stragglers from the east.

For two days nothing happened. Then Krüger's 58th Panzer Corps swept below Baraque de Fraiture and the extreme right flank tried to take the crossroad in a dozen vicious sideswipes as it brushed by.

Although Parker himself was seriously wounded, his small force held off a dozen raids, and Krüger's men, not realizing how important "Parker's Crossroad" was, continued to the west, figuring some other unit behind them could easily mop up.

Now on the morning of December 23, a much more determined assault began from three sides. Major Elliott Goldstein, Parker's executive officer and now in command, knew the end was near. His force had been dangerously whittled down, ammunition was almost gone, and two of the morning's prisoners were officers from the powerful 2nd SS Panzer Division. He decided to take the two prisoners as evidence of a major threat and go north to find some help.

Simultaneously Major General James "Slim Jim" Gavin, commander of the 82nd Airborne Division and the youngest major general in the army, was learning of these attacks from one of his own patrols. Although his main mission that day was to hold while the men of the Fortified Goose Egg retreated through his lines, he saw that the hills his men held a few miles northeast of the crossroad would be outflanked if the 2nd SS Panzer Division seized it. He also guessed the Germans would continue north up the road toward Liége, cutting off not only his own division but almost all of Ridgway's corps.

Even though the crossroad was in 3rd Armored Division territory and though his own thin line extended in a great 44,000-yard semicircle all the way from Stoumont, he ordered Captain Woodruff of Company K, 325th Glider Infantry, to rush to Baraque de Fraiture.

That morning a great German victory hung on the actions of a few men and a few guns at a dreary road junction.

To compound the confusion of the battle which was developing at Baraque de Fraiture, earlier that morning Hodges decided to transfer the 3rd Armored Division from Ridgway's corps to the VII Corps of "Lightning Joe" Collins.

General Maurice Rose's 3rd Armored Division still "held" the mountainous wooded territory from Baraque de Fraiture fifteen miles west to Hotton. A fantastic assignment for an armored unit, it had been born of desperation. The three task forces which Rose had thrown out to delay Krüger's panzer corps while Collins' corps tried to get behind the Germans had done their job well in a bold bluff. But now two had been driven to the north and the third, Task Force Hogan, was still surrounded in the ridge village of Marcouray, three miles north of La Roche.

At 10:00 A.M. Sam Hogan, the colonel from Texas, was listening to a radio report from Division. It was cheerful news: the engineers, clerks, and other rear-echelon men were still holding out at Hotton and reinforcements from Colonel Howze had almost reached that besieged town; and Combat Command A, released from tracking down von der Heydte paratroopers, had finally closed in on Manhay, a road junction village six miles north of Baraque de Fraiture. This last news cheered Hogan for it meant the muscle of the 3rd Armored Division was now in the fight. But his answer to Division was not so cheerful: he was almost out of plasma, bandages, food, and ammunition.

Rose's answer soon came: "There'll be an air resupply drop tonight. And we're also going to shoot in plasma and bandages. Be watching for them."

Hogan went to the door of his command post. It was perfect flying weather. Perhaps things weren't as bad as they seemed. Suddenly an armored car rolled past. It was filled with Germans. Hogan ducked back inside. A second armored car, its occupants as nonchalant as if they were parading in Berlin, shot by. Hogan called the outpost on the southern end of town.

"Two Kraut armored cars coming through," he shouted, then rang the northern outpost and asked, "What the hell happened?"

"I didn't check the gun on my tank this morning, Colonel," apologized the outpost commander. "The Krauts rolled into town without any warning and as I started to lay on the lead car and traverse, the damn thing wouldn't move. Guess moisture on the turret froze."

Hogan, ordinarily easygoing, tongue-lashed the commander, then hurried to the southern part of town. One German armored car was blazing, its occupants running toward haystacks and hedgerows. Hogan saw his men flushing out the Germans one by one. Five gray figures made a frantic dash for the ditch and dove in face down.

An American lieutenant ran up to the ditch, pulled out his .45, and shot one of the Germans in the back of the head.

"Stop!" shouted Hogan.

But the lieutenant, taking careful aim, murdered a second German who lay helplessly sprawled out. He went to the third. This man got to his feet, eyes terrified. As the lieutenant aimed his pistol, another American knocked the gun from his hand.

Hogan angrily dressed down the lieutenant and went back to his command post. A likely prospect for imminent capture, he now had two Germans, shot in the back of the head.

In his command post near Marche, General Collins had just learned that in addition to his other considerable worries he had another responsibility, the 3rd Armored Division. In other words, he now commanded a snakelike corps line from Baraque de Fraiture almost all the way to the Meuse.

Two days before, Montgomery had ordered Collins to circle behind the entire battlefield with three divisions—the 75th, the 84th, and the 2nd Armored—and to avoid contact with the enemy. The 75th, an infantry division, which was supposed to close in to the right of Maurice Rose's 3rd Armored, was still miles to the rear. The 84th Infantry Division, next in line, had pulled into position in front of Marche, but in spite of Montgomery's orders, was already fighting.

Its opponents were from Krüger's 116th Panzer Division. These same Germans had run into such hot opposition at Hotton from Rose's rear-echelon clerks and engineers that Krüger had ordered his panzers to disengage and make their breakthrough a few miles to the west, where, according to spies, there were no American troops.

The 116th Panzers had followed orders. To their dismay (and that of the marshaling 84th) the two forces were now meeting with a solid bump.

A moment after this news was relayed to Collins, Field Marshal

Montgomery, wearing a parachutist's red beret instead of a helmet, walked into his command post.

"I just got a report from Bolling of the 84th," said Collins. "He's run into Germans north of Marche."

Montgomery frowned. "I told you I didn't want you to get committed in defense action. You're my strategic reserve." He cautioned Collins to avoid further trouble and to fall back if necessary. Under no circumstances was there to be a counter-attack. This should come only when the German had run his course.

A few minutes after Montgomery left, Major General "Gravel Voice" Ernie Harmon, commander of the 2nd Armored Division, entered.

"I just talked with Monty," said Collins, who had great respect for the Field Marshal in spite of their conflicting military philosophies. "He told me again not to get committed. Ernie, you're to lay quiet for about a week and get ready for a surprise counterattack."

"That sounds good to me," said Harmon in his deep rasping voice. His 14,000 men were tired from continuous fighting. They'd rushed 70 miles overnight and needed a long rest.

Half an hour later Harmon was back in his own command post, a chateau northwest of Marche. He told his officers the good news and sat down to a leisurely lunch. While Harmon was drinking coffee, a lieutenant with a bloody bandage crudely bound around his head pushed his way in. Harmon recognized him as Lieutenant Everett Jones, who had been sent that morning to reconnoiter the area to the south.

"My patrol was fired on, sir," said Jones excitedly. "There were at least two Mark IV tanks. The Krauts are only ten miles away and they're coming like hell!"

If the Germans were ten miles to the south, that meant they were already ten miles *west* of Marche. They must have circled below that town and headed straight for the Meuse. Harmon made a quick decision. Hatless, he ran across a snowy field to a grove of trees where a tank battalion was bivouacked. "How soon can you crank up and move out?" he called to a company commander.

"If radio silence is lifted, General, five minutes."

"Radio silence is lifted here and now. You get down that road to a town called Ciney. Block the entrance and exits of town. The whole damn division is coming along right behind you!"

Within five minutes seventeen Shermans roared south, throttles wide open. Close behind were thirty-seven more.

Harmon was at a telephone. "Joe," he was saying quite happily, "I'm committed!"

On the other end of the line his corps commander, Collins, was nodding, but not too happily. Ernie had done the right thing, but would Monty agree?

7

It was 2:00 P.M. Six miles north of Baraque de Fraiture, at Manhay, Major Elliott Goldstein was pleading with Lieutenant Colonel Walter Richardson of the 3rd Armored Division. "Colonel, my people are going to be overrun if you don't give me help."

Richardson looked at the two captured 2nd SS Panzer Division officers Goldstein had brought from the crossroad as persuaders. He nodded and picked up a phone. "Brew," he said, "they need a hand down at Baraque de Fraiture. Crank up a platoon of tanks and have a look." He turned to Goldstein. "Major Brewster is a couple of miles down the road. If he can help, he will."

An hour later General "Slim Jim" Gavin was on the ridge a mile northeast of Baraque de Fraiture. His 82nd Airborne riflemen were scattered in foxholes 200 yards apart; there was little antitank defense. Defending this important ridge from a major attack would be impossible. Yet he couldn't steal a single man from another section of his bulging twenty-five-mile division line.

Heavy mortar fire began digging up the hills. Then even louder sounds of attack came from the southwest. Baraque de Fraiture was really getting shellacked. He ducked into a company command post and telephoned Captain Woodruff, commander of the airborne company he'd sent to beef up the crossroad defenses that morning.

"We're under terrific attack, sir," shouted Woodruff above the noise of battle. "I don't know how long I can hold out."

Gavin hurried across fields, into a pine woods. He wanted to see if things were really desperate. The roar of German 88s was shattering as he crawled through underbrush to the edge of the woods. One hundred yards beyond he saw a smoking mass of ruins, Baraque de Fraiture. German tanks and infantrymen were attacking from three sides.

There was nothing one man could do. He crawled to the rear.

Two majors, Goldstein and Brewster, were racing toward the same crossroad in a jeep. A mile above their destination, several filthy artillerymen stopped them.

"The enemy broke through," cried one excitedly. "The road-block's been wiped out!"

Goldstein and Brewster got out of the jeep and continued south through the woods. Perhaps the men were exaggerating and they wouldn't be too late. They plowed through snow until they came to the edge of the woods. A huge tank, marked with a black cross, suddenly rumbled over a rise, aimed its 88 at them, and fired.

The two ran, speeded on by the near miss. They were too late— no doubt about it.

Stoumont was the only bright spot in Ridgway's XVIII Airborne Corps line that day. The General stepped out of his jeep, his ever present Springfield rifle in his right hand, and walked into the beautiful modern chateau situated on the ridge between Stoumont and La Gleize. He was quickly briefed by General Harrison: the 82nd Airborne was closing in; the 30th Division, helped by the 740th Tank Battalion, was pushing in from the west.

"Our attacks from the west and east bogged down today," said Harrison. "But tomorrow I'm going to try one from the north." From these wooded hills his men could approach La Gleize without being seen.

Their conversation was brief and loud, for two howitzers and a great 155-mm. cannon, dug in next to the chateau, were lobbing tons of high explosive into Peiper's final stronghold at La Gleize.

This one cannon was giving Peiper more grief than any other gun he'd run up against. His men were in an almost constant state of shock from its pounding. In addition he was low on ammunition and out of fuel.

The day before he had radioed: "Almost all our Hermann is gone. We have no Otto. It's just a question of time before we're completely destroyed. Can we break out?"

Now a day later, an answer finally came: "If Kampfgruppe Peiper does not punctually report its supply situation it cannot reckon on a running supply of fuel and ammunition. Six Koenigs-tigers ready for action east of Stavelot. Where do you want us to send them?"

Peiper was disgusted at the unrealistic message. "Send via air lift to La Gleize," he replied sarcastically. And then added, "We must be allowed to break out immediately."

There was a pause. "Can you break out with all vehicles and wounded?"

Peiper felt a surge of hope. It was the first indication that the High Command didn't expect him to die uselessly in La Gleize. "Last chance for breakout tonight," he radioed. "Without wounded and vehicles. Please give permission!"

Convinced that this permission would soon come, Peiper made breakout preparations. Then he had Major Hal McCown brought from the cellar containing the American prisoners.

"We've been called back," said Peiper, hiding the desperation of the situation.

"Well, Colonel," said McCown, "I've always wanted to ride on a King Tiger."

Peiper smiled but didn't say they would all be walking. "My immediate concern is what to do with the American prisoners and my wounded." He promised to release all the prisoners except McCown. In exchange the Americans would release the German wounded at Stoumont and La Gleize.

McCown was dubious. "I have no authority to deal with you. I doubt very much if my commander will agree. After all, Colonel, you're not in a very good bargaining position."

"I know," said Peiper. "But I'd like to go ahead with the plan in hopes your commander will agree."

An agreement was drawn up. McCown, again insisting his signature meant nothing, signed. Peiper signed and then hurried outside to the radio car to find out if permission to leave had been received.

"Where main line of resistance?" his radio officer was asking with nervous insistence. "Where covering position? May we break out? I repeat, may we break out?"

The receiver finally crackled. Then a voice said, "State when and where you will cross our lines." But as Peiper and the radio man were about to congratulate each other, the message continued. "You may break out but only if you bring all wounded and vehicles."

Peiper angrily pointed at the radio car. "Blow up the damn thing!" Then he said, "Permission or not, we're breaking out of here on foot."

8

At 3:26 P.M. six B-26's of the 322nd Bombardment Group approached a town nestled in hilly forested country. The flight leader glanced down. Even on this clear day he hadn't been able to locate his primary target, Zulpich, Germany, a railhead for Brandenberger's Seventh Army, but he concluded he was over Lammersum, only six miles northeast of the target. As his plane swept over the center of town, thirteen 250-pound General Purpose bombs dropped from the bomb bay. The other five planes of the flight dumped their loads.

The streets of the town erupted from the bombs. All pilots noted, with pleasure, that the results were excellent.

Twelve thousand feet below, dazed American soldiers of the 30th Division and hysterical civilians were crawling from the wreckage of Malmédy, Belgium—39 miles away from Lammersum.

Many were no longer able to crawl.

Moments later General Hobbs, commander of the 30th Division, was angrily talking by phone to an air force general. Hobbs was bitter. It wasn't the first time he'd been bombed by the 9th Air Force. His men had already dubbed it "the American Luftwaffe."

The air force general was dismayed. "It can't happen again," he promised.

General Matthew Ridgway's XVIII Airborne Corps began at this unfortunate town. About twenty miles southwest, near the middle of his line, the gloom of early night was falling over Vielsalm. Since morning the streets had been clogged with vehicles retreating from the Fortified Goose Egg. Clarke's men had passed through. Now trucks, tanks, and jeeps of the other two combat commands of the 7th Armored, CCA and CCR, were rolling past Hasbrouck's schoolhouse command post.

A few miles south, Colonel Gustin Nelson had been trying to

contact Hasbrouck all afternoon. Under attack since noon, his men of the 112th Regiment were stretched several miles east of the Salm River. They were to stand fast as a screen until all but Task Force Jones, the rear guard covering the retreat of Hoge and Reid, had passed through safely. Nelson had strict orders to stay in position until General Hasbrouck himself gave the order to withdraw. Then he was to move fast so that the road would be clear for Task Force Jones.

For several hours no friendly troops had passed through. Every half hour Nelson had been radioing Hasbrouck that he was sure that all of Hoge's and Reid's troops had escaped through his lines. No answers were received.

"As usual," grumbled a GI in the message center, "the 112th is unreported, unsung, and unrelieved."

Now German tanks were blazing away not 200 yards from Nelson's command post. And still the order to withdraw didn't come. Never again would he take an order like that without violent protest.

Desperate reports came from the 1st and 2nd Battalions. The Germans had punched through in several places. Nelson made up his mind. He ordered an immediate withdrawal. But as the 112th Regiment vehicles approached the main highway running north to Salmchâteau, it was discovered that this road was already crowded with vehicles of Task Force Jones, the last unit to escape from the southern sector. As Nelson's vehicles elbowed onto the highway, Tigers and Panthers poked out of the hills to the east. Soon shells began falling into the jammed column. Terror swept from vehicle to vehicle as Task Force Jones and Nelson's regiment, both using the same road, crawled up toward Salmchâteau.

In Vielsalm, Hasbrouck imagined his message ordering Nelson to withdraw had been received two hours before. Shells were falling in the streets and the roars of German tanks could be heard. Hasbrouck packed his papers and, with the last members of his staff, walked down the stairs of the schoolhouse.

A few miles east of town Lieutenant Colonel Moe Boylan, in charge of the force covering the retreat of the 7th Armored Division, had just learned that all that stood between Vielsalm and the onrushing Germans were two machine-gun squads and his small rear guard. And the situation was even worse to the south.

German tanks had broken into Salmchâteau. This meant that the slow-moving column of Task Force Jones and the 112th Regiment, already threatened from the east and south, was now blocked in the north. Another American debacle was in the making.

Boylan sent a platoon of light tanks to Salmchâteau to try to blast a way for these two trapped units. He spread the rest of his men in a thin shield east of Vielsalm, hoping he could hold long enough for everyone to pull through.

As Hasbrouck stepped out of the schoolhouse a German tank appeared around the corner and fired at a half-track and two jeeps parked in front of the building, motors running. The half-track burst into flames. Hasbrouck and his staff jumped into the jeeps and raced toward the bridge crossing the Salm. The pursuing tank fired again. There was an explosion just ahead of Hasbrouck's jeep, blowing a motorcyclist off his vehicle. The two jeeps careened down the cobblestone street and crossed the bridge.

At the abandoned supply depot, civilians of Vielsalm were patiently shoveling coal into buckets and toting them home. Life under the Germans would be hard and every piece of coal precious.

The road below Salmchâteau was an inferno. Colonel Nelson, discovering that the escape route up through the town had just been cut off, worked his way to the head of his column. Using a light-tank company as a spearhead he drove a trail to the west.

It was now dark. But a full moon and the blaze of burning vehicles lit the way as the 112th Regiment found a bridge, crossed the Salm River, and then wheeled across snowy fields and over frozen marshes.

Task Force Jones was also probing for an escape to the west. The column hurried blindly down a dirt road which soon dwindled to a cow trail leading into the Salm River. Half a dozen tanks and trucks trying to cross became mired. The rest of the column turned north and, after a few miles, came to a ford. The column crossed the Salm and headed west. Half an hour later it entered the darkened village of Provedroux.

The commander of the lead Sherman tank, noticing parked vehicles on the main street, ordered a halt. Then he saw they were German. He shouted, "Fire!"

The town was soon in chaos as Americans and Germans milled around confusedly. An American half-track burst into flames. The men tumbled out, looking for cover. One was Sergeant John Banister of the 14th Cavalry Group but for the past two days a member of Task Force Jones. In eight days he had missed death a dozen times.

An American tank destroyer rolled by, decks covered with infantrymen firing rifles. "Climb on, soldier," called its commander from the turret. "This one's going out."

Banister ran after the vehicle. Someone grabbed his hand and pulled him aboard.

"Know who you're riding with?" asked the man who had helped him, pointing at the commander. "Lieutenant Bill Rogers."

"Who's he?"

"Why, hell," said the other proudly, "he's Will Rogers' boy."

American tanks, half-tracks, trucks, jeeps, and men on foot had now turned to the north, hoping to cross the east-west highway from Vielsalm before they were caught from behind.

An hour later Rogers' tank destroyer reached the road. Banister saw a bazookaman digging a foxhole. Dirty, unshaven, unperturbed, exhausted, he could have posed for Mauldin's "Willie." "Are you looking for a safe place?" he drawled.

"Yeah," said Banister.

"Well, buddy, just pull your vehicle behind me." He hitched up his droopy pants. "I'm the 82nd Airborne. And this is as far as the bastards are going."

In Vielsalm, it was now time for Colonel Moe Boylan to withdraw his rear guard across the Salm River. He stood at the bridge counting the last of his vehicles.

"Is that all?" shouted an engineer attached to the 82nd Airborne Division.

"As far as I know," said Boylan. "You can blow her now."

Boylan's vehicles, all low on gas, lined up at a fuel dump. A message came over his radio. "Deadshot Six, cease fueling and prepare to move out." It was his operations officer.

"This is Deadshot Six," replied Boylan. "I'm not moving until I refuel. Who the hell orders me to move out?"

"Workshop Six," was the answer. Workshop Six was General Hasbrouck.

"Roger out," Boylan said in a small voice. A few minutes later his column drove up the rise.

An MP stopped him. "You Colonel Boylan?" he asked. "General Hasbrouck wants to see you."

Boylan, expecting a dressing down, slowly walked into a temporary command post, a farmhouse. Hasbrouck came toward him. The General threw an arm around Boylan's shoulder. "Thank God, Boylan, you're here," he said. "You got everyone out."

There was a deep rumble. The bridge at Vielsalm had blown. The Battle of the Fortified Goose Egg was over.

In Versailles Eisenhower had just finished writing a telegram to Hodges.

Please transmit the following personal message from me to Hasbrouck of the Seventh Armored QUOTE The magnificent job you are doing is having a great beneficial effect on our whole situation. I am personally grateful to you and wish you would let all of your people know that if they continue to carry out their mission with the splendid spirit they have so far shown, they will have deserved well of their country. UNQUOTE.

4. DAY OF DECISION

24 December 1944

1

The 2nd Panzer Division was still pushing on due west against no resistance. Its only apparent enemy was its own supply system. For several days gasoline and oil had been doled out by can. The tankers were frustrated; with full fuel tanks they could long since have dashed across the Meuse.

Several hours before dawn of December 24, the division's spearhead drove through the fog along the road leading to Celles. The commander looked at his map by flashlight. From Celles it was only five miles to the Meuse.

At this important junction stood a pleasant inn, the Pavillon Ardennais, owned by Mme. Marthe Monrique. The day before she had seen frightened American engineers hastily lay a single daisy chain of mines across the road in front of the inn, then retreat toward the Meuse in jeeps.

Neighbors told her she should hide in the woods like the other townspeople because there wasn't an American soldier on this side of the river. But Marthe could speak German and she was determined to keep the Boche from destroying the inn.

At 6:00 A.M. she was awakened by an explosion. She turned on the lights and looked out. A German tank was smoldering. Two German officers, seeing her light, walked to the inn. "How many kilometers to Dinant?" asked one.

It was useless to lie. There was a sign just across the road. "Ten kilometers," she said in German.

"Good! We must be in Dinant before noon. How's the road?"

"The Americans mined the whole road." Like so many women in the Ardennes, she was a good actress. "They've been working night and day burying mines in the road—for miles."

The officer asked about the main highway several miles north.

"Oh, that's also mined. And there are thousands of American soldiers hiding just over the hill!"

The German tankers, conquerors of Clervaux and Noville, were alarmed by Marthe Monrique's fairy story. Their column turned off into the woods and coiled up.

2

About forty air miles east of this stalled spearhead of the 2nd Panzer Division, another unit often mistaken for it by Allied Order of Battle teams was continuing its attack north after the victory at Baraque de Fraiture.

The 2nd SS Panzer Division was now only four miles below the next junction on the Bastogne-Liége highway—Manhay. This village was also the point where "Lightning Joe" Collins' VII Corps met Ridgway's XVIII Airborne Corps. For the next twenty-four hours this undistinguished settlement of a hundred houses would be a point of bitter dispute not only between Americans and Germans but between American units.

Task Force Richardson, of the 3rd Armored Division, presently held Manhay. Its commander, Lieutenant Colonel Walter Richardson, had been told the boundary between the two corps was the north-south Bastogne-Liége highway and that everything west of the road was his to defend. East of the road belonged to the XVIII Airborne Corps.

Richardson, like his best friend in the division, Sam Hogan (still surrounded in Marcouray ten miles to the southwest), came from Texas. There the resemblance ended. Hogan, a graduate of West Point, had gone through training relaxed and sure of himself. Richardson, a reserve officer, spent the week ends studying. He was serious, intense, and determined to be a top-rank commander.

Richardson was called to the phone at 9:00 A.M.

It was Major Olin Brewster, commanding a roadblock on the Bastogne-Liége highway at Belle Haie, just four miles to the south. "Rich, things are really popping down here." In code and double-talk he explained that he'd knocked out several 2nd SS Panzer armored cars which were trying to come up through the deep cut in the road he was defending. Fortunately the woods were so thick on both sides of the road that all German vehicles were road-bound.

"P-47's are buzzing us," went on Brewster. He had laid out friendly identification panels, but he didn't think the American planes had spotted the heavy concentration of German tanks getting ready to smash through the block.

Richardson hung up. The men at Belle Haie were all that stood between the Germans and Manhay. He quickly called Major Bill Zech, his battalion executive ten miles to the west at Erezée, gave him Brewster's position and the probable position of the German tanks, and told him to alert the air force.

Less than an hour later Richardson's phone rang again. It was Brewster. The P-47's had made their strike. "It must have been a good one," he said. "The whole damn area is black with smoke!"

The news encouraged Richardson, who had no idea an entire panzer division was trying to drive up through his lines. "I'm going to send you another company of infantry," he said. "Attack and retake Baraque de Fraiture."

The 2nd SS Panzer Division had suffered a sharp jolt. Between Brewster's tanks and the P-47s, nine big German tanks were now burned-out wrecks. But this was only a temporary setback. The SS men had already backed up the bulk of their armor, turned to the west, and circled around Brewster's roadblock. Tanks and men were now slowly pushing across snowy fields toward the village of Odeigne. If they couldn't smash straight up the highway, they would take Manhay from the southwest.

3

Twelve miles farther up the Bastogne-Liége highway, the fate of Manhay was being determined by Matthew Ridgway in a stone farmhouse near Werbomont. Although he commanded three full divisions and sizable units of three more, his XVIII Airborne Corps line, extending from Malmédy to Manhay, was presently held by only two divisions—the 30th and the 82nd Airborne. The rest of the corps, the men from the Fortified Goose Egg, were resting from their exhausting escape.

Even though the great Goose Egg existed no longer, the 82nd Airborne Division still bulged far into the German lines. Gavin's five-mile line was stretched to the breaking point and it was obvious he had little strength near Manhay. It was just as obvious that Manhay was the next German objective in this unexpected drive to the north.

There was only one thing to do, though Ridgway hated to do it. He would have to use the worn-out escapees from the Fortified Goose Egg. He scanned the map and found Malempré, a village several miles southeast of Manhay. He would put Bill Hoge's people there.

But the big problem was the area from Belle Haie up to Manhay. Yesterday Manhay itself belonged to the 3rd Armored Division of Joe Collins' VII Corps. Today it was Ridgway's. To clarify jurisdiction of the Bastogne-Liége highway, the boundary between the two corps had been pushed back a mile west of the road.

To this important area he would have to send the men who had come out of the St. Vith battle in the best shape: Combat Command A of the 7th Armored Division.

An hour later an open car, with no MP escort, pulled up before Ridgway's farmhouse. Montgomery stepped out and grinned at the American guards who grinned back. Montgomery's mission was simple. He had come to straighten out Ridgway's lines. The 82nd Airborne Division bulge within the Bulge was an abomination to his neat precise mind. He told Ridgway the 82nd had to be withdrawn to a sensible line of defense, the road running from Trois Ponts to Manhay.

Ridgway said little. A disciple of constant attack, he was still able to follow Montgomery's reasoning. He also knew the Field Marshal had made up his mind and that argument would be useless.

The two men shook hands. Montgomery returned to his car, again gave a comradely wave to the GIs, and told his driver to head for Courtney Hodges' new command post.

At 1:30 P.M. Ridgway's commanders—Gavin, Hasbrouck, Hoge, and several others—crowded into the farmhouse at Werbomont.

"Starting after darkness," Ridgway said somberly, "Combat Command A of the 7th Armored will withdraw to Manhay and the 82nd Airborne to Trois Ponts."

Most of the commanders nodded approval but Gavin started to protest. His 82nd had never retreated and didn't want to start now. Ridgway gave him a sharp look.

After the meeting, Ridgway sat down and began to write. His troops had to know that once they withdrew to the line ordered by Montgomery they would not retreat another step. There they would stand, fight, and defeat the Germans.

His proclamation concluded with these words:

> In my opinion this is the dying gasp of the German Army. He is putting everything he has into this fight. We are going to smash that final drive here today in this Corps zone. This command is the command that will smash the German offensive spirit for this war. Impress every man in your division with that spirit. We are going to lick the Germans here today.

4

At Manhay, Richardson was talking with his combat commander, Brigadier General Doyle Hickey. Neither was aware that this area was no longer in their corps or theirs to defend. Hickey, calmly puffing on his pipe, was telling Richardson of the 3rd Armored Division plan of defense when a colonel wearing a 7th Armored Division patch drove up.

The newcomer told Hickey he had just been given the job of defending all the territory around Manhay. Pointing to an overlay he showed the puzzled Richardson and Hickey that the 7th Armored now controlled the area a mile to the west as far as the village of Grandmenil, east as far as Malempré, and south to Belle Haie. (He as yet knew nothing of Ridgway's recent order to withdraw to Manhay.)

Both Hickey and Richardson were unfavorably impressed by the 7th Armored colonel. He didn't seem to be at all worried about the Belle Haie roadblock four miles to the south. And Brewster's safety would depend on his decisions.

Hickey got into his jeep, still unable to believe such an unrealistic corps line had been drawn. "I'm going to check with General Rose," he said, and left.

Half an hour later he was back. "I met General Rose near Grandmenil," he told Richardson. "That 7th Armored colonel is right. This is his territory."

The two men walked across the street to a stone house, the command post of the 7th Armored colonel. "Where do you intend to defend?" Hickey asked him.

"I like the hills north of Manhay," said the colonel.

Hickey, angered by his apparently bored, complacent attitude, pointed to the high ground south of Manhay, and said curtly, "*That* will have to be defended by your people, Colonel. Otherwise Brewster at Belle Haie and Task Force Kane to his right will be exposed."

"Well, all right." The colonel was reluctant. "I'll send my tanks to those hills to the south."

Hickey, followed by Richardson, walked back to his jeep. He was still disturbed. "You work out detailed arrangements with him," he told Richardson. "But don't pull out Brewster until I give you the word."

"Brewster's awfully short of infantry. My whole task force is played out. The men are ready to drop."

"It doesn't make any difference," said Hickey, without removing his pipe. "General Rose just told me we were to hold at all costs."

"Do you mean all costs *regardless*?"

"I meant just what I told you."

"Yes, sir." Richardson turned and determinedly headed again for the 7th Armored command post.

The colonel, now sitting behind his desk reading *Stars and Stripes*, wasn't pleased to see Richardson.

"Are you sending your people to the high ground south of the village?" prodded Richardson.

"Of course I am," said the colonel irritably. At that moment 7th Armored tanks roared past the house, heading south.

"I'd suggest the change-over be made more quietly. If the Jerries hear your tanks cowboying like that into position, they'll attack."

"I know my own business. I'm not a damned bit interested in having some light colonel advise me. When I want advice I'll ask for it!"

Richardson turned and walked out. Manhay was going to catch hell—and so was Belle Haie.

5

Montgomery's car was just pulling up to Hodges' new command post in Tongres. In a few minutes he was telling the First Army commander of his withdrawal orders that morning to Ridgway. Then he offered the British 51st Highland Division as a backstop to Collins' corps.

"Collins' situation," he went on, "is very critical. And I very much fear we'll have to consider a general withdrawal."

He went to the big wall map and pointed to Andenne, a town on the Meuse thirty miles northwest of Marche. Then he pointed to Hotton, where the 3rd Armored Division had recently thrown back the 116th Panzer Division.

"If need be Collins can swing back his entire right flank on the Andenne-Hotton line."

Hodges was incredulous. Swinging back Collins' right flank 45 degrees to the north was like opening the door to the Germans advancing below Marche. "That will open the Meuse from Namur to Givet," he said.

"Don't worry," said Montgomery reassuringly. "British troops will be back there." Like many British, he considered the resistance of Americans to retreat an emotional approach to battle. "And let me say once more, I want Collins to avoid contact with the enemy as much as possible. I want Joe to keep backing off until the German has run his course. And then"—he drove his fist into the palm of his left hand—"attack."

When Montgomery left, Hodges and his staff mulled over the situation. Hodges had great respect for the Field Marshal but he didn't like fighting a battle by backing off. Neither would his generals—particularly Collins and Harmon.

A few minutes later, at 2:30 P.M. at the VII Corps command post, Collins' deputy, General Willie Palmer, was having a phone conversation with Harmon.

"One of my patrols," said the commander of the 2nd Armored Division excitedly, "just spotted Kraut tanks coiled up near Celles. Belgians say the Krauts are out of gas. They're sitting ducks. Let me take the bastards!"

Palmer was aware of Montgomery's warnings about avoiding contact with the advancing Germans. Collins would have to approve such a radical decision. "Joe is out visiting all his divisions. He's now on his way to your command post. Wait until you see him, Ernie."

A few minutes later Palmer's phone rang again. It was Harmon. *"We've got the whole damned 2nd Panzer Division in a sack!* You've got to give me immediate authority to attack!"

"Well," said Palmer slowly, "you can make preliminary preparations. But you've got to wait for Joe's final decision."

Twenty minutes later Palmer's phone rang. It was Kean, Hodges' chief of staff. To clarify the muddled state of affairs, Colonel "Red" Akers was on his way down with a verbal message to Collins. "Joe is authorized to change his defensive line," continued Kean guardedly. "Do you see a town A and a town H on the map?"

Palmer looked at his map. Instead of picking out Andenne and Hotton, he thought Kean was referring to two towns to the south. "Yes," he said. "I have them!"

"Those will be the new line."

Excitedly Palmer hung up, inferring that since the new line was south, Harmon was being allowed to attack. He dictated this information to Collins.

Not long after the message was dispatched, Palmer's phone rang again. It was Kean. "I've been thinking it over, Willie, and I doubt if you understand me. Now get this. I'm only going to say it once. *Roll with the punch.*"

Palmer, bitterly disappointed, hung up. If the VII Corps was to "roll with the punch," that meant a withdrawal. He looked again at the map and this time found Andenne. On a carbon copy of the previous message to Collins, he wrote in "Andenne," then added a note: "He meant pivot *back*. You can use Ernie any way you need but roll with the punch. . . . You better come home! P."

At the command post of the 2nd Armored Division, Collins had just received Palmer's first message permitting the assault on Celles. While he and Harmon were discussing details of the attack, the second message arrived. When Collins read the admonition to "roll with the punch" he groaned. It ruined all his plans.

"I've got to get back to my CP. I don't know what this whole thing is about yet." When he saw Harmon's face fall he added, "As of now we'll still attack. But hold things until I give you the final go-ahead."

The shadows of early dusk lengthened as Collins headed for his own command post. Soon he would have to make the most important decision of his career, a decision that might affect the outcome of the whole battle. The safest course would be to watch and wait. But if he waited, even a few hours, the 2nd Panzer tanks might sneak out of the trap or the 9th Panzer and Panzer Lehr, both pushing forward as fast as they could to reinforce this advance division, might join up and turn Harmon's attack into an American debacle.

When Collins reached his command post, Hodges' personal courier, "Red" Akers, was already there.

"You're authorized to pull back to the Andenne-Hotton line," Akers told him. "But this line has to be held at all costs."

Collins shook his head worriedly. "That will open up the whole road network west of Marche and give the Germans the Meuse from Givet to Namur!"

Akers repeated Montgomery's promise that British troops would be waiting on the other side of the river. Then he assured Collins that he had more latitude to use his own discretion than Kean's guarded telephone message implied.

But Collins remembered the celebrated case of von Moltke's courier, Lieutenant Colonel Hentsch, at the First Battle of the Marne in 1914. Hensch, like Akers, had carried a verbal message to von Kluck. The latter, misinterpreting the message, had retreated, saving the French from probable annihilation. Von Kluck, because he hadn't insisted on written orders, had been blamed for the classic mistake.

Collins was determined not to make the same mistake. He turned to Akers and said, "I want you to dictate a written statement." A few minutes later he was handed a document signed by Akers:

> For the time being, the VII Corps is released from all offensive missions and will go on the defensive with the objective of stabilizing the right flank of First U.S. Army. Commanding General, VII Corps, is hereby authorized to use all forces at his disposal to accomplish this job. Commanding General, VII Corps, is authorized, whenever in his opinion he considers it necessary, to drop back to the general line: Andenne-Hotton-Manhay.

Collins read the statement carefully, and then discussed it with his staff. Several thought it was an invitation to attack, others that it implied only defensive action.

Collins studied the message again. Apparently he could make either choice. He knew no one could criticize him if he went on the defensive. But if he attacked and failed, his army career could be ruined. It was the biggest gamble of his life.

He stopped the heated discussion. "I've made up my mind."

The others, the great majority in favor of attack, leaned forward expectantly.

"We'll proceed with the attack on the 2nd Armored." He turned to Akers. "I want you to tell General Hodges this decision is entirely mine. I'll take all responsibility."

A call was put through to Harmon. In double-talk Collins told him to attack Celles in the morning.

There was a roar of delight from the other end of the line. "The bastards are in the bag," shouted Harmon. "In the bag!"

6

The spearhead of the 2nd Panzer Division was at Celles. But the rear echelon was billeted many miles to the east in Bande, six miles southeast of Marche.

Sitting on a hillside overlooking the Bastogne-Marche highway, Bande was an ordinary-looking village. It had been a center of resistance during the occupation. In reprisal the houses located along the main highway were burned down. Before further reprisals could be taken, Hodges' First Army had liberated Belgium.

The Abbé Jean-Baptiste Musty and his young students of the Bastogne seminary were also in Bande, trapped there two days before by the 2nd Panzer advance to the Meuse. Ever since he had finished celebrating high mass at the village church late that morning, Musty had been trying to find four of his charges. During mass the four young philosophy students and sixty-six other boys and men of the village had been rounded up by Gestapo agents and taken to the Rulkin sawmill located on the main highway.

Wehrmacht and even SS officers billeted in the village had protested, asking the men wearing the black and white patch of the SD (the Security Service of the SS) what they intended to do. But it was obvious these were special troops of Himmler come to exact reprisals.

Musty walked down the hill from the main village to the section of burned-out houses which lined both sides of the highway, and approached an SD officer.

"Pfaffe," shouted the officer, pulling out a pistol. "Get out of here and fast, you black soul!"

Musty sadly walked back up the hill to the main part of town. Mme. René Tournay, wife of a Bande innkeeper, passed Musty carrying two overcoats. She went to the Rulkin sawmill, for she was sure the seventy men and boys were going to be sent to Germany as slave laborers.

An officer stopped her, promising to give the coats to her husband and the son of their landlord. "Get me some cognac," he demanded. When she protested she had none, he laughed. "People like you always have cognac hidden somewhere. I know, I'm in the Gestapo."

Mme. Tournay hurried to the upper town, soon returning with three bottles of champagne. "Won't you also free my nephew, Xavier Tournay?"

"People don't bargain with me," said the officer angrily. "I'm not a Jew."

Inside the sawmill another officer had just learned one of his prisoners, Armand Toussaint, was a farmer. "Farmers always have wine," said the officer. "We need some for our Christmas celebration. If you bring me twenty bottles I'll free you and your son."

Toussaint hurried to his farm. While he was collecting the wine, a Wehrmacht officer billeted in the house stopped him. "Don't go back to the sawmill," warned the officer. "Let me go. I'll fix things up."

The German officer left, but returned in a few minutes, dejected. "There's nothing I can do for you, monsieur," he said sadly. "Those people down there are strangers. You'd better take them the wine."

Toussaint returned to the sawmill with the wine. To his amazement, he and his son were freed. But the other men were divided into two groups. The older men were left in the mill. The young men were marched to the rear of the Rulkin house and lined up in three rows. There were thirty-three.

Guards went from man to man taking all possessions: watches, money, pocketbooks, handkerchiefs, and rosaries. The prisoners were ordered to raise arms over head and cross them. Then they were marched down the main highway to the Café de la Poste. They were lined up again in three rows, facing the highway. Six soldiers guarded the prisoners while an officer opened the door of the burned-out Bertrand home next to the café.

Heavy flakes of snow began to fall slowly, melting on the prisoners' faces, whitening their caps and bare heads. The day was dying fast.

A small middle-aged sergeant put his hand on the shoulder of the last man of the third row and led him to the Bertrand house. The other prisoners had no idea what was going on at their backs. Then there was a shot.

The sergeant returned, tapping the next man. Soon there was a second shot. Now the men lined up knew they were being murdered one by one.

"Let's try and escape," whispered Leon Praile, a tall well-built young Belgian of twenty-one. "We'll attack the guards. It's our only chance."

No one answered.

Praile turned and saw the sergeant leading one of his neighbors through the doorway of the Bertrand house. The SD officer grabbed the Belgian, brought up a machine pistol, and shot him in the neck. Then with his knee he kicked him into the yawning wreckage of the cellar.

Praile, the twenty-first, felt a hand on his shoulder. He saw the sergeant was crying. As the two neared the doorway Praile suddenly hit the German in the face, knocking him to the ground. He ran up the highway thirty yards, then darted to the right across the road, jumped the hedge, and waded across a stream. He disappeared into the dusk safely.

On the highway the massacre was continuing. Soon thirty-two bodies sprawled in the Bertrand cellar. Several still moved. The SD officer emptied the clip of his machine pistol into the writhing mass. Then there was no movement.

As snow began to cover the bodies, the six guards went from house to house ripping up planks. As they were piling three layers over the human mound, an SS officer, Lieutenant Spaan, passed. He was on an errand of mercy. Billeted at the Godfrainds' in the main part of Bande, he was trying to free his host who had been arrested that noon. He saw the gruesome tidying up in the cellar, and wisely looked away.

At the sawmill he pleaded with the SD men for the third time that afternoon. They indifferently brought out Godfraind and told Spaan to take him home for Christmas.

"Be happy your husband is alive," Spaan told Mme. Godfraind a few minutes later, then added, "I am very sad." His comrades called out, asking him to join their Christmas celebrations. But Spaan shook his head and slowly walked to his room.

About eight miles to the east, Spaan's Army commander, Hasso von Manteuffel, was holding a phone conversation at a chateau near La Roche. He was talking to Jodl at the Führer's headquarters.

"Time is running short," said the little general in his clipped accent. "Brandenberger's Seventh Army isn't far enough forward to cover my left flank. I expect a heavy Allied attack any moment from the south. You've got to let me know this evening what the Führer wants. The time has come for a complete new plan. I can't keep driving toward the Meuse and still take Bastogne."

"The Führer won't like this news," said Jodl anxiously.

"It's the damn truth," said Manteuffel brusquely. "The most we can do is reach the Meuse. We've been delayed too long at Bastogne. Anyone can see the Seventh Army is too weak to hold off a heavy attack from the south. Besides, by this time the Allies are sure to be on the other side of the Meuse in strength."

"But the Führer will never give up the drive to Antwerp."

There was still a chance for a great victory, Manteuffel said, *if* they would follow his plan. "I'll wheel north, on this side of the Meuse. We'll trap all Allies east of the river."

Jodl was shocked at the proposal.

"Give me reserves and I'll take Bastogne, reach the Meuse, and swing north."

"Well," said Jodl slowly, "I'll speak to the Führer."

"Now. Every minute counts. If I swing north fast, the plan will work. If we wait, the American VII Corps will have time to prepare."

"Be assured, my dear Manteuffel," was the answer, "the Führer will be told immediately."

Manteuffel hung up. A shell exploded near the chateau. Another came closer. He walked down into the cellar, joining the rest of his staff. Everyone was sitting on the floor in dejection.

7

At Manhay, Walter Richardson, the lieutenant colonel from Texas, was at a highway bridge a few hundred yards south of the crossroad, supervising the placing of demolitions.

His jeep driver ran up. "Colonel! I think the 7th Armored people are pulling out."

"They can't. They haven't said anything to me about it."

"Well, sir, they are!"

Now Richardson could hear the faint noise of motors as retreating American trucks and tanks approached from the darkness. He hurried back to the crossroad. In front of the 7th Armored Division Command Post he met a captain.

"What's going on?" asked Richardson.

"We're moving out to the high ground north of Manhay."

Richardson, angry and worried, strode into the command post. The 7th Armored colonel was packing up papers.

"We'll lose everything if you pull out now," said Richardson.

The colonel explained curtly that he had just received orders from Ridgway to pull back. He was now forming a new defense line that ran east-west through Manhay.

Richardson exploded. "But that'll mean Brewster and all his people will be wiped out!"

The colonel, ignoring Richardson, went back to his packing.

Richardson hurried to his jeep, where Captain Maxwell, who had a platoon of light tanks at the crossroad, was waiting. "Notify Brewster over the radio that some changes are occurring. But he's to stand fast." Then Richardson made contact with Major Zech on his own jeep radio. As he was briefing Zech on the new situation, retreating 7th Armored tanks began coming in from the dark hills south of Manhay. "I'm afraid we're going to get an attack." The Germans usually attacked when they heard tanks moving at night. Tanks attracted tanks. "Contact General Hickey and inform him of the situation."

Richardson then found his artillery liaison officer and told him to have the 54th Field Artillery send a section of M-7s to the road west of Grandmenil to back him up.

The retreating traffic was getting heavier; a sense of desperation had seized many of the drivers; those behind wanted to move faster than those in front.

Richardson went back to the 7th Armored command post to make a last appeal. The house was empty. Even the copy of *Stars and Stripes* was gone. He ran back to his jeep, and reached General Hickey personally by radio.

After hearing the facts, Hickey paused a moment. Then he said placidly, "You will hold as long as you have anything to fight for, Rich. This word has come down from General Collins."

"Yes, sir." Richardson hung up and called Brewster. "Fight with everything at your disposal, Brew," he said.

"Enemy tanks are moving across the main road to my rear," reported Brewster. The Germans had circled around him, through Odeigne, and should soon be approaching Manhay. In addition to his other troubles his two radio sets were acting up. On one the receiver was dead and on the other the transmitter.

"Don't give an inch unless I approve it," said Richardson.

There was a pause as Brewster ran to the transmitter. "But Rich, the situation is hopeless!"

"I don't give a damn. You'll still have to fight."

Though Richardson had made many enemies in training, by now his men had learned he was a good man to have on their side. They had also learned he never gave an order thoughtlessly.

"Roger," said Brewster.

Within an hour the dark crossroad at Manhay was a scene of din and chaos. In addition to the 7th Armored, elements of General Bill Hoge's combat command were streaming in from the east.

Richardson now knew the Belle Haie roadblock was useless. He radioed Brewster to get out fast.

"It's about time," was the wry answer. "All my tanks have been knocked out except two Big Boys and one light."

"Try to get through the 82nd Airborne sector at Malempré." Richardson did not know that town was already in possession of the 2nd SS Panzer Division. "Do the best you can, Brew. Keep me posted as long as your radio works."

Shooting, getting louder every minute, burst from the woods less than a mile to the south as German tanks fired directly at the crossroad.

Snow began to fall in a red haze as 7th Armored tanks roared up the pitch-black road paying no attention to a shouting, gesticulating 7th Armored lieutenant colonel.

"What the hell's happening to your troops?" asked Richardson. According to plans, the 7th was supposed to form a defense on an east-west line through Manhay. But these tanks and half-tracks were speeding by so fast it was obvious they wouldn't stop for miles.

"We're not abandoning Manhay," said the harried 7th Armored officer. "We're going to reorganize!" He stepped onto the road waving his hands. A tank roared past. The retreat became even wilder as German tank fire blasted the roadside houses.

A 7th Armored captain ran up. "Jerry tanks and infantry are streaming up the highway!" he shouted, then ran to the north.

The other 7th Armored officer again tried to stop the wave. Then, in desperation, he jumped onto a passing vehicle.

Richardson and his few men were now the only ones not running. "Send your platoon over to Grandmenil," called Richardson to his light-tank commander, Captain Maxwell. "Warn Kane to get the hell out."

Maxwell sent five tanks to Grandmenil—a mile to the west—and then placed his own tank at the crossroad, to wait for orders.

Richardson was telephoning the demolition detail at the bridge at the southern outskirts. "Blow the bridge, Goddard," he ordered.

"I've been hit," reported the lieutenant in charge of the detail. "All my men are dead."

In the light of flares Richardson now saw the bridge. Crouched infantrymen, obviously German, were running across it. Then, to his horror, he saw a huge, low-slung Tiger suddenly swing onto the highway and sneak into the long line of retreating American vehicles. A second big tank, marked with crosses, joined the American column.

Richardson waved to the passing Americans, pointing at the German tanks. No one paid any attention to him. On the hill leading north the two Tigers suddenly swung slightly out of line and began raking the crowded American tanks and cars with their machine guns and 88s. Confusion became panic as American vehicles broke across the fields looking for safety.

In fifteen minutes Manhay was momentarily deserted except for Richardson and Maxwell. They found four Sherman tanks abandoned by the 7th Armored and climbed into one.

"Tigers!" shouted Richardson as a platoon of German tanks crept up the road toward him. In his ledger one Tiger equaled at least four Shermans.

Maxwell trained the Sherman's 76 on the leading German tank. Richardson fired although he knew a Tiger was usually vulnerable only between the wheels, at the ammo rack or the engine compartments. The round bounced harmlessly off the front of the oncoming tank.

It stopped, turret moving around looking through the dark for its attacker. Richardson loaded the 76 again. But the gun jammed. By now German flares lit up the crossroad. The Tiger's big gun slowly traversed toward Richardson's tank.

"Bail out," cried Richardson. He and Maxwell scrambled to the road just as their tank exploded. Rifle and machine-gun fire followed the two Americans as they piled into the back seat of Richardson's jeep.

The driver, Walker, dropped his rifle and stepped on the gas. Richardson and Maxwell, kneeling on the back seat, fired their carbines at two pursuing tanks. The jeep careened west, shielded by a curtain of gently falling snow.

Two minutes later it stopped where the first houses of Grandmenil clustered around a road branch. Richardson looked back through the snow at Manhay. Houses burned with a dull pink glow. Friendly shells from Erezée were exploding with flashes, made fantastic by the snow.

"Well, sir," said the jeep driver, "we got out of there just in time. But we lost *our* shirts and *your* cot."

"Not my safari cot!" Richardson groaned. Somehow this made him angrier than his near escape from death. He turned to his tank platoon leader. "Maxwell, you stay with one light tank. I'm going over and see Matt Kane."

He hurried up a dirt side road toward a stone house. This was the command post of Task Force Kane. A tall slender lieutenant colonel was sitting at a table in the kitchen, studying a scrap of map by the light of a coal-oil lamp.

A radio was playing music from the B.B.C.

"Hi, Rich, things are in a nice mess. I've lost complete contact with my people in the south."

Richardson leaned over the map. "No use both of us staying in this thing," he said. Kane had only a medical detachment and a few headquarters people in Grandmenil.

"I'm not leaving you here alone," said Kane.

"You're getting the hell out."

"I won't go."

"We agreed this afternoon," said Richardson, "that this was my pigeon. Now I'm telling you to get the hell out."

Kane reluctantly rose. "Well, Rich, you've got the command." He gathered his few possessions. "Good luck. See you." At the door he paused. "What a hell of a Christmas." Then he left.

Richardson noticed the music coming from the radio. Bing Crosby was singing "White Christmas." If he ever got out he'd never listen to that song again.

Richardson hurried back to the road branch. Maxwell pointed to a little rise. "I think Krauts are over there."

The deep rumble of motors came from the east. "Diesels. Sounds like two Krauts coming." Richardson ducked behind a house and ran to the next house. Then he heard a noise. Two forms came through the snow from the north. They were American tank destroyers.

"You belong to me," he called out. The lead destroyer leveled its gun at him. "Hey, don't shoot!"

It stopped. A young lieutenant in the turret cupped his hand and called, "I'm glad to see you."

"I'm taking you over. Put one into position over there." Richardson pointed. "Use the other as cover."

The noise of Diesels was louder but the swirling snow and wind made them seem to come from several directions at once. He saw a dim low silhouette coming across a field to the northeast. It moved so fast he was sure it was a Panther. The second tank destroyer, jockeying for a covering position, was unknowingly moving in that direction.

"Shoot at anything that moves," shouted Richardson to the lieutenant in the first destroyer. Then he rushed through the snow toward the second destroyer which was innocently heading for the Panther.

Bullets arched over Richardson's head from the ring turret of this tank destroyer. Fortunately the gunner couldn't shoot low enough because of the back deck.

"You damn fool, stop," shouted Richardson.

The tank destroyer slowly backed up; its commander, a young frightened lieutenant, hopped out. Richardson pointed to the field. "A Panther will be there any minute. Don't try to get him from the front. His sighting is a lot better than yours."

The lieutenant nodded excitedly, then ran back to his vehicle and climbed in. Richardson felt sorry for him. He'd have little chance against the Panther's deadly 75.

Far out in the field Richardson saw a dull glow. Something was burning—probably tanks from the 7th Armored Division. The two Tigers which had sneaked into their column must have scored heavily.

Walker ran up. "I just heard tanks from the southwest. And I think General Hickey's trying to get you on the radio."

"This is Five to Six." It was Brewster. In double-talk he said he'd left Belle Haie and headed northeast for Malempré which Richardson had assumed was still held by Ridgway's corps. He'd moved out with infantry in front and almost immediately had the tank covering the rear knocked out. Then at the edge of Malempré, another tank had been lost. He'd tried getting into town two different ways and lost two more tanks.

"This front is really fluid as a goose, Rich. They got my last Big Boy. What'll I do?"

"Use your own judgment, Brew. I'm for you. Walk out the best way you can. You've done enough."

"This is the last message you will receive from this station. Out."

Then another voice in stilted English came over the radio. "I know where you are. Your name is Richardson." The voice laughed. "We've known you for a long time. We're going to get the officer and men you were just talking to. Then we're going to get you, Richardson. You know what we'll do when we get you." The German laughed again.

"Go to hell, you Kraut bastard." Richardson turned off the radio. He'd known for a long time there was a price on his head for "atrocities." Atrocity meant you'd killed a lot of Jerries.

There was a blast to his left. He turned just in time to see the covering American tank destroyer fire a round into the side of an approaching Panther. The German, shrouded in smoke, suddenly flamed up.

There was a deeper blast. Richardson knew this came from a Panther 75. As the tank destroyer backed up frantically, there was a second 75 shot. The American vehicle flew apart with a tremendous detonation. Another Panther had sneaked down from the north and thrown a round into its ammunition rack.

The first American tank destroyer, the one in position, fired. The round hit the front plates of the Panther. Sparks flew but the Panther rolled forward. Its long 75 belched. The tank destroyer tipped over, smoking.

Richardson shouted to Maxwell at the road branch, "Get your tank back to Erezée as fast as you can!"

As Maxwell's light tank headed up the mountain road to the west, Richardson switched on his radio and made contact with Zech in Erezée.

"Give me all the artillery you can right on top of Grandmenil."

There was a pause as Zech relayed the message to Colonel Frederick Brown, Chief, 3rd Armored Division Field Artillery; then another pause as Brown passed a message to Richardson.

"Brown says it'll come right on your head," warned Zech.

"Tell Ted I might as well lose my head. I'm about to lose my ass." He turned to Walker who was sitting in the driver's seat. "Now it's time for us to get out of here. But go slow. We don't want to make any noise."

Walker cautiously guided the jeep onto the main highway. On all sides they could hear the deep roar of German tanks.

"Help is on the way," said Zech over the radio. "A column of 75th Division doughs. Be on the alert."

On the left the noise of approaching tanks quickly became deafening.

"Walker," shouted Richardson, "barrel-ass out of here!"

The tires screamed as the jeep jumped forward. Two Tigers swung onto the road and chased after them. Then came a terrifying series of overlapping explosions to the rear. Richardson turned. A TOT—a time-on-target—had landed on Grandmenil. The village was suddenly a shambles.

The jeep headed up the steep hill west of Grandmenil as machine-gun bullets from the Tigers spattered its rear. After half a mile it turned a sharp curve.

"Halt!" cried out a frightened voice.

The jeep stopped. Richardson saw a dozen infantrymen carrying bazookas. Behind them was a long line of riflemen.

An infantry lieutenant colonel trotted toward him.

"Get the hell off the road," said Richardson. "Kraut tanks coming! Put your bazooka teams in the ditch and your riflemen on the high ground to the right. The rest hold in reserve."

The infantry officer—a battalion commander of the brand-new 75th Division—nodded. "I'll take over now," he said excitedly.

Richardson waved, nudging Walker to move on. It was hard to imagine, but his job was over. From here in, it was up to the infantry. The jeep slowly climbed up the hill. Behind he heard the crump of bazookas.

The jeep stopped in front of a roadside house, regimental command post of the infantrymen. The guard at the door saluted sharply. Richardson winced. This was obviously their first day of battle. He reported to a colonel wearing pinks and a forest green blouse, his chest brilliant with medals from World War I. Richardson started to tell him the situation.

"Oh, never mind," said the other, "have a cup of coffee."

Richardson knew this was no place for him. He went back to his jeep and soon was in his own regimental command post at Erezée. He borrowed a sleeping bag, putting it on the floor next to an operating table.

He hadn't slept for three nights. He should have dropped off instantly but his mind was a whirlpool. He kept living over what had happened at Manhay, Belle Haie, and Grandmenil. He'd gone into the tangle with a complete battalion of tanks: 65 mediums and lights. He probably didn't have a dozen left.

He closed his eyes. What was happening on the road west of Grandmenil? Were those green 75th Division doughs holding? And what was happening to Brewster? He'd recommend him for a Silver Star.

Finally, exhausted, he fell asleep.

5. "IN THY DARK STREETS"

Christmas Eve—Christmas Day 1944

1

Bastogne was outwardly peaceful on Christmas Eve, but by now the men in the surrounded town had given themselves a new title: the Battered Bastards of the Bastion of Bastogne.

At his command post, General McAuliffe was talking to General Middleton on the phone. The strain of the past week was evident on his face. "The finest Christmas present the 101st could get," he was saying somberly, "would be a relief tomorrow."

"I know, boy," answered Middleton just as somberly, "I know."

The 3,500 civilians trapped in the town were trying to settle down in their cellars for another night. Hundreds were huddled on the damp floors of the great seminary cellar. The sisters of the clinic circulated in the flickering candlelight, trying to comfort the old people and the children. Living in the cellar on filthy mattresses, crowded but cold and infested by lice, was hardest on the old. Several had already died; several had gone mad; some were nearing the point of madness or were so petrified by fear they could no longer take care of personal needs. Carbolic acid, mixed with water, had been sprinkled around but it did little to counteract the nauseating stink of human excrement.

But the young people played cards, laughed, and joked. The older ones were now interrupting the games, telling the youngsters they had no right to be so flippant and ordering them to be quiet.

Suddenly the drone of planes drowned out the arguments. A stick of bombs dropped near the seminary. More bombs fell, even closer. The lamps and candles blacked out. Overhead came the thunder of falling timbers and stones. A snowstorm of dust filled the cellar.

An old man banged the sides of his bed, screaming wildly. Then he shook the bed next to him. A woman jumped up and grabbed the long hair of one of the sisters, screaming, "Let me out of here!"

This bombing was the worst. Soon dozens of buildings were burning. The improvised military hospital, hit directly, was a mass of debris. Volunteers were digging for the dead and dying patients entombed in the wreckage. The command post of Team Cherry was destroyed. Four junior officers—including two survivors of the Longvilly ambush, Captain Ryerson and Lieutenant Hyduke— were killed.

Fred MacKenzie, of the Buffalo *Evening News,* leaped up the steps leading from McAuliffe's underground command post as falling bombs seemed about to collapse the cellar. When he had been invited a short week ago to accompany the 101st Airborne to Bastogne for a story, he never dreamed it would be as an eye-witness to battle.

Ahead of him was Daniel Olney, the General's jeep driver. The little corporal's movements reminded MacKenzie of a fat wood-chuck hustling to his burrow. The reporter was seized in a spasm of laughter.

He went back into the command post. At the switchboard a soldier beat time with his feet as he hummed, off tune, "Santa Claus Is Coming to Town." He continued into the operations room.

Colonel Kinnard, looking too young for his rank, pulled a sheet of paper from a typewriter. "What do you think of my composition, Mac?" He handed the paper to the newsman. "It's a Christmas message to the men."

Merry Christmas!

What's merry about all this, you ask? We're fighting—it's cold—we aren't home. All true but what has the proud Eagle Division accomplished with its worthy comrades of the 10th Armored Division, the 705th Tank Battalion and all the rest? Just this: We have stopped cold everything that has been thrown at us from the North, East, South and West. . . .

Allied Troops are counterattacking in force. We continue to hold Bastogne. By holding Bastogne we assure the success of the Allied Armies. We know that our Division commander, General Taylor, will say: "Well Done!"

We are giving our country and our loved ones at home a worthy Christmas present and being privileged to take part in this gallant feat of arms are truly making for ourselves a merry Christmas.

MacKenzie looked down at Kinnard. "You should be a writing man," he said.

Kinnard smiled, pleased by praise from a professional. "Pretty good, huh?"

"Fine."

"We'll see what General McAuliffe thinks of it in the morning."

MacKenzie then noticed the situation map on the wall his friend from Buffalo, Danahy, had recently finished. It was an overlay in red and green. The red showed the enemy positions completely surrounding Bastogne. In green Danahy had scrawled across the defenders' positions, MERRY CHRISTMAS.

A few blocks away a soldiers' chorus was singing in the vaulted chapel of the Abbé Musty's great seminary. Soldiers and officers were standing in the transept. Slivers of bright moonlight filtered through holes in canvas covering broken stained-glass windows. Snow sifted through cracks as the men sang:

> O, little town of Bethlehem,
> How still we see thee lie.

Wounded, lying on the cold floors, wrapped only in colored parachutes from the supply drops, listened silently.

> Yet in thy dark streets shineth
> The everlasting light;
> The hopes and fears of all the years
> Are met in thee tonight.

There was a pause. Then the choir began singing, "Silent night, holy night." The wounded, covering the entire floor up to the altar, joined in.

There was an explosion in another part of town but the singing continued. Most of the men were thinking of Christmas at home.

In the foxholes surrounding Bastogne in a great wavering line, the "Battered Bastards" felt a solemnness that midnight. The hard-boiled joking stopped. There was no bravado. Men silently shook hands. Many felt this was going to be their last night.

2

On the northern shoulder of the front at Malmédy, Christmas Eve was being celebrated in many strange ways.

An American truck loaded with presents was just driving up to the civilian hospital. The GIs had given up their own Red Cross Christmas presents in token of their sorrow for the hundreds of civilians killed in the accidental bombing of Malmédy that after-noon by the U.S. Ninth Air Force—the second in two days.

An officer and four men brought the presents into the hospital. The children, delighted, clapped their hands; the sisters, smiling broadly, tried to express their thanks in German and French.

The five Americans were led to a room lit only by candles. In the center was a large table covered with a white cloth. The sisters knelt around the table—then, in German, softly sang "Silent Night."

There were tears in the eyes of the Americans.

Two Germans—Skorzeny's men—were creeping across the snowy wastes that lay between Ligneuville and Malmédy. They were volunteers trying to recover Germans killed in the fruitless attack of December 21.

The two men silently moved onto the battlefield. It was dotted with snowy mounds. They tried to lift a dead comrade, but his body was frozen to the ground. The men pulled out trench knives and dug out the body. They lifted their heavy stiff burden and brought it to a jeep hidden behind a hill. They returned for another, then another and another, always getting closer to the American lines.

The battlefield was quiet, as if in tribute to the Holy Night, but the two men were afraid that gunfire would soon light up their work. They picked up a body. Just as they were starting for the rear again, they heard a crunching noise—someone walking over the snow toward them. Rooted by terror, they stood like statues, clinging to the frozen body.

The noise came closer. Dark figures approached from nowhere. The two men suddenly stared into the surprised faces of an American patrol. The Germans waited silently, expecting to be shot. The Americans, only a few feet away, turned and passed on as if they were good householders merely checking to see if the front door was locked.

The two men felt an overwhelming sense of brotherhood with the Americans who had just passed. They carried their comrade to the jeep and headed for Ligneuville. As they left, a grenade, shot from an American rifle, lofted harmlessly into the air, a salute fired by an honor guard.

3

In Germany there were many celebrations.

Colonel Descheneaux, commander of the captured 422d Regiment of the 106th Division, was brought from his tiny cell in an ancient castle and lined up with other American officers.

"Because I ordered you from Limburg, you men were spared from yesterday's terror raid by your Air Force," said the castle commandant. "The building you left was hit. Fifty American officers were killed by Allied bombs." A bugler came forward and played taps. Then Red Cross packages were handed to each of the Americans and Descheneaux, as senior officer, read a few passages from the Bible. The prisoners were returned to their 6' x 8' cells.

Descheneaux examined his Number 10 package. There were six packs of cigarettes—priceless for exchange—sugar, powdered milk, oleo, jelly, K-2 biscuits, Spam, corned beef, pâté, salmon, raisins, 4 bars of chocolate, and cheese. He fingered each treasure.

He prayed that his wife Betty and his daughter Joey were happy and comfortable far off in Maine. He prayed they wouldn't find out about his capture until after the holidays. Then in the dim light he looked and looked at their pictures.

Alan Jones, Jr., now wearing a tattered French overcoat and cap, was in a locked boxcar. It was so cold the bars of the one tiny window were covered with ice. As yet the Germans hadn't discovered he was the son of the division commander. But he was worried more about his father than himself. A rumor had swept the train that the General had been captured and killed.

Fifty others were crammed in the barren car. For two days they had had no food or water. Most of the men were also from the 106th Division, and except for grousing about food and water and the cold, the talk had been of the battle on the Schnee Eifel.

It had been bitter, violent talk. The men felt they had been forgotten. The promised supply drops had never come. The surrender itself was bitterly discussed. Many of the men could see no reason for it. They had given up without a fight. What would the people back home think? There was ugly talk about Cavender and Descheneaux.

Probably the unhappiest was a man in a fur-collared flight jacket who sat by himself in a corner. He was an air force pilot who had come up to the 423rd the day before the battle to visit his brother, a GI.

"Captured as a damned infantryman," he kept saying. He considered his mates in the boxcar as accomplices in the greatest atrocity of the war, his capture.

Suddenly there was a drone overhead—American bombers. Now came the warning whistles of falling bombs. Then shattering explosions. The boxcar shook. The fifty men in the locked car were terrified.

"Let's sing," said someone in a quavering voice. The men got half through "Jingle Bells," then other bombs whistled down. The singing stopped abruptly.

"My God, let's pray," said someone.

A bomb landed with a thud right beside the car. It did not explode.

4

At 1:00 A.M., Christmas morning, a strange double military action was taking place in the northern part of the Ardennes. Both sides were falling back.

Following Montgomery's order to "tidy" up, "Slim Jim" Gavin's spirited 82nd Airborne Division was withdrawing north to the Trois

Ponts-Manhay highway. As Gavin went from unit to unit, he was amazed to find that though the move irritated these men who never before had taken a backward step in battle, they were as aggressive and confident as ever.

And coming south across that same road was another unit aggressive even in retreat, Kampfgruppe Peiper. Before dawn of December 24, Peiper had led his 800 men and the captured American, Major Hal McCown, out of La Gleize. Behind, true to his promise, Peiper had left the 130 American prisoners. He also had left in the gutted village all his own fuelless vehicles, smoldering tombstones to the drive to the Meuse.

As Kampfgruppe Peiper slowly plodded over a wooded hill, McCown felt he couldn't go much farther. They must have already traveled twenty miles since leaving La Gleize and he'd eaten only four small biscuits and two swallows of cognac. He staggered. The regimental surgeon handed him a piece of Charms candy. The sugar gave him renewed strength.

Several hours previously Colonel Peiper had left the column with some of his staff. The main group was now led by a young captain who marched without a break. Peiper had stopped the column every hour and solicitously checked the men. The new leader exhorted the men to greater effort, laughing at any show of weakness.

McCown, carrying only an empty canteen, didn't know how the men with heavy packs and mortars managed to keep up the pace over the rugged terrain. One man dropped to his knees, exhausted.

"If you fall behind, you'll be shot," warned an officer.

The man crawled on his hands and knees.

Several times that dark night there had been brushes with Americans. The wounded from these fights were supported by comrades over the steep snowy trail.

Artillery fire began falling several hundred yards to the south in front of the column. The men stopped, puzzled, little realizing that this came from the 82nd Airborne Division, withdrawing toward them.

Suddenly small-arms firing broke out. Tracer bullets flashed overhead. McCown dropped to the snow. Machine-gun bullets chopped down the nearby trees. Then mortar began falling. Commands in German and English seemed to come from all sides.

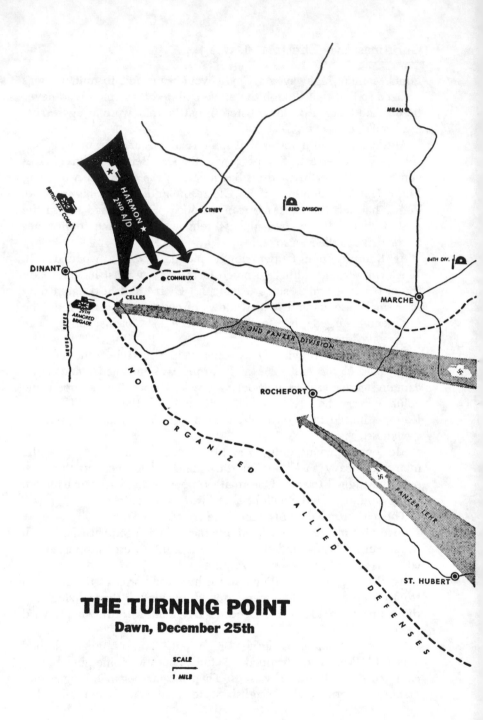

MEAN

83RD DIVISION

84TH DIV.

BRITISH XXX CORPS

HARMON 2ND A/D

CINEY

DINANT

CONNEUX

CELLES

MARCHE

29TH ARMORED BRIGADE

2ND PANZER DIVISION

ROCHEFORT

NO ORGANIZED

PANZER LEHR

ALLIED

ST. HUBERT

DEFENSES

THE TURNING POINT
Dawn, December 25th

SCALE

1 MILE

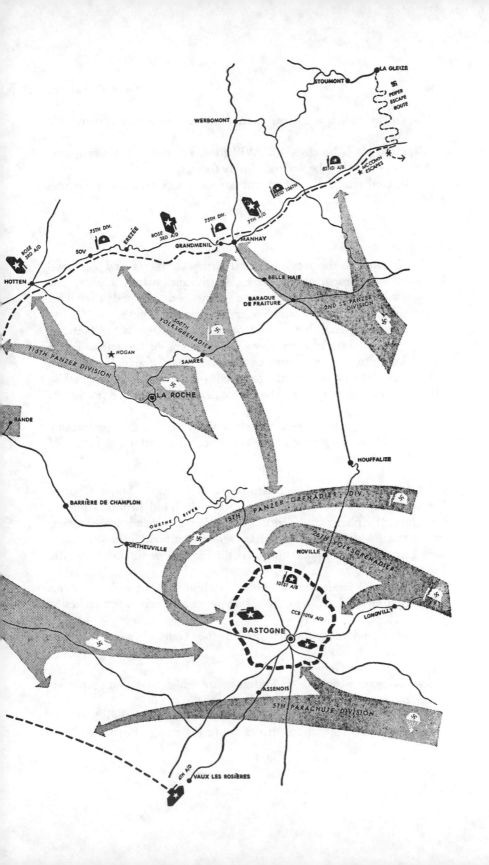

McCown lay still a moment, then crawled cautiously toward the American fire.

After 100 yards he stood up. Whistling a popular American song as loudly as possible, he walked slowly forward.

"Halt, God damn it!" called out a voice. McCown knew he was safe.

5

Forty air miles to the west, General Ernie Harmon's 2nd Armored Division was preparing to strike south and attack Celles, the village where Marthe Monrique's story had stopped the Nazi spearhead the day before only five miles from the Meuse.

As Harmon's men rolled down toward the great pocket of German tanks, the American tankers knew the outcome of the entire battle might be riding in their turrets. Several miles above Celles, one column swung east of the village to cut off a possible retreat while other columns converged on the German pocket from the northwest and north.

At first light of day the tip end of the Bulge began to tremble from a great far-flung tank battle that could determine the future of "Watch on the Rhine."

Later that morning, Omar Bradley and his aide, Major Chester Hansen, were en route to Montgomery's Holland headquarters in the General's plane, the *Mary Q.* Bradley's mission was to persuade the Field Marshal to start a general attack from the north and take the heavy pressure off the southern shoulder of the Bulge.

The *Mary Q* landed at St. Trond, Belgium. It was almost noon when Bradley and Hansen, in a borrowed staff car, approached a Dutch village.

"What's happening today?" asked the General when he saw gaily dressed Hollanders.

"It's Christmas, General."

Soon he was in the modest Dutch house which was Montgomery's command post. The Field Marshal was most cordial.

"I hope I can get to Bastogne," said Bradley after they had discussed the general situation. "But I doubt if I can go farther without replacements." He hoped that Montgomery would soon join the Third Army attack with one from the north.

"At the moment," said Montgomery, "I simply can't pass over to the offensive. There will be at least one more enemy blow on my flank. When the German has exhausted himself, then I'll attack."

There was nothing more Bradley could do. He stood up. The two parted as cordially as they had greeted.

Deeply disappointed, Bradley and Hansen started on the long dangerous trip down to Luxembourg City.

6

It was a bleak Christmas for American prisoners. Not long after noon a long line of men captured in the Ardennes curved up a snow-covered hill deep in Germany. Near the head of the column was Colonel Hurley Fuller.

There had been no system of march and halt—just a steady grueling trudging ahead. The Americans, weak from hunger and exhaustion, had difficulty keeping in the line of march. Men from the rear kept shouting to slow down but the German guards pressed on. Word was passed to Fuller that several prisoners had fallen by the side, unable to keep moving, and had been shot. Even those who stopped to relieve themselves were bayoneted in the buttocks as they squatted.

"I'm going to halt the column," Fuller told the other officers. He turned around, held up both hands, and shouted, "Halt! Fall out on the right."

The order was passed on down the long line. The flustered German guards didn't know what to do.

"We're taking a ten-minute break," said Fuller, as if he were still commanding his own regiment.

The guards, completely confused, talked excitedly as the entire column fell out. Three German officers, who had been several hundred yards ahead of the column, ran back.

Fuller was leaning lazily against a snowbank.

The officer in charge of the march, a major, shouted a command in German. An American private came up to Fuller. "Sir, he says he's going to shoot you!"

"Tell him we're exhausted." Fuller, settling deeper in the snow-bank, looked up at the infuriated major. "Tell him that if he'll let me control the march, we can make better time and maintain better discipline."

As this was translated, the major's eyes widened with astonishment. He advanced angrily. Fuller merely stared at him.

"Verrückte Amerikaner!" cried the major, waving his arms. He spoke rapidly to the American private, then in disgust walked away.

The GI looked at Fuller in amazement. "Colonel, he said *you're* in charge!"

Fuller, pleased that the march would now be run properly, stood up. "All right, men, fall in."

The prisoners were lining up when the German major returned with a small but heavy suitcase and handed it to the nearest American. As the march progressed, Fuller noticed the suitcase being passed from prisoner to prisoner. It would wind up at the end of the line.

An hour later Fuller stopped the column for another break. Soon an excited guard led a GI to the head of the column. The GI was carrying the suitcase. It hung open, empty.

The German major hurried up. Shouting angrily, he struck the American in the face with his riding crop.

Fuller caught the major's arm.

"He claims the American soldier stole everything," said the interpreter.

"What was in the suitcase?" asked Fuller.

"Cheese and butter."

Fuller laughed.

The major's face turned red. He raised the riding crop as if to strike Fuller, then suddenly burst out laughing and threw the empty suitcase into a snowbank.

Not far away Major Don Boyer was being interviewed in a German village. Boyer kept repeating his name, rank, and serial number.

His interrogator was exasperated but not angry. "But I know you're in the 38th Armored Infantry Battalion of the 7th Armored Division. Why don't you admit it?" When Boyer said nothing the German offered him coffee and cake.

Boyer refused for fear the food might be drugged.

The German was disgusted. "Ach, you and your damned 7th Armored Division! If it hadn't been for you, we'd be in Liége tonight. Take him away."

A tall SS officer pointed at Boyer's galoshes. "Take them off," he ordered.

"No."

"We don't have to treat you as a prisoner until your Red Cross card is dispatched. Now take them off."

Boyer shook his head stubbornly. The officer shouted a command. A bayonet was jabbed in Boyer's back. Then the officer struck him in the face. Boyer fell. He was picked up, knocked down again.

"Now will you give me the galoshes?"

Boyer tried to say "No," but no word came out. Soldiers pulled off the galoshes. Two GIs picked Boyer up and helped him into a nearby church. They laid him on a pew, a prisoner but still at war.

7

In an Ardennes chateau near La Roche, Hasso von Manteuffel was eating his Christmas dinner—American K-rations. Just a year ago he had spent the holidays in luxury as the Führer's house guest.

He was talking with Major Johann-Mayer, Hitler's adjutant, rushed to La Roche because of the phone call to Jodl the night before. Manteuffel brusquely reviewed the Fifth Panzer Army situation. The 2nd Panzer Division was cut off by Harmon's 2nd Armored Division. Two units were rushing to the rescue—the 9th Panzer from the west and Panzer Lehr from the southwest—but the prospects were not bright.

"The drive to Antwerp must be abandoned at once," he continued. If Hitler gave his immediate permission, the Fifth Panzer Army could wheel north and still trap the Allies east of the Meuse. It would be a great victory, but time was running out.

Johann-Mayer, convinced by Manteuffel's arguments, telephoned Jodl at the Führer's headquarters, and gave his personal estimate of the situation. Johann-Mayer then handed the phone to Manteuffel.

"The Führer hasn't made his decision yet," Jodl told the Baron.

"But you know a decision has to be made now or it may be too late." Manteuffel made no attempt to hide his anger. "What's more I need immediate replacements."

"I can only give you one more armored division," said Jodl. "And remember the Führer doesn't want you to move back one foot. Go forward! Not back!"

Manteuffel banged down the receiver.

8

Less than five miles north of Manteuffel's chateau, "Hogan's 400," surrounded in Marcouray, were also eating a Christmas dinner of K-rations.

There was no panic. Hogan's easygoing confidence had permeated down to the last man. But their situation was now hopeless. The sorely needed plasma and bandages shot in by American artillery had landed on target two days ago, but the distance had been so great the contents of the shells had been pulverized. And yesterday the air drop had failed. As the flight of C-47s was dispersed by German anti-aircraft located in nearby La Roche, the supply parachutes drifted far from Marcouray. Later in the day, a German jeep flying a white flag had come into Hogan's lines with a demand for surrender. The Texas colonel was told he was surrounded by three divisions. If he doubted it, he or any other officer would be taken on a tour of the German lines.

"We have orders to fight to the death," said Hogan. "Since I'm a soldier I will obey orders. Tell your commander to go to hell."

Not long after the austere Christmas dinner, Hogan received a radio message from his division commander, General Maurice Rose: "Destroy equipment and make your way out as best as you can. Good luck."

Hogan knew they'd certainly need it. But he didn't pass on his doubts. He ordered the men to drain oil from the motors of their vehicles and put sugar in the gas tanks. Then a few at a time, so that the Germans wouldn't guess what was happening, motors were started and run until they froze. The weapons were also destroyed, the breachblocks dropped into wells.

There were still three problems: the wounded, the prisoners, and the two Germans shot in the back of the head.

Captain Louis Spiegelman, the battalion surgeon, volunteered to stay with the wounded; the two murdered Germans were buried in the frozen earth under a rosebush. Then the fate of the prisoners was debated. Hogan hated to turn them loose so that they could fight again. "On the other hand," he added, "this is hardly the appropriate time or place to knock them off. Pretty soon we all might be prisoners ourselves." He decided to have the walking wounded guard the prisoners until the column escaped from town, then free them.

It was deep dusk when he radioed a résumé of the plan to his combat commander. A moment later came the answer: "Wait."

Hogan tried again and got the same answer. As he was about to order the radio destroyed a message started: "Paratrooper patrol will attempt to meet you and guide you through the lines. Password for tonight, FINAL. Countersign, EDITION."

At 6:30 P.M. it was dark enough to leave. Hogan ordered the men to ditch helmets and other noisy equipment, and to blacken their faces with burnt corks. Then the column quietly headed out the northern end of town. Phil De Orio, Hogan's orderly, formerly bell captain at the Algonquin, New York City's famous theatrical hotel, suddenly had a pang of remorse. He had purposely left Hogan's prize possession, a rubber mattress, in the cellar of the command post because he was tired of inflating it. He ran back to the cellar, folded the mattress, and stuffed it in his belt. He would give it to the Colonel, wrapped up as a surprise Christmas present.

Hogan said good-bye to Captain Spiegelman and the wounded. Then, as he fell in at the end of the long column, he heard the deep roar of a Diesel motor. A German tank was coming. A rocket crashed into the center of the village. "Hogan's 400," with Hogan at the tail end, ran into the woods.

Fifteen miles north, a major of Hogan's division, with torn uniform and haggard face, was just stepping into General Rose's command post at Barvaux. It was Olin Brewster. The past twenty-four hours, most of them spent at the Belle Haie roadblock defending Manhay, had been the roughest in his army career. He'd had to burn up the last of his few tanks and vehicles and filter through the enemy lines on foot. But he had saved every man.

He went into the office of the operations officer. Colonel Sweat looked at the grubby tattered figure. "My God, Brew, we thought you were dead!"

A few minutes later Brewster entered General Rose's office. Rose, immaculate in riding breeches and shiny boots, looked across his desk. His handsome face stern, he said, "What happened?"

Brewster, startled by the cool manner, told of his fight at Belle

Haie, the escape to Malempré, and the final decision to burn up his last few vehicles.

Rose, an aggressive commander of great personal courage, insisted on the same qualities in his subordinates. "Why did you destroy government equipment?"

"Sir, I felt sure I could return a good group of trained men to fight again. I felt we couldn't have fought our way out."

Rose's face was accusing. "Major, I call that misbehavior."

Brewster, stunned, automatically walked out of the room. He headed toward the mess hall, for the hot Christmas turkey dinner he had been dreaming about all day. He was served Spam.

Brewster's battalion commander, Walter Richardson, was just then crawling into his sleeping bag.

"Hey, Rich," called someone, "the General wants to see you on the double at Barvaux."

As Richardson was driven over the dark road to the division command post, he guessed that Rose either wanted him to launch a new attack or give him a personal commendation for the action at Manhay and Grandmenil. As he passed through the hallway of Rose's command post, several staff officers averted their eyes.

"Rich, the General wants to see you," said a staff officer in an official tone. Now he knew he was in hot water.

He walked into Rose's inner office. The General, behind his desk reading documents, silently waved him to a seat. When Richardson sat down, a glaring white light hanging from the ceiling struck him full in the face. This was like the third degree. He felt a surge of resentment.

A staff officer, taking notes, didn't look up but muttered, like a ventriloquist, "Hello, Rich."

Rose looked up and said in a cold tone, "I understand Brewster walked out and left a lot of your equipment. And I understand you lost a lot more. Now I want the answer."

Richardson controlled himself. "I told Brewster to leave his stuff and get out with his men. It was *my* order. I was more concerned for the lives of the men. He'd put up a helluva fight and I told him just to do the best he could." He stared at Rose.

"What about those abandoned tanks on the hill north of Manhay?"

"Those were 7th Armored tanks, sir." He told tersely about the 7th Armored colonel at the crossroad.

Rose's face began to thaw. "Oh, yes. Hickey gave me a rundown on him. I told Bob Hasbrouck and he assured me in no uncertain terms that he'd take care of that colonel." He looked at Richardson and almost smiled. "I believe I have a better picture now."

Richardson saluted and left. The staff officers in the outer office were now eager to talk, but he angrily brushed past them.

In his office, General Rose was dictating to a staff officer. "Prepare the papers," he said. "I want Brewster court-martialed for cowardice."

9

Twenty-five miles to the east, Christmas was drawing to a close in Malmédy. Men of the 30th Division and civilians were digging for survivors of another friendly bombing—for the third day in a row.

6. "WE CANNOT FORCE THE MEUSE"

26 December 1944

1

Midnight of December 25 was bitter cold. Several miles northwest of Marche the winter moon cast a bright light on the Chateau of Verdenne. Hoar frost glistened on a knocked-out Panther sitting near the iron gates. The second Christmas holiday was beginning with a rare silence.

In the great cellar of the chateau, its owner, a Belgian with Polish ancestors, the Baron Charles de Radzitsky d'Ostrowick, his daughter, fifteen refugees from the town, and thirteen tankers of the famed Greyhound Division, the 116th Panzer, sat in the light of a single candle. One of the tankers, wounded painfully in the right leg, asked for water.

"Aren't you going to get him any?" finally asked the Baron.

The other tankers, dazed by the bitter fighting since Christmas Eve, didn't answer. They didn't know whether Germans or GIs held the upper floors. The Baron picked up a bucket and started up the stairs. No one stopped him. Two days before, as he was preparing a Christmas party for the GIs of the 84th Division billeted in the village, firing had suddenly broken out and he was told to hide in the cellar. Since then the chateau had changed hands five times.

The Baron stepped into the great hallway. Moonlight streamed through a jagged hole in the ceiling. The stately main room was chaotic. Priceless pictures lay on the floor smashed; bullet holes pocked the walls; furniture passed down for generations was heaped in broken piles. The billiard table, legs sawed off, stood in the middle of the room, its green cloth matted with blood. A few operating tools, with dark red stains, were scattered at one end.

Dead eyes looked at the Baron from the floor. It was a German. Near him lay an American, fists clenched, a blank look on his face. The dead held the upper floor.

The Baron sickened as he stepped over the debris to the door. Here thirty bodies—American and German—were stacked as if for future reference. He picked his way through the human refuse to the courtyard. Outside, bodies were so thick he climbed onto a wall. He had to stop, vomit. Then he went on, found water, and returned to the safety of the cellar.

Two miles northwest of the chateau, Company A of the 233rd Infantry Regiment of the 84th Division was marching briskly out of a large communal barn. The men were griping. Their long-awaited Christmas dinner had still not arrived. The latest rumor was that the Krauts had made a daring morning raid on Marche and stolen all the turkeys.

The column stopped. "All right," said a platoon leader nick-named Rabbit, "We're going to attack. Get rid of overcoats and overshoes."

Private John Shaw, son of a professor of music, carefully hid his coat and galoshes under a bush. Like others in his division he'd been in combat only a month but he knew from hard experience the value of warmth after battle. He carefully noted the bush.

Shaw adjusted his glasses, and then joined the men marching across a railroad track up a small hill. It was a bitter night and he soon regretted giving up the coat. It was unreal, marching in the bright moonlight, across the gleaming white countryside. Since mid-afternoon they had been rushed from one place to another, given a dozen different orders.

They followed a dirt road to a thick woods. Silent men from an-other company watched, with a pleased expression, as Company A passed through their ranks. Not a word was spoken but Company A knew they were thinking, "Better them than us."

Ahead were gently rolling, snow-covered fields. Shaw could now see a group of houses, blacked out but glistening in the moonlight. It was eerie. He was afraid. He passed a burned-out tank, menacing even in death. The column turned left. Suddenly a wall loomed ahead, and behind it was the dark ominous shadow of a stately chateau.

There was a whispered order. The men sat down in a long line while a tiny group of officers huddled in conference. Shaw wondered if they had any idea what they were conferring about. He pulled out a box of K-rations and opened it with a knife.

Then without orders many started firing at the blank wall. Shaw, flattening himself on the snow, fired once. It seemed silly so he didn't waste any more rounds. Others must have had the same feeling, for the firing soon petered out. A rumor passed back. The chateau was owned by some Polish baron who was sympathetic with the Krauts.

Shaw's platoon was led to the right, around the chateau. They walked till they came to the north side of the great structure. There, in front of a tennis court, they met comrades coming from the other side.

"No one knows what's going on," said Shaw to his platoon leader, Rabbit. "We'll all be killed."

"I know, I know," said Rabbit nervously, but hurried on. The 75 men were stretched in a 100-yard line. Behind them were officers and noncoms.

"Fire from the hip," whispered Rabbit hoarsely. "Walk slowly and shout. That will scare the Krauts."

"This is idiotic," said Shaw. Rabbit started to answer, then shrugged his shoulders. Shaw tilted his canteen for a final drink. The water was frozen. His throat burned.

"All right, move out!" cried Rabbit.

The long wavering line moved into the thick woods. Shaw found himself screaming wildly like the others as he fired from his hip. After ten yards he came to thick underbrush. He dropped to his knees and crawled, still shouting, "Come on out! Hey, we got you!"

He crept over the snow through matted growth for twenty yards. Suddenly there was a pop. A flare exploded, lighting up the woods starkly. Other flares went off. Shaw looked to both sides. He saw other frightened men on their knees, completely exposed. A few yards ahead were deadly-looking German tanks. Shaw flopped on his face as machine-gun bullets tore through the underbrush. The big guns of the tanks blasted.

Shaw felt a sting in his left leg. The man on his left rolled over clutching his knee. The man on his right, a Mexican, moaned, then suddenly was dead.

Shaw was afraid to move. Red tracers were flitting over his head in angry waves. The men of Company A screamed in terror. Abruptly the German machine guns stopped. A man crawled forward dragging a bazooka and turned a frightened face to Shaw.

Suddenly there was a great roar as German tank motors burst into action. It was terrifying. "Give me the bazooka!" shouted Shaw. The other man, in a quavering voice, explained about the safety catch, then scrambled into the brush.

The noise of tanks deafened Shaw. Those who could move were running frantically through the woods, easy prey to burp guns. Shaw crawled toward a dirt road. He'd never fired a bazooka but he had a sudden urge to shoot at a tank. The ditch alongside the road had been filled with brush, probably by the Germans. He didn't know what to do. He decided to shoot the bazooka straight down the road. But he couldn't. It seemed pointless without a target, and he was afraid. His glasses were ripped off by the brush. He spent an agonizing few minutes until he luckily found them. He turned and hurried down the road away from the enemy, his wounded leg throbbing.

Two other GIs burst out of the woods. One, seriously hurt, was supported by the other. "Let's get out of here," yelled the wounded man.

The three hustled down the road to the edge of the woods. To the right rose the menacing chateau. Beside it was a German tank, glistening with hoar frost.

"My God, look at that!" said the unwounded man. Shaw thought it was a dead tank. They decided to take a chance and ran across the snowy field to another patch of woods. Shaw's throat was parched. He got a stick, poked the ice in his canteen, but he couldn't get a drop. Disgusted, he threw the canteen away.

A young lieutenant suddenly emerged from the dark and grabbed Shaw urgently. "You've got to go back and get the wounded."

"I'm wounded," said Shaw.

"And I'm helping these two," said the unwounded GI.

The three brushed past the distraught lieutenant. Nothing could have driven them back to those woods. They hurried down the hill, but they could still hear the moaning and screams of the wounded in the woods. They crossed railroad tracks. Shaw saw a battalion aid station and went in.

"We can't take care of anyone not critically wounded," said a tired doctor. Shaw walked to the main highway leading to Hotton. He felt drunk, then he felt nothing.

When he opened his eyes he was in an aid station. A lieutenant grabbed his arm. It was Rabbit, tearfully wringing his hands. He kept saying, "I'm sorry! I'm sorry!"

Shaw knew he should tell Rabbit it wasn't his fault. But he remembered the Mexican and the others screaming in pain and fear. He couldn't say a word.

2

On a rugged hogback ridge, about five miles east of Verdenne, Sam Hogan, the lieutenant colonel from Texas, was being pushed up a slippery incline by his orderly, Phil De Orio, and his jeep driver, Gast. Sliding up and down the rugged ridge in his fur-lined British flying boots had exhausted Hogan. The three had started at the tail end of the escaping column. Now they were more than a mile behind the others.

Hogan fell. "My feet have given out. You two go on without me."

The two enlisted men refused. Hogan would never have abandoned them. The three huddled together, covered only by Hogan's trench coat, and tried to sleep.

Soon it was daylight. Around them were empty shell cases, the odds and ends of military and personal equipment. They were on the field of a recent battle.

Hogan limped up a hill and saw a village. A voice that sounded like English grew louder. The three crept closer. "Down five zero. Fire for effect!"

They were in American lines. They walked boldly across a field. Then a frightened voice shouted, "Halt, drop your guns!" The three eased their guns to the snow. "Move forward with your hands up!"

Hogan, followed by the others, moved forward toward a chicken house. He saw two infantrymen wearing a strange patch.

"He wanted to shoot first," said one of the infantrymen. "I wanted to talk first and *then* shoot!"

"Glad you won the argument," said Hogan.

Soon Hogan and his two men were in a jeep bound for Barvaux, command post of the 3rd Armored Division. There they were given a boisterous reception by other gaunt-faced men of the task force. The march-out of "Hogan's 400" had been a great success.

"We only lost one man," an officer told Hogan.

"Yeah," said a sergeant, his face still blackened with soot, "and he was killed by a 75th Division sentry. 'The Six-Bits' and they ain't worth two-bits. What a bunch of crumbs!"

Hogan was brought into General Rose's office. Rose shook his hand. "But why were you the last one out?" he asked.

Hogan hesitated. He thought of several heroic answers. He said, "Because my feet hurt."

Outside Phil De Orio was indecisively looking at the rubber mattress he'd carried out of Marcouray. If he returned it, he'd only have to keep inflating it till they reached Berlin. He threw Colonel Hogan's prize possession into a campfire.

A few miles away Hogan's best friend, Richardson, was storming into the command post of his combat commander, General Hickey. He had just learned Major Brewster was under arrest, facing charges of "cowardice in the face of the enemy."

"Brew deserves a Silver Star," said Richardson angrily. "What are you going to do?"

Hickey calmly puffed his pipe. "The charges against Brewster require an affidavit signed by one of his commanders that he believes the accused guilty as charged. Either you or I will have to sign it."

"You know damned well *I* won't!" said Richardson.

An hour later, Hickey was ordered to Rose's command post. Rose, immaculate as ever, his face stern as stone, shoved some papers at Hickey. "I'd like you to sign these," he said.

Hickey slowly, deliberately read the papers—charges against Brewster. He handed them back to his division commander. "I can't sign these charges."

Rose was incredulous. "I never thought *you* would be disloyal to me."

"This is simply a case of loyalty to you and your views, General, or to my conscience and sense of justice." He looked steadily at Rose. "I think these charges are very unjust. I will never sign them."

3

It was now 11:00 A.M. In Luxembourg City, Patton had just summoned his inner planning group. As each man entered the conference room, Patton, puffing on a long cigar, nodded but said nothing. There was an air of excitement and expectancy. Patton knew how to set a stage.

"I asked you to come here to consider a proposal that has just been made by Field Marshal Montgomery," he said in a quiet voice that added to the suspense. "Now I want your frank opinion. General Eisenhower has asked me personally to get that opinion for him." He cleared his throat and pointed his cigar like a revolver. "Montgomery thinks the First Army has no offensive power left and won't have for three months. He thinks the only possible offensive is by us—the Third Army. And he doesn't think we have enough troops." Montgomery, he continued, suggested holding action all over the Ardennes.

The others were stunned. The operations officer was the first to explode. "It's fantastic. The psychological effect of such a plan on our troops would be disastrous!"

"You're absolutely right." Patton was delighted at the reaction. His high-pitched voice rose shrilly. "Goddam, our men aren't trained to withdraw. But Eisenhower wants your opinion. He knows *mine*." He turned, jammed the cigar in an ash tray. "But goddam it, if this plan goes through, the war is over and the Germans will win it!"

There was silence.

"Those people up north have plenty of offensive power," suddenly blurted out one man. "All they have to do is get off their butts and fight."

"Of course they've got plenty of offensive power," said Patton. "That's just a lot of goddam crap. All they need to fight is the order to fight. But, of course, they won't fight if Monty won't give the order. Certain of those gentlemen up north, and I mean SHAEF, have been associated with him so damn long the only thing they know how to do is sit on their dead asses, regroup, and pivot on somebody else."

He picked up his cigar. "I better get the hell out of here. I'm making too many speeches. You talk it over among yourselves and give me a brief report as soon as you can." He jammed the blunted cigar in his mouth and strode out. It was a good exit.

The discussion was brief. With angry unanimity the Montgomery plan was rejected as unsound and ill-advised. The recommendation was equally brief: hold all positions and counterattack immediately.

4

Patton had promised to be in Bastogne and Wiltz by Christmas. Both were still held by the Germans.

On the eastern outskirts of Wiltz earlier that morning a young man in a torn stained American uniform staggered across a snowy field. He had no idea where he was for he was delirious from hunger, cold, thirst, exhaustion, and pain. He couldn't feel his feet or legs. He wasn't even sure he was walking. Only a stubborn spark kept him moving.

His name was Ralph Ellis and he came from California. He was a private from Hurley Fuller's lost regiment and had escaped from Munshausen, one of the strongpoints protecting Clervaux.

Since the afternoon of December 17 he had been hiding by day, escaping to the rear by night. Already he had narrowly missed capture half a dozen times. He scooped up a handful of snow and ate it. It made him sick. He retched painfully but there was nothing to vomit.

He sat down and rested. Some town was ahead and he could just make out houses on the hill in the darkness before dawn. He didn't care what town it was, or who held it. He needed food and shelter. He walked boldly toward a little green house. It was probably empty for no smoke was coming from the chimney. Inside he discovered a half-filled box of GI oatmeal. Not daring to build a fire in the enameled kitchen stove, he ate the oatmeal uncooked with sugar, floating it down with a half bottle of red wine. Nothing had ever tasted so wonderful.

He went upstairs and found a bed with a feather mattress and a huge fluffy quilt—a "stepdecken" the Luxembourgers called it. Crawling into bed with his last strength, he pulled the quilt over him. In this sea of feathers he was in heaven.

A few blocks away in the attic of an elderly couple, the Balthasar-Wageners, another 28th Division soldier was being given medicine by a fragile-looking blond Luxembourg nurse. In the rooms below them, a dozen German soldiers were now billeted. But Sergeant George Carroll, still weak from a shoulder wound, felt safe under the care of the girl, Mlle. Anna. He had never met anyone like her before.

Half a mile up the hill in Upper Wiltz, a third 28th Division soldier, Sergeant Lester Koritz, was planning his escape from the German hospital located in the castle. The day before, the young nieces of the two spinster Goebel sisters had come to the castle under the pretext of looking for schoolbooks. They had found their friend, Koritz, and given him the key to the tobacco shop. Soon the hospital would be evacuated to Germany. In the confusion of departure, he decided, he would make his break for freedom.

Near the bottom of the hill leading to Grand' Rue, in the post office building, Josephine Thein and her two children were sleeping in the Kremers' bed. There was a great explosion outside. More shells fell. She heard the angry drone of planes, then the whistle of bombs.

Josephine wakened her two children, for something told her she had to hurry. A bomb fell, shaking the building. Fragments smashed through the window into the apartment. She grabbed the children and pulled them into the hall. There was a splintering crash, then a roar. The apartment filled with rubble, a cloud of dust. She looked with horror at the bed so recently occupied. It was covered with debris.

"Oh, Mary, Mother, help me!" cried four-year-old Edy.

Josephine pulled the children down the corridor. There was a deep cellar under the post office itself. The three went past a gate into the main cellar. Inside she saw officers busily giving orders, men at a telephone switchboard.

"Is that Windbride?" said a sergeant wearing earphones. "Yes, this is Monika. Hello, Dida. Have found new toys but they are unusable." The sergeant glared at her. She pressed against the wall, trying to look inconspicuous. Above she could hear the crash of bombs and shells.

She fished through her bundle for a package of tobacco, then tentatively held it out to the sergeant. "The children are afraid," she said, "and it's so cold upstairs."

The sergeant muttered but shoved the tobacco in his pocket. An officer passed. "What are those civilians doing here?" he asked angrily. "Get them out."

Josephine led the children out of the cellar. In the corridor she filled her baby carriage with a few possessions. She decided to make a run for the Carmes house a block away. It had a good cellar.

A German, wounded and swearing, staggered from the street into the corridor.

"Help me take the carriage into the street," she said.

"I haven't time." He tried to pass her.

"You must help me," she pleaded.

He looked at her and then the children. "No sense! Just like my wife." He picked up the carriage and carried it into the street. "Be careful, crazy housewife," he said solicitously.

Josephine wheeled the carriage up the cobblestone street, her two children clinging to her skirts. A neighbor, Louis Steinmetz of the Red Cross, ran to her, shouting, "Don't stay in the streets! Bombs are falling!"

A plane flashed by. Seconds later there was a great explosion. Another plane swooped down, its machine gun jabbering. German soldiers fell on all sides.

"Come with me," cried Steinmetz, grabbing the carriage.

Suddenly there was a demoniacal shriek. A Jabo was heading straight for them. Josephine screamed. She knew she was going to die. She hid her head under Steinmetz's coat. The children hid under their mother's skirt.

The American plane swooped like a chicken hawk at them. Suddenly, as if the pilot had caught a glimpse of the baby carriage and the woman, the fighter-bomber shot up without firing its machine guns. It banked, came back, spied a group of running Germans a hundred yards up the street. Its machine guns spat. German soldiers screamed, threw up their hands, and dropped on the street, reddening the dirty snow.

Josephine Thein, her two children, and Steinmetz ran into the
Carmes house, into the safe cellar.

This was Wiltz on the day after Christmas.

5

In Bastogne, at 1:00 P.M., Fred MacKenzie, of the Buffalo *Evening
News,* was walking aimlessly in the compound of the Belgian Barracks. He saw the smoke of battle rising on all sides. It was like
being in the center of a stinking hell. The disgust of war overwhelmed him. He'd accepted assignment to the overseas job because of his deep patriotic convictions, his hatred of the Fascists
and the Nazis.

General McAuliffe came across the courtyard, his face set with
worry. "I suppose you wish you were out of here," he said con-
versationally as MacKenzie fell in at his side.

"General, if others have to stay here, I can." MacKenzie couldn't
restrain an acid tone.

"Come on," said McAuliffe. "Let's go down to the cemetery."

The two crossed the road to the walled-in town cemetery. Mc-
Auliffe stopped at the snow-covered grave of Lieutenant Colonel
James La Prade, killed at Noville.

"He was a splendid man and a very fine soldier," said McAuliffe
distantly. "We're fortunate to have done so well without him." He
looked down at the grave as at an old friend, then passed on to
where German prisoners were digging other holes in the frozen
ground. "Are they being fed?" he asked a guard.

"Yes, sir, as good as us."

"Be sure not to neglect them," said McAuliffe.

Then he and the newsman slowly recrossed the road.

Five miles south at that moment, 1:30 P.M., Colonel Creighton
W. Abrams was standing on a hill looking toward Bastogne. His
37th Tank Battalion was the spearhead of the 4th Armored Division driving up from the south to relieve Bastogne. He was
scheduled to attack a village several miles to the northwest. But
he was down to twenty medium tanks, only enough for one good
assault. Should he take a chance and ask permission to blast
straight north toward Bastogne?

A great roar filled the air. Soon clouds of C-47s flew overhead looking like fat geese. Hundreds of brightly colored parachutes burst over Bastogne. Gliders zoomed toward the ground. Flak burst on all sides; several planes flamed and crashed, but the flights kept coming on.

Abrams' mind was made up. He returned to his tank, the "Thunderbolt IV," and radioed Hugh Gaffey, commander of the 4th Armored Division. He asked permission to attack straight north.

At 2:00 P.M., Gaffey telephoned Patton. "Will you authorize a big risk with Combat Command R for a breakthrough to Bastogne?" he asked.

"I sure as hell will!"

A few minutes after 3:00 P.M., Abrams was handed a message. His face was impassive but his eyes glinted. He shoved a big cigar in his mouth. It stuck out aggressively like another gun. "We're going in to those people now," he said as he stood up in the turret of his tank. "Let 'er roll."

The chain of tanks, armored cars, and half-tracks jerked forward. Tanks in the lead, followed by half-tracks filled with infantry, the column went through a patch of woods and started down a steep slope.

Lieutenant Charles Boggess, a veteran at thirty-three, was in the lead with his nine Cobra Kings, forty-ton Shermans. Soon he was on the outskirts of a village, Assenois. He called for artillery support, then he gave the order to attack. The nine tanks headed straight for the town, all guns firing. Friendly artillery dug up the streets as Boggess and two other tanks broke through; but a half-track next in line, catching fire, blocked the way.

Infantrymen jumped off other half-tracks. Private James Hendrix, a nineteen-year-old boy from Arkansas with red hair and countless freckles, ran forward. Somewhere in the smoke ahead, he knew, two 88s were raising hell with the tanks. They had to be knocked out. Hendrix charged, yelling, "Come on out!"

One German poked his head from a foxhole. Hendrix shot him in the neck. He ran to the next hole, bashing in the head of a terrified German with the butt of his M-1.

Hendrix quickly searched him and found a book of American matches. He ran on, still shouting. As the lone GI charged through the smoke with his rifle, the two crews of the 88s came forward holding up their hands in surrender.

By 4:30 P.M. Boggess, followed by two other Cobra Kings, was heading for the woods north of Assenois. The barrel of his 75 was hot. Gunner Dickerson had used it like a machine gun, throwing in twenty-one rounds in the few minutes it had taken to blast through the village. The bow machine gunner, Kafner, played his gun around fir trees ahead. In the fast-approaching dusk, dim figures ran, fell.

Boggess saw a concrete blockhouse painted green. He ordered Dickerson to put three rounds into it. The concrete flew apart. A hundred yards farther Boggess saw colored parachutes draped over the fields, in the trees. Then he saw foxholes ahead. But he had no idea whether they were held by friends or foes. He stood up in his turret and shouted, "Come here! This is the 4th Armored."

There was no answer. The tanker called again and again. Several helmeted heads slowly, suspiciously rose. Then a single figure came forward.

"I'm Lieutenant Webster of the 326th Engineers, 101st Airborne Division. Glad to see you." The paratrooper, grinning broadly, extended a hand.

Boggess leaned down and shook hands.

The men of Bastogne were now in Patton's Third Army.

6

At 4:35 P.M. Private Hans Ulrich Leske, of the nebelwerfer battalion of the Hitler Youth Division, started on foot for St. Vith. His column had been rerouted around it, for the men had been told St. Vith was a "hospital town."

It was almost dusk as he plowed through snowdrifts, still more than a mile from his destination. Then he heard a great roar. To the west a cloud of bombers, lowering as if for a run, was coming toward St. Vith through the red rays of the setting sun.

"Achtung! Bomberangriff!" he shouted as the first planes dropped markers.

Three hundred British Lancasters and Halifaxes dumped their loads. The ground shook, like an earthquake. Fir trees toppled down. To Leske's horror St. Vith seemed to rise in the air to meet the planes.

The Lancasters and Halifaxes, mission accomplished, wheeled and started back for England where children were celebrating Boxing Day. In their wake, the ruins of a town burned. Slowly, as if sleepwalking, two women crept out of a cellar. Their faces were pale, shocked. A few other people of St. Vith crawled to the surface. They were deaf, dazed. A thousand people had been in the cellars. Two hundred were dead.

Leske shakily got to his feet. A vast red cloud was drifting westward from St. Vith, a cloud of dust lit by the dying rays of the setting sun. He was transfixed. It was apocalyptic.

7

It was a day of Allied might. The snows of the Ardennes ran red with the blood of "Watch on the Rhine." Nowhere was carnage greater than in the Celles pocket a few miles from the Meuse River. Here Harmon's 2nd Armored Division was battling the 2nd Panzer Division in a hundred small engagements. That afternoon there had been a bad moment for Harmon as a powerful armored force from Panzer Lehr rolled from the southeast to the rescue of those in the Celles pocket. But rocket-firing British Typhoons, led to the advancing column by a tiny American Cub, routed the rescuing Panthers and Tigers.

Although a great German defeat was now in the making, there was still hope for the 2nd Panzer. Comrades of the 9th Panzer Division were driving to their rescue from the west. Already they were less than fifteen miles away. By dusk the tank battle still hung in the balance.

8

In Berlin they had been arguing about "Watch on the Rhine" at the Führer's headquarters since morning. Jodl was now saying, "Mein Führer, we must face the facts squarely. We cannot force the Meuse."

The 2nd Panzer was near disaster at Celles. Kampfgruppe Peiper had been trapped in the Amblève Valley and had escaped only by luck. Elsenborn Ridge—held by the American 1st, 2nd, and 99th Divisions—could not be penetrated. The 116th Panzer was stalled near Verdenne. Patton had just opened a narrow corridor to besieged Bastogne.

On all fronts in the Ardennes it was the same story. The Germans were either pulling back or were stalled. For the moment it was a static struggle. Although the tide had not yet turned, the great offensive had been temporarily checked.

Everyone at the portentous meeting had a plan. Hitler listened to them all. Then he spoke. "We have had unexpected setbacks—because my plan was not followed to the letter." There was bitter sarcasm in his voice. Then his face changed. "But all is not yet lost. Model can still cross the Meuse *if* Brandenberger's Seventh Army regains its equilibrium in the south; *if* Bastogne is taken; *if* Manteuffel and Dietrich wipe out the great Allied force we have caught in the bend of the Meuse."

He issued new orders: Manteuffel was to turn to the northeast, thus outflanking most of Hodges' First Army; Dietrich was to continue his vigorous attack in the Manhay-Hotton direction.

"I want three new divisions and at least 25,000 fresh replacements rushed to the Ardennes." Hitler looked at the semicircle of faces. Granted the Allies could not now be wiped out in a single dramatic blow as planned, "Watch on the Rhine" could still be turned into a deadly battle of attrition. And this would certainly bring about an overwhelming political victory for the Nazis. The Great Dream was not yet abandoned.

In Luxembourg City, Omar Bradley was trying to reach Eisenhower by telephone. But the Supreme Commander was on his way to Holland to see Montgomery. In his place, Eisenhower's chief of staff, Bedell Smith, was called to the phone.

"Damn it, Bedell," said the usually calm Bradley, "can't you people get Monty going on the north? As near as we can tell this other fellow's reached his high-water mark today. He'll soon be starting to pull back—if not tonight, certainly tomorrow."

"Oh, no, Brad, you're mistaken." Smith had just read a stack of apprehensive estimates from Montgomery's 21st Army Group. "Why, they'll be across the Meuse in 48 hours."

"Nuts!" Bradley hung up. He was disgusted with the way SHAEF was dancing to Monty's tune. Disturbed, he sat down and wrote a letter to his old friend Courtney Hodges, now serving under Montgomery. Bradley made it clear that though he had no control over Hodges, he would view with misgivings any plan of First Army's to give up any terrain which might be favorable for future operations.

As Bradley went to bed, he hoped the aggressive spirit of the southern half of the Bulge would travel northward.

PART FOUR
Twilight of the Gods

1. QUEEN OF BATTLE

27–28 December 1944

1

By the morning of December 27 the fog of war covering the Ardennes had lifted. The battle, no longer fluid, had resolved itself into obvious well-defined lines.

On the northern shoulder, Montgomery now had Hodges' First Army stretched firmly from Monschau to Celles. On the left—the east—flank, Gerow's V Corps was still holding along Elsenborn Ridge. In the center, Ridgway's XVIII Airborne Corps was actually on the attack, retaking the key crossroad of Manhay. On the right flank "Lightning Joe" Collins' VII Corps had not only stopped Manteuffel's drives at Celles, Verdenne, and Hotton but was beginning to regain ground.

On the southern shoulder, Bradley's situation was not tidy but he was making steady if slow progress: his troops—Patton's Third Army—were widening the narrow Bastogne corridor a few yards each hour and were also only a mile below the Café Schumann crossroad in the drive on Wiltz.

2

That morning Eisenhower was in a Paris railway station choked with security officers, armed sentries, and Military Police. The night before, the train he was supposed to have taken to Belgium had been bombed.

The new train finally pulled out, but not before Eisenhower had again complained about the elaborate protective measures. His annoyance was heightened at the first stop when he saw a squad of GIs jump into the snowbanks, rifles at the ready.

"I'd consider it miraculous," he told the officer in charge, "if any ambitious German murderer could determine in advance that he'd find his prospective victim on a particular railway train at a given moment, at a given spot in Europe. Get those men out of the cold."

Eisenhower was en route to a meeting with Montgomery to discuss the scheduled counterattack from the north. For a week Bradley and Patton had been urging the Supreme Commander to get some action from Montgomery. The Field Marshal, they insisted, was losing the Battle of the Bulge by his maddeningly slow preparations.

But Montgomery had problems the Third Army people knew nothing about. His troops—that is, Hodges' First Army—had taken the full fury of the "Rundstedt Offensive." In a fight for survival, Hodges had been forced to throw in relieving divisions piecemeal, using up supplies and reserves with no thought of future operations. To turn over abruptly to the attack would take complete regrouping and refitting.

In spite of this Eisenhower knew that on Christmas Day Hodges himself had urged Montgomery to counterattack within a week or ten days.

Montgomery had replied, "But, Hodges, I don't see how you can be ready by then."

"I've talked to Joe Collins," said Hodges, "and he assures me he can be ready."

"But will that give you time to regroup properly?"

"Marshal, we don't do things the same as you British. In an operation like this we regroup on the line of attack."

Montgomery had remained dubious, and plans for the great counterattack were still indefinite.

3

At three o'clock that afternoon Fred MacKenzie of the Buffalo *Evening News* watched the 4th Armored tanks roll up into Bastogne. For the moment, the siege was broken, but it was apparent the real battle was just beginning.

MacKenzie was about to leave with a truckload of glider pilots. He said good-bye to his friends, shoved his bag and typewriter into a truck, climbed in and sat down thoughtfully next to a young glider pilot. He was coming out with the hottest news story of the war—the only correspondent at a key battle—and yet he felt no sense of achievement. He had seen too much death.

The convoy pulled away. The glider pilots, bright-eyed and jaunty, shouted to those left behind. A shell exploded to their right. MacKenzie and a C-47 pilot jumped nervously. The young glider pilots laughed.

"I've been here over a week," grumbled the C-47 pilot to MacKenzie. "These kids are just tourists."

The glider pilots were now pointing out the grim signs of battle as they neared the perimeter. German tanks, burned black, stood in the snow looking like great dead animals. Hundreds of black craters pockmarked the fields. Snow-covered mounds, once men, dotted the landscape.

"They act like it was some sort of picnic," said MacKenzie.

The C-47 pilot nodded somberly. "I never knew before what it was to fight on the ground."

The trucks, moving targets on the Assenois highway, rolled south, hurried on by explosions on both sides of the road.

Heading north on the same road was a jeep. The driver was Staff Sergeant Charlie Kartus; in peacetime he owned three shoe stores in North Carolina. The man next to him was a major general. In the back was a captain, the general's aide. It was starting to get dark and Maxwell Taylor, commander of the 101st Airborne Division, urged Kartus to put on more speed. Taylor had been in Washington, D.C., when the battle started and had flown to France on Christmas Eve in a freight-carrying C-54 transport. On landing he had asked permission to parachute into Bastogne, but Bedell Smith had refused.

The jeep was stopped by an outpost guard near a farmhouse. The three men went inside, and joined several correspondents and 4th Armored Division officers grouped around a big tiled stove.

"You'd better not go into Bastogne yet," warned one of the armored men. "The corridor is so narrow you can spit across it. The Jerries have this road zeroed in good now."

"I have to get in tonight," said Taylor, and then added, "I've got room for one of you correspondents."

Cornelius Ryan of the London *Daily Telegraph* shook his head. "No volunteers today, General."

Half an hour later, Taylor walked down the stairs to McAuliffe's cellar command post. The staff of the 101st was having a pre-dinner cognac.

"Well, boys," he said, after boisterous greetings, "you're heroes."

"Who, us?" asked McAuliffe.

"Everybody's been worried about you. Just what is the condition of the division?"

"No damned reason to be worried about us," said McAuliffe. "We're ready to attack."

4

At the tip of the Bulge, not long after midnight, General Ernest Harmon was sitting in a half-destroyed Belgian farmhouse near Celles writing out a personal report to his commander, Courtney Hodges.

The three-day battle between Harmon's 2nd Armored Division and the 2nd Panzer Division was over.

Harmon wrote:

Attached is a list of the spoils we took—including 1,200 prisoners. Killed and wounded some 2,500. A great slaughter.

The list was formidable: 405 vehicles, including 88 tanks and assault guns; and 75 heavy guns—the complete division artillery. More important, the spearhead of the offensive had been smashed. The Germans would not cross the Meuse.

Harmon wearily signed the report, then leaned back and relaxed for the first time since he'd arrived in the Ardennes. He felt little elation. It had indeed been a great slaughter. But the price had been high.

5

At five o'clock the next morning, December 28, a great barrage began falling on the hills above Wiltz. Private Ralph Ellis of California and Hurley Fuller's regiment was still hiding in the green house at the edge of town. He woke up in the feather bed, startled. The Americans must have returned to Wiltz.

Excitedly he got out of bed. Painfully he pulled on a pair of knee-length rubber boots ransacked from a closet. He put on his field jacket, his helmet, grabbed his M-1 and stumbled down the stairs. He pushed open the door and ran outside. But there were no GIs anywhere. Puzzled, he crossed the ruins of the bridge across the Wiltz River, then staggered up the hill toward Upper Wiltz.

He hurried through the morning darkness toward two soldiers in front of the post office. They had bedrolls under their arms, rifles slung over their shoulders.

When he was ten feet away he realized something was wrong. Their helmets looked like coal scuttles. The soldiers, seeing Ellis, reached for their rifles but his M-1 was at the ready. Their hands shot up.

"Speak English," he said. In the darkness he still wasn't sure. He was answered by a torrent of German. From inside the post office he could hear other German voices. He got behind the two men, prodding them with his M-1 until they broke into a trot. Then he turned and ran back down the hill, to the green house.

A mile away, at the castle, the last American wounded were being loaded into trucks for evacuation to Germany. The pressure on Wiltz had become so great that Brandenberger had already left town. Major Henry Huber, a surgeon from New York, and Lieutenant Zerha, a surgeon from Vienna, were supervising the litter bearers.

A figure came up to Huber in the dark courtyard. "If I get the chance," whispered Sergeant Lester Koritz, "I'm going out the back way and hide."

Huber held out his hand. "Good luck."

Koritz walked unconcernedly into the basement. He hid in a corner until all the patients were evacuated. When there was silence, he crept upstairs out the back door of the basement. He had to hurry. It would soon be dawn.

He climbed up a wall, then jumped to the deep gully behind the castle. He carefully picked his way down a steep winding path until he saw the rear of the houses on Grand' Rue. He followed an alley up the slope that led to the street. He intended to leave the alley at Grand' Rue and then walk the hundred yards to Number

27, the Goebel sisters' tobacco shop, but the streets were filled with Germans, moving silently among a line of vehicles.

He turned back to the alley as the first light of day came from the east. He had to hide. Part way down the gulley he saw a tiny wooden building. Soon he was inside a bee house.

He peeked out of a small window. A long line of German tanks was slowly heading south for battle. Shells began to fall in the gully. Koritz was annoyed. The American artillery could not hit the tanks on Grand' Rue because of the peculiar topography. Shells burst closer, shaking the bee house. Koritz hugged the floor. As one concussion wave after another washed over, he prayed.

Several miles southwest of Wiltz snuggled a small dejected village of yellowish cement houses. This was Nothum, an innocent-looking, snow-covered cluster of buildings lying less than a mile below one of the most important crossroads in the Ardennes, Café Schumann. The roar of artillery, the same artillery that was threatening Koritz, shook snow from the trees. A few minutes ago the new-fallen snow around Nothum had been white. Now it was as spotted with black as a printer's apron.

In the woods just south of the village, infantrymen of the 26th Division were preparing to assault Nothum. Then they would take Café Schumann and drive toward Wiltz.

Lieutenant James Creighton, executive officer of F Company, of the 101st Regiment, felt uneasy about the attack. It was a dark dawn. He knew that the good weather which had started on December 23 had ended. It would also be the end of air support. The next days would be bad ones for doughboys. Machines of all kinds would be of little use in the snowdrifts of these hills. The battle would be won or lost by infantry, Queen of Battle.

And the men of his company were infantrymen only by title. Of the original Fox Company which had started on the dash across France, there weren't a dozen left. Most of the company had been captured in Lorraine. Outside of Lieutenant Larkin (the company commander), Creighton, and eleven noncoms, no one had any combat experience. Eighty of the men were raw replacements, drafted from rear-echelon outfits—ordnance, heavy bridge, field artillery and anti-aircraft. Few had fired an M-1 since basic training; they were in poor physical condition and their morale was

even worse. They all felt they had been sent up front as punish-
ment.

They had. When Patton, bleeding for infantry replacements,
ordered that the best 10 per cent of each rear-echelon outfit be
sent up front, the "eight-balls," of course, had been selected. The
American Army, in this respect, was the same as the German.

Creighton scanned the reluctant riflemen, crouching, steeling
themselves for the attack. They looked cold, unhappy, and scared,
and they held their rifles distastefully. They knew nothing about
skirmish lines and their only arm-and-hand signals were for double-
time and "I have to go to the john."

The night before, when they had tried to take Nothum in their
first action, everything had gone wrong. The battalion plan had
been skimpy. There had been no coordination. The men had
stood out in the bright moonlight in their dark uniforms. A scout
had stumbled over a trip wire of a booby-trapped Teller mine and
been blown to pieces. Then German artillery had plastered their
positions. The tanks supposed to support them had bogged down.
Finally the whole battalion had been pulled back 1,000 yards into
these woods.

Now it was about to start again. Fox was to circle behind Nothum
from the left and take "Cemetery Hill," which lay between the
village and the Café Schumann crossroad. Easy Company was to
attack Nothum itself and George Company was to circle right
of the village and take Café Schumann.

Actually E and G Companies were no better off than F; in fact
the entire 26th Division was in bad shape. Less than two weeks
previously it had come to Metz for four weeks' rest and training. But
after only two days the division, its 4,000 unhappy replacements
still untrained, had been hurriedly loaded into 2½-ton trucks and
open trailers and rushed north to the Ardennes.

The barrage stopped. Lieutenant Larkin stood up. He was so tall
his fatigue pants didn't even reach the top of his combat boots. Larkin turned for a moment and then loped across the field. The men
followed unenthusiastically. As Larkin reached the crest of the
ridge overlooking Nothum, machine-gun and rifle fire came from
the town and "Cemetery Hill" beyond. The men dropped to the
snow, pinned down along a fence line. Now heavy machine-pistol
fire came from the reverse slope.

Creighton could see only an occasional white flash. The Germans in their snow capes and helmet covers were almost invisible. He crawled forward to where Larkin was peering studiously at two houses a hundred yards forward.

"If we can occupy those houses," said Larkin, "we can bring fire directly onto the Jerries." He picked a squad, then quietly said, "Let's go."

As Larkin and his squad entered the first house, its roof seemed to explode. Smoke poured out the windows. Larkin backed out of the door dragging a wounded man. Five others were pulled out and brought back to the fence line.

Larkin ordered the frightened men to dig in fast. He picked up a field phone and called for mortar fire. To Creighton he said, "Try and make contact with the 1st Battalion on our left." Then he added in mild complaint, "This isn't so good."

Creighton wriggled through the snow to the left to make sure the Germans hadn't infiltrated in the gap between battalions. American mortar shells flew overhead, landing with hollow thumps. To the north he saw white figures—the enemy—carefully pulling back a few yards. Creighton crawled for almost 300 yards until he found the 1st Battalion. Then he crawled back to report to Larkin. As he scrambled up the ridge, heavy fire broke out. There were screams. When Creighton reached the fence line, he saw sixteen GIs sprawling along the fence in grotesque attitudes. Most were dead. Several, who were badly wounded, looked at him with shocked eyes, their faces yellow. One—his stomach laid open, his entrails stretched up over a branch—smiled with embarrassment as he tried to stuff them back. Rifles, bazookas, grenades, packs, gas masks were strewn around like the refuse of careless picnickers.

Larkin lay under a shattered tree. A medic, his hands shaking, was putting a bandage on a flowing wound. There was an explosion almost overhead as a shell was detonated by a branch. Shrapnel from this tree-burst rained down. Creighton saw a white tank at the foot of the hill, its 88 smoking. It fired again. Creighton grabbed Larkin under the shoulders and gently dragged him down the south side of the hill. Then he picked up Larkin's phone and called Battalion. "This is Fox. Lieutenant Larkin is a casualty. He's not the only one. Send litter bearers."

"We'll send you bearers," promised a voice. "Creighton, you take over Fox."

Fox was his. He checked Larkin's wound and then, stooping down, ran back up the hill to reorganize the fence line.

Heavy German firing started on the left. "The 1st Battalion is catching hell," he told the only other surviving officer in the company, a former music teacher. "There's a big gap between us. I'm going to make a personal reconnaissance and see what's over there. You hold fast."

The music teacher nodded uncertainly as Creighton moved off.

Twenty minutes later Creighton was back. But the fence line was almost deserted. He counted only three heads. Creighton jumped into the first shallow foxhole.

"The other g-guys took off," said a scared replacement. It was a man Creighton had known only a week. He was a little sunken-chested New Yorker who had complained almost incessantly on the long march to the front. He was constantly asking to fall out. Creighton had had to carry his M-1 the last three days.

"You stay here until I get back," said Creighton. "You understand?" The soldier nodded. Creighton ran back to the bottom of the ravine. Men were crouching in terror behind bushes.

A sergeant, sweating and swearing, herded half a dozen toward Creighton. "Christ, sir," he panted, "they never saw a dead man before. And when they heard that shooting and shouting from the 1st Battalion they took off like rabbits." It was Love, the communications sergeant. He lowered his voice. "You can't blame the poor bastards."

"I'm not blaming them. Just get them back on the hill. And where the hell is my exec?" Love shrugged his shoulders. Creighton scoured the bushes and found a dozen more refugees. He pushed them ahead of him up the hill. As he neared the top, there was a burst of fire, several horrible screams, and silence.

Creighton crawled forward. He was sure the Krauts had overrun the three men on top of the hill and now sat in their foxholes. But he had to go on. If he retreated, Fox Company would go to pieces. He reached the crest and looked over. The hypochondriac from New York was kneeling in his foxhole clinging desperately to the butt of a Browning automatic. His face was white.

"What happened?" asked Creighton.

"I d-don't know! Some G-G-Germans came over the hill. I fired at them." Creighton peered over the edge of the foxhole. Ten feet away was a German almost cut in two by a burst from the BAR. Six feet behind him was another German, his body sprawled out crablike. Halfway down the hill a third knelt in the snow, the front of his white cape red. He moaned as he bobbed his head from side to side.

"You did all right." Creighton turned. The hypochondriac was vomiting.

Sergeant Love slithered into the foxhole. "What'll we do now?"

Creighton peered down the enemy side of the hill. "Call up some Shermans to knock out that Jerry tank down there."

"Then what?"

"Then we attack—as planned."

Love's mouth dropped open. "With these eight-balls?"

Creighton adjusted his glasses. "With these eight-balls."

While waiting for the supporting tanks, Creighton worked out a plan of attack for his reluctant warriors. The 3rd Platoon, the one originally on the hill crest, had been shot to pieces. It would stay in place as support while the 1st and 2nd Platoons attacked down the hill, and then up the next hill to a small walled cemetery.

The 1st and 2nd Platoons were half led, half pushed into the foxholes along the fence line. At 4:15 P.M. an artillery and mortar barrage opened up. Friendly shells flew over Fox Company, landing in the German positions. Then there was a rumble from behind. An American tank slowly, cumbrously, climbed the hill. As it reached the crest, panzerfausts blasted from the German side of the hill. The Sherman fired into the two houses, then, still buttoned up, suddenly swung to the left. To Creighton's horror, it began firing directly down the fence line with 75s and machine guns. Men of the 1st and 2nd Platoons, crouching ready for attack, were caught in its fire. Creighton plunged across the snow to the Sherman. He hammered on its side with his carbine. But the firing continued. He jumped onto the tank's deck and kicked the barrel of a machine gun. The turret cautiously opened.

"You damn fools," he shouted, "those are my men!"

At that moment the preparation barrage stopped. It was time for the attack, but the men refused to move. The valley below Creighton was now crisscrossed by bands of tracers and exploding shells. It was like looking into the bowels of Hell. Since the men would never move into this death trap without an example, Creighton stood up and shouted the slogan of Fort Benning, the infantry school, "Follow me!"

He ran down the hill, certain he would never come back alive. Dirt and snow splattered all around him as he ran full speed to the bottom. Here he spotted a stone wall and slid behind it.

"Well, we made it," said someone next to him. It was Sergeant Love. Creighton felt elated. He turned, ready to lead his men on another charge to the next objective, "Cemetery Hill." No one was behind.

"For Christ sake, we're alone!" In his anger he forgot fear. The two turned and climbed back up the hill, ignoring the bullets ripping on all sides. Their men, crouching in foxholes, only stared at Creighton and Love.

"Now listen, you sons of bitches," said Love. "This time you follow the Lieutenant and keep up with him. If you don't *I'm* going to shoot you."

Creighton and Love hurried down the line, pulling the terrified riflemen out of their foxholes. Once more Creighton led the attack. This time the men followed for Love was behind them with his carbine.

Once started the GIs ran, anxious to get out of the heavy fire— and away from Love. They followed Creighton across the valley and up toward the cemetery on top of the next hill. White figures popped up from nowhere, and retreated to the north. Fox Company followed, too scared to shout or shoot. In five minutes they had taken their objective. "Cemetery Hill" belonged to Fox.

6

Because of snow and heavy bombings, Eisenhower's train didn't reach Hasselt, Belgium, until noon of December 28. Montgomery greeted him in a chipper, confident manner.

After reviewing the situation and indicating the position of his general reserves, Montgomery walked to a big wall map. "I'm beginning to assemble Collins' corps once more. When he's ready I'm having him attack in the general direction of Houffalize." He pointed to a town fifteen miles north of Bastogne.

Eisenhower brightened.

"But I can't go over to the attack quite yet."

"Why not?"

"I've just received information the German intends to make at least one more full-blooded smash at my lines. I'm confident I can beat off the attack," he quickly added, "but I want more time to get my reserve ready to follow in on the heels of the German just as soon as we turn him back."

Eisenhower didn't like the timing of a great counterattack to depend on the action of the enemy. "Don't you think there's a good possibility the German might *not* attack again in the north?"

Montgomery shook his head. "I feel it's a practical certainty." In any case, he said, he could use the time to reorganize, re-equip, and refresh his troops. He asked if Eisenhower didn't agree that the first task was to make sure of the integrity of the northern lines.

"Well," said Eisenhower, "I do agree that the best thing to do is strengthen the front, reorganize your units, and get thoroughly ready for a strong counterblow. In the meantime you'll be prepared in the event of another German attack." He paused. "When can you get started?"

"New Year's Day," replied Montgomery with no hesitation. And then he added, "Or shortly after—the second or third."

The meeting was concluded. The men shook hands cordially. Eisenhower had other business. With the long-awaited northern attack more or less settled, he now had to coordinate it with a strong attack from the south. He dictated a radio message to his chief of staff, Bedell Smith:

> Release to Bradley at once the 11th Armored and 87th Divisions, and organize a strong Bastogne-Houffalize attack.

The third and last phase of the Battle of the Bulge was fast approaching.

7

An equally important meeting was going on in Germany at the Führer's daily conference. Von Rundstedt was trying to persuade Hitler to abandon "Watch on the Rhine" and retreat before the Montgomery offensive started.

"I suggest," he said, "that the Fifth and Sixth Panzer Armies withdraw to a defensive line east of Bastogne."

Hitler was infuriated at the suggestion. "Only the offensive will enable us once more to give a successful turn to the war in the West. We will renew the drive to the Meuse just as soon as I've carried out the next phase of the over-all plan—Operation 'Nordwind.'" He admitted that the attack on the Ardennes hadn't resulted in the decisive success he had expected, but his sarcastic tone implied that von Rundstedt, who had been little more than a figurehead, was to blame. "On the other hand," he then told his generals, "there *has* been a tremendous easing of the situation. The enemy has had to abandon all his plans for a winter attack. He is severely criticized at home." He paused, pursed his lips in a little private smile. "Already he has had to admit that there is no chance of the war being decided before August, perhaps not before the end of next year. This means a transformation in the situation such as nobody would have believed possible a fortnight ago." He pointed at a huge wall map. "The Americans have been forced to withdraw 50 per cent of their forces from other fronts to the Ardennes. And the line here is now extraordinarily thin." He jabbed a finger at a point in the map a hundred miles to the south—Alsace. "Here we will strike in a few days with 'Nordwind.' Its certain success will automatically bring about the collapse of the threat to the left of the main offensive in the Ardennes"—he looked around at his commanders—"*which will then be resumed* with a fresh prospect of success."

The Führer paused. "In the meantime, Model will consolidate his holdings and reorganize for a new attempt on the Meuse. And he will also make a final powerful assault on Bastogne. Above all, we must have Bastogne."

By midnight nine panzer and volksgrenadier divisions began to converge on the town Hitler wanted at all costs.

2. CANDIDATES FOR DEATH

29–30 December 1944

1

In Wiltz it was half an hour before dawn of December 29. Private Ralph Ellis had no idea what time it was nor how many days he'd been in the little green house. His frozen feet throbbed. He was thirsty, starving. Anything was better than slowly dying in loneliness.

He tried to pull on boots but now his feet were too swollen; he had to cut off the toes of the boots. He staggered into the street. To walk he had to look down for there was no feeling in his feet.

At the communal well of Lower Wiltz he drank greedily from his helmet. He walked up the cobblestone street to a house, and opened the door. When a wave of warmth hit him, he backed out quickly. He opened the next door. It was unoccupied. Painfully he climbed to the top floor. He saw a bed with a mattress, headed for it, and dropped down unconscious.

A mile away on the ridge of Upper Wiltz, another GI, Lester Koritz, was huddled in the basement of the Goebel sisters' tobacco shop reading a pocket-size Overseas Edition of *Mr. and Mrs. Cugat* by candlelight. The night before he had crept out of the bee house, climbed over a series of fences and retaining walls, and entered the tobacco shop through the back door.

He was nodding over the book when he heard the sound of footsteps overhead. The cellar door opened.

"But who could be burning a candle downstairs?" said a woman in Luxembourg. It was Tante Elise. "Who's there?" she called.

"C'est moi," he said.

"Lester!"

For the first time, as he stood waiting to greet them, he thought of the danger these people were running for him. He would leave.

Elise came down the steep steps. Behind her were the smallest sister, Mariechen, the two nieces, Maria and Thesy, and finally their mother, the third Goebel sister.

"Are the Germans searching for me?" he asked.

"Oh, no," said Thesy. "Everyone in the castle is now gone."

"This is no place for a celebration," said Elise. They went upstairs to the "stuff," a cozy little parlor used only when special company called. The walls were hung with family portraits and photographs of the Grand Duchess Charlotte and her consort.

While Elise prepared a meal, the others told of mutual Wiltz friends; of their hectic flight to Boulaide and their sad return along the corpse-lined highway near Café Schumann.

It was a heavy meal of beef, and even included beer from the hotel across the street. Three or four times Koritz hid when the bell over the shop entrance tinkled and a German customer came in.

Koritz asked about the military situation.

"We don't really know," said Thesy. "Everyone thinks the Americans are four or five miles away near Café Schumann."

Mariechen's face wrinkled in worry. "You're not thinking of crossing the lines?" she asked.

"I'm not going to stay here and endanger you people."

"Soyez sage," she scoffed. "Why, that would be risking your life. You will stay here."

2

The situation at Bastogne was improving. The corridor was now a mile wide and ten tons of medical supplies had arrived the day before by glider. This was to be the last supply by air by the IX Troop Carrier Command; the road leading up to Bastogne was relatively safe. The night before, a 62-vehicle convoy had brought in ammunition, rations, mail, and PX items. Supplies and reinforcements continued to pour in all day of December 29.

At last Patton felt ready to launch the attack he hoped would bring a quick end to the Bulge. He had just been given two new di-

visions—the 11th Armored and the 87th. The next day he would
send these fresh troops north toward Houffalize.

Manteuffel was also planning an attack for December 30. Panzer
Lehr and the 27th Volksgrenadier Divisions were to strike at the Bastogne corridor from the northwest. Simultaneously the 1st SS Panzer
and the 167th Volksgrenadier Divisions would smash from the east.
This great pincers would meet several miles below Bastogne and
the town would again be surrounded—and set up for annihilation.

3

By 3:00 A.M., December 30, the two fresh American divisions scheduled to attack north were in position: the 11th Armored a mile west
of Bastogne and the 87th to its left.

The GIs of both divisions had little idea of what would happen to
them that day. They knew they were going into combat but had
little conception of what it would be like. The infantrymen of the
87th had seen their first action on December 13 in the Saar. The men
of the 11th Armored had never faced an enemy. They had been
rushed from England, moved to Reims to help set up a last-ditch defense line behind the Meuse River, then brought up front only half-
equipped for battle. Now in the darkness before dawn they huddled
in foxholes, waiting for they knew not what.

Pfc. John Fague, Company B, 21st Armored Infantry Battalion of
the 11th, tossed restlessly in his bedroll. He was runner for his platoon leader, Lieutenant Roy Stringfellow, who was presently getting
attack orders at company headquarters.

At 4:00 A.M. Fague heard Stringfellow talking to the platoon and
squad sergeants in a southern drawl. "There will be enemy artillery
fire and plenty of it. The Germans always advance their fire, so
keep the men moving."

Fague got up, packed his bedroll, and walked to the kitchen
truck. It was cold and he stamped his feet to keep warm. The food
was tasteless but he bolted it down. Soon others were wandering
around. Word was passed that they were to follow Baker Company
of the 22nd Tank Battalion at 6:00 A.M.

At 5:30 A.M. Sherman tanks suddenly roared past. There were
alarmed cries all over the company area. The 22nd had come ahead
of time. The men hastily threw equipment onto trucks and jumped

in. But the tanks were far out of sight before the company was on the road.

They came to a crossroad. A pudgy lieutenant colonel, their battalion commander, was standing there, looking out of place.

"Sir," called Lieutenant Stringfellow from his half-track, "which way did the tanks go?"

The colonel hesitated, then pointed ahead. Fague's vehicle, followed by the rest of the platoon, rumbled along this road. He noticed American tanks peeking from behind stone buildings. Abruptly they were alone. The entire area began to erupt from artillery fire. Something was wrong.

Stringfellow halted the company and tried to contact the main column by radio. Gray dawn slowly lit up the bleak snowy countryside. A ruined farmhouse smoldered near by. Next to it amidst the wreckage of a plane were two bodies.

Fague had never seen violent death before. It was a new, frightening, fascinating concept. With anxious curiosity he approached the scene. He looked down at the first dark heap and wished he hadn't. It was a German pilot, his face frosted with a ghastly faraway look. He was frozen stiff, his fingers white and rigid; his legs were broken and doubled up underneath him. His fleece-lined boots had been pulled off by looters and he lay in his stocking feet. The pockets of his uniform were pulled inside out. Most horrible was his right hand. The middle finger had been crudely cut off. Some GI had wanted his ring.

Fague went back to the half-track with a sick feeling in his stomach. Shells began to explode even closer. Shrapnel whistled overhead. He tried to make a few wisecracks. No one was in the mood for jokes. The men huddled together and kept their heads below the quarter-inch-thick armor plating.

Stringfellow, as tall and lanky as his name, peered over the sides. "Okay, we're turning back."

The column turned and raced to the rear. Now that they were moving, Fague was no longer afraid and he stood up. He noticed they were going through another division; they were infantrymen, wearing the bloody-bucket patch of the 28th Division. Most of these men looked almost hypnotized by exhaustion. Their beards were heavy, their rifles slung carelessly over their shoulders. Their faces became concerned, however, as they watched the 11th Armored vehicles racing to the rear. Fague saw some run to their own vehicles and start to pull out.

At last the column returned to the crossroad and utter confusion. Finally there was order and tanks crawled up the road to the right, followed a few minutes later by the half-tracks.

Soon Fague could hear the blasting of 75s—their own tanks. The half-tracks stopped; the men piled out, frightened but curious. As they formed a skirmish line across a hill, Fague saw American tanks burning at the edge of the woods.

"Fix bayonets," said Stringfellow. The men, with fumbling fingers, fastened bayonets to their M-1s. Fague felt a wave of fear. If they were fixing bayonets, the enemy must be near. Any minute now gray troops would probably come charging out of the woods. Shells began plopping on the hill. The American tanks fired, were fired on, and then began to retreat. The GIs lying in the snow had no idea what they were supposed to do.

"All right," called Stringfellow in a calm drawl. "Mount up."

The men never obeyed a command so fast. In seconds they had dashed back to their half-tracks and piled in pell-mell, flying over the sides on top of each other.

Sherman tanks were spinning, throwing up clouds of dirt and snow as they scurried to the rear over the rolling hills.

"Why the hell are you pulling out?" called Stringfellow to a passing tanker.

A major, standing in the turret, his face dazed, shrugged his shoulders.

The road back was a hopeless tangle. "Dismount," called Stringfellow. "Withdraw!"

The men piled out of the half-tracks in even greater panic. They scrambled to the rear, down into a protected ravine.

The entire 11th Armored Division was stalled. When Patton learned of this, he angrily got into a jeep and headed for the Bastogne area to find out what had gone wrong.

The western jaw of Manteuffel's pincers, aimed at the corridor, had rammed into the 11th Armored. The same thing was happening to the eastern jaw. It had run into a veteran, battle-tested American infantry division, the 35th. Harry Truman's old division had been brought up to help widen the corridor to the right. Positioned several miles below Bastogne it was elbowing to the east toward dense woods known to be filled with Germans. At dawn, these Germans, the infantry elements of the eastern jaw, attacked. Immediately behind them was a unit rushed down at Hitler's orders from the Stavelot-Ligneuville area, the 1st SS Panzer Division. (It was minus, of course, Kampfgruppe Peiper, which was still recuperating from its escape.)

At 7:00 A.M. Hitler's "Own" Division swarmed into Villers-la-Bonne-Eau, a village five miles south of Bastogne. Two 35th Division companies were quickly surrounded. German tanks and infantry attacked in wave after wave, but the GIs held. Mainly because of these two companies, Manteuffel's eastern attack began to bog down.

At 8:00 A.M. the commander of the 1st SS Panzer Division, Oberführer Mohnke, shawl over head to fight the morning cold, angrily called to find out why his tanks hadn't pushed beyond Villers. They should already have made contact with the western jaw and cut the corridor. Soon the morning fog would lift and the panzers would be easy targets for Jabos and rocket-firing fighters. Word came back: an Ami division had gotten into Villers first.

Lieutenant Eberhard Kosch of the Tank Artillery Regiment of the 1st SS Division was sitting in his tank, waiting to hear what was going on at Villers. His radio operators, crowded below him, had contact with five artillery observers and Kosch was ready to call down the fire of forty batteries.

"Sir," said one radio operator, "contact with the tanks at Villers is broken."

Kosch swore. He ordered his tank driver to roll forward. The Panther raced toward Villers, bouncing crazily over the rough road. The half-dozen antennae, waving dangerously, threatened to snap off.

"You can call down the artillery whenever you're ready, Kosch," came the impatient voice of his commander over the radio.

"Yes, s-s-sir," said Kosch. It was almost impossible to talk in the bouncing tank.

Another voice came on the line. "What's the situation?"

"I'm trying to find out," said Kosch irritably. "Who is this?"

"Model." It was the commander of Army Group B. "I want to know what's going on between Villers and Bastogne."

"I'm going up to see for myself, sir!" Kosch hung up, trying to

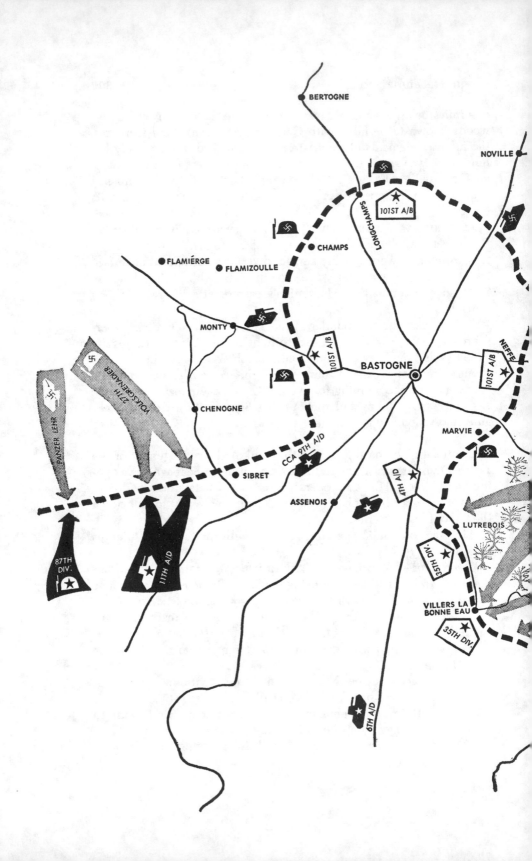

ATTACKS ON DECEMBER 30TH

HOUFFALIZE →

CLERVAUX →

SCALE
1 MILE

LONGVILLY

MAGERET

NIEDERWAMPACH

WARDIN

BRAS

NOERTRANGE

WILTZ

1ST SS PANZER

WILTZ R.

CAFÉ SCHUMANN

157 VOLKSGRENADIER

HARLANGE

35TH DIV.

26TH DIVISION

SAUER R.

BOULAIDE

80TH DIV.

keep from being mashed against the sides of the tank as it darted from side to side to avoid fallen trees.

Finally the tank reached the edge of the woods. Kosch stood up in the turret. In the open area ahead German tanks were wildly careening over the snow, trying to dodge flower-bursts. Eight were already aflame; tiny figures, clothing afire, were escaping through the hatches.

Kosch's vehicle pulled up to the first burning panzer. A young lieutenant, coat smoldering, his face scorched, pointed an accusing finger at Kosch. "Seven cannons fired at me!"

Kosch was wild with frustration. He had forty batteries behind him, and still didn't know where to fire. The phone rang.

"Well, what's going on?" It was Model again.

"The whole situation is confused, sir. You just can't tell friend from enemy."

One of Kosch's operators nudged him, saying, "Seven tanks have reached the outskirts of Bastogne, Lieutenant. But they're catching hell from artillery and infantry. The commander says his own infantry jumped off the tanks and ran to the rear." He held up an earphone. Kosch could hear someone screaming, "God damn it, send me some infantry! My damn infantry, the scum, ran off!"

Kosch took the phone. "We'll do what we can. I'll forward your report."

"Forward my ass!"

Kosch hung up. The phone rang a minute later.

"I can't stay here any more!" It was the same tank commander. "I have only five vehicles. They'll be knocked out in a few minutes. I've got to move out!" His voice was frantic. "Please, please give me artillery fire. I'd rather have our own fire on top of me than the goddam Amis crawling up my ass. Everything here is fouled up!"

Kosch quickly called fire on the tank commander's own positions. The phone rang again. "We're getting out! Keep pouring it on!"

Kosch was afraid to call for more fire. The situation ahead had become even more confused because of the huge rolls of smoke billowing from the battlefield. He saw figures coming across the snow. Friends or Amis?

Suddenly the wind switched to the east. The battlefield cleared. Kosch saw dozens of white-starred vehicles and men in forest green.

"Amis!" he shouted. He quickly passed the word to the rear,

giving the proper coordinates. In three minutes, forty batteries opened up in a thunderous barrage. The battlefield was again covered with black smoke. Damaged panzers limped back under this protective cloud and white-robed infantrymen began to dig in.

Kosch turned his tank and headed for his own headquarters at Bras, four miles east of Bastogne. Halfway there, one of his phones rang. A tank commander was on the wire.

"Kosch, twelve Shermans with infantry have just come through my position. They're driving toward Bras!"

"Are you sure?"

"Take my word as a good friend. I think they're from that damned 4th Armored Division."

"But what the hell are *they* doing that far east?"

Kosch turned his tank and drove in the direction of the reported breakthrough. A mile east of Bras he saw ten Shermans coming from Bastogne. It was impossible. A German division was supposed to have that road under control. Excitedly he called back the news and asked for fire. Two rocket batteries opened up. He saw one of the tanks hit, but the rest came on.

"What the devil do you think you're doing?" It was the division chief of staff screaming over one of the phones. "You're firing at our own tanks!"

"They're Shermans."

"How could Shermans be that far east? Cease fire and report to the commander's headquarters at once."

A few minutes later Kosch was standing in the commander's office.

"Just who do you think you are, Kosch?" shouted the commander. "The Field Marshal gave us permission to fire on Bastogne. But that didn't mean you could waste shells as you like. And on our own tanks too. You'd better keep your damned tired eyes open after this."

The roof exploded. Plaster rained down. A beam fell in. The division commander and his chief of staff dove under the heavy table.

"Tank fire!" shouted a sergeant at the door.

Kosch looked out a window. Shermans were just outside.

"General," said Kosch sarcastically, "don't be afraid. They are *our own* tanks."

Kosch laughed as he watched the staff officers scramble. Again he looked outside. He felt more comradeship for the men in the Shermans than for those in his own uniform under the table.

4

Ten miles southeast of Bastogne the fighting that day in the 26th Division sector was just as bitter. Jim Creighton's Fox Company was attacking Café Schumann from "Cemetery Hill," just to its south. Creighton ran forward, clutching a grease gun. It was cocked, the cover down to keep dirt out of the chamber. He turned the corner of the first house.

Ten feet away a German, holding a rifle, was staring at him in wonder. Creighton pulled the trigger on his gun. Nothing happened. The German was also having trouble with his rifle. Both men simultaneously spun and ran back where they had come from.

On the other side of the house, Germans were coming out of the cellars hands over head. The men of Fox Company were shouting and joking as if they'd just won a football game. More Germans poured out of the cellars, eager to surrender.

Fox had caught an entire company by surprise and was now stripping 105 captured Germans of watches, wallets, Lugers, and medals.

"Let's get going," called Creighton. He started up toward their main objective, Hill 490, just to the north.

Although this thickly wooded hill was only several hundred feet higher than the surrounding terrain, it commanded the entire area from Café Schumann to Wiltz. Besides its obvious strategic importance, Hill 490 was also an invaluable observation point. It had to be taken.

But no one was following Creighton. "God damn it!" he shouted, almost crying in anger and frustration. "Come on!"

Still no one paid any attention to him. The Fox riflemen were too busy fighting each other for souvenirs.

It was just beginning to get dark in nearby Wiltz. On Grand' Rue, people were leaving their homes for safer cellars. German soldiers, engrossed by their own problems, did not notice that among a small group of women hurrying along the sidewalk was an American soldier draped with bedclothes. The five women with much chatter and arm waving convoyed the American into the May Furniture Store. Sergeant Lester Koritz, formerly of the 28th Division, in spite of protests that he was endangering his Luxembourg friends, had finally found a permanent hiding place.

A mile away, in Lower Wiltz, another 28th Division GI, Ralph Ellis, was in a daze. Pain from his frozen feet was almost unbearable. The pangs of hunger were sharp. He hobbled to the window of the top floor of the building on the Rue du Pont. He had three hand grenades. He would wait for a staff car and then drop them. It would be the end of him, but he would take some Jerries with him. He lined up two grenades on the floor and held the other, ready to pull the pin. Two German soldiers and two civilians—a man and a woman—came out of a basement grocery store and stood under the window. The soldiers, pulling a little cart filled with bottles of schnapps, were arguing with the man and woman. Ellis became fascinated by the argument in a language he couldn't understand. It was like watching a foreign movie. He carelessly leaned out of the window. As he did the woman looked him in the eye. Ellis pulled back his head and fell, half-conscious, on the floor.

He heard the cart rattle away, then footsteps on the stairs. The door opened and the man and woman stared down at him. They talked but he couldn't understand. The man, short and powerful like a wrestler, tried to make signs of friendliness.

The woman, plump and attractive with a merry face, smiled. Ellis tried to smile as she leaned down and carefully pulled off his tattered socks. Green fluid ran from his swollen feet. The woman's smile died.

Somehow the two Luxembourgers convinced Ellis they were friends and that they would return soon. When it was dark the two did come back. They slipped a pair of civilian pants over his GI trousers and a coat over his field jacket. Then, one on each side, they supported him down the stairs and out into the street. At the next house he was led down a flight of steps to a cellar grocery store and into a cozy, delightfully warm dining room.

The woman smiled and pointed to herself. "Meisy," she said.

Ellis pointed to himself: "Ralph."

The short powerful man joined in the pantomime: "Louis."

5

In Versailles that night, Eisenhower knew the Battle of the Bulge was far from over. He was rereading a cablegram he had received

earlier in the day from his good friend, and commander, George
Catlett Marshall, Chief of Staff of the U.S. Army.

> They may or may not have brought to your attention articles in cer-
> tain London papers proposing a British deputy commander for all
> your ground forces and implying that you have undertaken too much
> of a task yourself.
>
> My feeling is this: under no circumstances make any concessions of
> any kind whatsoever. You not only have our complete confidence but
> there would be a terrific resentment in this country following such
> action. I am not assuming that you had in mind such a concession.
> I just wish you to be certain of our attitude on this side. You are
> doing a fine job and go on and give them hell.

The day before, Montgomery had sent him a letter suggesting
that the Allied forces in the Ardennes offensive be placed under the
control of one commander. The key to future success, according to
Montgomery, lay in the assignment of all available offensive power
to the north for a single powerful advance to the Ruhr.

Eisenhower was beginning to lose his patience. In fact, he was
close to an emotion he considered a luxury, anger.

Near the storm center of the battle, Troy Middleton, whose VIII
Corps now consisted of the 87th, the 11th Armored, and the 101st
Airborne Divisions, was just driving up to an advanced headquarters of the 11th Armored Division to find out why their first day of
attack toward Houffalize had failed so dismally. While Middleton
was in an inner office with the commander, his driver slumped in a
chair outside to catch a few minutes' sleep. No sooner had he
dropped off than someone stepped heavily on his feet.

The driver woke angry. "Why, you son of a bitch," he cried, "don't
you know I'm trying to sleep?" Then he saw he was looking up at
George Patton.

Patton leaned back and laughed. "Son," he said, "you're the first
son of a bitch I've met today who knows what he's trying to do."

3. "BRAVE RIFLES . . ."

31 December 1944–2 January 1945

1

On the south (the American) side of Hill 490, men of the 26th Division were trying to sleep in their frigid lonely foxholes. They were exhausted by the almost constant fighting of the past week, but whenever they dropped off to sleep a moan from no man's land would awaken them. If anyone from either side tried to creep out to help the wounded, a chatter of machine guns broke out. The fight in these snowy hills just south of Wiltz was a bitter one, with no mercy given or expected.

Creighton's company, Fox, still held the line near the Café Schumann crossroad.

At 6:00 A.M. German mortar and artillery began to dig up his sector. Then as the first light of day came over the hills, Creighton saw ghostly figures flitting among the woods. The white-caped Germans drifted forward expertly, shouting only enough to terrorize the Americans; not enough to give away their positions. Suddenly a great white wave rose, screaming wildly, and rushed straight for Fox Company.

Creighton was sure his company—F for fouled up—would now pile out of its foxholes and tear for the rear. But M-1s and BARs spit flames. Not one Fox Company man broke and ran. A second wave of attackers ran down the hill. Once more Fox Company held. A third attack came, and was thrown back.

Now fire from the 101st Field Artillery Battalion dropped between Fox and the Germans. Mortar shells—81-mm.—fell so fast their explosions became a continuous din.

Creighton crawled up to the first foxhole. Two bearded grubby men, their stiff bodies raised, were peering out front at the piles of dead Germans only yards away. "Y'know," said one thoughtfully, "if we use armor-piercing ammo next time, we'll go right through the trees."

The other, nodding sagely, began to load his magazine with black-nosed cartridges.

Creighton went to the next foxhole. There they were discussing ways to improve their positions. In the next hole a man painfully wounded in the arm was telling his buddy, "I'm staying."

Creighton tried to convince the man the extreme cold was dangerous to the wound.

"The Krauts are liable to come down that hill any minute, Lieutenant," said the man. "Anyway, it's just a scratch. Whatya want me to do, apply for a Purple Heart?"

Creighton said nothing but moved on. Fox Company had abruptly come of age.

2

In Versailles that afternoon Eisenhower was writing Montgomery a letter. He was willing to leave one U.S. Army under 21st Army Group on the basis of military necessity and as a token of confidence in the British commander but that was all. He added that he was disturbed by Montgomery's constant predictions of failure unless his plans were followed in their entirety.

Eisenhower ended the letter declaring he would deplore "the development of such an unbridgeable gulf of convictions between us that we would have to present our differences to the Combined Chiefs of Staff. The confusion and debate that would follow would certainly damage the good will and devotion to a common cause that have made this Allied Force unique in history."

As soon as Montgomery received this letter, he sat down and wrote a reply. He was distressed if his previous letter had proved upsetting. There were probably many factors involved in the command question which he didn't know about. He pledged his 100 per cent cooperation in backing any decision the Supreme Commander might make.

In Ziegenberg, Germany, that afternoon, Otto Skorzeny, whose "Trojan Horse" Brigade had been relieved by an infantry division at Ligneuville on December 28, was received for the second time that day at Hitler's field headquarters. That morning he had been summoned to make a personal report to the Führer. But on seeing Skorzeny's eye bandage Hitler had insisted his favorite commando immediately consult his personal doctor, Stumpfecker.

Skorzeny's wound was freshly bound when he reported to Hitler in the afternoon. To his amazement the Führer was full of enthusiasm.

"We are now going to start a great offensive in the southeast," Hitler said and then explained briefly about Operation "Nordwind." Following this new offensive in northern Alsace the attacks in the Ardennes would be resumed.

Skorzeny left the conference room much more cheerful than he had entered; but he was puzzled, and not a little worried, by the Führer's excess spirits. Was Hitler deceiving himself or was he under the influence of Professor Morell's injections?

Only that day Dr. Rudolf Brandt had told Skorzeny he considered Morell's injections and stomach pills extremely dangerous. "I recently analyzed one of those stomach pills," he said. "It contained arsenic. I warned the Führer but he wouldn't listen."

In another German town General Student was reviewing the survivors of Kampfgruppe von der Heydte. Two hundred and forty had managed to escape from the Ardennes and now stood in three lines while Student thanked them for their "worth-while, successful mission."

The men in the ranks knew what a dismal failure it had been, but they gladly accepted their Black Crosses and fourteen-day leaves.

A few of the veterans, like Hans-Jurgen Isenheim, were ordered to report to a special conference room. There they were told by a young eager officer that when they returned from leave they were to be assigned to their most important mission of the war. "Early in February," said the officer, "the leaders of the democracies will meet in Yalta. They think we know nothing about it but you men

will make a para-drop. You will kill Roosevelt, Churchill, and
Stalin."

3

By nightfall the situation at the foot of Hill 490 was still critical. A
new line had been set up after the ferocious morning attacks, but
those in the rear were preparing for the worst. All available troops
were now digging breakthrough defenses several miles to the south.

Up front, James Creighton's Fox Company was getting ready for
another attack. Creighton wasn't there. He had found a sled in one
of the buildings at Café Schumann and was using it to evacuate the
badly wounded. Creighton was now on his way back to the front;
this time the sled was loaded with ammunition, two BARs, and a
bag of mail.

As he dragged the sled through the deepening dusk, huge soft
flakes of snow began to fall. Nebelwerfer and artillery fire broke out.
He hurried forward; another Jerry attack was coming.

When he reached his improvised command post, a dugout, he was
told the communication section had just run a line into the company
area. He was called to the phone and briefed: the situation was serious all over the regiment; in case of a general retreat the going
would be rough and the rifle companies would have to hold to the
last man; Division had only two Bailey bridges on hand in case of
a retreat back across the Sauer River; the challenge for the night
was READERS, the countersign DIGEST.

It was a gloomy picture for New Year's Eve.

Cries came from the top of the hill as white-robed Germans
loomed up. Creighton quickly called for artillery and mortar. It was
almost impossible to see the approaching enemy in the early darkness. The men of Fox Company held off until the last moment, then
loosed a withering fire.

The attackers fell back.

Creighton crawled forward to the 2nd Platoon positions. A sergeant was clutching his arm, swearing. Creighton had always disliked this man—for his tiny black mustache, for his fancy scarfs and
tailored uniforms, and especially for his brown-nosing at battalion
headquarters.

"Well," said Creighton, "you got your Million Dollar Wound.
Move back." He took the sergeant's carbine.

"Balls to you, Lieutenant." The sergeant snatched back the weapon.

Creighton shrugged his shoulders and went to the next hole.

The second attack began. Creighton's men were almost out of ammunition and the Germans kept boring in. The attack was stopped only by a pinpointed barrage from the 101st Field Artillery. But a few minutes later a third, much stronger, attack was launched.

The Germans came on relentlessly. Creighton emptied his carbine and looked for more ammunition. He saw two of his noncoms dash from their foxholes to grab weapons from dead or dying Germans and then slither back to their holes.

The company perimeter defense was broken in two places. A rifleman stood up, aiming his M-1 at two charging Germans. It jammed. A wounded comrade in the next foxhole flung him his carbine. The rifleman grabbed it and loosed a burst as the Germans leaped with fixed bayonets. Both white-robed attackers flopped at the edge of the foxhole, dead.

Creighton's phone rang. It was General Harlan Hartness, the assistant division commander. "How are things?" he asked.

"We're pretty busy, sir."

"Will they break through?"

"That's hard to say, General."

"Well, keep on the phone. If the Germans break through you, we've got to know right away. Do you understand?"

"Yes, sir." Creighton hung onto the phone, though he was impatient to get up farther front and see what was going on. Another wave of Germans started down the hill. Creighton disconnected himself from Division and rang the battalion artillery liaison officer. "Give me artillery fire, fast." He called for it almost at the edge of the perimeter line.

"For God's sake," said the artillery officer. "I can't do that! It's inside the safety limit for artillery."

"Damn it all, bring it exactly where I call for it," said Creighton angrily. "It's our only chance. We're in foxholes and the Krauts aren't."

A minute later friendly shells were exploding only yards beyond Fox Company. The GIs were showered with snow and dirt. The Germans, caught in the open, were slaughtered by the tree-bursts. The survivors turned and ran back up the hill.

There was now deadly quiet. Creighton crawled forward. His men were still dazed by the terrific barrage. But there had been only one casualty—a single slight shrapnel wound in the buttocks.

Creighton's phone rang again.

"How did we do?" asked a worried voice. It was Battery B.

"You only got one of my men," said Creighton. "And he was sticking his ass up too high."

The man on the other end seemed to sigh.

"Fox Company thanks you," said Creighton and hung up.

A moment later he crawled to the most forward foxhole. Though it was dark, light reflected from the snow. Before him was a scene of utter carnage. Bodies were sprawled in grotesque positions, already freezing like ice statues. Five men in white were stretched in a straight line, frozen in flight. The barrage had caught a German machine-gun team, still carrying weapons and equipment.

Dark figures were now creeping from the Fox Company lines, collecting armfuls of light weapons and ammunition. Two GIs were hanging a German body upside down from the crotch of a tree—a warning of what would happen to the next attackers. Creighton didn't stop them. The night before, men of that platoon had sneaked out to pull back a wounded comrade. When they touched the wounded man there had been a great explosion—he had been booby-trapped.

A wounded German was led into the company lines, his face yellow, his eyes wild, the entire top of his skull sheared off. Creighton saw it was useless to question him and finished checking his count. He now had forty men. He crawled over to the 2nd Platoon to see how the sergeant with the mustache was doing.

The sergeant was lying in his foxhole dead, his mouth open, his tiny mustache frozen. Creighton slowly crawled back to his own dugout.

An artilleryman was waiting in the dugout. He handed Creighton a big paper bag.

"What the hell's this?" Creighton opened the bag. It was filled with doughnuts.

The artilleryman grinned cockily. "Battery B wants to wish Fox Company a Happy New Year."

4

Just before midnight eight German divisions rushed from their Sieg-fried Line positions with great élan and attacked the Seventh U.S. Army near the boundary of northern Alsace. Operation "Nordwind," designed to take Allied attention from the Bulge, was launched.

To the north, in the Ardennes, a tremendous artillery barrage sud-denly erupted at the stroke of midnight. George Patton had ordered that every available gun fire a New Year's salute.

Just south of Bastogne, within hearing of Patton's thunderous bar-rage, Red Cross worker Fran Alden, eight months pregnant, was celebrating her New Year's Eve at an abbey which was now the 16th Field Hospital, attached to the 6th Armored Division. The wounded from the second battle of Bastogne were coming in stead-ily. In addition to her regular Red Cross work she undressed the wounded, gave them baths, shaved them, and assisted at operations. She was not at all squeamish in the presence of the most mangled. These days were the high point of her existence. She had never been more useful.

As yet she had told no one of her marriage in England, knowing she'd be sent out of the European Theater of Operations. And as yet her height, her erect carriage, and a remodeled Eisenhower jacket had camouflaged her condition. Late at night, when his own work with the 6th Armored Division trains was over, her husband, Major Ken Alden, would come to the hospital and try to persuade her to go to Paris and get the proper rest and treatment. She always put him off. First it was impossible to leave before the Christmas party for the wounded. Now it was the New Year's Eve party.

That night Fran played the piano in the chapel on the second floor of the great abbey while the ambulatory patients sang. The music drifted down the halls to those in the beds: "Auld Lang Syne," "Down by the Old Mill Stream," "Don't Sit under the Apple Tree," "White Christmas."

As counterpoint came the distant deep thunder of artillery from the Bastogne battle.

After the party, the commander of the hospital jokingly asked, "When are you and Ken going to get married?"

She showed him the wedding ring she wore around her neck on a chain. "We were married in England. I'm going to have a baby in a month."

He was amazed, then angry. "What do you mean coming up here —eating cold rations, working twenty hours a day, handling the worst cases?"

"But I love it."

"But why take such a risk?"

"If you had the chance to be with someone you love, wouldn't you take a risk? I'm not hurting anyone by staying. Haven't I done my job?"

"Yes . . ."

"You can't make me leave now at a time like this. Give me another week."

An orderly wheeled a patient, prepared for operation, past them. Shrapnel had grazed his heart. That afternoon Fran had spent an hour calming his fears. He was not yet nineteen, and his face was white—and scared. "Fran," he said, "you promised to hold my hand while they operate."

"Don't worry. I'll be right in." She looked inquiringly at the commandant.

"Oh, all right," he said reluctantly. "But next week you're leaving." Fran hurried into the operating room.

In Berlin, at exactly 12:05 A.M. on January 1, Adolf Hitler began to shout shrilly but confidently into a microphone:

> Our people are resolved to fight the war to victory under any and all circumstances. . . . We are going to destroy everybody who does not take part in the common effort for the country or who makes himself a tool of the enemy. . . . The world must know that this State will, therefore, never capitulate. . . . Germany will rise like a phoenix from its ruined cities and this will go down in history as the miracle of the 20th Century!

> I want, therefore, in this hour, as spokesman of Greater Germany, to promise solemnly to the Almighty that we shall fulfill our duty faithfully and unshakably in the New Year too, in the firm belief that the hour will strike when victory will ultimately come to him who is most worthy of it, the Greater German Reich!

5

"Nordwind," the new offensive a hundred miles south of the Bulge, wasn't Hitler's only surprise of the New Year.

Fighter pilots of the Luftwaffe did not celebrate New Year's Eve, as usual, at night-long parties. Instead they were ordered to bed early.

At 5:00 A.M. on January 1, they were awakened and briefed. Every fighter plane that could fly was to take off in a desperate attempt to knock out Allied air in the West. It was an attack personally planned by Göring and Hitler: Operation "Hermann," or the "Big Blow." Each pilot was assigned a special target at a specified airfield. There would be no deviations. If the carefully worked-out plan were followed exactly, Allied air would be dealt a crippling blow. The pilots, many of them with only a few hours of solo flight, were enthusiastic. At last they were on the offensive.

At 7:45 A.M. more than 1,100 Focke-Wulf 190s and Messerschmidt 109s took off from snow-covered fields in four massive formations. Led by Junker 88s, they headed toward the Ardennes under strict radio silence. At the Rhine the shepherding Junkers turned back and the inexperienced pilots were guided west by colored smoke, searchlights, and "golden rain" flares.

The four great waves dropped dangerously low and were soon skimming over the snowbound Ardennes at tree level. Now enemy radar would be useless and the surprise attack complete and devastating.

At 7:45 A.M. Lieutenant Colonel John Meyer, commander of the 487th Fighter Squadron, based near Aschen, Belgium, stepped out of the operations office. Meyer had just become the leading American ace in Europe. With the jet-propelled Arado 234 he'd knocked down the day before he now was credited with 35½ enemy aircraft.

His twelve planes, scheduled for a dawn patrol over St. Vith, were still waiting for the sun to burn off the fog. He went to the mess hall, had a quick cup of coffee, then hustled to the runway. It was beginning to clear from east to west.

"It's good enough to go," he finally told his men at 8:05 A.M. "Remember, this is just the same old patrol." He climbed into his P-51 Mustang, "Petie." His crew chief, worried as ever, made last-min-

ute checks like an anxious mother sending her son to school in a
storm. As Meyer was taxiing, he saw bursts of flak at the far end of
the field.

He called Marmite control. "Anything coming?"

"No, not a thing," replied the radar warning station.

Meyer gave his plane the throttle. But before it could lift from the
runway, there was a roar ahead. A Focke-Wulf 190 suddenly rock-
eted toward the "Petie" at tree level. Meyer knew he didn't have a
chance.

But the Focke-Wulf abruptly pulled up, did a wing-over, and attacked an empty C-47 parked at the edge of the runway.

Astounded at his luck, Meyer roared into the air. While his wheels
were still retracting he came up behind the Focke-Wulf and fired a
burst. The German exploded and crashed into the ground with a
pinwheel skid.

Behind Meyer, others in HUNter Squadron were zooming up, attacking waves of Germans. Meyer saw Germans everywhere. The
sky was wealthy with targets. He picked one, again a 190. But every
time he got on the Focke-Wulf's tail, friendly ground fire tore
through the wings of the Mustang. A big hole suddenly opened in
front of his cockpit. He decided not to come from behind but to
shoot the German from about 20 per cent deflection. Finally he cor-
nered the Focke-Wulf and exploded it with his last belt of ammunition.

By 10:30 A.M. it was all over. The surprise had been so complete
that twenty-seven Allied bases from Brussels to Eindhoven were in
ruins and almost 300 Allied aircraft knocked out.

The Big Blow had been an astounding success—but suicidal.
Three hundred German fighter pilots, including fifty-nine leaders,
had been killed. The Luftwaffe was now kaputt.

6

That morning Patton issued an emotional order of the day to his
men. In closing, he said:

> I can find no fitter expression for my feelings than to apply to you
> the immortal words spoken by General Scott at Chapultepec when
> he said: "Brave rifles, veterans, you have been baptized in fire and
> blood and have come out steel."

The green troops of the 11th Armored Division—baptized in snow and ice as well as fire and blood—were standing around half-tracks just short of Chenogne, the same goal as yesterday, eating while they stamped their feet to keep warm.

Someone remarked, "This is a helluva way to start the new year."

Pfc. John Fague threw down his half-finished can of C-rations. He and his buddy, Jim Cust, had had to dig three different foxholes the night before. Now they were exhausted.

Cust wasn't eating either. "One of us is going to die today," he said.

Fague, frightened by his friend's matter-of-fact tone, tried to laugh it off as a joke. But Cust repeated, "One of us is going to die."

Sergeants grouped their men. The attack on Chenogne was almost ready. Half-tracks, tank destroyers, tanks, and medical jeeps massed behind the infantrymen.

Fague felt worse than he had the day before. The medical jeeps gave him an uneasy feeling. He kept thinking of what Cust had said.

Great hollow booms came from the rear. Shells, preparation for the attack, began falling on Chenogne. The tanks maneuvered in position across the reverse side of the hill. Fague and the other infantrymen began to deploy in a skirmish line behind the tanks. Today the 2nd and 3rd Platoons of B Company were on the line. Fague's platoon, heavily hit the day before, hung back in reserve.

Cust nudged Fague. His young, intelligent face was creased with worry. "Let's stick together. Sort of look after each other."

Fague nodded nervously.

Lieutenant Stringfellow, his lanky figure bent with weariness, came up to the two. "Stick by me, boys. I'm running out of gas." He handed Fague his walkie-talkie.

The roar of tanks mingled with the shouts of sergeants. The attack was on. Tanks and men reached the crest of the hill, then went down the other side.

The village exploded with answering fire. All along the hill men cried, "Medic! Medic! Bring a stretcher!"

German mortar fire dropped on the attackers. Cust and Fague carried wounded back over the hill. Then as the morning wore on the reserve platoon got mixed with the rest of the company and the two men found themselves in the middle of the attack, running into the streets of Chenogne.

Machine-gun fire broke out somewhere on the right. A bullet

creased Fague's thumb and smashed into the upper hand guard of
his rifle. He spun around, fell.

"Come on!" The platoon sergeant was shouting at him, pointing to
a house thirty yards ahead. "That's where it's coming from. You and
Cust go up and toss some grenades in that building."

The two ran forward, crouching by the walls of the house. Cust
threw a grenade at an upper window. It hit the ledge and fell back.
Cust flopped on the snow. The grenade exploded only ten feet away
but the fragments flew up.

Cust got up shakily, unharmed. He smiled weakly at Fague.

Fague threw his grenade. It also fell down. He jumped into a
doorway to escape the blast.

"Come back," Sergeant Ferguson called. The two ran back just as
a Sherman began shelling the house.

Safe in the ditch, Fague looked around for his friend. Cust was
nowhere in sight. "Where's Jim?"

The sergeant pointed to the hedge. A figure was lying under it.
Fague scrambled forward, oblivious of the machine-gun bullets
ripping on both sides of him.

Cust was lying on his back. His eyes were glassy, as if staring at
something very far away. His teeth protruded, his skin was drawn
tightly over his face. It didn't look anything like the Jim Cust he
knew.

The house was now in flames from the tank.

"They're coming out of the basement," shouted a man from a
Sherman. Those in the ditch stood, weapons ready. It was the first
time Fague had really felt like killing a human being.

Soldiers in gray poured out of the house, choking from the smoke.
The first, a medic, waved a German Red Cross flag and shouted for
mercy. Half a dozen M-1s cracked. The medic staggered and
dropped to the snow. He lay still. From the cellar came the terrified
shouts and screams of suffocating men. As the Germans rushed out,
they were cut down. Soon a ring of bodies formed around the doorway.

Then hysterical women and children burst from the cellar. The
GIs held their fire. When the Belgians saw the Americans, guns
ready, they huddled against the wall, thinking they too would be
shot. Several were wounded but had to be held forcibly by the GIs
to be bandaged.

At last the women realized the savage "Sammies" wouldn't murder them. They went frantic with joy. But when the shelling resumed, still distrusting the Americans they grabbed their crying children and ran across the snow to the woods.

Germans were surrendering all over Chenogne. Fague saw a white flag waving from a stone house. Then a man boldly appeared. "Come on," yelled Fague, waving him forward. The German, followed by a dozen others, shuffled wearily down the road. Soon over sixty prisoners were lined up.

"Not here," said a sergeant. "The others hiding in the woods will see. Take them over that hill."

Fague knew they were going to be shot for word had been passed down to take no prisoners. He watched volunteers march the prisoners just out of town into a field. He turned his back and hurried to the half-track where he found a can of C-rations. He tried to thaw out the can on the vehicle's exhaust pipe but he gave it up as a bad job.

The word came to continue the attack toward the important Bastogne-Marche highway. He walked up the road—the same road the sixty prisoners had walked not long before. In the snowy field beside the road were the dark forms of lifeless bodies.

A jeep raced up the hill. Its driver, an officer, shouted something to a man ahead of Fague. The man turned. "Did you hear that? Somebody fouled up. We're supposed to take prisoners."

Fague didn't answer. But he turned and looked again at the sixty-odd mounds in the snow.

7

Next morning the 26th Division was ordered to take Hill 490.

At 5:00 A.M. the battalion commander's voice was only a drone to Lieutenant James Creighton of Fox Company. He shook his head and pinched himself to stay awake.

"The attack will kick off at 0600," said the commander. "The battalion objective is the high ground at Hill 490."

Both Creighton and the Easy Company commander had bitterly protested the attack. Their companies were down to platoon strength; the men were suffering from trench foot, exposure, and pure exhaustion. There was no protest from George Company. That outfit had gone to pieces several days before when its commander, a good soldier, had cracked, refusing to lead his men to what he insisted was suicide.

The battalion commander knew that his people were in no shape for attack, but the order had come from above that Hill 490 would be taken at once. "E, F, and the remnants of G will attack on a 200-yard front on the right of the main highway to Bastogne," he said. "C Company of the 1st Battalion will attack from the buildings at Café Schumann and keep left of the road. Creighton, you'll guide on the road and assault Hill 490 with E and G on your right. Any questions?"

The two company commanders bundled up and pushed out into the bitter cold.

"I'm not holding back anything," said Creighton. "I want to put as many men up on the line as possible."

"Same here."

The two wished each other good luck, and started back for their own companies. Creighton called together his few remaining noncoms. They were so dazed from sleepless nights and the shock of incessant artillery that he had to repeat the orders three times. Then, to be sure, he made each man recite the orders.

At 5:30 A.M. Creighton lined up Fox Company along the right side of the highway at the Café Schumann crossroad. Across the highway he could see the dim shapes of men from the 1st Battalion. It was comforting to know he had a solid left flank. His men stood, half sleeping, their heads nodding, too exhausted to know they were slowly freezing to death.

At 5:45 A.M. there was a gargantuan roar. The entire 101st Field Artillery had broken into simultaneous action. It was awesome even as it winged overhead harmlessly.

At 6:00 A.M. the barrage stopped. From the shattered woods ahead came the screams and moans of wounded Germans. Creighton led the attack, amazed to find that almost every tree had been cut down to waist-high height. Nothing happened for 150 yards. Then came a blast of machine-gun and rifle fire. Two men near Creighton dropped to the snow.

On the left side of the road it was worse. C Company of the 1st Battalion had been caught in open ground.

Suddenly a German self-propelled gun, sticking its nose out of the far edge of the clearing at the base of Hill 490, laid down low devastating fire. Then a flak wagon came alongside the gun, raking Fox Company with its 20-mm. multiple guns.

Creighton rushed forward. He felt a strange numbness but didn't realize he'd been hit. He knew only that something had to be done about the self-propelled gun. There was a roar from the flak wagon. Creighton found himself on his knees in a cloud of smoke; he staggered to his feet, then dropped. He felt himself being rolled over. Sergeant Love's serious face was staring at him.

Creighton sat up. Half his field jacket had been blown off; one pants leg had been sheared off, the hairs on his right leg shaved as if by an expert barber.

"Are you all right?" asked Love.

"Sure." Creighton blinked and shook his head to clear his thoughts. "I'm going up to the company. You go back for tanks. We've got to get that damn SP."

Love didn't want to leave but he knew it was useless to argue with a man like Creighton. At Café Schumann he found two tanks and pointed out the location of the flak wagon and self-propelled gun; then he ran back toward Hill 490. Fox Company was digging in but he could see one man deliberately walking from foxhole to foxhole. It was Creighton, blood running out of both ears.

"Get down!" cried Love.

But Creighton walked on, exhorting his men, until he stepped into a shell hole and disappeared from sight. Love found Creighton in a crawling position half out of the hole, but unconscious. The Sergeant draped the Lieutenant over his back and staggered back to Café Schumann.

For Creighton the battle was over. And Hill 490 was still German.

8

In Paris the French had been completely baffled by McAuliffe's retort at Bastogne. But the Agence de Presse Française announced that evening it had solved the problem. "Nuts!" simply meant, "Vous n'êtes que de vieilles noix." That is, "You are nothing but old nuts."

McAuliffe was at the Hotel Scribe in Paris, headquarters of Allied correspondents, resting from an all-day session of press conferences. His frank friendly manner had won the reporters. He was easy and affable; his youthful vitality was a welcome relief from the gloom of the previous week.

Consequently news stories were already taking on a confident, almost boastful tone, implying that the Battle of the Bulge was as good as over.

In Berlin Hitler, infuriated by the stand at Bastogne and by Mc-Auliffe's one-word message, had just demanded that von Rundstedt take the town immediately, at all costs.

Rundstedt was now talking on the telephone to Model. "You must continue the attack on Bastogne. I don't care how heavy your losses are. The Führer insists you encircle the town and wipe it out. He wants you to attack either from the west to the southeast or from the southeast toward the northwest."

"That's not possible," protested Model. "The enemy is too strong southeast of Bastogne and the terrain is unsuitable for tanks. Why can't I attack with the 9th Panzer Division from the north, the 12th SS Panzer Division from the northeast, and the Führer Escort Brigade from the east?"

The suggestion was relayed back to the Führer. Hitler considered the change and agreed.

4. IN DUBIOUS BATTLE

3–8 January 1945

1

Heavy ground fog covered most of the Ardennes at dawn on January 3. Sleety rain was punctuated with wild flurries of snow. In spite of the somber weather which was closing Allied airfields, there was a feeling of excitement and hope in the Ardennes. This was the long-awaited day of full-scale counterattack. Two American armies and one British corps were poised for assault.

At exactly 8:30 A.M. the First Army struck on a 25-mile front against the middle of the northern shoulder of the Bulge.

"Lightning Joe" Collins' VII Corps, regrouped and refitted after its bitter fight to stop the Nazis at Manhay, Hotton, Marche, and Celles, carried the burden of the attack. Harmon's 2nd Armored Division rolled west of the Bastogne-Liége highway carrying the 335th Infantry Regiment of the 84th Division on its tanks. The remaining two regiments of the 84th and the 290th Infantry Regiment of the 75th Division plowed through knee-high snow in close pursuit, their job to consolidate the gains. A similar attack was going on east of the same highway. Rose's 3rd Armored Division, with the 330th Infantry Regiment of the 83rd Division attached, was also heading for Houffalize. Behind them followed the rest of the 83rd Division.

To the east of Collins' corps, one division of the XVIII Airborne

Corps, the 82nd Airborne, was plunging through snowdrifts to protect the left flank of the 3rd Armored Division.

Simultaneously the British XXX Corps, commanded by Lieutenant General Sir Bryan Horrocks, was attacking the western tip of the Bulge with the 6th Airborne Division, veterans of the Normandy drop, and from the south Patton continued his drive up toward Houffalize.

The great triple attack—from north, west, and south—struck with fury. On all sides the Germans fought tenaciously, yielding every yard of snow at heavy cost to both sides. They were dug in with their usual efficient use of terrain.

The Allies came forward slowly for the dense fog eliminated air support and cut down the use of artillery. Tanks and self-propelled guns slipped and skidded on the icy trails and roads, often crashing into each other and holding up columns for hours.

It was obvious by mid-morning that the road to Houffalize would be a rugged one.

2

Early in the afternoon Patton's situation grew worse. The Germans unexpectedly attacked five miles north of Bastogne near Longchamps.

At 1:10 P.M. the phone in the command post of Company D, of the 502nd Regiment of the 101st Airborne Division, rang.

"I hear something," reported Sergeant Lawrence Silva from his outpost. He called a few minutes later. "I can see fourteen tanks. Down the road from Compogne. There're eighteen tanks! No, twenty!"

Hitler's all-out assault on the Bastogne salient had begun in earnest.

"I can't tell you any more," Silva said in a muffled voice.

"Why not?"

"There's a tank right over my foxhole. I'm lying flat on my stomach."

The German tank pivoted over Silva's foxhole. But the hole was too deep, the ground frozen hard as a rock. Thwarted in its efforts to crush the paratrooper, the tank now parked over the hole, its motor roaring. Carbon monoxide flooded the foxhole. In a few minutes Silva was dead.

By nightfall, Patton's lines in the Bastogne area were almost where they had been in the morning, despite heavy losses. He was angry, disappointed, and chagrined.

Opposite him, Manteuffel's lines were also unchanged at the cost of much German blood. He too was disappointed.

Neither realized that what had taken place was that rare military event, a full-scale meeting engagement: two opposing attacks colliding head-on.

Ten miles to the southeast, Patton's drive on Wiltz was also stalled. That night Hill 490 was still German.

Fox Company was being pulled out of the line for a rest. Through the darkness the remnants of Lieutenant James Creighton's company headed for Nothum. A few days before they had numbered 176. Now there were twenty-seven.

They were being led out by Lieutenant De Roller of Battalion; their last officer, Creighton, was in a field hospital. The bedraggled, battle-weary column passed the battalion command post. No one came out to see them slog by.

De Roller was disgusted as he stepped aside and watched Fox Company head for the rear. Practically every man a hero and there was no one to give them a word of cheer or a single "Well done."

He shrugged and went into the warm command post.

3

January 4 was another bad day for the Allies. Montgomery's drives from north and west were slowed almost to a standstill by snow, ice, and continued stubborn resistance.

Patton was making even less progress. As his troops renewed their attack up toward Houffalize that morning, Manteuffel resumed his all-out assault on the Bastogne area.

The strongest German onslaught came five miles southeast of town. Here a stubby finger of heavily wooded German territory stuck down between Bastogne and Wiltz. The 6th Armored Division, at the tip of this finger, was hit with such ferocity it fell back—the first time since landing in Normandy. But by 1:00 P.M. the German attack had subsided and Major General Robert Grow, the division commander, decided it would be safe to make an orderly with-

drawal to a new, more defensible line. He ordered it to start at 3:00
P.M.

By sheer chance one of the most feared maneuvers in battle
started a few minutes after 3:00 P.M. As the Americans began falling
back, the Germans unexpectedly renewed their attack.

The early darkness added even more terror to the retreat. The
dense woods, the lonely trails, even open fields were fearsome
places. Some, particularly the new replacements who had yet
found no comrades to trust, were running back in sheer panic.
Others pulled back slowly, making the Germans pay for each yard
of advance.

The Germans, tanks and men camouflaged in white, surged forward in triumph. They were hungry, frozen, low on supplies and
ammunition but high in morale.

Colonel John Hines, of Combat Command A, was working tire-
lessly to organize the most critical area, the division's right flank.
He ordered antivehicular mines buried all along the highway.
Flares with trip wires were scattered freely all along the broken
front. These, when tripped, would give the alarm, and expose the
enemy to fire, yet would not kill any returning GIs.

Reports from men drifting back from the front were alarming.
Entire units, claimed many wild-eyed refugees, had been cut off
and were being wiped out. Back at Division, General Grow had no
clear idea of how great his casualties were. But he did know it was
the worst day in the history of his 6th Armored Division.

The retreat of the 6th Armored wasn't the only reverse on George
Patton's front. For the savage meeting engagement was at its climax. Violent German attacks had struck all along the Bastogne
front. In particular the 17th Airborne Division, in their first real day
of action a few miles west of town, had been dealt shocking casualties, some battalions losing 40 per cent of their men.

Ordinarily the most optimistic of American generals, Patton was
now in a despondent mood. Each man lost that day weighed heavily on him. He sat at a desk and wrote in his diary, "We can
still lose this war."

But at the front, later that night a strange thing began to take
place where the day's disaster had been greatest. Men stopped run-

ning, and were digging in. Terror was being replaced by anger.

Not far behind the 6th Armored Division breakthrough area, Colonel John Hines was in a stone house where refugees from the front were thawing out their frozen rifles and frozen bodies.

One man, his face covered with blood and dirt, his eyes two bitter holes, was saying, "I used to wonder what I was doing in the army. I didn't have anything personal against the Krauts, even if they were making me live in a freezing, frigging foxhole. But I learned something today. Now I want to kill every goddam Kraut in the world. You know why? To save my own ass."

4

There was a new GI in the Ardennes.

The good-natured, rather careless, supremely confident GI who had known one victory after another since landing in Normandy; who assumed he would be well clothed, well fed, and well led; who accepted it as his heritage to outgun and outmachine the enemy, was gone. Since December 16 he'd had few days of the overpowering air support and air cover he'd taken for granted; his clothing didn't keep out the cold; his boots were traps for trench foot; his tanks were outnumbered; often his machines were immobilized by cold, snow, and terrain.

He was cold and hungry. He had just fought a humiliating series of retreats where terror roamed far behind the lines. He had tasted defeat.

But he had learned bitter lessons that were beginning to pay off. In this first major winter battle ever fought by Americans he had learned that the wounded die fast in the zero cold. He had learned in a few weeks that cold is a living enemy and must be fought.

Medics had learned to tuck frozen morphine Syrettes under their armpits; to put plasma under the hoods of trucks and jeeps. Infantrymen were saving their hands from frostbite by cutting four oversized mitten patterns from blankets and sewing them together. Trench foot, which was cutting down more Americans than bullets, was beaten with muffs made from blankets. At night the men learned to take off their soggy combat boots and socks, massage their feet, and then pull these blanket "tootsie warmers" on, topped by overshoes.

They learned how to dry socks and shoes: heat pebbles in a can;

dump the hot pebbles into the wet socks and the socks into the shoes.

They learned that ordinary field jackets were little protection against the biting winds of the Ardennes. Inner linings were made of blankets sewed to the inside.

They learned that two wool shirts were equal in warmth—and less bulky to fight in—than a shirt and overcoat. But the shirts had to be switched every night, the one next to the body, wet from perspiration even in the coldest day, taken off and hung up to dry.

They learned what tramps and people of depression days had long known, that paper was a good insulator. A few sheets of newspaper wrapped around the chest between shirts was a buffer against the rawest wind.

They also learned to wear shoes and overshoes that were a little too big; for tightness, cutting off circulation, brought on almost instant trench foot. They would stuff paper between shoes and arctics—a trick long used by hunters. The paper not only anchored their misfit footgear but retained body heat.

They learned to heat food over a "flambeau"—a wine bottle filled with gas with a wick of twisted rags.

The facts of cold, long known to men of Minnesota and Maine, were passed on to men from Alabama and Texas. Frozen toes, ears, noses were rubbed gently to start circulation. The old wives' remedy of rubbing snow on these frozen parts often brought on gangrene. Hands stiff from cold, unable to trigger a gun, were placed under armpits. To survive a night in a freezing foxhole many a man lived by covering his head with a blanket and trapping his own warm breath.

The GIs learned not to eat snow except in very small doses or their stomachs would become chilled. Tankers learned that their great friend, Calvados, was their great enemy in the cold. For alcohol brought body heat to the surface, causing radiation and deadly chilling.

They learned that cold metal would sweat when brought indoors, and then quickly freeze when taken outside. All weapons and ammunition were left outdoors, protected only from the falling snow.

They learned the big lessons too. That their tanks should be whitewashed to blend with the snow; that they should wear sheets like Halloween ghosts.

Mechanics, with Yankee ingenuity, soon learned how to make

their machines work under sub-zero conditions. Where rubber tracks were unavailable for tanks, great metal cleats were welded on steel tracks to conquer ice and snow.

But the greatest lesson was one learned from the enemy: to hate. Word of the Malmédy Massacre, of the massacres of civilians at Stavelot, Trois Ponts, and Bande, passed from man to man, and from unit to unit. Until the Ardennes the GI had fought a civilian's war. Now he was learning to kill without remorse or pity.

5

On January 6, not far from Montgomery's troops attacking down toward Houffalize, a stocky man who was smoking a cigar as if it were a weapon had just finished writing a cablegram to his old friend, Admiral Q. He signed it, "Colonel Warden."

The man was Churchill and his friend was Roosevelt. The Prime Minister, overseeing the great counterattack which had started on January 3, had just come from a meeting with Eisenhower. He was worried about rumors of conflict between Eisenhower and Montgomery. "He and Monty," said the cablegram, "are very closely knit, and also Bradley and Patton, and it would be disaster which broke up the combination, which has in 1944 yielded us results beyond the dreams of military avarice."

He began another message, this one to a stocky man in Moscow, known to Colonel Warden and Admiral Q as UJ: Uncle Joe. Eisenhower had mentioned how anxious he was to get help from the Russians to take off the pressure from the Ardennes battle. But his liaison officers in Moscow had failed to learn when the Russians would start their next offensive. "You may find many delays on the staff level," Churchill had told him. "But I expect Stalin would tell me if I asked him. Shall I try?"

"The battle in the West is very heavy," he was now writing. "I shall be grateful if you can tell me whether we can count on a major Russian offensive on the Vistula front, or elsewhere, during January."

Eisenhower's troubles that day were many and varied. But his most aggravating problem was the rising insistence of the British Chiefs of Staff and Montgomery that he appoint a deputy—someone like Montgomery—to command all the field forces.

By now there was a near break between SHAEF and Montgomery's 21st Army Group. Tact and reason, Eisenhower had recently told his staff, were useless with Montgomery. In a rare burst of anger he thumped the conference table. In spite of his conciliatory letter of December 31, Monty now apparently wanted a showdown. He could have it. The matter would have to go to Churchill and Roosevelt. They could decide between Montgomery and him. But one would have to go.

General de Guingand, Montgomery's chief of staff, had shuttled between SHAEF and the 21st Army Group the past week, carrying messages, listening to both sides. Taken aside by Bedell Smith, he was warned that Eisenhower had reached the end of his patience.

De Guingand passed on this information. The Field Marshal was amazed. The Americans just didn't understand him. His campaign for one field commander wasn't for personal advancement. Hadn't he stated many times he would be willing to serve under Bradley if that capable man were chosen? The Americans couldn't understand that he was motivated not only by the need to win victories but to win them with the minimum loss of life. And it was for this reason that he had refused to start his attack until all was ready.

Montgomery wrote a brief but friendly message to Eisenhower. The Supreme Commander's authority would be accepted at once, without argument. As far as he was concerned, the matter—just as disagreeable to him as to the Americans—was dropped.

But on that day, January 6, the London papers revealed for the first time that Montgomery had taken charge of the northern half of the Battle of the Bulge.

The *Mail* headlined:

MONTGOMERY: FULL STORY OF BREACH BATTLE
British Halted Drive to the Meuse Line.

That paper editorialized, "This is the crucial part of the Western Front since General Rundstedt started to push, and the knowledge that Marshal Montgomery is now in full control there will be received with relief in this country."

The next day, Montgomery invited all correspondents attached to the 21st Army Group to Zondhoven, Holland, for a press conference. As they settled in their seats in an icy hall, Montgomery entered briskly. He wore the maroon beret of the British airborne

forces, a paratrooper blouse belted over his gray sweater and farm
corduroy slacks. He was in such high spirits he relaxed his most inex-
orable rule. He invited the surprised reporters to light up.

Then, brimming with enthusiasm and good will, he told of the
deep wedge the Germans had driven into the American lines.

> As soon as I saw what was happening I took certain steps myself to
> ensure that *if* the Germans got to the Meuse they would certainly
> not get over the river. I carried out certain movements so as to pro-
> vide balanced dispositions to meet the threatened danger; these were,
> at the time, merely precautions. That is, I was thinking ahead.
>
> Then the situation began to deteriorate. But the whole Allied team
> rallied to meet the danger: national considerations were thrown over-
> board; General Eisenhower placed me in command of the whole
> northern front.
>
> I employed the whole available power of the British Group of
> Armies; this power was brought into play very gradually and in such
> a way that it would not interfere with American lines of communica-
> tion. Finally it was put into battle with a bang and today British
> divisions are fighting hard on the right flank of the First U.S. Army.
>
> You thus have the picture of British troops fighting on both sides of
> American forces who have suffered a hard blow. This is a fine Allied
> picture. The battle has been most interesting; I think possibly one
> of the most interesting and tricky battles I have handled, with great
> issues at stake.

He continued his analysis with high tribute to American commanders. And the U.S. soldier, he said, was "a brave fighting man,
steady under fire, and with the tenacity in battle which stamps the
first class soldier. . . . I never want to fight alongside better soldiers." These men, he thought, should get the basic credit for stopping Rundstedt. Then he turned to a new subject, harmony.

> I want to put in a strong plea for Allied solidarity at this vital stage
> of the war. . . . Nothing must be done by anyone that tends to
> break down the team spirit of our Allied team. . . . I am absolutely
> devoted to Ike. We are the greatest of friends. It grieves me when
> I see uncomplimentary articles about him in the British press. When

Rundstedt put in his hard blow and parted the American Army, it was automatic that the battled area must be untidy. Therefore, the first thing I did when I was brought in and told to take over was to busy myself in getting the battle area tidy—getting it sorted out. I got reserves into the right places and got balanced—and you know what happened. I reorganized the American and British armies. . . .

It [Collins' VII Corps] took a knock. I said, "Dear me, this can't go on. It's being swallowed up in battle."

I set to work and managed to form the corps again. Once more pressure was such that it began to disappear in a defensive battle. I said, "Come, come," and formed again. . . .

You must have a well balanced, tidy show when you are mixed up in a dog fight. You can't do it nohow—I do not think that word is English—you can't win the big victory without a tidy show.

Although Montgomery pleaded for solidarity, the conference had the opposite effect. Most American correspondents were irritated at what they considered a patronizing tone in the speech. Even some British correspondents misinterpreted Montgomery's delighted, almost impish manner.

Repercussions were immediate. The more outspoken American correspondents were soon wiring home indignant stories.

Hugh Shuck of the New York *Daily News* finished his cable, TO BORROW EXPRESSION OF AMERICAN GENERAL TONY MCAULIFFE, "NUTS TO YOU, MONTY."

But the day also brought good news. "Colonel Warden" received an answer to his message of the day before to "UJ."

The Russian offensive, wrote Stalin, had been postponed by bad weather. "Nevertheless," he continued, "taking into account the position of our Allies on the Western Front, G.H.Q. of the Supreme Council has decided to accelerate the completion of our preparation, and, regardless of weather, to commence large-scale offensive operation against the Germans along the whole Central Front not later than the second half of January."

Churchill passed on this welcome news to Eisenhower, then wrote his reply to Stalin:

I am most grateful to you for your thrilling message. I have sent it over to General Eisenhower for his eyes only. May all good fortune rest upon your noble venture.

6

On the morning of January 7, Patton's drive to the north toward Houffalize—bogged down by snow, ice, and stubborn Germans— was resumed. The 17th Airborne Division, veterans of three days of battle, were to spearhead the attack with three regiments abreast.

In the center was the 513th Parachute Infantry, its objective Flamierge, five miles northwest of Bastogne. Three days before, it had won and lost the village in a bitter fight. Flamierge, which lay a few hundred yards north of the important Bastogne-Marche road, was holding up the march to Houffalize. It had to be taken.

Soon after dawn the 1st and 3rd Battalions prepared to attack the strategic village from thick woods a mile below the highway.

Pfc. Kurt Gabel, born in Germany but a recent graduate of Hollywood High School, was just finishing a cold breakfast. Unlike some of the other outfits, Headquarters Company of the 1st Battalion had had few casualties as yet. The morale was high. They were still "gung-ho."

"Okay, let's move out," called a sergeant.

As Gabel climbed out of his foxhole and moved toward the wide-open field to the north, great explosions burst on all sides. Branches fell to the snow. Shrapnel from tree-bursts sprayed the men. Gabel heard a noise like steel bees flying and flung himself into the nearest foxhole. It was already occupied by a dead man.

As the crash of artillery died down someone called, "Medic!" To his left a man was sitting next to a tree, his right leg severed above the knee, blood gushing onto the snow. It was a friend—a man who had just shared his breakfast.

Gabel took off his belt and made a tourniquet.

"You'd better move out, Kurt," said the wounded man.

Gabel ignored him and shouted, "Medic!" He then pulled his friend's bayonet from its scabbard, put a knot in the tourniquet and turned it.

"Oh, hell, I'm going to bleed to death anyway," said the other.

A litter team strolled through the woods. Both men were smoking.

"Get your asses up here," called Gabel angrily.

The men double-timed to the tree and laid the wounded man gently upon the litter.

"I'll see you in Paris," said Gabel.

"Okay." His friend smiled and wanly waved a hand. He would die in five minutes and knew it.

Gabel waved and moved to his left through the woods. He had to find the rest of the company. Soon he came to a dirt crossroad in a cut. As he was standing indecisively a column of men came over the hill to the left.

"What outfit is this, sir?" Gabel asked the platoon leader, a lieutenant.

"Second Platoon, F Company."

"Can I go along with you?"

"We're the assault platoon for F Company."

Gabel didn't want to be alone. "Can I go along?"

"Hell, yes. Go with the bazooka team."

The platoon moved along the little road. Soon it was open country. To the north rose a small snow-covered hill. After a hundred yards the lieutenant called, "Spread out in squad diamonds."

Eight-man squads left the road, spread into the field, and started up the hill. The bazooka team plodded through snow almost up to the knee. Then at the top of the hill Gabel saw, half a mile ahead, what looked like a viaduct running east-west. It was the elevated Bastogne-Marche highway.

The air was suddenly alive with a terrifying screech.

"Hit it!" cried the lieutenant. The men hugged the snow.

One nebelwerfer rocket landed near Gabel, throwing him into the air. He turned his head. The man next to him was dead. It was the first time in his life Gabel had been really frightened.

A captain plunged through the snow. "Get up, goddam you," he shouted. "This is no place to sleep. Do you want to get killed?" He kicked one man. "Move out on the double." He picked up one man by the collar.

Gabel and the rest of the bazooka team reluctantly ran across the open field, finally flopping into an irrigation ditch two hundred yards from the raised highway.

The lieutenant, his face white, jumped into Gabel's ditch. "Move forward as far as you can and cover the road as we move up."

Gabel looked ahead for his next objective, a shell crater fifty yards this side of the road.

"Fix bayonets!" called the lieutenant excitedly.

All along the irrigation ditch there was an ominous clicking noise as the paratroopers fastened bayonets to rifles.

Gabel, followed by a man carrying the tube and a man carrying six rounds, scrambled out of the ditch and ran toward the crater. A sharp noise, like a motorcycle in low gear, broke out—a German machine gun. Then a deeper, slower voice answered—American.

Snow flew up all around the three men but they reached the crater safely. Gabel peeked over the edge. In a depression along the side of the road he saw a row of well-camouflaged German foxholes. Then from the rear he heard a shout, "Let's go!"

Thirty paratroopers in a long line leaped from the irrigation ditch. Bayonets glistening, they ran through the snow screaming, "Geronimo!"

As the attackers approached the road, twenty-five Germans popped out of foxholes, hands over head, shouting, "Kamerad!"

Several paratroopers thrust their bayonets into the surrendering prisoners. One trooper, trying vainly to pull out his bayonet, finally released the flip and left his bayonet in the dead man's chest.

Gabel and the bazooka team headed left toward a small group of farmhouses. As they approached, fifteen Germans ran out, hands over head.

The rest of the platoon was trying to cross the elevated road and push further north, but a German machine gun, dug in on a rise on the other side of the road, opened up. Four GIs fell on the road wounded; the rest jumped to the south side of the highway and hid. A moment later two medics crawled onto the highway to get the wounded. They were shot.

Gabel ran up to the lieutenant who was wringing his hands in despair. "Sir, let's use the prisoners as a shield."

"That isn't in accord with the Geneva Convention."

"Neither is shooting medics."

"Well, all right."

In good German, Gabel told the prisoners to line up in a column. "Get your hands high. Move out slow. Get up on the road." Holding a tommy gun on them, he covered the prisoners from the ditch as they marched down the elevated highway. "If you move off the road, I'll cut you down."

The prisoners waved toward their own machine guns and shouted, "Don't shoot!"

Gabel halted the column when it was a shield between the wounded men and the German machine gun. Medics ran up the road and quickly brought the wounded back to safety. Gabel then marched the prisoners back to the farmhouse. There he saw a colonel sitting on the front steps, calmly smoking a pipe. He had graying hair and clear blue eyes. To Gabel he seemed old, almost thirty-five.

"Sir," said Gabel, saluting. "I'd like permission to go back to the 1st Battalion."

Lieutenant Colonel A. C. Miller was only five feet five; his helmet came over his eyebrows; his jump boots almost reached his knees. The GIs called him "Boots and Helmet." "There are Germans between us and the 1st Battalion," he said. "You stick with me."

After dark Colonel Miller and Gabel toured the sector around their tiny group of farmhouses. It was bitter cold and clear. In the bright light of stars they could see shattered Flamierge just ahead. It looked dead.

The two returned to the farmhouse. Men were huddled on the floors trying to find warmth. A sack of straw had been piled up for the Colonel's bed.

Miller pointed to it. "Lie down and get some sleep."

"That's yours, sir."

"Never mind."

Gabel, exhausted by the day's fighting, flopped down.

The Colonel took off his overcoat, covered the enlisted man. "Get a good night's rest, son. I'll wake you in the morning."

Sleepily Gabel watched Miller sit at a kitchen table and in the light of a candle, pore over a map. He felt relaxed and safe. Nothing could happen to him as long as "Boots and Helmet" was there. He fell asleep.

Just before dawn the next morning, January 8, Gabel was awakened by shell fire. Then he heard a field phone ringing.

Colonel Miller picked it up. "Are you sure they're tanks? What do they look like? Infantry with them? Hello, LP! LP!" He put down the phone and turned to an officer. "Have somebody run down the wire to LP2."

Gabel, now wide awake, went outside. The cold cut like a knife. It was painful even to breathe. Somewhere in the dark tanks rumbled.

The Colonel's driver ran past. "I'm going upstairs to get the Colonel a curtain," he said. "The old man wants to camouflage himself like the Krauts."

The two hurried to the second floor of the house and pulled down white curtains. Dawn was just breaking as Gabel ran outside and gave the Colonel a curtain. Miller cut a hole in the middle of the material and stuck in his head. Gabel imitated him.

German tanks were now roaming on both sides of the highway. Infantrymen in white slowly, ominously followed.

A major ran up to Miller. It was his executive, Irwin Edwards. "I suggest you move your headquarters back to the woods, Colonel," he said in a formal manner.

The barn behind them suddenly exploded.

"You get the battalion together, sir," said Edwards. "I'll collect all the stragglers and send them along to you."

"Good idea," said Miller excitedly in his high-pitched voice. "I'll have them dig in and hold on!" An 88 round hit the house, showering them all with rubble. "Okay, Gabel," he said. "Now we can go."

The two headed across the open field that had been won the day before in the bayonet charge. The little colonel, the curtain billowing behind like a great sail, plunged through the knee-deep snow, ahead of Gabel. The sharp chatter of machine guns and pings of rifles joined the blasts of the 88s. Men dropped in the snow. Gabel's throat was raw. He felt he couldn't take another breath. A GI fell. Gabel dodged around him, stumbling over the camouflaged curtain. He ripped it off, got up, and chased after Miller.

The Colonel turned. "What're you doing, Gabel?"

"I fell down, sir."

"How about firing your weapon once in a while at the Krauts?"

"Yes, sir." But Gabel had no desire to fire; he'd have to clean his piece if he did. He was interested only in escaping. He threw away his gas mask, knife, and canteen. Nothing helped. His lungs felt as if they would burst; his legs were as heavy as lead. But he knew the Colonel wouldn't let him stop running. Only a bullet or fragment could do that. He wished he'd get hit so that he could rest.

In desperation he ditched first-aid pouch, compass, poncho, magazine, and finally his overcoat.

Suddenly the woods loomed up. He found himself on the ground, panting—safe. Colonel Miller was looking down at him. His camouflage curtain was riddled with bullet holes but he looked fresh and unruffled.

"Can I take a break, sir?"

"Go ahead. See you later."

Gabel looked out on the field. It was dotted with dark, still heaps —comrades. Ahead lay the elevated highway and beyond that Flamierge. Around him the remnants of the assault company, panting in painful gasps, rested. Of the original 200 men he could count only twenty. And the road to Houffalize was as far away as it had been the previous morning.

7

In New York that morning papers were headlining the Montgomery press conference. As expected, anti-British papers were indignant. But the *Times* commended editorially, "No handsomer tribute was ever paid to the American soldier than that of Field Marshal Montgomery in the midst of battle."

This calm reasoning was not felt in Luxembourg City. Third Army and 12th Army Group men were angry. They had just heard a B.B.C. broadcaster giving Montgomery credit for saving the Americans from disaster:

> It is the most brilliant and difficult task he has yet managed. He found no defense lines, the Americans somewhat bewildered, few reserves on hand and supply lines cut. . . . The battle of the Ardennes can now be practically written off, thanks to Montgomery.

This broadcast, and Montgomery's failure to tell newsmen that the split in command was only temporary, brought a wrathful delegation into Bradley's office: Major Hansen, Bradley's aide; Lieutenant Colonel Ralph Ingersoll, editor-on-leave of the New York paper *PM*; and Major Harry Munson, General Allen's aide.

"You've got to get something on record that tells the whole story of this change-over in command," Hansen indignantly told Bradley. "Until you do the American people will have nothing to go by except Montgomery's statement which certainly leaves a questionable inference on the capabilities of the U.S. command."

Bradley was as angry as his staff. Earlier that day he had personally complained to Eisenhower of the distortion of fact in certain British papers. The London *Mail* that morning had headlined its story on the Bulge:

MONTGOMERY FORESAW ATTACK
ACTED "ON OWN" TO SAVE DAY

Then it went on to say, "Apparently the situation was so desperate that Field Marshal Montgomery, using his own initiative, threw in all his weight and authority and asserted his leadership which was accepted by those around him."

"Well, I can do one of two things," Bradley told Hansen, Ingersoll, and Munson. "I can take a statement to Ike and ask him to approve it. He may or he may not. If Ike lets me go ahead and we get into trouble over it then he hangs with me. On the other hand, we need not put Ike on the spot. I can release a statement here without clearing it with SHAEF and take the consequences myself —if there are any." He paused dubiously.

"After all," said Ingersoll, "Montgomery spoke to the press yesterday."

Bradley was still doubtful.

"Do you suppose Montgomery cleared his interview with Eisenhower?"

"You know damned well he didn't." Bradley looked out the window at the spires of the Luxembourg cathedral, then turned. "Okay," he said. "I'll do it."

In Berlin, Hitler sat hunched at a desk. He looked bitterly at the paper in front of him. It was a realistic report from von Rundstedt of the Ardennes situation. He picked up a phone and said in a low voice, "I authorize a withdrawal to the Dochamps-Longchamps line."

Within an hour panzer units at the tip of the Bulge did an about-face, hurrying to get east of the Bastogne-Liége road.

The Great Dream had ended.

Now the question was: Would the hundreds of thousands of Germans, the thousands of panzer and self-propelled guns in the Ardennes be caught in a sack? Would the attempted retreat be another Stalingrad?

In the Ardennes not far from the battle-torn hills west of Wiltz an open jeep marked with three stars was slowly pushing through a seemingly endless column of trucks heading north. The trucks held doughs of the 90th Division, chilled to the bone, on their way to spearhead an attack through the tired Yankee Division to take Hill 490.

In the jeep was Patton. The next day, January 9, he was to begin another general all-out attack. The VIII Corps would continue the drive up to Houffalize and these men of the III Corps would smash toward Wiltz and St. Vith.

When the men recognized Patton, they leaned out of the trucks, cheering wildly. The General's face broke into a smile. He waved. But he could hardly hold back the tears. Tomorrow many of those now cheering would be dead—because of his orders.

5. JUNCTION AT HOUFFALIZE

9–16 January 1945

The GIs had already nicknamed this stage of the fighting the "Bitter Battle for Billets." They had to be driven out of their comparatively warm cellars each morning to attack. Once in the cold they pressed forward savagely to the next group of cellars, fighting not for ground or glory but for a place to get warm.

By the morning of January 9, men of Hodges' First Army were already noticing the effects of Hitler's order to pull back. Although their advance to the south was slow, it was steady. In six days they had covered half the distance to their goal, Houffalize.

That morning, Patton's double attack kicked off. Gains of one and two miles were made in the drive north up toward Houffalize; and bloodstained Hill 490 was finally taken by fresh troops of the 90th Division in the attack toward Wiltz and St. Vith.

2

In Luxembourg City, Bradley was holding his press conference. First he explained why he and Eisenhower had thinned out the lines in the Ardennes. It had been, he said, "a calculated risk."

Then he explained with some heat why Montgomery had been given half of the battlefield:

> The German attack cut both our direct telephone communications to the First Army and the direct roads over which personal contact

was normally maintained. The weather prevented the making of frequent personal contacts with First Army by plane. It was therefore decided that the 21st Army Group should assume *temporary* command of all Allied forces north of the salient. This was a *temporary* measure only and when the lines are rejoined, 12th Army Group will resume command of all American troops in this area.

This, Bradley hoped, would clear the air once and for all.

In spite of the obvious fast approach of Allied victory, there was a strange sense of depression in the Luxembourg capital. Most felt the war would last another year.

This gloom was caused by war weariness, the stories of suffering from refugees of occupied towns, and the mysterious bombardments that had been going on since December 31. Although little damage was done from the twenty or so shells that exploded in the streets each night, their inexplicable origin was causing near panic. No known cannon had such a range.

It was the newest German "superweapon," the V (Vergeltungswaffe) 3, nicknamed by its gunners, "Tausenfüssler"—thousand legs. Originally designed to fire on London from the Belgian and Dutch coast, its barrel was 492 feet long. What gave the giant cannon its nickname were the 96 small lateral tubes that stuck out from the main tube. These tubes contained explosive charges for supplementary propulsion, giving its 165-pound projectile a range of 80 miles.

Now Hitler was using a junior version of this fantastic weapon—only 197 feet long—in an effort to knock out Bradley's and Patton's command posts.

3

That afternoon Louis Steinmetz, Red Cross worker and partisan, walked up the steep hill from Lower Wiltz to the Clinique St. Joseph. Ralph Ellis, the American soldier he and his sister-in-law, Meisy, had brought to the grocery store, was in great pain from frozen feet. Louis had already amputated part of one toe with a razor blade and for the past week had been making daily trips to the hospital for ointment.

He walked up the steep narrow path to the rear of the big building. The frail blond nurse, known only as Mlle. Anna, again brought him a jar of pomade.

"Your friend is still in pain?" she asked.

"Oh, yes." He told her more about his friend, a citizen of Lower Wiltz who worked in the tannery.

"I don't believe you," she said. "You've got an American in your house. You can trust me."

Louis said nothing. He knew only that she was a refugee from a neighboring village. She might be a Boche-lover.

"I've got one too." She told about George Carroll, still hiding in the attic of the Balthasar-Wagener house on Rue Plank. "But you've got to help me get him out of there. The house is already full of German soldiers. Now they want to use the attic. Only yesterday we had a narrow escape. Blood from the American's wound dripped through the ceiling. By good luck M. Balthasar cleaned it up in time."

Louis agreed. "While the Germans are eating their dinner tomorrow evening, you go into the house, and bring him to the street. I'll be waiting."

Fifteen minutes later he was back in the grocery store. Ellis, wearing a suit belonging to Meisy's son, sat in a rocking chair in the back room repairing a large wall clock damaged by the last bombing.

Louis excitedly told about the other American in town.

Meisy came in from the store. "Bring him here, Louis. It will be nice for Ralph." She looked at Ellis as if he were her own son. "He is so lonely to talk to someone who understands."

The door of the store burst open. There was a stamping of heavy feet. Meisy started for the store but before she reached the curtain which separated the two rooms, a heavy-set German feldwebel was standing there.

"What do you want?" she asked.

"We've come to sleep here."

"That's impossible. We have no place. Can't you see I only have one room for myself and the son of my sister sitting there." She pointed to Ellis who had closed his eyes, pretending to sleep.

The big German, followed by another, pushed into the little room. Both wore SS insignia. "We've got to come here." The feldwebel went to Ellis. "What's a young fellow like you doing in civilian clothes? Why aren't you in the Army?"

Ellis opened his eyes. If he spoke a word they would know he was American. Meisy shoved between them. "Don't you see the poor boy is sick?"

"Let him speak for himself."

"How can he?" cried Meisy. "He was hurt in one of the American bombings. Now he can't say a word." She suddenly became indignant. "And don't think you're going to stay here. I don't have a thing for you to eat. Haven't you a mother in Germany?"

"Why, yes," said the feldwebel.

"I also have a son in the war." She pointed to a picture of Josi in German uniform. "He's a comrade of yours. What would your mother say?"

The feldwebel backed away, like a scolded boy. "We didn't mean anything."

Meisy steered the two SS men out of the room and into the store. "Now, here's an apple for each of you and that's all I can give you."

"Thank you, mutti," said the feldwebel. He and his comrade bumbled out of the front door.

Meisy returned to the inside room. "Don't be afraid, Ralph," she said in Luxembourger. "Now I'm your mother. I'll take care of you."

Ellis understood only one word, "Ralph." But he knew what she meant.

Meisy turned to Louis. "I hope some mother, somewhere, is doing the same for my Josi."

The following evening the door of Meisy's grocery store opened. Ralph Ellis sat up alertly in his rocking chair. A moment later Louis came in supporting a man in his early thirties wearing civilian clothes. The newcomer, about Ellis' own size, was pale and tired. His shoulder was bandaged.

"I'm George Carroll," he said.

Ralph got out of his chair. "I'm Ralph Ellis." They shook hands. It was good to hear an American voice.

4

On the morning of January 11, General Sir Bryan Horrocks' XXX Corps resumed its attack. The 51st Highland and the 6th Airborne Divisions hammered at the west end of the Bulge.

The 5th Seaforth Regiment was told to take Mierchamps no matter what the cost. The tempo had to be quickened. The men of this historic unit made no comments, except to each other, but went forward across the featureless valley that lay in front of their objective. They expected to be slaughtered for there was little cover.

But only a few scattered rifle shots rang out. A German machine gun chattered briefly. It was soon wiped out. The men of the 5th Seaforth closed in on Mierchamps. Seventy Germans eagerly came out of the cellars hands over heads. The Seaforth had taken the village surprisingly at almost no cost.

Later that day another British unit seized the village of Bande, scene of the Christmas Eve massacre. The Abbé Musty, head of the Bastogne school for young men, told the first officer, "Germans have murdered a large group of boys."

"Why?"

"Who can say?" Musty was still tortured by the thought that but for him, his four dead students might be safe.

Soon Musty, the schoolteacher, the mayor, and British soldiers were at the Bertrand house on the highway. Three Tommies jumped into the wrecked cellar, tearing away planks heavy with snow. Underneath were thirty-four bodies, frozen stiff.

The British officer, his face pale, turned to a sergeant. "I want every man brought down here. I want them to see what kind of enemy we're fighting."

The Allied military picture that day of January 11 was good.

But the Bradley-Montgomery situation had reached a dangerous stage. The London *Mail* was irritated by Bradley's remarks. In an editorial titled, "A Slur on Monty," it criticized Bradley for stating that Montgomery's assignment was temporary, and that American troops would soon revert to 12th Army Group. The plea to make Montgomery commander of all ground forces was renewed.

> Montgomery is good enough to be given the position of responsibility in an emergency, but when the danger is over and the ravages of

the enemy made good his services are no longer required except in a comparatively subordinate capacity.

Must he again be pushed back into the semi-obscurity which was his lot in the weeks before the Ardennes link was snapped by the enemy?

At the same time Brendan Bracken, chief of British press affairs, was vehemently denying that the broadcasts heard by Bradley and thousands of GIs sharply criticizing American handling of the Battle of the Bulge were of British origin. The Germans had obviously cut in on the B.B.C. Home Service Program.

"I need hardly tell you," Bracken told Eisenhower, "that the B.B.C. would never broadcast anything which would be offensive to American troops or to the Commander-in-Chief."

These were difficult days for Eisenhower. The Bradley-Montgomery imbroglio was causing him more distress and worry than any other similar problem in the whole war.

Bradley came to Versailles. "You must know," he told Eisenhower, "after what happened I cannot serve under Montgomery. If he is put in command of all ground forces you must send me home. For if Montgomery goes over me, I will have lost the confidence of my command."

Eisenhower replied, "I thought you were the one person I could count on for doing anything I asked you to."

"You can, Ike. I've enjoyed every bit of service with you. But this is one thing I cannot take." He didn't add that Patton had already told him, "If you quit, Brad, then I'll be quitting with you."

5

On January 12, the most exciting news of the day came from Russia. Field Marshal Konev's army group, after one of the most thunderous artillery barrages in history, was advancing on the Upper Vistula. Fourteen infantry divisions and two independent tank corps were striking at the Baronov bridgehead. To the north a hundred other Russian divisions were also moving up for attack. Germany, caught between powerful forces on east and west, would soon be crushed.

But there was also a great victory in the Ardennes. The 90th Division, with Hill 490 taken, suddenly turned northwest and drove into the base of the German finger still sticking down between

Wiltz and Bastogne. Simultaneously the 6th Armored and 35th Divisions drove from the other side.

By afternoon the two forces met near Bras. The cankerous salient had been snipped off and almost 15,000 first-rate German troops—including most of the 5th Parachute Division—trapped.

The Battle of Bastogne was abruptly over.

Bradley and Patton were now more than eager to renew the main attack up toward Houffalize. There was another incentive for quick action. Eisenhower had told them that once the north and south linked up, the First Army would be returned to Bradley's 12th Army Group.

On that day Bradley was somewhat surprised to be handed a letter from Montgomery. He was even more surprised when he read:

> My dear Brad,
>
> It does seem as if the battle of the "salient" will shortly be drawing to a close, and when it is all clean and tidy I imagine that your armies will be returning to your operational command.
>
> I would like to say two things:
>
> *First:* What a great honour it has been for me to command such fine troops.
>
> *Second:* How well they have done.
>
> It has been a great pleasure to work with Hodges and Simpson: both have done very well.
>
> And the Corps Commanders in the First Army (Gerow, Collins, Ridgway) have been quite magnificent; it must be most exceptional to find such a good lot of Corps Commanders gathered together in one Army.
>
> All of us in the northern side of the salient would like to say how much we have admired the operations that have been conducted on the southern side; if you had not held on firmly to Bastogne the whole situation might have become very awkward.
>
> My kind regard to you and to George Patton.
>
> Yrs. very sincerely,
> B. L. Montgomery

Bradley put down the letter. It was obviously an effort to forget the past. As far as Bradley was concerned the past was also forgotten. There was a much bigger problem in hand: the final destruction of the German Armies.

6

The next day, January 13, Hodges launched a fresh attack from the north. Now Ridgway's entire XVIII Corps joined the battle to wipe out the Bulge. The 30th Division struck from Malmédy. The 106th Division—that is, the 424th Regiment and the attached 517th Parachute Regiment—crossed the Amblève River at Stavelot and headed south through deep snow. To their right, Collins' VII Corps continued its attack on Houffalize, driving to within two and a half miles of the final goal.

That morning Patton launched a new attack up toward Houffalize in the hopes of a quick junction with Hodges' men. He also pressed his III Corps attack on Wiltz and St. Vith. By now he realized it was impossible to storm Wiltz directly from the south. This time he was circling around the hill mass that had cost the 26th and 80th Divisions so dearly and was attacking from the west.

The civilians in the occupied towns of this drive were nearing the end of their endurance. For almost a month they had been living like animals in icy cellars with death always overhead. They slept on cement, dirt, or if lucky, bags of potatoes or coal. The simplest acts of life were difficult: moving, breathing. There were no bathroom facilities. Bathing, shaving, even washing teeth was impossible. For toilets there were helmets and cardboard boxes. Even at these times there was no privacy. But this was no time for false shame. Only one thing mattered: to survive.

Man was proving again he was the most adaptable animal on earth; but there was a limit and it was approaching.

At the half-wrecked church of Lower Wiltz, a Nazi police official was telling the pastor, Canon Prosper Colling, "I want you to evacuate all your people to Wilwerwiltz by tomorrow morning."

Colling, a small wiry man of sixty-three, was used to talking back to Nazis. "Impossible," he said. "I can't move 4,000 people that fast."

The Nazi was furious, as much by Colling's lack of fear as by the answer. "An order is an order!" he said, then slammed the door.

Colling went into the cellar. The occupants looked at him fearfully. Their spirits had to be raised. This last news would cause panic. He turned over an empty cabbage barrel and laid a piece of paper on it. Then he began to write. The people looked at him curiously. Had he gone mad?

In a few minutes he handed the paper to his assistant. "Go up to the parish office and type it," he said. The typewritten copy was soon returned. Colling stood up. "I am making a promise to Our Lady of Fatima," he said. "A promise to build a shrine to the Sacred Heart and Our Lady of Fatima on the slopes of Bassend, if we are all saved."

He signed the paper. All the men over twenty-one eagerly signed. The gloom in the cellar was gone. Canon Colling was a man whose word could be believed.

"Go all through the town," he said. "Tell the people that I have composed a special prayer—a novena. Every day they will pray: first, the Song of St. Sebastian, patron of our town; then the Credo; Pater Noster; a prayer for repentance; and finally the song, 'I'm Christian and I'll Stay Christian.'" With such a busy program, he figured, they would have no time for fear. The information spread from cellar to cellar. By the time it reached Upper Wiltz, people were assured that if they kept the pledge to build the shrine, the Germans would leave town on the birthday of their patron, St. Sebastian. A new spirit of hope swept Wiltz. Almost every citizen believed without reservation that liberation would come on January 20.

The next morning German police officials rescinded the order to evacuate the town. No reason for this sudden change was given, but the people were sure the vow taken by Canon Colling and the men of Wiltz was already bearing fruit. Even the town's few skeptics wondered if there could be something in the vow.

7

On the morning of January 15, Montgomery and Hodges were well pleased with their attack from the north. The 84th and 2nd Armored Divisions had reached the banks of the Ourthe River just west of Houffalize. Their goal was only a rifle shot away.

But Patton's troops driving up north were having trouble again. They were still ten miles below Houffalize. Unhappy to think Montgomery's troops would probably reach the common goal before him, Patton drove up to the front early that afternoon to speed the attack. On the way he saw a frozen German machine-gunner, arms extended, holding a loaded belt of ammunition. Then he noticed black objects sticking out of the snow. He stopped his jeep and went out to investigate. They were the toes of dead men—Germans and Americans. The quick freezing had turned them claret-red. "It was a nasty sight," he wrote in his diary.

At 5:15 P.M. a half-track pulled into the shattered streets of Bertogne, a village seven miles northwest of Bastogne. A small, neatly dressed major with an intelligent face stepped from the vehicle. Though he looked like a typical headquarters officer, Major Michael Greene disliked his command post assignment as executive officer of the 41st Cavalry Reconnaissance Squadron of the 11th Armored Division. He wanted to be up front.

Greene looked around. He had been told to close headquarters at Monaville and drive to Bertogne where Colonel Foy had set up the advance command post.

A jeep dashed into town. Two men jumped out: Brigadier General "Hunk" Holbrook of Combat Command A, and Colonel Williams, the division chief of staff.

Greene came forward. "Colonel Foy is up forward with Troop C," he said in a clipped, precise voice.

Holbrook shook hands with the young major not yet four years out of West Point. Greene's father was a good friend. "Mike, we have a mission—an extremely important mission—a *must*, directed by General Patton. Someone must get up to Houffalize tonight and contact the First Army as it comes down from the north."

"This is a delicate, difficult assignment," cut in Williams. "Houffalize is more than ten miles behind enemy lines. But someone has to get through to establish contact with the 2nd Armored Division as it comes down from Achouffe. They may already be there. General Patton wants this mission accomplished without delay. And he wants this division to do it."

The general surveyed young Greene. Physically he appeared too scrawny to last very long. But he came from good stock and could be trusted. "Mike, I want you to lead the mission. This is your chance to get a good medal."

"Yes, sir," said Greene. He didn't care about the medal. It was his chance to get from behind a desk.

It was pitch dark when seventeen light tanks of F Company assembled in the village of Rastadt, two miles east of Bertogne. Accompanying the tanks was a reconnaissance platoon from Troop A. They had been told to wait in Rastadt for Major Greene, who had been delayed when his half-track was destroyed by a mine.

The infantry commander was a big burly lieutenant with a four-day growth of whiskers. A string of grenades hung around his neck; an eight-inch knife was stuck in his boots. This was "Big Gene" Ellenson, former football star of Georgia, still exhausted from two rough days of battle in Les Assins woods, where he and Sergeant Fred Till had personally captured eight Germans. He was presently in a belligerent mood for he didn't like the idea of plunging into the dark, German-infested woods ahead.

As Ellenson was telling the tank company commander, Captain Harold Mullins, what he thought, men burst out of the woods ahead.

"The Krauts are all over the place!" shouted a wild-eyed doughboy.

Then a captain, his face blackened from powder burns, hurried up to them. "You can't go fifty yards up that road without being blown to hell."

Ellenson was disgusted. Woods on both flanks. Germans on the forest trail ahead. There were only two ways to go, straight up or back where they came from. "The hell with the deal," he told Mullins. "I'm going back and tell them they'll need a lot more than a few light tanks and armored cars to get into Houffalize." He put on his helmet. "I'm going to tell Major Greene to blow it out his barracks bag. I'll be damned if I go up that trail tonight."

"We are all going up that trail tonight."

Ellenson swung around. It was Greene, looking neat and efficient. His voice was precise. "And *you* are going to lead the way."

The unkempt Ellenson, towering above Greene, glared at his superior. No two officers could have been more different. Ellenson ruled his platoon by being stronger and tougher than anyone else. No one saluted or called him "sir." Just as dirty and battle-worn as his men, he was "Big Gene" to everyone.

Greene looked coolly at Ellenson. "We're moving out immediately. *Nothing* will impede our progress. If any vehicle is knocked out, push it off the trail. If any man is wounded he'll have to take care of himself."

Ellenson said nothing.

Task Force Greene started up the forest trail, deep in drifted snow, and plunged into the no man's land ahead. Ten miles to the northeast lay Houffalize. What lay between nobody knew. Seventeen light tanks, fifteen armored cars, six assault guns, fifteen jeeps, six half-tracks, and 450 men disappeared up the dark mysterious road.

Breaking trail was Ellenson, and at his heels Major Greene.

At 6:30 the next morning, January 16, Greene and Ellenson looked down into the Ourthe River valley. According to Ellenson's map Houffalize should be less than a mile away.

It had been a rough night. As Ellenson led the way on foot, he kept expecting to hear the chatter of machine guns, the ping of rifles. The tension mounted as nothing happened.

Behind him, Greene, still showing no emotion, was wondering if his would be another "Lost Battalion." It seemed as if he was being sucked into a trap. The first light of day was graying the sky as the long column rumbled down the hill into the valley.

"Look!" Ellenson pointed to the east. Through the dispersing morning fog, Greene saw a town perched on a ridge.

The two men hurried across a field to a highway. A marker stood at the side of the road: HOUFFALIZE.

"Well," said Greene in a matter-of-fact tone, "we're in Houffalize." He held out his hand. Ellenson shook it.

As they started back to the main column, Ellenson saw movement on the hill to their right. "Hey, Major, there's someone up there. It looks like an OP to me." He saw a man in a white camouflaged suit sitting beside an automatic gun. The Third Army had different passwords and countersigns. This could be ticklish. He shouted several GI expressions to show he too was GI. But the guard was obviously asleep.

"Let's get up there," said Ellenson. "It's probably a 2nd Armored patrol." He called back to his mainstay, Sergeant Till, standing in an armored car. "We're going up the hill." Then, armed only with a flashlight, he plodded up the steep bank.

Greene, who wore a .45 pistol, followed.

When they were twenty feet from the foxhole, Ellenson said, "Hey, are you 2nd Armored?" The man in white stood up. Then in alarm he swung an automatic gun at them and shouted, "Haende hoche!"

"I gather he wants us to put our hands up," said Ellenson.

"We'd better put our hands up then," said Greene. He turned to the German. "We-don't-understand-German," he said slowly. Then he shouted to Till, "This is a German up here. Fire at him."

The German called out an order. Greene stuck his hands up. Just then Till fired the anti-aircraft machine gun from the turret of the armored car. As the German jerked his head in alarm, Ellenson threw his flashlight. Then he let himself fall over backwards and slid down the hill. Greene jumped behind a log, pulled out his pistol, and fired.

The German escaped to the north while Greene and Ellenson ran in the other direction. Suddenly shooting came from Houffalize. Task Force Greene had been discovered.

For an hour a fire-fight raged. Then Ellenson came up to Greene. "Major, look." He pointed to the high ground on the north side of the Ourthe River. Less than a mile away men were walking to the east. They could be First Army men—or retreating Germans.

"Send a patrol over there," said Greene. "Tell them to proceed cautiously."

A patrol set out. Others, wanting to be the first to meet the First Army, had to be forcibly restrained. While Task Force Greene waited tensely, a jeep drove up from the rear. Two men approached.

"We're correspondents." They showed Greene their cards.

"This is a hell of a place to be," he said.

"We wanted to be in at the closing of the Bulge."

"Well, this is the right place."

"Is this Houffalize?"

Greene pointed down the road. "That's the town signpost over there."

"Major, is it okay with you if we walk up to the sign? Then we can dateline our story Houffalize."

"It's pretty quiet now. Come on." The three walked the fifty yards to the sign. The reporters took down Greene's name and his home town, Philadelphia. Mortar fire began to fall. "We'd better get out of here," said Greene. The three men hustled back to cover.

The reporters thanked Greene. "It was a pretty good experience," said one.

"Well, I'm glad you lived through it," said Greene drily.

Men were running over the snow from the north. It was the patrol returning. "That's the 41st Infantry of the 2nd Armored up there," said the leader excitedly. "We made contact at 0905!"

The First and Third Armies had at last met. In one big bite half of the Bulge had been eliminated and about 20,000 Germans cut off.

Ellenson looked at Greene and grinned.

"All right, Ellenson," said Greene. "Let's not stand around doing nothing. Let's move into Houffalize."

6. "ALLES KAPUTT!"

17–23 January 1945

1

On January 17, the day after the junction of the First and Third Armies at Houffalize, George Patton was in a belligerently cheerful mood. He spent the morning wheeling the troops he'd used in the Houffalize drive to the east. Then he visited those troops already attacking toward Wiltz and St. Vith—the 6th Armored, 90th, and 26th Divisions. "I know you're tired," he told them, "but you'll have to keep fighting."

Finally he went to his right flank. For weeks there had been a static but deadly battle of attrition in the Echternach-Diekirch area. Now he called on the three divisions of the XX Corps—the 4th, 5th, and 80th—to join in the common attack and drive straight north.

The fighting went well that day and by evening there was a feeling of triumph in all echelons of the Third Army. The Battle of the Bulge was nearing completion, and in a few hours, at midnight, Hodges' First Army would revert to Bradley's control. Then the entire battle would be fought on the American plan.

2

At 5:30 P.M. a shell landed on the top floor of the May Furniture Store on Grand' Rue in Wiltz. Three Germans, now bivouacked on the second floor, hurried toward the cellar and safety.

Mariechen Goebel, hearing the Germans, ran ahead of them. Sergeant Lester Koritz was sitting in a rocking chair in the second room of the cellar reading a popular novel, *Mon Oncle et Mon Curé*.

"You must hide, quick," cried Mariechen. "The Prussians are coming here!"

Koritz scrambled to the back of the little room. The Luxembourgers flung bedclothes over him as the three Germans came down the stairway.

When the shelling slacked off, one of the German soldiers approached Mariechen's niece, Maria. "You think Amis are pretty nice, don't you?"

Maria, sitting only a yard in front of the hidden Koritz, nodded.

"Well, it's not true. That's propaganda."

"Oh, no," said Maria. "We knew many American boys—very well too."

"Not like me. I tell you I had to rub noses with the damn Amis. Why, in Normandy I was so close to them I could have reached out my hand and touched them."

Mariechen laughed. "We hei," she whispered to Maria.

The shelling was over. The German near Maria stood up. "Well, we've got to get upstairs and prepare potatoes for dinner." The three Germans left.

Koritz stuck his head out from the pile of covers. "What does 'we hei' mean?" he asked.

Mariechen laughed, "It means, 'Like here.'"

The following noon Mariechen ran from her tobacco shop into the Mays' cellar. "Lester," she cried, "you must leave. The Germans have ordered the upper part of town evacuated by tomorrow. They're planning to use our cellars for pillboxes." Then she told him she'd gone to Father Wolff, the priest of Upper Wiltz. "He told me he'd find someone to take you to Lower Wiltz."

A few hours later Koritz was being led along a narrow cobblestone street by Mlle. Anna. He wore a civilian coat over his uniform. As they passed row after row of damaged homes, she said, "It was such a beautiful town."

He turned, thinking she was blaming him (all the damage had been done by American artillery and bombs), but on her pale face was the sad understanding smile of a medieval religious painting.

Though they'd met only ten minutes before, he knew she could be trusted.

As they approached the big hospital, he said, "How can you walk through the streets when it's so dangerous? Even soldiers hide when the shells come in. Aren't you ever afraid?"

"No, I'm not ever afraid."

They entered the Clinique. As they walked down a bleak corridor, lined with cots, each patient glanced up, smiling at Anna as if she were unexpected sunlight in a dark garden. She brought him to an empty room. "Wait here," she said. "Someone will soon come and take you the rest of the way. Bonne chance!"

Two blocks away Josephine Thein was foraging for food. There was nothing left in the Carmes cellar. She was digging for potatoes in the snow behind the Adler villa when she heard music coming from the house, a phonograph playing a tango.

She knocked on the door. The music stopped. She pushed the door open a crack. "I am a mother," she said. "I'm hungry. I've come to find food for my children."

"Come on in!"

She walked into the house and saw two young SS officers lolling on a cot. "How can you play music now?" she asked.

The younger one flung up a hand hopelessly. "Alles kaputt! All I want now is to dance a tango with a nice girl before I die." He stood up and held out his arms.

"How can I dance a tango with you? I'm a poor wife with two children waiting for me in a cellar and a husband at the front, perhaps dead. I'd rather you gave me something to eat for my children."

"When the Americans come, you'll be free. But we . . ." He despondently pointed to his SS insignia. "We can't return to Germany. We must fight. All we can do is kill ourselves." He patted his pistol. "That's why I want one little dance with you, dear woman."

"Haven't you anything to eat for my children?"

"Everything for your children." He handed her a little jar of butter. "This is my last ration." He turned to his comrade who was emptying a flask of brandy. "Get her everything we have."

The other lazily got up, returning in a minute with a round box of Quaker Oats and a small bag of sugar.

"That is everything we have to eat," said the young SS man. "Do . . . you think it's possible for us to hide in your cellar?"

She shook her head regretfully. They were SS, but they were human beings. "You'd scare my children to death."

He nodded sadly. "Ach, so. You are right." He shrugged his shoulders. "Alles kaputt, dear woman, alles kaputt!"

It was now almost dark. At the little room in the hospital Lester Koritz wondered if he'd been forgotten. The door slowly opened. Germans? Two men quickly entered and closed the door. One was short and powerful. This was Louis Steinmetz. The other was very tall and thin. His name was Josy Bier. Koritz smiled. They reminded him of Mutt and Jeff.

Louis looked at the GI suspiciously. "Let me see your dog-tags."

"Anna said he was all right," said Josy.

Louis was still dubious. But he said, "Well, let's go then."

"If we meet anyone," said Koritz, "shall I do any talking?"

"No, no. Just nod your head and say, 'Yo, yo,' every so often. And don't turn around. Josy will go first. Then you, then me."

The three men went out the back of the hospital and started down the steep narrow path through back yards and gardens that led to Lower Wiltz. Josy tripped over a German telephone wire.

Louis, with a sharp kick, broke it. He smiled impishly at Lester. He saw another wire, broke that. And another.

"For God's sake, Louis," whispered Josy. "Not now."

The three continued down the path until they reached a cobblestone street. Suddenly a group of German soldiers came around the corner and headed for them.

"What'll we do?" whispered Josy.

The Germans drew closer. There was a weird whistling noise. Then a shell exploded a hundred yards away. The Germans scattered. The three hurried down the deserted street, went over the wrecked bridge that spanned the Wiltz River, and started up the Rue du Pont.

Two other Americans, Louis explained, were hiding a few houses away in the grocery store of his sister-in-law, Meisy. There wasn't room for a third, so Koritz would stay at Number 60, the home of a baker named Nic Schambourg.

"But when it gets dark," promised Louis, "I'll bring you up to meet Ralph and Georges."

3

On January 19, a blizzard reminding North Dakota men of home, swept the Ardennes. In places snow drifted head-high. Every available piece of American equipment was thrown into road maintenance. But only a few routes could be kept open.

Winter, not the Germans, was now stalling the American drives on St. Vith from both sides of the Bulge. Icy gusts blew over the Ardennes, making life miserable for soldiers of both uniforms, for civilians, for animals. Winter was king, the entire battlefield a frozen world of white dunes. Snow muffled the sporadic sounds of war, making a new world of white silence.

4

It was 10:00 A.M., January 20, the birthday of St. Sebastian. This was the day the "Miracle of Wiltz" was scheduled to take place.

At the half-destroyed church of Lower Wiltz, old Canon Prosper Colling was singing High Mass. When he noticed whispering among the hundred people in the congregation, he became angry. Another garbled bit of war news, another wild rumor. As he was about to reprimand his people, he heard the clomping of hobnails on cobblestones. It was a noise known to almost everyone in Europe: Germans on the march.

Someone ran into the church and shouted, "The Boche are leaving!"

The people laughed, cried, and hugged one another. Canon Colling, closing his eyes, thanked God.

Inside Nic Schambourg's house, Sergeant Lester Koritz also heard the marching feet. Peering out a window, he saw lines of infantry retreating to the east, some pulling children's sleds loaded with loot.

He waited until dark, for wandering groups of Germans—in retreat as dangerous as in attack—still roamed the streets. Then he ran the few yards up the Rue du Pont to Meisy's grocery store. He had already met the other two Americans and he wanted to celebrate with his comrades of the 28th Division.

As he came into the back room Meisy was triumphantly crying,

"Yesterday I dropped my best plate and broke it. I told you it was an omen of good luck."

Mlle. Anna came in, her pale face flushed from excitement. As she efficiently put a clean bandage on Carroll's shoulder, he looked gratefully at her. "Tell Anna she's the best nurse in Europe, Les," he said.

Koritz translated the message into French. Anna laughed. "Oh, he just means I'm the best nurse he's had in Wiltz." She affectionately patted Carroll's wounded shoulder.

There was a clatter of boots at the doorway.

"Prussians!" cried Meisy. She opened the trap door in the floor. The three Americans scurried into the cellar.

Meisy closed the trap door and pulled the dining-room table over it. A big German private, his face wan and starved, came into the room. "I want something to eat." He looked around desperately.

Meisy, a shawl over her head, was bent over. "I'm just an old lady," she said in a quavering voice. "And I don't have a scrap to eat."

"Every Luxembourger has food in the cellar."

"You fool, can't you see I'm too poor to have a cellar?" She pushed him back into the grocery store where she handed him part of a sausage. "Now leave and stop bothering a poor widow."

Like a tramp begging a handout, the German went to the next house.

5

The great retreat was on. At last there was no doubt. For several days Dietrich's Sixth Panzer Army had led the way east. Manteuffel's army, recently confident and conquering, now joined the full retreat.

Everyone was in retreat—except a few picked infantrymen, left behind in shattered buildings or lonely foxholes to slow down the relentless Americans. These men of the rear guard—for the most part picked because they were very young, old, or useless—fought gallantly, in lonely hopelessness. They knew they had been abandoned so that the best fighting men could escape beyond the Westwall. It was simple German logic to save the best. The same thing had happened in France.

Boys of fourteen and fifteen were found, rifles frozen to their hands, feet black with putrefaction; men in the fifties were found in cellars, faces the color of port wine, the blood of their wounds frozen.

Those who retreated also suffered. Their columns were blasted by marauding aircraft and pursuing artillery. No man who had fought in the Ardennes would ever forget the cruel, overpowering Ami artillery.

A new Allied invention had been used for the first time in this battle: shells equipped with the proximity fuse. A British invention, manufactured in the United States, it was not only a lethal weapon but its surprise action was shattering to morale. The ordinary shell exploded on contact. The new shell exploded several seconds before contact, scattering fragments in a much more deadly pattern.

Rivers of men and machines flowed slowly toward the Fatherland. Great lines of trucks, tanks, and self-propelled guns rumbled cast over icy roads and trails clogged with snowdrifts. Long, discouraged lines of infantrymen trudged in the powdery snow, pursued by death from the Americans or the bitter weather.

6

The Germans in the Ardennes were caught in a deadly nutcracker: the First Army in the north, the Third Army in the south, and now one man in charge, Omar Bradley.

By January 21 the snowstorm had stopped and big advances were being made everywhere. From the north, the men of Hasbrouck's 7th Armored Division had joined the attack. A month before they had been driven out of St. Vith. Now they were rapidly approaching that key town.

Patton's VIII, III, and XX Corps were also making strides toward the same goal from the west, southwest, and south. They were less than twenty-five miles away. The 17th Airborne Division was taking part in the western attack on St. Vith. Early that morning four men who had been in the savage Flamierge fight were asked to go back and show a Graves Registration burying detail where the dead were; they now lay hidden under a thick blanket of snow.

Pfc. Kurt Gabel was one volunteer. By late morning the burying detail reached the edge of the woods where the 513th Parachute Regiment had launched its attack of January 7.

"Move out, the same way you attacked," the four volunteers were told. "As you come across bodies, group them together. If you find Germans stack them separately."

The four 17th Airborne men began their slow sad journey across the white wasteland. Gabel, following his original trail, had no difficulty finding American bodies. He lined up five neatly. He tried to straighten out the sixth. But it was frozen in a foetal position.

At noon he opened up K-rations. As he ate a piece of cheese, he lay down next to the bodies to rest. Their cheeks were ruddy with mock health.

It seemed unfair to him to be lying here eating cheese while they stared at the brightly shining sun with eyes coated with ice. He should be lying there staring glassily too.

He looked again and again at them, until they seemed alive. He held out a piece of cheese to the nearest, catching himself as he was about to say, "Want a bite?"

As Gabel ate the cheese he noticed tears running down the dead man's cheeks. The ice covering the dead man's face was melting.

Gabel turned away and examined the man frozen in the same position he'd entered the world. It was someone he knew—a man who had once cheated him out of a room at the Milestone Club in Kensington. They had almost had a fist fight.

Gabel looked around the field. The others on the grave detail were also eating their lunches as they lay in the snow. It was impossible to tell who was alive or who was dead. Gabel felt he could never get off the snow. He might as well be dead himself.

A whistle blew. The men slowly got up and went back to their dismal job. Trucks moved onto the field. The Graves Registration men began loading the frozen bodies. One grabbed the feet of a corpse, the other its shoulders. "One, two, three, heave!" shouted the first man. The body, as hard as a board, was flung onto the truck.

Gabel saw himself being picked up and flung onto the truck like a piece of cordwood.

One of the airborne volunteers walked toward the loaders. His face pale and full of hate, he said, "You do that once more and I'll b-blow your brains out."

The loaders said nothing. But they lifted the next body up tenderly, carefully placing it on the truck—as if it were a man.

7

In Wiltz at 4:30 P.M. the three American soldiers—Koritz, Ellis, and Carroll—were sitting in the little room behind the grocery store. Meisy burst in and excitedly cried in French, "American troops! Coming down the street!"

Koritz skeptically went into the street. There had already been two baseless rumors that the Americans were coming. A squad of soldiers was filing down the hill from Noertrange, rifles cradled.

"GIs!" he shouted to his companions. As the squad drew near, he yelled, almost hysterical in his joy.

The newcomers eyed Koritz coldly.

Koritz showed his dog-tags, then his pay book. The leader, a sergeant, slowly smiled. "We're the 101st."

"The airborne?"

"Hell no, the 101st Regiment of the 26th Division."

"The good old Yankee Division," said Koritz.

Louis Steinmetz ran out of the grocery store, waving a bottle in the air. "Schnapps! I've been saving it for a celebration."

Other citizens of Wiltz came out of their cellars, surrounding the American infantrymen. This was the ninth day of prayer to St. Sebastian. Everything Canon Colling promised had come true.

But the GIs looked at them with hard eyes. No one had bothered to tell them this was Luxembourg, an ally. The street signs, the store windows were German. The people spoke German, so they were Krauts.

A GI bumped into a slender girl hurrying up the Rue du Pont toward Meisy's. When she apologized, he shoved her into the snow. "Damn Kraut bitch," he said and then spit on Mlle. Anna.

8

The next day, January 22, the two-pronged attack on St. Vith gathered momentum. From the north the 7th Armored Division approached Hünningen and was only three miles away. From the south Patton's men converged on Trois Vierges. The distance between the First and Third Armies diminished with every hour.

That day Allied planes found the roads near Vianden and Dasburg choked with tanks, armored cars, and horse-drawn artillery pieces, and attacked them with rockets and high explosives. The destruction was appalling: 536 vehicles were damaged, 1,177 completely destroyed.

Patton telephoned Bradley. He was in an impatient, insistent mood, for he smelled final victory. "Brad, you've got to urge all armies to attack all-out now. No matter how the hell fatigued; no matter how many losses we have to take. *Now* is the time to strike."

In Wiltz it was a day of celebration and sad leave-taking. Ralph Ellis kissed Meisy good-bye. There were tears in her eyes for Ralph was finally safe. She hoped her own Josi was safe.

Carroll was saying good-bye to Anna.

Then the two men got into an ambulance, one hesitantly, the other expectantly. Ellis could hardly wait to get to a telegraph office. He wanted his wife, Nadine, to know he was safe.

The third man, Lester Koritz, was saying good-bye to his many friends in Upper Wiltz: the Goebel sisters, their two nieces, the Mays. "From now on," he told them, "Luxembourg is going to have two ambassadors in the United States—the official one and myself." He tried to thank them for what they had done for him.

"Oh, we're used to it." Little Mariechen laughed mischievously. "We've been hiding our own Luxembourg young men for four years."

9

On the morning of January 23, Combat Command A of the 7th Armored Division was poised near Hünningen for the final attack on St. Vith, which lay less than two miles to the south.

Then General Hasbrouck changed his mind. He phoned Bruce Clarke who still led Combat Command B. "Bruce," he said, "you got kicked out of St. Vith. Would you like to take it back?"

Clarke would. He quickly organized three task forces, ordering them to attack at 2:15 P.M. simultaneously from three directions.

At 1:45 P.M. Clarke walked to a hill a few miles east of St. Vith and looked down at the wreckage of the town. Suddenly there was a great concerted roar: the artillery preparation. In a few minutes his attack would begin. As he started back to his jeep he noticed a car almost covered with snow. It was the old Mercedes-Benz he'd driven from Eubach.

He paused thoughtfully. Where were all the men he had preceded into St. Vith on that hectic day of December 17?

Many were dead.

Many were prisoners in Germany. Major Don Boyer was still alive, but he was nursing sore thumbs. The day before, he had been strung up for objecting to the way things were being run in his prison camp.

With him in Germany were thousands of others captured in the Battle of St. Vith, on the Schnee Eifel, and at Clervaux.

Colonel Descheneaux, after an exhausting march, had finally arrived at Oflag 79, but he had picked up tuberculosis.

Judge Hoban, captured near Wiltz, was writing a postal card. His term as judge in Scranton would soon expire. Now he was filing his personal nomination papers.

Hurley Fuller was marching down a road in Poland. The roar of guns of the approaching Russians could be heard and Fuller was making plans. Among the guards there were two officers: one a typical Nazi; the other an amiable man named Paul Hegel. Fuller decided he would frighten the Nazi and make a deal with the friendly German. It was almost time for him to take over the marching prison camp and join the onrushing Russian allies.

At Oflag 13 B in Hammelburg, young Alan Jones, son of the commander of the 106th Division, was watching a new load of prisoners detruck. One was an old friend, Bud Bolling, the son of General Alexander Bolling of the 84th Division. The two sons of generals shook hands.

"Have you heard from your mother in Washington recently?" asked Jones eagerly. Bolling nodded. "Has my wife had her baby?"

Bolling thought. "Yes, Mother said something about a baby."

"Well, what was it?"

"I don't know. Just a baby."

10

Late that afternoon a veteran of the Schnee Eifel battle was discovered near Meyerode. In dense woods, not far from the six-way trail behind Maraite's house, two villagers found the body of a big American lieutenant encircled by seven Germans. It was Lieutenant Eric Wood, Jr.

Several miles to the southwest, Clarke's columns were converging on St. Vith. The Germans, down to small arms and machine guns, fought hard but by 5:45 P.M. the three American task forces pushed into the town.

Many snipers still hid in the rubble. It was almost midnight before St. Vith once again belonged completely to Combat Command B.

Colonel Bob Erlenbusch wearily walked toward his command post. The capture of St. Vith was a historic occasion but he doubted if anyone would feel like having even a token celebration. He looked over the ruins in the moonlight. They were tombs to fallen comrades. Then he walked into the wrecked kitchen that was his headquarters. The men were toasting cheese sandwiches.

The Battle of the Bulge, except for the miserable job of mopping up, was over. The fighting soon passed on to the east, into Germany, leaving behind two tiny ravaged countries, destroyed homes and farms, dead cattle, dead people, dead souls and dead minds. The Ardennes was a vast charnel house for over 75,000 bodies.

Troopers of the 17th Airborne Division were marching up to a Luxembourg church.

"Sit down in place," ordered a company commander.

The men, among them Pfc. Kurt Gabel, sat on the snow-covered cobblestones. The chaplain assured them their dead would always be close.

The company commander cleared his throat. "Everyone on your feet." Then, "Bat-tal-ion, ten-hut! Present arms!"

There was a mass noise of weapons. Taps were blown by a single bugler. Tears ran down Gabel's face as he thought of his dead friends at Flamierge. He looked around furtively. Everyone was crying. The back of his company commander was heaving.

Then he heard his commander's voice shakily cry out, "Or-der arms!"

The battle was over.

"Watch on the Rhine," like a great bleeding beast, was crawling back to the Fatherland. Men staggered over the snow, feet wrapped in burlap bags, women's shawls wrapped around their heads. They walked on numb feet, pursued by icy winds, bombs, and shells. Behind lay a waste of tanks, trucks, and guns—abandoned for lack of fuel or minor repairs.

The wounded and sick plodded east: some with rotting insides, noses bulbous from cold, louse-ridden, their oozing ulcers freezing; some with pus running where once ears had been.

The columns passed fields and woods filled with the dead and dying. An American soldier stood frozen, his arms outstretched as if begging. Some German signalman with a macabre sense of humor had passed wires through the stiff fingers. Now he stood— a frozen pole.

But none in the great retreating columns had a glance for such sights. Escape was the only thought. The great sad parade wound east. Breath formed a crust of ice on each man's collar. They shuffled east on frozen feet, hearts dead, bodies diseased. Dysentery rode their columns. And behind in the snow it left its pitiful blood-hued trail.

The will of the German soldier was broken. No one that survived the retreat believed there was the slightest chance of German victory. Each refugee of the Battle of the Bulge brought home a story of doom, of overwhelming Allied might, and of the terrible weapon forged in the Ardennes: the American fighting man.

Three and a half months later, on May 7, Germany surrendered.

EPILOGUE

1

Because of Hitler's desperate gamble in the Ardennes, the lives of thousands of British and American fighters were spared. If Hitler had not insisted on the "Big Solution," if he had hidden behind the Siegfried Line, the Allies would have had to smash through fortifications well protected by the armies that were broken to pieces in the Ardennes.

If victories are measured in lives saved, the Battle of the Bulge was a great one.

The battle was won not by chance, by force of numbers, or by overpowering air superiority. It was won by the GI, by his ineffable qualities. The things that made him a poor garrison soldier—independence, cockiness, love of luxury—made him finally a deadly fighter.

The Bulge was an unorthodox battle. Lines were nonexistent or fluid. It was a series of isolated actions, connected only by the direction of attack. Americans were surrounded. A few miles away Germans were surrounded. Communications were unreliable. Divisions, regiments, battalions, companies, at times even one or two men fought lonely battles that determined great issues. In this kind of fight, the American soldier excelled. The independence, which got him into trouble in camp, paid off in the Bulge.

His love of luxury made him a poor soldier in his first moments of battle. But in the Bulge he soon learned that there was only one way to survive: he had to fight. And he fought, not for political or ideological reasons, but for his life.

The GI went into the war with a basic philosophy—to do as little as possible. He was always only as good as he had to be. In the Bulge he had to be very good, but he was such a curiously complex soldier that even today most Germans think he was a bumbling enemy. They still firmly believe that what beat them were overwhelming numbers of bombs and shells, a mass of machines and materiel. Many Germans still resentfully insist that it was a slovenly, cowardly, expensive way to fight. But the GI never cared about the chivalry of war. He wanted only to win and go home.

With all its obvious faults the United States Army in World War II was a powerful, democratic army. Built from scratch overnight, it survived stupidities, civilian complacency, bureaucracy, Congressional meddling, countless mistakes, politics, and growing pains. Many of its officers were fumbling and incompetent. But the school of battle soon destroyed or winnowed most of these. The army that won the Battle of the Bulge and raced through Germany was hard and tough—run by hard and tough men. If necessary it could have been harder and tougher.

Much has been written of the failure of American G-2 officers to foresee the battle. The rather primitive, naïve American Intelligence system, based largely on procedures used by the Pinkertons in the Civil War, was not at fault; the sophisticated British system was just as blind. The blame should not even fall on Hodges, Bradley, and Eisenhower, nor on the architects of strategy, Roosevelt and Churchill. The entire Allied world must share the blame. On the night of December 15, 1944, it breathed the air of complacency, optimism, and self-delusion.

There were many isolated facts pointing to "Watch on the Rhine." But they did not fit into a meaningful picture. For the basic premise —that Germany was capable of mounting an all-out offensive— was unacceptable to everyone in authority. What led the Allies to the edge of disaster in the Ardennes was not so much a failure of Intelligence as of imagination.

2

Many of the Allied participants of this story went on to greater fame. Eisenhower became President of the United States; Montgomery, chief of SHAPE; Bruce Clarke, commander of the Seventh Army in West Germany; Maxwell Taylor, Chief of Staff of the Army; James Gavin, the public conscience of the Army.

Many stayed in the service: Don Boyer of St. Vith; Mildren and Morrow of the twin villages; Creighton of Fox Company; Hogan of Marcouray; young Alan Jones. Many now help run corporations: Collins, Hoge, McAuliffe. Others are in education: Troy Middleton is President of Louisiana State University; Private John Shaw is an English professor at Hiram College; "Gravel Voice" Ernest Harmon, to the amazement of his war colleagues, is President of Norwich University.

Michael Greene, whose task force blazed a trail to Houffalize, is now a lieutenant colonel in the Regular Army. His assistant, "Big Gene" Ellenson, is line coach of the University of Miami football team. Linus Hoban, re-elected while in a German prison, is still a judge in Scranton, Pennsylvania. Major Olin Brewster of Belle Haie lives in Temple, Texas. He was not court-martialed—but only because Richardson (now back with the 3rd Armored Division in Germany) and Hickey (retired in Pass Christian, Mississippi) continued to refuse to endorse General Rose's charges. Rose, himself, was killed soon after the Bulge while far up front with his tankers.

Bradley, after heading the Veterans Administration, lives in Washington, D.C. So does Jones, commander of the 106th Division, and he has finally recovered from his heart attack there. So do hundreds of others, including John Hines, Bedell Smith, Robert Hasbrouck, and Robert Grow.

San Antonio, Texas, is another mecca for the retired. Hodges and Leonard are close neighbors. One of Hodges' hunting companions is Hurley Fuller. On January 29, 1945, Fuller not only took command of his group of prisoners but a large number of captured Italian generals and the East Prussian village of Wugarten. He barricaded the village and the next day turned it over intact to the onrushing Red Army. With typical Fuller impetuosity, he made the friendly German guard, Paul Hegel, an American soldier and a citizen of Texas. Hegel, disguised in an American uniform, was safely escorted through Russia and then to Italy. Later Fuller was investigated by an inspector general for aiding an enemy. But when the investigation revealed that Hegel had made the lives of the captured Americans easier, Fuller was exonerated.

By coincidence Hegel, who owes his life to Fuller, now lives in Oberursel/Taunus on Füllerstrasse.

Many of the German survivors of the Bulge are now dead. Model committed suicide; Rundstedt died in an old folks' home near Wienhausen.

At the Malmédy Trial in Dachau in 1946, Peiper was sentenced to hanging and Dietrich to life imprisonment. The trial, unfortunately, was a poor advertisement of American justice. Some of the accused were beaten and given mock trials to frighten confessions out of them; witnesses of dubious mentality were called.

Colonel Willis M. Everett, Jr., of Atlanta, Georgia, was appointed Chief Defense Counsel. Infuriated by the undemocratic methods, he fought hard for his clients. At great effort he brought Hal McCown from the United States to tell what he had seen as a prisoner in La Gleize. This testimony uncovered the so-called atrocities of that village as a fabrication and cast doubt on much of the prosecution's case. Even so, forty-two of the defendants were sentenced to be hanged, twenty-three to life imprisonment.

Instantly a storm of protest went up, not only in Germany but in the United States. Led by Senator Joseph McCarthy, many of whose constituents were of German stock, there was a long, explosive investigation.

Because of poor preparation, shocking irregularities, and impassioned pleas for vengeance rather than facts, the Malmédy Trial pleased no one. Many of the documented atrocities went unpunished; men innocent of atrocities were thrown into prison.

Colonel Everett, convinced there had been a miscarriage of justice, did not rest. He spent the next ten years and over $40,000 of his own money fighting for a fair trial. In 1957, due in large part to his efforts, Dietrich and Peiper were freed. Both now live, under probation, near Stuttgart.

The Malmédy Trial is still a cause célèbre in Germany. In 1957, the *Revue*, a weekly magazine, printed a sensationalized, highly inaccurate version of the trial which was widely read and discussed. Enemies of the United States continue to point out that Malmédy is a good example of American justice.

To other Germans, the Battle of the Bulge and the entire war are forgotten history. Bayerlein, who missed taking Bastogne by minutes, runs a carpet shop in Würzberg. A few blocks away at the famous university, Baron von der Heydte teaches International Law.

Manteuffel is in politics. One of the heads of the Deutsche Partie, he was until the 1957 elections a member of the Bonn Senate. He has lost none of his vigor, sharpness of mind, or outspokenness.

Skorzeny lives in Madrid under a Nansen Passport. A successful engineer, he cherishes the dream of coming to the United States and teaching his former enemies the commando tactics that made him famous. In many respects he is already Americanized. When I visited his home, he cooked dinner and then did the dishes.

Most of the civilians in the story are alive. Fran Alden, the pregnant Red Cross girl, got to Paris just in time to give birth to a son. She now has seven more.

In Luxembourg and Belgium, with little money and much ingenuity and determination, the people are still clearing away the wreckage of battle and rebuilding homes, factories, and bridges. The bridge at Trois Ponts is almost finished but Stavelot still hasn't enough money to reconstruct its ancient stone span.

The people of Wiltz have completely rebuilt their town. It is once more a center of tourism in the Ardennes. There is now an outdoor theater behind the castle. In this romantic setting, plays, operas, and musicales are presented every summer in an International Festival of Theater.

Meisy's grocery store prospers. Her son, Josi, survived the war and gave her two grandchildren. Louis Steinmetz, her brother-in-law, drives an American car. He is doing well in the wholesale grocery business. Eugène Weber still runs his drugstore and the Boy Scouts. He also runs the Festival. The Goebel sisters are all well, as are their nieces. M. May died in an automobile accident recently and Maria May entered a nunnery.

Canon Colling, at seventy-eight, has retained his vigor and keenness. When asked if he, like the other citizens of Wiltz, was absolutely convinced the Germans would leave on St. Sebastian's birthday, the old man smiled and said, "I *hoped*."

The shrine, as promised, stands on the hill overlooking Wiltz, a permanent tribute to an indomitable people. Its cross is made of shrapnel from American shells.

One civilian is no longer in Wiltz. A few weeks after the battle, Mlle. Anna died of tuberculosis. But the three soldiers she helped will never forget her. Lester Koritz is public information officer for the California Division of Highways; and Ralph Ellis is an engineer for Lockheed at the Missiles and Space Division in Sunnydale. By coincidence, the third man, George Carroll, recently moved to California. All now live within a hundred-mile radius.

3

To gather the material for this story I traveled almost 100,000 miles: to a Senatorial hearing chamber in the Capitol Building; to former President Harry S. Truman's office in Independence, Missouri; to the West German Senate building in Bonn; to the gas chambers of Dachau; to West Point; to the Players' Club on Gramercy Park, New York City; to great castles and huts in the Ardennes; to jails; to SHAPE headquarters in Versailles; to the Pentagon; to Louisiana State and Norwich Universities; to the grammar school of Meyerode; to a slate mine in Vielsalm; to the baths of Spa; to the winding Siegfried Line; to the battlefields of Wiltz, St. Vith, Krinkelt, Manhay, Bastogne, Clervaux, Celles, La Gleize, and the Schnee Eifel.

I heard Dr. John Fague's story of the 11th Armored Division while he operated on a cow, a horse and a dog; the Baron de Radzitsky d'Ostrowick's while he finished breakfast in the servants' quarters of his beautiful gutted chateau in Verdenne; Fred MacKenzie's in the office of the Buffalo *Courier-Express;* Matthew Ridgway's at the Mellon Institute in Pittsburgh; the Rupps' in their chalet behind the Hotel du Moulin.

This book could never have been written without the help of many people and many organizations.

Libraries contributed greatly to the book: the Historical Archives in Alexandria, Virginia; the libraries of the Army Historical Section at Fort McNair, Washington, D.C. and at Karlsruhe, Germany; the Air University Library at Maxwell Air Force Base; the Library of Congress; the Main Branch of the New York Public Library (Charles Dornbusch); the British War Museum; the Historical Library of the British Army; the U.S. Army Infantry School Library at Fort Benning, Georgia (Ruth Wesley); and the Red Bank, New Jersey, Public Library.

I read hundreds of books, after-action reports, and unofficial battle accounts. Those which proved most valuable were: *Luxembourg in der Rundstedt-Offensive* by Prof. Joseph Maertz; *Les Deux Libérations du Luxembourg* by Lt. Colonel E. T. Melchers; *La Bataille de l'Amblève* by Marcel Bovy; *St. Vith, the 7th Armored Division in the Battle of the Bulge* by Donald P. Boyer, Jr.; *The Preparations for the German Offensive in the Ardennes* by Percy Ernst Schramm; *Dark December* by Robert Merriam; *Bastogne: the First Eight Days* by S. L. A. Marshall; *St. Vith: Lion in the Way* by Colonel R. Ernest Dupuy; and the student monographs of the Fort Benning library.

Veteran organizations invaluable in finding survivors of the battle were the American Legion, the Veterans of Foreign Wars, and the following Division Associations,

Infantry: 1st (Arthur Chaitt), 4th (Gerden Johnson and Iz Goldstein), 26th (H. Guy Watts), 28th (Ray Carpenter, Major John McDonald), 30th (John P. Carbin, Jr.), 35th (Mahlon S. Weed), 75th, 80th, 83rd (Lawrence Redmond), 87th, 90th (Milt Sears), 99th (Major General Walter Lauer), 106th (Douglas Coffey).

Armored: 2nd (Colonel R. F. Perry), 4th (Anthony J. Passanante), 6th (Edward Reed), 7th (Johnnie Walker), 10th (J. Edwin Grace), 11th (Kenneth W. Hanlon).

Airborne: 17th (W. A. Roncone, Charles Worrilow), 82nd (A.R. Pattullo), 101st (George B. Woldt, Colonel Leo Conner).

Since only a small percentage of the material gathered was used I would like to thank the hundreds interviewed whose stories don't appear in the book. Men like Sid Salins (99th), Ted Black (3rd Armored), Steve Prazenka, Embert Fossum and Paul Gaynor (28th), Al Blumberg and James McCrorey (6th Armored), Robert Bowen (101st Airborne), and James Peale, Jr. (26th) spent hours telling of their experiences. The accounts of such men actually make the heart of the story.

It would be impossible to list all the individuals who helped. Here are a few: Major Victor Walker, who gave me the idea of writing this book; Major General Harry P. Storke, Brigadier General Chester Clifton, Colonel James Chesnutt and Lieutenant Colonel John Chesebro of the Office, Chief of Information, U.S. Army;

Major James Haslam, who arranged most of my European appointments and drove me through the Ardennes on his leave; Major James Sunderman, Magazines and Books Branch of the U.S. Air Force; Colonel Laurence Macauley and Dr. Albert Simpson of the Air University; Karola Gillich of Munich; Elisabeth Philipp of Würzberg; Maggie Dieschbourg and Eugène Weber of Wiltz; Joseph Geiben of Diekirch; Marcelle Koeune of Bastogne; Dr. Maurice Delaval of Vielsalm; Dr. Jacques Clesse of Trois Ponts; M.T. Urbain-Choffray of Houffalize; Henri Demoulin of Stavelot; Major Herbert Trattner and Mrs. Trattner, Barbara Gore, Judge Jacob Wice and Dr. Hugh Cole of Washington, D. C.

Finally I would like to thank Professor Fred Stocking, John Jamieson, and Gerald Simons for their constant encouragement; and Rogers Terrill and Robert Loomis for editing four complete drafts of the book.

4

There are many impressive monuments to the Battle of the Bulge in the Ardennes: the Patton Memorial in Ettelbruck; the shrine to those murdered at Baugnez; the beautiful memorial at Bastogne. My favorite is on a lonely foot trail several miles from the village of Meyerode. Here in the middle of a dense forest lies a moss-covered mound in the form of a cross—the exact spot where 1st Lieutenant Eric Wood, Jr., died. Across the path is a small monument built by the people of Meyerode. On it in English (mistaking his rank) they have chiseled, "In January 1945 died here in heroic struggles by the German Offensive Eric Fisher Wood Captain U.S. Army."

Every day some villager walks to the monument and puts fresh flowers in a Mason jar.

There are other monuments in the Ardennes too—the thousands of foxholes, dotting the countryside like open graves. These holes still tell the story of the battle. In them can be found rotting ration cans, gas masks, rifle clips, bits of camouflage material, boots, and even occasionally the pitiful remains of a human being, forgotten for many years. These foxholes are the most appropriate monuments to the GI.

INDEX

Abrams, Col. Creighton W., 284, 285

Achouffe, 360

Alden, Fran, 323, 324, 383

Alden, Maj. Ken, 323

Allen, Brig. Gen. Frank, 152

Allen, Maj. Gen. Leven, 86

Allied Units

6th Airborne Division (British), 334, 355

17th Airborne Division, 336, 343, 371, 372, 376, 385

82nd Airborne Division, 55, 86, 87, 102, 115, 159, 166, 199, 214, 218, 223, 224, 228, 229, 234, 238, 239, 240, 250, 262, 263, 334, 385

101st Airborne Division, 55, 86, 87, 115, 118, 121, 150, 164, 169, 209, 293, 316, 334, 385

2nd Armored Division, 226, 227, 242, 243, 245, 266, 269, 287, 294, 333, 360, 363, 364, 385

3rd Armored Division, 166, 173,

Allied Units (*cont.*)

199, 200, 224, 225, 226, 228, 240, 242, 279, 333, 334, 381, 385

4th Armored Division, 7, 206, 208, 219, 284, 285, 292, 293, 313, 385

6th Armored Division, 323, 335, 336, 337, 357, 365, 385

7th Armored Division, 33, 34, 35, 36, 41, 45, 48, 53, 55, 60, 62, 67, 68, 69, 128, 130, 152, 159, 184, 215, 224, 231, 232, 235, 239, 240, 241, 249, 250, 251, 269, 273, 371, 373, 374, 385

9th Armored Division, 4, 7, 25, 34, 62, 112, 114, 119, 128, 141, 159, 161, 169

10th Armored Division, 49, 86, 115, 150, 164, 169, 209, 385

11th Armored Division, 302, 306, 307, 308, 316, 327, 360, 384 385